D0082584

Ethical Decisions for Social Work Practice

 Brooks/Cole Empowerment Series

NINTH EDITION

Ralph Dolgoff
University of Maryland, Baltimore

Donna Harrington
University of Maryland, Baltimore

Frank M. Loewenberg
Bar-Ilan University

 **BROOKS/COLE**
CENGAGE Learning™

Australia • Brazil • Japan • Korea • Mexico • Singapore • Spain • United Kingdom • United States

BROOKS/COLE
CENGAGE Learning

Ethical Decisions for Social Work Practice, Ninth Edition
Ralph Dolgoff, Donna Harrington and Frank M. Loewenberg

Senior Publisher: Linda Schreiber-Ganster

Acquisitions Editor: Seth Dobrin

Associate Editor, Market Development: Arwen Petty

Assistant Editor: Alicia McLaughlin

Media Editor: Elizabeth Momb

Program Manager: Tami Strang

Content Project Manager: Greg Johnson

Design Director: Rob Hugel

Art Director: Caryl Gorska

Print Buyer: Linda Hsu

Rights Acquisitions Specialist: Dean Dauphinais

Production Service: PreMediaGlobal

Text Designer: PreMediaGlobal

Text Researcher: Don Schlotman

Copy Editor: Paula Bonilla

Cover Designer: Jeremy Mende

Compositor: PreMediaGlobal

For product information and technology assistance, contact us at **Cengage Learning Customer & Sales Support, 1-800-354-9706.**

For permission to use material from this text or product, submit all requests online at **www.cengage.com/permissions**. Further permissions questions can be e-mailed to **permissionrequest@cengage.com**

Library of Congress Control Number: 2010941396

Student Edition:
ISBN-13: 978-0-8400-3410-6

ISBN-10: 0-8400-3410-5

Brooks/Cole
20 Davis Drive
Belmont, CA 94002-3098
USA

Cengage Learning is a leading provider of customized learning solutions with office locations around the globe, including Singapore, the United Kingdom, Australia, Mexico, Brazil, and Japan. Locate your local office at **www.cengage.com/global**.

Cengage Learning products are represented in Canada by Nelson Education, Ltd.

To learn more about Brooks/Cole, visit **www.cengage.com/brookscole**.

Purchase any of our products at your local college store or at our preferred online store **www.Cengagebrain.com**.

Instructors: Please visit **login.cengage.com** and log in to access instructor-specific resources.

Printed in the United States of America
1 2 3 4 5 6 7 15 14 13 12 11

CONTENTS

PREFACE   ix

PART 1
INTRODUCTION TO ETHICAL DECISION MAKING   1

CHAPTER 1
Ethical Choices in the Helping Professions   3
Social Work Competencies and Practice Behaviors   6
Ethics   8
Contemporary Interest in Professional Social Work Ethics   8
Ethical Problems in Social Work Practice   9
   Goal Setting   12
   Role Conflict   12
   Value Dilemma   12
Can Professional Ethics be Taught?   14
About this Textbook   16
Pretest: How Much Do I Know About Social Work Ethics?   18

CHAPTER 2
Values and Professional Ethics   23
Values   23
Professional Values   24
Ethics   25

Morality 26

Professional Ethics 27

Law and Ethics: The Problem of Unethical, But Legal, Behavior 29
  Characteristics of Law 30
  Differences between Law and Ethics 31
  Conflict between Law and Professional Ethics 31

Malpractice and Unethical Behavior 33
  Protection against Malpractice Suits 37

Who Needs Professional Ethics? 38

Codes of Professional Ethics 41

A Brief History of Codes of Professional Ethics 43
  U.S. and International Codes of Ethics 44

CHAPTER 3
Guidelines for Ethical Decision Making: Concepts, Approaches, and Values 50

Foundations for Ethical Decision Making 52
  Ethical Relativism 52
  Ethical Absolutism 53
  Different Approaches of Two Social Workers 54

Contemporary Approaches to Ethical Decision Making 56
  Clinical Pragmatism 56
  Humanistic Ethics 57
  Religious Ethics 58
  The Ethics of Caring 59
  Feminist Ethics 61
  Virtue Ethics 62
  Confucian Ethics 63
  Hindu Ethics 63
  Summary of Contemporary Approaches 64

Personal, Group, Societal, and Professional Values 64
  Clarifying Personal Values 65
  Clarifying Group Values 67
  Clarifying Societal Values 68
  Clarifying Professional Values 68

CHAPTER 4
Guidelines for Ethical Decision Making: The Decision-Making Process and Tools 72

Ethical Assessment Screen 74
  Protection of Clients' Rights and Welfare 74
  Protection of Society's Interests 75

The Least Harm Principle 76
  Efficiency and Effectiveness 77

Rank Ordering Ethical Principles   78
    Application of Ethical Decision-Making Screens   82
    The Importance of Identifying One's Own Hierarchy of Principles   85
Summary and Conclusions   86

PART 2
ETHICAL DILEMMAS IN PROFESSIONAL PRACTICE   89

CHAPTER 5
Client Rights and Professional Expertise   91
Who is the Client?   91
Professional Expertise and Self-Determination   94
Self-Determination   96
Ambiguity and Uncertainty   101

CHAPTER 6
Value Neutrality and Imposing Values   106
Client/Worker Value Gap   107
Value Neutrality   109
Value Imposition   111
Making Judgments About Values   114
The Inevitability of Values   115

CHAPTER 7
The Professional Relationship: Limits, Dilemmas, and Problems   119
Professional Relationships and Special Duties   119
    Limitations on Professional Judgments   120
    Democratization and the Rights Revolution   121
    A Disappearing Sense of Privacy   122
Limits of the Professional Relationship   122
Client Interests Versus Worker Interests   124
Dual Roles Within the Professional Relationship   125
    Reconsidering and Further Defining Dual Relationships   126
Sexual Relations with Clients   128
Students and Sexual Relations   132
Touching   133
Other Social Relations   133
Truth Telling and Misrepresentation   134
Diagnosis and Misdiagnosis   138

Compassion Fatigue, Secondary Traumatic Stress, and
Psychological Indifference as Ethical Limitations   141
Sources of Help   143

CHAPTER 8
Confidentiality, Informed Consent, and the Duty to Protect   146
Privacy And Confidentiality   147
  Other Social Workers   149
  Colleagues from Other Fields   149
  The Community   150
  Administrative and Electronic Records   150
  E-Therapy   151
  Insurance Companies and Third-Party Payers   152
  Police   152
  Relatives   153
  Clients   154
  Limits to Confidentiality   155
Health Insurance Portability and Accountability Act
(HIPAA, 1996)   156
Health Information Technology and Clinical Health Act
(HITECH, 2009)   157
Child Welfare and Confidentiality   158
Privileged Communication   159
Informed Consent   160
  Disclosure of Information, Voluntariness, and Competence   161
  Community Organizing and Informed Consent   166
  Ways of Consenting   166
Duty To Protect   167

CHAPTER 9
Social Justice, Limited Resources, and Advocacy   173
Commitment to Social Justice   174
  Time   174
  Inequality and the Distribution of Scarce Resources   174
  Societal Responses to Distribution of Scarce Resources   179
  Discrimination and Diversity   180
  Discrimination and Adoptions   182
Limited Resources   184
  Ethical Problems in Allocating Limited Resources   185
Social Justice and Clinical Social Work   186
Ethical Dilemmas in Advocacy   187
  Case Advocacy   187
  Cause/Class Advocacy   188
  Advocacy as Whistle Blowing   190

Advocacy and Privatization of Services 191
Cyberactivism (Electronic Advocacy) 192
Conclusion 193

CHAPTER 10
Organizational and Work Relationships 195
Relations with Professional Colleagues 196
Practitioner Impairment 200
Adherence to Agency Policies and Regulations 202
Non–Social Work Employers 204
Social Work and the Military 204
Social Workers Not in the Military but in War Related Activities 206
War and Pacifism 207
Other Non–Social Work Settings 207
Social Work Administration and Supervision 210
Dual-Role Relations with Supervisors 211
Other Conflicting Obligations 212
Supervisor Ethics and Liabilities 214

CHAPTER 11
Social Work with Selected Client Groups 217
Intimate Partner Violence 217
Elder Abuse 220
End-of-Life Decisions 222
Assisted Suicide 224
Clients Living with HIV and AIDS 225
Biases About AIDS 226
Confidentiality and HIV/AIDS 226
Social Work Advocacy for Clients Living with HIV 226
Technology in Direct Practice 227
Religion and Spirituality 231
Religion, Social Work Values, and Secularism 231
Spirituality and Social Work Practice 233
A Plurality of Identities and Client Groups 235
Discrimination and Misdiagnosis 236
Culture and Treatment 236

CHAPTER 12
Changing World, Changing Dilemmas 241
Managed Care and Mental Health 241
Technology 246
Research and Evaluation in Practice Settings 248
Evidence-Based Practice (EBP) 250

Private Practice   253
   Client Dumping   253
   Misrepresentation   254

Practice in Rural or Isolated Settings   254

Macro Practice   257
   Community Groups   257
   Community and Societal Issues   258
   Community Organizing   261

CHAPTER 13
Whose Responsibility Are Professional Ethics?   267

Resources that Support Ethical Decision Making   268
   Clients' Bill of Rights   268
   Agency Risk Audits   268
   Peer Review and Committees on the Ethics of Social Work Practice   270
   Accountability Systems   271
   Training and Consultation   271
   Agency Appeals Procedures and Ombudsmen   272
   Professional Associations   272
   NASW Professional Complaint Procedures   273

Ethics Advocacy, Human Services Agencies, and Interdisciplinary
Teams   274

Conclusion   276

Returning to the Beginning   276

APPENDIX A
Additional Exemplars   278

APPENDIX B
Glossary   293

BIBLIOGRAPHY   296

INDEX   319

PREFACE

Every day, social workers and other human service professionals are faced with stressful, even traumatic situations, such as child abuse, domestic violence, family tensions, the homeless, persons with chronic mental illness, and suicide. These concerns have become almost commonplace. However, in recent years, challenges of a different nature have included service in war zones, military service, and the very difficult issues that arise for veterans, disabled and otherwise. Natural events, such as Hurricane Katrina and the earthquake in Haiti, as well as human created disasters, such as the Deepwater Horizon event, called for extra efforts by social workers and other human service workers. Most of the attention paid in these latter two cases focused on concrete problems such as housing, food, safety, prevention of disease, and physical medical care. In addition to the many physical concerns, individuals and families lost their businesses and jobs and were beset by physical and mental stresses. These disasters called on social workers to provide services when resources were in short supply, requiring creativity and perseverance. The many and diverse social and economic needs will not soon be met sufficiently; they will have lingering effects for many years.

At the same time, the United States and other countries have been going through a "Great" Recession, reminiscent in many ways of the Great Depression of the 1930s. There is high unemployment; many people are without work, and jobs are hard to find. There are projections that our nation has entered a period of slow economic growth where the competition for available funds becomes intense. If these predictions prove to be true, human services will have to compete for scarce funds with all other societal needs. The coming few years may not produce enough so that the social welfare needs of the population will be sufficiently met, certainly not as they have been for the last several decades. What special ethical dilemmas do social workers encounter when there are too few social workers, when the needed resources are in very short supply, and many people and their families are living under great stress? How does a social worker pick and choose when faced with great human need and a reality of resources not equal to the needs? How can a social worker choose between individuals, families, groups, and communities?

Under these circumstances, how is a commitment to equality enacted? What is the meaning of social justice in these harrowing situations? What should be done for the non-squeaky wheel? Should social workers in these circumstances shift the priority of their roles to advocacy and intervention with governments—local to federal—or should they operate case by case in a situation in which one has to choose between families and communities because social workers and resources are not available everywhere nor available in sufficient quantities? Or, to what extent should social workers consider ways of developing cooperative efforts to maintain food supplies, businesses to sustain individuals and groups, and exploring new ways of confronting an era of shortages? What are the ethical ways in which to proceed? These are questions that have to be considered by social workers and will be considered throughout this book. Our questions are not meant to fault any person but to point out how pervasive the requirement of ethical decision making is for social workers and other human service workers during these times of disasters *and* economic troubles.

For this reason, more and more social work educators and the professional community are concerned with ethical conduct, as well as the preparation of students and professionals to recognize ethical dilemmas when they occur, to be prepared to assess these dilemmas, and to deal with them correctly. We believe that concern for ethical conduct should be included in every curriculum for professional education. Those who teach in the area must keep in mind Thomas Aquinas's caution that when it comes to ethics "we cannot discuss what we ought to do unless we know what we can do" *(Commentary on De Anima,* I,1.2). In other words, teaching the theory of ethical action is not worth much unless we also teach the skill of making ethical decisions. In this book, therefore, we will follow this dual focus. Some have said that virtue cannot be taught in a college classroom and that ethical dilemmas cannot be resolved by textbooks. However, we believe that the principles and techniques of ethical assessment and ethical decision making do have a place in a professional curriculum.

At the same time, we agree with those who have suggested that the concern of instructors should be less focused on presenting solutions to dilemmas than with efforts to encourage students to: (a) be alert to discovering and perceiving ethical issues; (b) be clearer about the values that affect their decision making; and (c) consider competing arguments, in examining both the strengths and limitations of their own positions, and in reaching thoughtfully reasoned conclusions. Our approach to ethical decision making is designed to assist social workers in reasoning carefully about ethical issues, to help them clarify their moral aspirations at the level demanded by the profession, and to achieve a more ethical stance in practice.

NEW TO THIS EDITION

The ninth edition is part of Cengage Learning's new Empowerment Series, an initiative to help instructors and students link the material in this book with CSWE's 2008 Educational Policy and Accreditation Standards. In Chapter 1, we discuss the most relevant policies. Each chapter begins with an overview of which educational policies are addressed and ends with competency notes that summarize how the chapter addresses the specific educational policies. Educational Policy 2.1.2 is about applying social work ethical principles (CSWE, 2008), and this entire book addresses this educational policy. Educational Policy 2.1.3 is about critical thinking, and we have exemplars, questions, and critical thinking exercises in every chapter to emphasize critical thinking and to encourage you to engage with the material presented in this book. We hope that as you are reading you take the time to stop and think about each question that we have asked—it will take you longer to read this book if you do so, but you will gain much more than if you just read through the material as quickly as possible.

Although the main emphasis of this book is on Educational Policy 2.1.2, several other Educational Policies are addressed in the book. Specifically, Educational Policy 2.1.1 on identifying as a professional social worker and conducting oneself accordingly (CSWE, 2008) is addressed in almost every chapter because we believe that behaving ethically is an integral component of professional social work. Within this policy, several practice behaviors are addressed in the book: advocating for clients' access to services is discussed in Chapters 5, 9, and 12; personal reflection is discussed in Chapters 2, 5, and 13; and roles and boundaries are discussed in Chapters 7 and 12. Diversity (Educational Policy 2.1.4) is discussed in Chapters 1 through 3, 9, 11, and 12; specific practice behaviors of recognizing the impact of culture's structures and values (2.1.4a) are addressed in Chapters 3 and 6; eliminating (or perhaps more accurately recognizing and minimizing) the influence of personal biases and values (2.1.4b) is discussed in Chapters 2, 3, and 6; and recognizing the importance of difference in shaping life experiences (2.1.4c) is discussed in Chapter 6. Advancing human rights and social and economic justice (Educational Policy 2.1.5) are discussed in Chapters 9 and 12. Finally, engaging in research-informed practice (Educational Policy 2.1.6) is addressed in Chapter 12.

The exemplars presented, as well as the critical thinking exercises at the end of each chapter, have been prepared to heighten students' sensitivity to the ethical aspects of social work practice, to aid them in developing a personal approach to such issues, and to help them consider the essential elements in ethical decision making in professional practice. Suggestions for additional readings also appear at the end of each chapter. In addition, we provide Internet sites so readers can look for additional information on many topics.

In our continuing effort to make this book more useful, this edition has been completely updated and includes the latest research. We have added to or augmented material on the following topics:

- Information regarding the NASW Code of Ethics has been updated and used throughout the edition, including increased attention to cultural competence and social diversity.
- New references and updated research are used throughout the text.
- Substantially more international content has been added, including websites for various international organizations and rights covenants.
- The chapters have been re-ordered to improve the flow of material and so that more general concepts such as determining who is the client and client rights and values are introduced before specific content about ethical standards (e.g., confidentiality).

- Chapter Two has been greatly expanded to include a comparison of the Code of Ethics of Great Britain and that of the United States, more material on International Codes of Ethics, and the Code of Ethics of the International Federation of Social Work. The New Zealand Code of Ethics has been introduced, with its Maori parallel emphasis.
- Chapter Three has a greatly expanded discussion of several contemporary approaches to ethics, including caring, feminist, and virtue ethics; as well as new sections on Confucian, Hindu, and post-modern ethics.
- Chapter Four has expanded discussion of the social control role in social work; the ethical principles screen has been updated to include social justice and we have added content on variation in individual hierarchies of ethical principles.
- Social justice has been given more emphasis throughout the book, especially in Chapters 4 and 9.
- Information on HITECH has been added, as has a discussion of health disparities, and societal responses to the distribution of scarce resources.
- Cyberactivism is discussed in Chapter 9.
- Emphasis has been added on social work in the military in general, in war, and after leaving service, as well as mandated dual role relations.
- We introduce the issue of pacifism.
- Information on technology in practice has been expanded in Chapter 11.
- Increased attention to religion and spirituality has been added to Chapter 11.
- The section on community organizing has been expanded in Chapter 12.
- We discuss social work in rural and other isolated communities in Chapter 12.
- Research is reported on the implementation of social work ethics audits.
- Discussion of ethics and advocacy in agencies in a time of accountability, quality control, and risk management has been added.
- We expanded and updated suggested readings and Web resources.
- We introduce the issue of whether the rules of dual role relationships have been undergoing a change, and should be further changed.
- New exemplars have been introduced in Appendix A.

In addition to the many exemplars of ethical dilemmas provided throughout the book, one particular family situation is considered several times in the book from different perspectives. Additional information is provided each time we return to this exemplar. Finally, we have included a pretest with answers for readers at the end of the first chapter.

We have retained the two ethical decision screens in this edition. We have received numerous comments that the screens have proved helpful in the rank-ordering of ethical principles and ethical obligations, thus helping social work practitioners identify priorities among competing ethical obligations. Our intent has been to suggest some principles and guidelines that can substantially help social workers making ethical practice decisions, and we have been gratified by the wide use of the screens. Although ethical and moral perfection remains an unattainable goal, social workers—like everyone else—must continue to strive toward that goal.

The exemplars in this book are taken from the real world, but none of them occurred in exactly the way described or to the people identified in each situation. No names or other identifying information came from social agency records or from social workers who worked with these people. Many new exemplars have been added to reflect newer areas of practice. Needless to say, the exemplars do not always typify good or desirable practice. They were chosen simply to illustrate ethical problems occurring in the world of practice.

We thank our colleagues and students for helping us think through many of the issues involved in social work ethics. We also want to thank the peer reviewers for their very helpful feedback on this edition. They are Professor Thomas Chalmers McLaughlin, University of New England; Professor Joel Farrell, Faulkner University; Professor Mary Montminy-Danna, Salve Regina University; Professor Bart Grossman, University of California at Berkeley; and Professor Dennis Ihara, Hawaii Pacific University.

Our thanks and appreciation to the Health Sciences and Human Services Library of the University of Maryland, Baltimore; to the Milton S. Eisenhower Library of the Johns Hopkins University; and Maxine Grosshans, librarian, at the University of Maryland, Baltimore Thurgood Marshall Library at the School of Law for her generous assistance. Dr. Howard Altstein, Dr. Eva Sivan, Pat Hicks, Dr. Kathleen Walsh, and many students over the years shared with us ethical dilemmas they encountered in practice situations.

We are pleased that our ninth edition is being published by Cengage Learning. We appreciate the helpfulness of those who have worked to bring this edition to fruition.

We thank our friends, families, and spouses who have continued their everlasting patience with our not-so-minor foibles. We especially are proud that one edition of our book was translated into Chinese and that another edition was translated into Korean. Finally, we thank each other for the cooperation and support we have given each other through various editions and for the learning we have gained through our work together.

Ralph Dolgoff
Donna Harrington
Frank Loewenberg

Introduction to Ethical Decision Making

PART

I

ETHICAL CHOICES IN THE HELPING PROFESSIONS

CHAPTER **I**

As a social worker, what is the ethical way to respond to each of the following situations?

- Your client tells you that he intends to embezzle funds from his employer.
- You believe that one of the residents of the detoxification center that you staff is potentially violent and may become a danger to other residents.
- As a military social worker, you have been counseling a 19-year-old enlisted man. His young wife is pregnant, and neither of them have relatives nearby who could help after her rapidly approaching delivery. The enlisted man asks that you claim that he is unable to go with his unit to Afghanistan so that he can be present for the birth and help his wife afterward.
- A client who is HIV-positive tells you that he has unprotected sex with his wife because he does not want her to know about his medical condition.
- You discover that another social worker knows about a child abuse situation but has not reported the case to Child Protective Services as required by law.
- You are a social worker in an employee assistance program. A client tells you that in this company women are paid 25% less for doing the same work as men. You make some inquiries and find that you, too, are underpaid. What should you do?
- A board member has helped your agency obtain a substantial grant that has made it possible to add services for adult alcoholics and their family members. He now wants you to report that more clients have been served by this program than actually participated so that the agency can receive a larger grant next year.
- A surgeon at a pediatric hospital strongly recommends that a child have surgery, but the child's parents refuse consent because of possible risks. The physician asks you to convince the parents to agree to let him operate regardless of risk.

Every social worker is confronted every day with the necessity of making decisions that involve ethical issues or dilemmas, although many are unaware of it or solve the ethical dilemma routinely. Sometimes a social worker may have an opportunity to think about all possible options and even, perhaps, to talk things over with a colleague or consult with an expert. More often, however, social workers—even student social workers—are alone when they must make difficult ethical choices. Due to the immediacy of the problems that face them, they cannot delay making decisions. At best, they have a few hours or days to consider what should be done. Throughout this book, we provide a number of exemplars of ethical dilemmas for you to consider, beginning with Exemplar 1.1.

1.1   PROTECTING A FAMILY SECRET

EP 2.1.2

Basanti Madurai came happily to the United States from southern India after marrying a man who claimed to be an engineer, but who was actually employed at a local gas station. She was only slightly familiar with English and unacquainted with U.S. culture when she joined her husband in her in-laws' home. Her new family forbade her to make friends. Moreover, she was almost never allowed to leave their home, where she was expected to stay and take care of their two small children. When her husband discovered shortly after they were married that she had brought less money to the marriage than he expected, he started verbally abusing her. Gradually, he also became physically abusive. Her in-laws were aware of his behavior but considered it acceptable and appropriate.

On her occasional walks in the neighborhood, Basanti was always under the gaze of friends and relatives. However, she managed to meet one young Indian woman at a local grocery. After a time, she began to trust her new friend and confided that she was practically a prisoner in her home and was being beaten by her husband.

On her own initiative, this new friend spoke to Ellen Ashton, a social worker for a family service agency that provides a mutual support group for South Asian women. The friend asked Ellen to speak to Basanti. When Ellen had an opportunity, she struck up a conversation with Basanti, telling her about her agency's support group. Basanti claimed that all was well at home. She added that she would not join such a group because she did not want to bring shame on her own family in India or on her husband's family. But she also mentioned that she wanted to try to make a better life for herself, her husband, and their children.

This situation poses a number of ethical dilemmas for Ellen Ashton. Can you identify some of these? Where will the social worker find help with the ethical aspects of this social work practice problem? How will she decide what course of action to follow? In this book, we consider a variety of professional ethical dilemmas. Social workers are confronted by a number of such problems, whose solutions should be consistent with ethical professional practice. We will briefly analyze several of these dilemmas.

Before we begin our analysis, please take a moment to write down what you think are the two or three most important dilemmas that the social worker must address. What, if anything, would you do, based on the friend's report that Basanti is being abused by her husband? You will refer back to these thoughts as we progress through the book. In most practice situations, you will gain additional information each time you meet with a client, and your view of the situation may change as you learn more. We will use a similar approach in this book, returning to the Madurai family several more times, providing additional information each time and asking how the new information changes the ethical issues involved.

The root ethical problem in this situation is that every social worker, including Ellen, fills two professional roles: (a) helper/enabler and (b) societal control agent. The conflict between these two roles triggers a number of ethical dilemmas. What is good for one participant is not necessarily what is best for another. A decision that is best for now may not be so for the long run. We also need to consider the degree of damage (e.g., harm to Basanti or others) that can be permitted to occur before the social worker must intervene. We will now consider two areas of dilemmas from this situation: multiple-client systems and competing values.

Multiple-Client System The National Association of Social Workers (NASW, 2008) Code of Ethics requires that every social worker give priority to her[1] client's interests and to her client's self-determination. These principles are undoubtedly relevant in this situation. But who are this worker's clients? What are her responsibilities toward Basanti, her children, her husband, his and her parents, as well as toward the community and society? To whom does this practitioner owe first obligations?

Competing Values Client self-determination, protection of human life, and enhancing the quality of life are three values to which all social workers are committed. As is so often the case, in this instance the social worker cannot follow these three principles simultaneously. But Basanti is not Ellen's client. What ethical questions does this present? For example, does a social worker have a societal legal obligation to report this situation? If the social worker intervenes to protect Basanti's life without her agreement, she undermines Basanti's self-determination and perhaps her long-term quality of life. Yet, if she does not do anything, Basanti may suffer serious harm from her husband's continued physical and emotional abuse. There may be good reasons for giving priority to one rather than the other of these values. Nevertheless, the social worker must first recognize this conflict as a dilemma and then seek to resolve it.

In addition to the competing values identified above, this situation confronts the social worker with other value dilemmas. Although she is committed to providing service to voluntary clients, she is not at all sure which professional values are relevant in this situation. She does not want to undermine Basanti's self-determination

---

[1] Some social workers are men; many more are women. In recent years, many writers have used terminology such as *his or her* and *she or he,* or they have used the plural form such as *social workers believe.* However, these usages are clumsy and often tend to interfere with the clarity of the message. Because most social workers are women, we will refer to the social worker as *she* (except in exemplars where the social worker has been identified as a man) and to the recipient of the service as *he* (except where the recipient is a woman). We hope that male social workers and female recipients will bear with our usage.

or her motivation to make a better life for herself. She also does not want to impose her own values on Basanti, her husband, and his parents. Should a social worker act upon the report of a neighbor, who may or may not have an accurate impression of the situation? Ellen clearly needs more information, but how can she obtain it if Basanti claims everything is all right and does not want to talk to her?

To summarize, in this situation, the social worker's ethics indicate that in her role as a helper/enabler, the first problem is to find a way to assess the level of risk. If she determines Basanti is at serious risk for physical abuse, she must consider how to intervene immediately. If she learns that the risk is not that great and immediate, she may seek ways to involve Basanti either in the group or in some other way. In this case, she must make certain Basanti is enabled to make her own thoughtful decisions, she must assist her to know and analyze alternatives, and she must facilitate access to helping systems that make these decisions possible. In her role as social worker, Ellen must not intervene unless she sees sufficient evidence of imminent danger.

There are many ways to prepare for this practice reality. First, it is important to recognize that every decision in social work practice includes ethical aspects. Next, social workers need knowledge and skill to clarify these aspects of practice in order to engage in effective ethical decision making. Knowledge and skill in this area (as in all other aspects of social work practice) must be developed and refined throughout a social worker's professional career.

This book has been written to help social workers, students as well as practitioners, become skilled in making ethical decisions. In preparation, every social worker must consider the following questions:

- Who is my client?
- What obligations do I owe my client(s)?
- Do I have professional obligations to people other than my clients? What are my obligations to my own family, my agency, and my profession?
- What are my own personal values? Are these values compatible with the profession's values and with societal values?
- What are my ethical priorities when these value sets are not identical or when they are in conflict?
- What is the ethical way to respond when I have conflicting professional responsibilities to different people?

SOCIAL WORK COMPETENCIES AND PRACTICE BEHAVIORS

In this chapter, we introduce the complex topic of ethical decision making and define what we mean by this important concept. Social work students and practitioners have repeatedly asked for guidelines to help them grapple with ethical practice issues. In the past, these requests were answered by the adoption of codes of ethics that were helpful in some ways but left too many questions unanswered. Most social workers know instinctively that ethics are supremely important. The priority of ethics for social workers is underscored by the Purpose statement of the Code of Ethics that "professional ethics are at the core of social work" (NASW Code, 2008) and are key for guiding practitioners' actions.

EP 2.1.2

As of 2005, 31 state regulatory boards required continuing professional education credits in ethics for maintaining social work licenses, and additional boards were planning such requirements. Effective in 2011, the Association of Social Work Boards (ASWB) will place greater emphasis in its examinations on the content areas of professional relationships, values, and ethics. On the master's level, the examination content in these areas will increase from 16% to 27%, whereas in the advanced generalist level the increase will be from 17% to 24%. Smaller increases have been announced for the bachelor's and clinical levels (retrieved from the Association of Social Work Boards, http://www.aswb.org/). Although the changes on the bachelor's and clinical examinations are minor, this represents an increase in the percentage of exam content focusing on professional relationships, values, and ethics of 11% at the master's level and 7% at the advanced generalist levels.

Ethical content and decision making are currently taught in all phases of social work education, including continuing professional education following graduation from educational programs. In an age when scientists have cracked the genetic code, put men on the moon, transplanted hearts, transferred an embryo from the test tube to the womb, and cloned sheep, almost anything is possible from a technological point of view. The key question now is no longer to decide what *can* be done, but what *should* be done. An increasing number of social workers have come to recognize that they, too, face questions that go beyond the techniques of social work. This recognition has made the subject of professional ethics more visible in the professional social work curriculum. Since 1982, the Council on Social Work Education (CSWE), the accrediting authority for social work education, has required the inclusion of content about professional practice values and ethics at all levels of the curriculum.

In 2008, CSWE revised the Educational Policy and Accreditation Standards (EPAS) to focus on core competencies and related practice behaviors (see http://www.cswe.org/Accreditation/Handbook.aspx for the CSWE 2008 EPAS Handbook). The "EPAS defines competencies as 'measurable practice behaviors that are comprised of knowledge, values and skills' (EP 2.1)" (Holloway, Black, Hoffman, & Pierce, ND). Under Educational Policy 1.1 – Values, the EPAS specifically identifies "service, social justice, the dignity and worth of the person, the importance of human relationships, integrity, competence, human rights, and scientific inquiry" among the core social work values (CSWE, 2010, p. 2). Because values are central to any discussion of ethics, we will discuss them throughout this textbook; indeed, we have already begun to do so.

Under Educational Policy 2 – Explicit Curriculum, the CSWE (2010) EPAS identifies Core Competencies; Educational Policy 2.1.2 is to "apply social work ethical principles to guide professional practice." Applying ethical decision making to social work practice will be addressed in every chapter of this textbook. In addition, this textbook addresses several other competencies, including critical thinking (Educational Policy 2.1.3), engaging diversity in practice (Educational Policy 2.1.4), advancing human rights and social and economic justice (Educational Policy 2.1.5), and using research-informed practice (Educational Policy 2.1.6). At the beginning of each chapter we will provide a brief introduction that identifies the specific Educational Policies that are addressed in that chapter.

ETHICS

What does the term **ethics** mean? The word comes from the Greek root *ethos*, which originally meant custom, usage, habit, or character. In contemporary usage, it deals with the question of what actions are morally right and with how things ought to be. **General ethics** clarify the obligations that are owed by one person to another person. Some obligations, however, are based on specific relations between two people (such as between a mother and her son), or they are based on a particular role voluntarily accepted by one of the parties. The latter are special obligations that apply only to those who have consented to accept that role. **Professional ethics** are a codification of the special obligations that arise out of a person's voluntary choice to become a professional, such as a social worker. Professional ethics clarify the ethical aspects of professional practice. Professional social work ethics are intended to help social work practitioners recognize morally correct practice and learn how to decide and act *ethically in any professional situation.*

CONTEMPORARY INTEREST IN PROFESSIONAL SOCIAL WORK ETHICS

Jane Addams, a pioneer social worker in the 19th and early 20th centuries, was aware of the importance of ethical practice. She understood that "action indeed is the sole medium of expression for ethics ... that the sphere of morals is the sphere of action, that speculation in regard to morality is but observation and must remain in the sphere of intellectual comment, that a situation does not really become moral until we are confronted with what shall be done in a concrete case, and are obliged to act upon our theory" (Addams, 1902, 2006). One of the paradoxes of our times is that interest in professional ethics is high, even while the level of morality of society seems low. In the last century, more people were killed by violence than ever before. Hitler's genocide was not a one-time aberration, but has been duplicated (though on a smaller scale) in Cambodia, Darfur, Rwanda, the Democratic Republic of the Congo, the Balkans, and elsewhere. At the same time, the Nuremberg Trials following World War II, the Civil Rights Movement of the late 1950s and 1960s, and the many rapid advances in computer technology and means of communication such as the Internet and satellite television have resulted in a greater awareness of human rights, including the rights of social work clients.

The current interest in social work ethics is, in part, related to this emphasis on human rights. It is also an expression of the maturation of the social work profession. The greater attention on social work ethics may also be the result of the rising concern of practitioners about the use of litigation by clients to resolve claims of ethical malfeasance and malpractice. Complaints and lawsuits against social workers insured by the NASW Insurance Trust have increased over the last three decades but have recently leveled off. Over the 40-year period since the inception of the social work professional liability program, through 2008, the three most frequent claims have been: incorrect treatment (23.65%), sexual misconduct (17.11%), and suicide of patient (or attempt at) (13.51%). (DeBenedetto, 2009).

Unethical conduct, corruption, and scandals in government as well as in industry have become commonplace. Almost daily, newspapers report unethical practices by corporate executives, legislators, scientific researchers, physicians, lawyers, accountants, and other professionals. The daily media headlines almost always involve ethical questions. In the past two decades, Americans have witnessed the impeachment of President Clinton, industrialists and accountants using ethically questionable and illegal accounting methods, insider-trading scandals, multiple Ponzi schemes, Olympic Games corruptions, new dilemmas in medical research, the use of drugs in sports, and questionable political fund-raising methods. Financial chicanery is found from Wall Street to Main Street. Ethical questions almost always are at the top of the public agenda. No wonder that courses in ethics are appearing everywhere—they are offered not only by universities but also by businesses, professional groups, and the military.

ETHICAL PROBLEMS IN SOCIAL WORK PRACTICE

Some have suggested that ethical problems occur only on very unusual occasions. They argue that in most practice situations a social worker requires only a high level of professional skill and insight because no ethical questions are involved. This is the approach to professional practice that was established by Sigmund Freud and that has been followed by generations of practitioners in all of the helping professions. The assumptions underlying this approach are supported by philosophers who argue that most actions do not involve any moral question but are instead the result of a free choice among a number of available alternatives. These alternatives are located in the "zone of moral indifference" (Fishkin, 1982), where, from an ethical viewpoint, it makes little difference which alternative is chosen. Other philosophers insist that there are ethical implications or aspects to almost every professional decision. We follow the latter approach because we believe that professional social workers are not mere technicians who solve mechanical problems (such as providing services or supplying information). They are, first and foremost, moral agents.

A closer examination of social work practice will reveal that almost all practice principles involve (or are based on) ethical principles. One of the sources for ethical problems in social work practice may be located in the multiplicity and contradiction of values that characterize contemporary society. Although we often speak of ethical problems, it would be more correct to speak of the ethical dimensions or ethical aspects of social work practice problems. In the past, it was assumed that ethical issues arose out of, and were limited to, the dyadic relationship between social worker and client. In addition to ethical problems that arise out of the traditional worker–client relationship, there are also ethical dilemmas that relate to others in the client's social system, even if they never interact directly with the social worker. The breakdown of consensus concerning societal means and goals, the increasing scarcity of resources that are available for social welfare, and the use of new technologies have intensified traditional ethical dilemmas and have also given rise to what may well be a new generation of ethical issues in social work practice.

In this textbook, we will examine both ethical problems and ethical dilemmas. Ethical problems raise the question: What is the right thing to do in a given practice situation? How can a social worker avoid unethical behaviors in that situation?

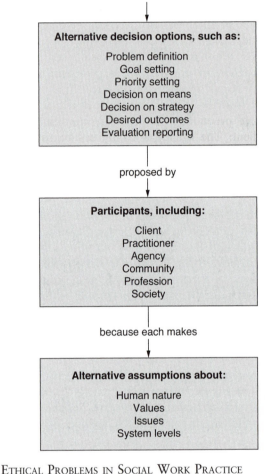

Ethical problems arise when there is a conflict about

Alternative decision options, such as:

Problem definition
Goal setting
Priority setting
Decision on means
Decision on strategy
Desired outcomes
Evaluation reporting

proposed by

Participants, including:

Client
Practitioner
Agency
Community
Profession
Society

because each makes

Alternative assumptions about:

Human nature
Values
Issues
System levels

FIGURE 1.1 | ETHICAL PROBLEMS IN SOCIAL WORK PRACTICE

Ethical dilemmas occur in situations in which the social worker must choose between two or more relevant, but contradictory, ethical directives or when every alternative results in an undesirable outcome for one or more persons. A seedbed for ethical problems in social work practice is portrayed in Figure 1.1. Any disagreement that different participants (e.g., relatives, professionals, landlords, employers, groups, and organizations) have with regard to alternate decision options or alternative assumptions will intensify the difficulties that social workers will encounter in ethical decision making. Examples of such difficulties occur in the following situations:

- A client wants a service that may affect another member of the family who does not want to receive that service: An adult daughter may want to place her aging father in a nursing home, but the father wants to remain in his own home.

- Conflicting values impinge on the decision facing the social worker: A young woman has asked you whether her fiancé (who is your client) is HIV-positive, whereas the client wants to keep this information secret.
- The community and the profession have different priorities: Everyone agrees that something must be done about domestic violence, but community leaders believe that better police protection is more important than providing prevention and treatment programs.
- The social agency prescribes a treatment modality based on one social work theory, although the practitioner knows that another approach is indicated for a particular client: The agency is committed to psychodynamic therapy, whereas research evidence indicates that, in the situation faced by a particular client, cognitive-behavioral therapy is usually more effective.

Some social workers try to ignore the ethical problems and dilemmas that arise in these and similar situations, either because they are uncomfortable with making ethical decisions or because they follow routinely a standard strategy. Other social workers are aware of the ethical aspects of these problem situations, but they are uneasy because they believe that they do not yet have the skill to deal with ethical problems of this nature.

EP 2.1.1

In summary, two causes of ethical problems are (1) competing values and (2) competing loyalties. Social workers may benefit from paying special attention to these causes.

Competing Values An ethical dilemma may arise when a practitioner is faced with two or more competing values, such as justice and equality or confidentiality and protecting life. An example of conflicts regarding self-determination and protection from harm is found in Exemplar 1.1. Conflicts regarding confidentiality are found in Chapter 8 (Exemplars 8.1 and 8.2), justice and equality in Chapter 9 (Exemplar 9.4), and protecting life in Chapter 12 (Exemplar 12.8). Similarly, in a time of rapidly shrinking budgets and an emphasis on evidence-based practice, no practitioner can ignore considerations of efficiency and effectiveness, even though these constraints may do violence to what is thought to be best for a particular client. A worker may feel equally committed to two values, even when both cannot be actualized in a specific situation.

Competing Loyalties When competing or conflicting groups make claims for the social worker's loyalties, the worker may face an ethical dilemma. To whom does Ellen Ashton (Exemplar 1.1) owe loyalty: Basanti Madurai, society, herself, the friend who reported abuse, the agency? The social worker represents both the society and the potential client, each having conflicting demands. There is little need to point to the more obvious examples of this cause of ethical problems. Even less blatant incidents, such as a request for giving preferential treatment to relatives and friends, can be problematic from an ethical point of view. Multiple loyalties are also a source of ethical quandaries when a social worker serves a multiple-client system, as is so frequent today. In these circumstances, identifying the person or unit that should receive priority becomes a crucial ethical issue.

Now let's examine several exemplars from social work practice. Consider how ethical issues arise in each exemplar. The ethical problems faced by the social worker who has been assigned to work with Blanca Gabelli in Exemplar 1.2 are similar to, yet different from, those faced by worker Ellen Ashton in Exemplar 1.1.

1.2	WHO DECIDES BLANCA GABELLI'S FUTURE?

EP 2.1.2

Blanca Gabelli, an 84-year-old retired physician, participates in a day treatment program and resides in an assisted living residence. Recently, she has become slightly more forgetful, falls more frequently, and has been somewhat less able to care for herself. She has also become increasingly irascible, and several staff members have complained about her demanding behavior. Your supervisor has asked you, her social worker, to arrange for her transfer to a nursing home because Blanca is a "pain," requires too much effort, and is upsetting staff members who have many other duties in the residential program.

Although you believe that Blanca is not yet in need of nursing home care, you contacted the only nursing home with a vacancy to arrange for her transfer.

Let's consider some of the ethical choices you might have made before making a decision.

GOAL SETTING

Who should set the goals in this situation? If you comply with your supervisor's demand, you and your supervisor determine Blanca's future while also undermining her sense of autonomy. Do you and your supervisor have an ethical right to do so? What part should Blanca play in deciding her own living arrangements?

ROLE CONFLICT

A social worker is often an agency employee. What are the implications if you do not comply with your supervisor's demand? Does your compliance undermine Blanca's sense of autonomy? Does the social worker's role require that you always comply with the suggestions of your supervisor or that you always serve as Blanca's protector? Whose interests and/or welfare should receive priority consideration: your supervisor's, the agency's, yours, Blanca's, society's?

VALUE DILEMMA

Your supervisor is demanding that you comply with the agency's decision. However, you and she have different assessments of Blanca's situation. Should you do what is best for the agency or what is best for the client? The agency wants to transfer Blanca, and you think she should stay in the assisted living facility and in the day treatment program. To whom do you owe loyalty? In what ways do your professional and personal values clash? Should you tell Blanca what your supervisor said? How honest should you be and with whom?

Another set of ethical problems faces Sharon Gillette, the social worker in the following exemplar.

1.3 | HURRICANE KATRINA, THE GILLETTE FAMILY, AND CHOICES

EP 2.1.2

For days, all one heard was that Hurricane Katrina was on its way. Social worker Sharon Gillette's husband was in Seattle on business and unable to find a flight to return to New Orleans. She could not decide whether to leave or to stay because her house was on higher ground. People in New Orleans and throughout the region were struggling with preparations for the expected storm. Sharon's child care provider, Mrs. Carlyle, called to say she was frightened and would not come the next morning because she had found a ride out of town with her son and his family. With her husband still away, Sharon finally decided it would be best for her and her children to leave New Orleans and stay with family in Texas until the storm passed.

Sharon phoned her supervisor to let him know that she would be leaving New Orleans and would return as soon as possible after the storm passed. However, her supervisor informed her that she was being asked to report immediately to the Civil Emergency Center in the Louisiana Superdome to assist the many people—both able-bodied and those with physical and other challenges—who would be forced to stay in New Orleans because they did not have a way to evacuate. People were confused and anxious; many were trying to contact loved ones.

What should Sharon do? Should she leave New Orleans for Texas as planned? Should she stay in New Orleans to help those in need? If she does stay in New Orleans, should she spend time trying to protect her home and children, or spend all her time helping those in the Superdome?

Competing Values Is it appropriate for Sharon to evacuate with her family, or should she stay in New Orleans to help those in need? What mother could go to work to help others while leaving her frightened and confused children alone at home? On the other hand, what are her obligations as a professional social worker to the families being served at the Emergency Center? Obviously, she cannot simultaneously evacuate with her children to another state and also remain in New Orleans working at the Emergency Center.

Ambiguity Although we now know the outcome of Hurricane Katrina, Sharon would have had to make some decisions before the storm actually hit without knowing what damage the hurricane would cause. She had to make choices without the benefit of the 20/20 hindsight we now have. Sharon would have been far less troubled by her decision if she had known that no harm would come to her children and/or if she had known for certain that her presence at the Emergency Center would make a critical difference in the lives of the hurricane victims.

What other ethical issues does this case pose? Where in the Code of Ethics can this social worker find help with the ethical aspects of emergency situations such as floods, hurricanes, outbreaks of violence, and war? How will the social worker decide what course of action to follow? The ethical dilemmas of this situation are relatively uncomplicated—as a social worker, Sharon has certain professional responsibilities toward her clients and her agency, especially in an emergency situation such as Hurricane Katrina. On the other hand, she also has responsibilities to her family, which in this case includes very young, frightened, and potentially at-risk children. Which of these two obligations has priority?

CAN PROFESSIONAL ETHICS BE TAUGHT?

Teaching professional ethics was traditionally based on the assumption that knowledge about ethics would lead to the acquisition of attitudes and values, and that these, in turn, would produce the desired ethical behaviors. This assumption needs to be tested. Is there any reason to think that studying ethics will motivate ethical behavior? Further empirical research is needed to discover whether and to what extent learning about ethics is helpful. Educators still do not know much more about value-and-ethics education than Socrates did 2,500 years ago when he told Meno that he did not know how values were acquired or whether they could be taught at all. These questions still require answers.

The widely accepted view is that attitudes determine behavior, but some leading attitude theorists teach the exact opposite—that is, they have proposed that behavior determines attitudes. Generally, theorists hold that our behavior is a direct consequence of our attitudes about the world, but revisionist theorists suggest that a person tends to select beliefs and attitudes that are in consonance with or support his or her behavior. Following the traditional theory, it is widely believed that social workers' values influence their professional practice, such as the selection of treatment methods. The CSWE requirement for curriculum content related to values and ethics is also based on the assumption that a student who learns to value professional ethics will, as a practitioner, choose to behave in ethical ways.

It may be that there is something to both approaches; some researchers have suggested that both the attitude–behavior and behavior–attitude models are far too simplistic and unrealistic (Deutscher, Pestello, & Pestello, 1993). Under some conditions, their relationship is reciprocal and/or reversed so that, at the same time, attitudes influence behaviors and behaviors influence attitudes. In addition, most attitudes contain a mix of positive and negative feelings embedded within them, thus creating complex dynamic systems in which attitudes are not singular and monolithic (Carver, 1999) as they interact with behaviors. However, more important is the fact that attitude is only one determinant of behavior; other causal factors include intentions, expectations of others, and beliefs about outcomes. Furthermore, situational constraints, vested interests, self-confidence, self-efficacy or perceived behavioral control, the ease or difficulty of performing a behavior, past experience and anticipated impediments and obstacles all affect the relationship between attitudes and behaviors (Ajzen, 2005; Manstead, 1996).

In the not-too-distant past, the transmission of professional ethics was not problematic because these ethics were transmitted by watching a master practitioner. This apprentice model was satisfactory for training professionals—as long as the novice practitioner faced the same types of problems as did the master teacher. Social work education, with its traditional emphasis on concurrent field instruction and educational supervision, suggests a partial continuation of the apprentice model. But this model may no longer be optimally effective in today's world of rapid changes. Innovative curriculum organizations and alternative teaching methods must be considered to supplement this traditional curriculum approach.

The impact of college and university courses on changes in values and ethics is not entirely clear. Feldman and Newcomb (1994), on the basis of an examination of more than 1,500 empirical studies conducted over four decades in undergraduate colleges and focused on general value systems in many different parts of the United States, reported some positive findings, although these differed for various types of colleges and curricula. One of their conclusions was that, with few exceptions, faculty members exerted an impact on values only "where the influence of student peers and of faculty complement and reinforce one another" (Feldman & Newcomb, 1994, p. 330). There are only a few empirical studies of value changes in professional social work education. These raise some questions about the efficacy of teaching values in academic courses.

While a number of studies, ranging from Varley (1963) to Judah (1979), report either negative outcomes or no significant changes, others report positive findings (Frans & Moran, 1993; Landau, 1999; Moran, 1989; Rice, 1994; Sharwell, 1974; Wodarski, Pippin, & Daniels, 1988). However, the usefulness of all of these studies is limited because they measured value changes as reflected by answers to a questionnaire, without attempting to assess ethical behaviors in practice settings. More recently, a review of the empirical social work literature related to the professional socialization of social work students (Baretti, 2004) produced contradictory findings that raise critical questions. Value acquisition or adherence may not increase with longevity and the degree of socialization in a profession—in fact, a decrease may occur. Neither does prolonged and intense social work education necessarily change students' value orientations in the desired direction (Baretti, 2004).

More than 50 years ago, Pumphrey (1959) noted that social work students viewed the teaching of social work values as something quite apart from (or even irrelevant to) practice. Many changes have occurred in the social work curriculum since Pumphrey undertook her study. During the interim, social work educational programs and the professional association, as well as a number of authors, have contributed to an expansion of interest in social work ethical decision making. In addition, ethical lapses in our society have also drawn attention to the ethical dilemmas that professionals encounter.

No academic course that is limited to thinking and talking about professional ethics will result in producing students who are more ethical practitioners. Thinking and talking must be supplemented by doing. Skill in using the decision-making tools that we will present in this book, as well as the discussions and exercises, should help to improve the ability of students and practitioners to reason more effectively about ethical issues, improve the quality of ethical decision making, and result in more ethical professional behaviors in day-to-day practice.

Earlier, we noted that ambiguity is an ever-present element in almost all social work situations. As daily life becomes more complicated, the level of ambiguity tends to rise. Because of this, we try to avoid giving pat answers. Instead, we hope to convey the need for tolerance of ambiguity when it comes to professional ethics. In professional practice there is rarely, if ever, only one correct answer to an ethical dilemma. Our approach is to focus on ethical applications in practice situations, rather than merely on the philosophical foundations of professional ethics. We agree with Hokenstad (1987) that instruction that is limited to ethics and values and does not at the same time concern itself with practice knowledge will not facilitate the development of ethical social work practice. The purpose of teaching professional ethics in a school of social work or in an in-service training program is not to develop philosophers or ethicists, but rather to train more effective and more ethical social work practitioners. The goal of such a program is to educate social workers who will be responsible for their own ethical professional conduct.

All social work educational programs are expected to provide specific knowledge about social work values and their implications, to help students develop an awareness of their own personal values, to clarify conflicting values, and to analyze ethical dilemmas and the ways in which these affect practice, service, and clients. The following are reasonable objectives for a course in professional ethics. As a result of such a program, students will be able to:

1. Become more aware of and more readily identify ethical issues in professional practice
2. Identify and grapple with competing arguments by examining their limitations and strengths
3. Learn to recognize the ethical principles involved in their practice situations
4. Develop a greater understanding of the complexities of ethical decision making
5. Be able to reach thoughtfully reasoned conclusions and apply ethical principles to their professional activities
6. Be able to clarify moral aspirations and standards and evaluate ethical decisions made within the context of the profession

ABOUT THIS TEXTBOOK

In this textbook, we try to help students acquire skill in analyzing ethical quandaries, become aware of the ethical aspects of practice, and learn techniques and tools useful for making better ethical decisions. We will not present detailed prescriptions for solving specific ethical problems, nor will we offer a cookbook approach that indicates what to do in every practice situation. Instead, we will offer various models to help social work students and practitioners gain skill in analyzing and assessing the ethical dimensions of practice problems so that they can develop ethically appropriate professional behavior. We will suggest several analytic schemes that may help social workers resolve the ethical dilemmas they face in practice.

It is important to recognize that ethical practice is not only the obligation of each individual social worker, but it is also the responsibility of the employing organization and of the profession, as well as a societal phenomenon and responsibility. Although ethical conduct is intentional behavior for which each individual bears responsibility, the professional peer group and the agency setting can and must encourage professional behavior that is ethical. Professional peers and agencies can facilitate or impede, empower or undermine, the implementation of ethical behaviors. For too long, professional ethics have been the exclusive concern of the individual social worker. Ethics must become the concern of the social group—in this instance, the concern of each social agency—as well as of the total profession. The following chapters will provide context and tools for ethical decision making.

In Chapter 2, we review the relation between values, general ethics, and professional ethics. Widespread concern about the relationship between law and ethics has led us to include a section on the relationship of ethical and legal behavior. We will also examine the manifest and latent functions of professional ethics, as well as present a brief history of the evolution of professional ethics in the field of social work.

In Chapters 3 and 4, we develop our decision-making framework. After briefly presenting several basic ethical theories and various approaches to ethical decision making in the helping professions, we will introduce two decision-making screens specifically designed to help in assessing the ethical alternatives that social workers face in their day-to-day practice.

The remaining chapters of this textbook are devoted to the presentation of a number of ethical problems, ethical dilemmas in professional practice, and tools for ethical decision making. Eight of the chapters in this section cover a variety of practice problems. Each ethical problem and dilemma is important in its own right, but no claim is made that any one of them is more important than any other. For each dilemma, we have presented some relevant background information to help the reader examine the ethical dilemmas that arise out of the exemplars presented. The decision screens developed in Chapter 4 should be applied in analyzing each of these ethical dilemmas.

In Chapter 13, we again discuss the question of who is responsible for professional ethics. From what we have written in this chapter and from the development of our argument throughout the book, it will not come as a surprise that we place the responsibility for professional ethics not only on each social worker but also on the employing organization and on the organized professional group. Exercises, suggestions for additional readings, websites of interest, and competency notes will appear at the end of every chapter. Additional exemplars and a glossary will be found in the appendices. In addition, at the end of this chapter, we include a pretest for the reader: "How Much Do I Know about Social Work Ethics?" Answers and explanations for each pretest question are presented after the competency notes at the end of this chapter.

Ethical issues will continue to cause discomfort even after this book has been completed: Every decision a social worker makes entails ethical risks. Perhaps the most agonizing of these risks is the danger of making a choice that may hurt or damage a client or someone else. Nevertheless, a fear of doing harm that leads to inaction can interfere with doing the right thing. We hope that the tools for ethical decision making that we present, as well as the discussions and questions that we raise, will alert social workers to their ethical responsibilities and help them become more skilled and more ethical practitioners.

PRETEST: HOW MUCH DO I KNOW ABOUT SOCIAL WORK ETHICS?

For each statement, circle true or false.

1.	The Code of Ethics of the National Association of Social Workers was created by federal legislation.	True	False
2.	An ethical dilemma is a question a client asks that you cannot answer.	True	False
3.	The NASW Code of Ethics is directed mainly at organizations and groups of social workers, not individual practitioners.	True	False
4.	Social workers must always decide between good and bad ethical choices. They seldom have to choose between two good or two bad ethical choices.	True	False
5.	Social workers are expected to know and comply with the Code of Ethics of the National Association of Social Workers.	True	False
6.	I know the mission of the social work profession and the profession's core values as identified in the NASW Code.	True	False
7.	The Code includes ethical standards that the social worker must follow as she relates to clients, colleagues, practice settings, individual professionals, the social work profession, and society.	True	False
8.	The Code's ethical standards are written in such a way that they seldom conflict with each other. But, when conflicts occur, the Code also includes ways to deal with these problems.	True	False
9.	If you are virtuous and of good morals, you will not have any difficulty making ethical decisions and living up to the ethical standards of the social work profession.	True	False
10	The Code of Ethics applies only to professional, licensed social workers.	True	False
11.	The Code of Ethics does not apply to social workers who are researchers, community organizers, social planners, and those who are employed in nonhuman service settings.	True	False
12.	Ethical decision making is scientific and rational, and it should be similar for all social workers facing similar situations and dilemmas.	True	False
13.	If you are an excellent social work practitioner, it is unlikely that you will experience any difficulty living up to the ethical standards expressed in the Code.	True	False
14.	Cultural diversity is an important consideration in social work ethical decision making.	True	False
15.	The personal values of a professional social worker play no part in ethical decision making.	True	False

CRITICAL THINKING EXERCISES

EP 2.1.3

1. Why should social workers be ethical in their professional practices?
2. If you had to create a Code of Ethics for the social work profession based on your experiences and knowledge, what would you select as the three most important general principles?
3. If possible, ask a social worker to describe her most recent use of the profession's Code of Ethics. What was the dilemma? What was her decision? How did she decide what to do?
4. Put yourself in the situation of Ellen Ashton (Exemplar 1.1).

   A. What ethical issues are involved in this exemplar?
   B. Without reference to the provisions of any code of ethics, what options are open to you?
   C. What do you think is the ethical thing to do?
   D. Do you think there is more than one ethical solution?

5. In Exemplar 1.3, does the Civil Emergency Center have an ethical responsibility to provide child care services for volunteers or employees who are called in on an emergency basis to deal with a disaster such as Hurricane Katrina, or the 2009 earthquake in Haiti, or the Gulf of Mexico oil-spill disaster of 2010?
6. Visit one of the websites listed below and review the Code of Ethics or other material provided about ethics. Compare the NASW Code of Ethics with the International Federation of Social Workers and International Association of School of Social Work Code of Ethics or one from another country.

SUGGESTIONS FOR ADDITIONAL READINGS

A short list of readings we consider particularly helpful is found at the end of each chapter. Emphasis is given to the more recent literature rather than to the classics. The readings may amplify points that have been made, present other points of view, or raise additional questions. Reference to an article does not necessarily mean we agree with it, but in each instance, we have found that the author has made a thoughtful contribution to one or more of the subjects discussed in the chapter. The articles are mentioned only by author and year; the full citation can be found in the bibliography at the end of the textbook.

Goldstein (1987) presents a critical analysis of the moral aspects of social work practice. Aguilar, Williams, and Aiken (2004) surveyed and compared the attitudes of social work practitioners and students to assess their attitudes toward appropriateness of sexual contact with clients, handling of colleagues who engage in sexual misconduct, and the extent of their educational preparation on sexual ethics. Brill (2001) suggests that a gap is growing between social work ethics and social work practice. Hugman (2003) explores the implications for social work as a result of postmodernism, which reflects a loss of legitimacy in universal perspectives and emphasizes the contingent and uncertain nature of social life. Clifford and Burke (2005) advocate an anti-oppressive ethics in social work curricula.

WEBSITES OF INTEREST

- The *Journal of Social Work Values and Ethics* (JSWV&E): http://www.socialworker.com/jswve/

This peer-reviewed, online journal "examines the ethical and values issues that impact and are interwoven with social work practice, research and theory development. JSWV&E addresses ethical and value issues that encompass the full range of social problems and issues that social workers encounter. The journal provides the necessary historical perspectives on the development of social work values and ethics, as well as present articles providing value and ethical dilemmas stemming from state-of-the-art developments."

- Association of Social Work Boards: http://www.aswb.org/

The codes of ethics for most organizations can be found on the web. Some codes of interest:

- National Association of Social Workers Code of Ethics: http://www.socialworkers.org/pubs/code/default.asp
- International Federation of Social Workers and International Association of School of Social Work: http://www.ifsw.org/f38000032.html
- National Association of Black Social Workers Code of Ethics: http://www.nabsw.org/mserver/CodeofEthics.aspx
- Clinical Social Work Association: http://www.clinicalsocialworkassociation.org/
- Clinical Social Work Federation: http://www.clinicalsocialworkassociation.org/
- Canadian Association of Social Workers: http://www.casw-acts.ca/practice/code3_e.html
- American Association for Marriage and Family Therapists: http://www.aamft.org/resources/lrm_plan/ethics/ethicscode2001.asp
- Australian Association of Social Workers: http://www.aasw.asn.au/document/item/92
- New Zealand Association of Social Workers: http://anzasw.org.nz/joining-in/anzasw-meetings/branch-meetings/

  The New Zealand Association has a bicultural partnership written into its organizational structure and Code of Ethics. The Code is published in Maori and English, and the organization and Code reflect Maori and Tauiwi (non-Maori) concerns. Interestingly, the organization is named: Aotearoa New Zealand Association of Social Workers, thus using the Maori name for New Zealand in the association name. Readers should take note that in the United States, the National Association of Black Social Workers, listed earlier, has similarly created its own unique Code of Ethics.

- American Counseling Association: http://www.counseling.org/Publications/

COMPETENCY NOTES

Identify as a professional social worker and conduct oneself accordingly: In this chapter, we introduced the idea of competing values and how they relate to ethical dilemmas for social workers.

EP 2.1.1

Apply social work ethical principles to guide professional practice: In this chapter, we defined ethics and introduced the approach to ethical decision making that will be developed throughout the book and may be used in practice.

EP 2.1.2

Apply critical thinking to inform and communicate professional judgments: Several exemplars asked you to consider and decide how you would respond to ethical dilemmas. In addition, the pretest and exemplars presented above also address critical thinking.

EP 2.1.3

Engage diversity and difference in practice: The pretest briefly addresses cultural diversity.

EP 2.1.4

PRETEST ANSWERS

1. **False.** The Code of Ethics was first promulgated in 1960 and consisted of a series of proclamations such as "I give precedence to my professional responsibility over my personal interests." In 1967, a principle pledging nondiscrimination was added. Several revisions followed. The most recent version of the NASW Code of Ethics will be discussed throughout this textbook.

2. **False.** A dilemma is a situation in which a social worker must choose between two or more relevant, but contradictory, ethical directives, or when every alternative results in an undesirable outcome for one or more persons.

3. **False.** The Code is directed to individual social work practitioners, although the Code may be used by employing agencies, state licensing boards, and courts under certain conditions.

4. **False.** Social workers encounter various dilemmas. A practitioner may have to choose between two goods of seemingly equal value or two ethical choices, both of which appear equally bad, or incorrect.

5. **True.** Social workers are expected to know and comply with the Code of Ethics regardless of where they are employed and in what role (e.g., practitioner, supervisor, administrator, consultant). Nonprofessional social workers may also be expected to live up to the standards of the Code in certain situations.

6. **Either True or False.** Only you—the reader—can answer this question.

7. **True.** These are the major sections of the Code in which ethical standards are set forth.

8. **False.** The Code has many standards. The large number of standards creates opportunities for dilemmas in which a practitioner may have to choose between herself and her agency, between the good of the agency and a client or patient, between a friendship and the impairment of a colleague, and so on. The Code does not include ways of dealing with these dilemmas.

9. **Either True or False.** The answer to this question depends on which philosophy of ethics, you—as a practitioner—think is most correct. There is one approach to ethics—virtue ethics—that suggests that personal character enables one to make ethical decisions, as if by nature. We will discuss these philosophies of ethics in Chapter 3.

10. **False.** It also applies to social work students and sometimes to those with a social worker title who lack professional training.

11. **False.** The Code of Ethics applies to all social workers, regardless of their employment roles.

12. **False.** Whether fortunately or unfortunately, ethical decision making is complex and—in addition to the Code and our education and training in its use—we all bring to our decision making our life experiences, our values and those of the groups we belong to, and our personal perspectives on the dilemma we are facing. Much depends on the context and on our knowledge and skill at identifying ethical dilemmas, as well as our ability to think through the dilemmas we confront.

13. **False.** All social workers at every level of experience face complex dilemmas. One may acquire more skill and become better able to deal with ethical dilemmas, but, because one is dealing with people and their circumstances, no social worker can escape struggling with ethical dilemmas throughout her career.

14. **True.** Social workers practice in our multicultural society. Clients, groups, and communities in the United States and other countries have backgrounds in various groups and many nationalities and cultures. For ethical practice, social workers should know the cultures of those they are working with, as these cultures impinge upon the situations they are confronting. In addition, a social worker should be aware of her own cultural and other diversity factors and how they affect her work and interactions.

15. **False.** As one can notice in several of the preceding answers, a social worker's values are a powerful ingredient of her professional self. Self-knowledge includes understanding as well as possible what values you believe in and how they affect your professional life.

VALUES AND PROFESSIONAL ETHICS

This chapter focuses on values and professional ethics and addresses the CSWE 2008 EPAS Educational Policy 1.1 on values and Educational Policy 2.1.2 on using social work ethical principles to guide professional practice. Specifically, Educational Policy 2.1.2 states that "social workers... make ethical decisions by applying standards of the National Association of Social Workers and, as applicable, of the International Federation of Social Workers/International Association of Schools of Social Work Ethics in Social Work Statement Principles." This chapter discusses both of these sets of standards.

The preamble to the NASW Code (2008) states that "the mission of the social work profession is rooted in a set of core values." This statement reflects the importance of values for social work. It is possible that few professions—perhaps with the exception of philosophy—concern themselves with values to the extent that social work does. Goldstein (1973) described social workers as "value laden individuals." For Vigilante (1974), social work values are "the fulcrum of practice." Viktor Frankl, a psychiatrist and creator of existential psychotherapy who died in 1997, also emphasized the centrality of values, not only for professional practitioners but for everyone. Life without values has no meaning, creating only an "existential vacuum." For Frankl, the "will to meaning" is considerably more important than the "will to pleasure" (Guttmann, 1996). The "will to meaning" suggests that humans should live with purposes that can give meaning to life, that is, by living in such a way that one's purposes and intentions give meaning to life through the expression of one's values.

VALUES

Social workers, like so many others, often fail to distinguish among such terms as **values**, **ethics**, and **morality** (or virtues). They use them rather loosely, as if all the terms have the same meaning. Values, however, are not the same as virtues.

Neither are values the same as ethics. One popular dictionary offers 17 definitions of *value*. Timms (1983) reviewed reports and publications from a number of social science fields and found no fewer than 180 different definitions for the term. A survey of the social work literature suggests that social work writers have used many of these definitions.

Maslow (1962) once observed that values are like a big container that holds all sorts of miscellaneous and vague things. Many philosophers have used the term *value* as if it meant the same as being interested and curious about something, but John Dewey used the term in a more precise way by noting that it must also include some element of appraisal or preference. Most social scientists have followed Dewey's definition, indicating that values are meant to serve as guides or criteria for selecting good and desirable behaviors. Kupperman (1999, p. 3) suggests that a value refers "to what is worth having or being" and that it "is preferable that it exist rather than not exist." Values enhance a life or the world and define "those conceptions of desirable states of affairs that are utilized in selective conduct as criteria for preference or choice or as justifications for proposed or actual behavior" (Williams, 1967, p. 23). Most writers draw attention to the differences among societal values, group values, and individual values. Usually, values at these different levels are complementary or reciprocal, though at times they may be in conflict. Within any one society, most people, most of the time, agree about a core of societal values.

PROFESSIONAL VALUES

Social work practitioners take their basic professional values from societal values—that is, from the values held by the larger society in which they practice. These professional values are most often compatible with societal values, but there may be important differences in emphasis, priorities, or interpretation. It stands to reason that, just as there is wide agreement about societal values, so there must be a wide consensus about basic professional values.

The central role that values play in social work has been recognized by many, as was noted at the beginning of this chapter, and professional values are considered to be primary in practitioners' decision making and action. The Code of Ethics of the National Association of Social Workers (NASW, 2008) summarizes the core values of the social work profession as follows:

1. Social workers elevate service to others above self-interest. (Service)
2. Social workers pursue social change, particularly with and on behalf of vulnerable and oppressed individuals and groups of people. (Social Justice)
3. Social workers treat each person in a caring and respectful fashion, mindful of individual differences and cultural and ethnic diversity. (Dignity and Worth of the Person)
4. Social workers understand that relationships between and among people are an important vehicle for change. (Importance of Human Relationships)
5. Social workers are continually aware of the profession's mission, values, ethical principles, and ethical standards, and practice in a manner consistent with them. (Integrity)
6. Social workers continually strive to increase their professional knowledge and skills and to apply them in practice. (Competence)

There is a general consensus about social work values. For example, most professional social workers agree that client participation, self-determination, and confidentiality are among the basic social work values. However, disagreements are likely to occur when it comes to implementing these generalized professional values. Social workers may disagree about priorities, specific objectives, and the means necessary to put these generalized values into practice. Furthermore, little is known about how social workers' personal and professional values are used for practice decision making and whether the adherence to particular values differs by practice setting or field (Csikai, 1999; Pike, 1996). Thus the value "enhancing the dignity of life" may be used by one social worker to support a client's request for an abortion or assisted suicide, whereas her social work colleague may call on the same generalized value to support her professional decision to try to persuade the client to undergo a full-term pregnancy or continue with palliative care. In fact, these examples illustrate how "nonprofessional" or "higher" values can affect practice decisions.

Bloom (1975) suggests that philosophic definitions of values do not really assist practitioners in the helping professions; according to him, the focus should be on "what values look like as expressed in action" (p. 138). Professional values that do not provide guidance and direction are only of limited use. Nevertheless, they are important because ethical principles and rules can be derived from these values. When framed as a professional code of ethics, such rules and principles may provide social workers with the ethical criteria necessary for making difficult decisions. Take note that ethical principles are always derived from values.

ETHICS

How to move from values to behavior is a problem that is not limited to professional practitioners. It is a more general problem that has become the focus of attention of ethicists. Ethics are generally defined as that branch of philosophy that concerns itself with human conduct and moral decision making. Ethics seek to discover the principles that guide people in deciding what is right and wrong. Another definition points to a key function of ethics: "Ethics is not primarily concerned with getting people to do what they believe to be right, but rather with helping them to decide what is right" (Jones, Sontag, Beckner, & Fogelin, 1977, p. 8).

Though the terms *values* and *ethics* are often used interchangeably, they are not identical. Ethics are deduced from values and must be in consonance with them. The difference between them is that values are concerned with what is *good* and *desirable,* whereas ethics deal with what is *right* and *correct.* A person's right to privacy, for example—a good and desirable thing—is an important value of U.S. society. One of the social work ethical rules deduced from this value states, "Social workers should obtain clients' informed consent before audiotaping or videotaping clients or permitting observation of services to clients by a third party" (NASW, 2008, 1.03f).[1] In the same manner, privacy is a desirable value, whereas informed

---

[1] Note: This reference is to the NASW Code of Ethics (2008) available at http://www.socialworkers. org/pubs/code/code.asp. All such citations encountered subsequently in this work refer to the same source.

consent and confidentiality are the ethical principles and the correct ways of practice that are derived from this value.

Even though values are meant to serve as guides for selecting desirable behavior, they do not always lead to these results because a person's behavior is not always consistent with his or her professed values. Social workers, like other professionals, at times practice in ways that are inconsistent with professional values or in ways that do not reflect societal values. For example, client participation in decision making is highly valued by social workers, yet some practitioners do not always make sufficient effort to involve their clients fully. One reason for the lack of congruence between values and behaviors may be that values are usually stated at a very high level of generality, whereas behaviors are very specific. Another reason for this incongruence may be the gap between professed (or public) and real (or personal) values of the person. What additional factors do you believe contribute to the incongruence between values and behaviors? Are there times when your own behavior has been inconsistent with your personal or professional values? If yes, what factors contributed to this incongruence?

There is broad agreement about the most generalized values, such as cooperation and success, but these are not sufficiently specific to help identify appropriate behavior patterns. The more specific a value, the more useful it will be as a behavioral guide. On the other hand, the more specific a value, the smaller the probability that it will gain wide acceptance. For example, everyone agrees that family life is a highly desired value—that is, everyone agrees as long as that value is not defined in more specific operational terms that may or may not reflect today's various types of families. This generalized value, however, does not help an adult son who has to make difficult decisions about how to care for his paralyzed, senile father without increasing the tensions that already exist between his present wife and his children from a previous marriage. Nor will the son's social worker find any specific ethical referents that may provide her with guidance in this situation; however, the rest of this book strives to provide her with the tools she could use in her decision making.

MORALITY

George Bernard Shaw (1932) once wrote, "I don't believe in morality." His reference may have been to traditional values and rules of behavior promulgated by some external authority, yet it is hard to conceive of life in a society that is essentially amoral.

Morality consists of principles or rules of conduct that define standards for acceptable behavior in a given society. One might hope that morality consists of a set of general rules that apply to everyone in a society. These rules are neither enacted nor revoked by a legislature but are accepted and changed by general consensus. They define the relationships among the members of a society. As Goldstein (1987) observed, "a moral sense ... involves not only individual thoughts and actions but relationships with others" (p. 181). Although in the United States there is a broad consensus about some issues, we are witnessing a growing diversity and multi-moralities. There are deep divisions in U.S. and other societies about such issues as euthanasia and the right to commit suicide, human cloning, abortion, gay and lesbian marriage, and the responsibilities of individuals, families, and governments. On another level, values are clashing among immigrant, racial, generational, religious, sexual-orientation, and ethnic and cultural groups, among others. Social workers are increasingly confronted by a diversity of values and moralities; they practice in a society where there is decreasing consensus about what is *the* proper moral stance.

EP 2.1.1

The CSWE 2008 EPAS expect every social work education program to provide specific knowledge about social work values. This curriculum content is based on the previously cited core values identified in the NASW (2008) Code of Ethics and their ethical implications. The educational goals of such content include assisting students to develop an awareness of their own values; developing, demonstrating, and promoting the values of the profession; and analyzing ethical dilemmas and the ways they affect practice, services, and clients.

The purpose of education that focuses on the core values of the profession is to help students understand and appreciate human diversity. This understanding and appreciation are the first steps to correct professional activity. Thus, knowledge and appreciation of race, color, gender, age, creed, ethnic or national origin, immigration status, disability, political orientation, gender identity, and sexual orientation (NASW, 2008) are important for professional purposes. Such groups represent a diversity of values and perspectives, and, for many social workers, raise value dilemmas, both for themselves and for their clients.

PROFESSIONAL ETHICS

Professional ethics provide the guidance that enables a social worker to transform professional values into professional practice activities. Ethical principles do not describe professional practice, but rather provide screens for assessing practice options for their rightness or wrongness. Codes of professional ethics identify and describe the ethical behavior expected of professional practitioners.

Professional ethics are closely related to, but not identical to, general societal ethics. Just as social work values are derived from the values held by society but are not necessarily identical to those values, so professional ethics come from the same sources as societal ethics but may differ from them in important details. There may be differences in priorities, emphases, intensities, or applications. Illustrative of these crucial differences are the ethical principles governing the relationships among people. Both societal and professional ethics stress the principle of equality, but professional ethics give priority to the client's interests, ahead of the interests of all others. Figure 2.1 summarizes these differences.

General Ethics: All persons shall be respected as equals.

Professional Ethics: All persons shall be respected as equals, but priority shall
                       be given to the interests of the client.

FIGURE 2.1   │   THE ETHICS OF INTERPERSONAL RELATIONSHIPS

For social workers, this professional ethics principle is expressed in the standard of the NASW Code of Ethics: "Social workers' primary responsibility is to promote the well-being of clients" (NASW, 2008, 1.01). The implications of this professional ethical principle for social workers and their practice are many because every social worker is almost continually forced to choose (knowingly or not) between general ethics and professional ethics. It is, of course, often easier to deduce and formulate an ethical principle in theory than it is to apply it in practice. The framers of the CSWE 2008 Educational Policy and Accreditation Standards (EPAS) recognized the importance of professional ethics for social work practice. They therefore mandated that the values and ethics that guide professional social workers in their practice should be infused throughout the curriculum. Figure 2.2 shows the overlap between general and professional ethics; do you think the overlap is accurately represented in Figure 2.2? If not, do you think there is more or less overlap than shown in the figure?

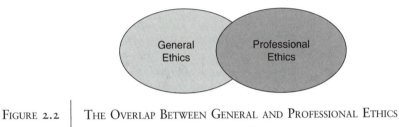

FIGURE 2.2 | THE OVERLAP BETWEEN GENERAL AND PROFESSIONAL ETHICS

Some social workers can discuss professional ethics at length at staff meetings but fail to see how these principles affect their own practice. Exemplar 2.1 analyzes the situation faced by one social worker; pay particular attention to the questions of professional ethics that this worker faces.

| 2.1 | DIANA CAN'T GO OUT |

EP 2.1.2

Alexia Macedonia is a single parent, the mother of three children ranging in age from 7 to 16. Her oldest daughter, Diana, is a 16-year-old high school student. Until the beginning of this school year, she received good grades, but at midterm she was failing all courses. She seems to have lost all interest in school. For the past three weeks, she has not been in school at all.

Alexia is a clerical worker in the town's only industry. She goes to work early in the morning before her children leave for school and returns home late in the afternoon, hours after the children finish school. Alexia is a good home manager, but she has no friends.

Recently, Alexia turned to the local family service agency to ask for help. She told the social worker that she did not know what to do about Diana's skipping school and her poor grades. By talking with both Alexia and Diana, the social worker learned that Diana has to stay home every evening and every weekend because her mother does not want to be alone. Even though Diana wants to go out with her friends, her mother never allows her to do so.

Alexia's social worker faced a number of practical and ethical questions, including the following: Who is the client? Whose interests should the social worker make a priority? Is it Diana or her mother, who made the initial request for help? Or both? Is it ethical for the social worker to intervene with Diana even though she has not asked for help and (on being contacted by the worker) claims to have no need for help? What other ethical considerations are evident in this case? For example, a social worker's primary responsibility to promote the well-being of a client does not mean that the welfare of other people should be ignored or harmed in order to satisfy the client's needs. Nor does the social worker's primary responsibility to the client relieve the social worker of her responsibility to the larger society and to the needs or problems of others who are not clients.

No profession can establish for itself ethical rules that grossly violate the general ethical standards of the community. If a profession fails to take into consideration general societal ethics, it risks severe sanctions, including the possible revocation of part or all of its professional authority. Yet society recognizes that practice requirements make it impossible for professional practitioners to follow the identical ethical rules that people generally are expected to follow. Social workers, for example, may ask the kind of questions that in general conversation might be considered inappropriate or even an invasion of a person's privacy. However, before asking such questions, a social worker must be certain that this information is necessary and that she can keep it confidential.

Society often sets limits on what a social worker may do. These limits can add to the ethical problems that social workers face. In a number of foreign countries, particularly in some of the developing countries, social workers have been jailed because they chose to follow professional ethics and used a practice modality contrary to their government's expectations. Their fate highlights the fact that ethical problems in professional practice are real and at times can result in dire consequences. In a number of countries, including our own, some social workers have lost their jobs, have not received promotions, or have been shunned because they practiced in accord with professional ethical principles and in this way ran afoul of agency rules and expectations or certain societal values.

LAW AND ETHICS: THE PROBLEM OF UNETHICAL, BUT LEGAL, BEHAVIOR

Within the United States, Congress and all state legislatures have passed a large number of laws that affect social work practice. At the same time, the various state and federal courts, including the U.S. Supreme Court, have handed down a number of decisions that are of critical importance for social workers. "Good intentions" and "ignorance of the law" are not acceptable excuses for social workers who break the law. Lack of knowledge not only exposes practitioners to possible litigation for malpractice but may also contribute to unprofessional and unethical practices.

The purpose of this section is to help social work students and practitioners understand the interdependence of law and practice. We will also explore a number of key legal principles that are of vital importance for social workers. Less attention will be paid to specific legal questions because (a) in many instances the law differs across countries and even in each of the 50 states within the United States, (b) law is constantly evolving, so if we were to discuss a specific law, there is a real possibility that it would be out of date even before this book is in the hands of the reader, and (c) we do not intend to make lawyers out of social workers.

CHARACTERISTICS OF LAW

The word *law* has been variously defined by different authorities. According to Albert (1986), laws are concerned with protecting people against excessive or unfair power—government as well as private power. Black (1972) emphasizes the social control aspect of law; for him, law defines the normative relations between a state and its citizens. Selznick (1961) considers justice to be at the very center of any adequate definition of law. Others note that law tells people what they can and cannot do. The law informs them what is likely to happen if they are caught doing something that is prohibited (Van Hoose & Kottler, 1985). Crucial characteristics of law are that it is enacted by legislatures, interpreted by courts, and enforced by the threat of punishment. Its observance is held to be obligatory.

Law changes continually. At any given time, it tries to reflect current knowledge and mores. The adaptation and change of law to reflect contemporary culture is exemplified by the evolution of the laws on abortion. When the California Supreme Court, in *People v. Belous* (1969), reversed the lower court conviction of an obstetrician who had been found guilty of procuring an abortion, it discussed at length the history of the statute that classified procuring an abortion as a crime. It noted that when the statute was enacted in 1850, almost every abortion resulted in the woman's death because of the complete lack of modern antiseptic surgical techniques. The legislature in the mid-19th century, therefore, limited abortions to those rare cases in which the danger to the woman's life from continuing the pregnancy was greater than the danger of her dying from the abortion. The court noted that, in the 1960s, abortions during the first trimester were relatively safe—in fact, statistically safer than going through with the pregnancy. For this and other constitutional reasons, the court reversed the conviction under what it considered the antiquated abortion statute and thus, in effect, revised the law in line with contemporary knowledge and technology.

In societies where the broad moral consensus has eroded, laws may be more effective than "moral persuaders" because they are enforced by the police power of the state. Following the enactment of the Personal Responsibility and Work Opportunity Act (1996), several states began to challenge former court rulings related to the provision of public assistance. These challenges placed restrictions on benefits for new state residents who were treated differently from those who had resided in the state for some time. In 1999, the U.S. Supreme Court held in *Saenz v. Roe* that states could not treat long-term and new residents differently in relation to public assistance benefits.

No matter how it is defined, law is of direct and immediate concern to social workers. There are many different ways in which law affects social work practice. Laws authorize payment for specified services; laws direct that certain social services be provided for all who need them; laws authorize professional social workers to engage in some activities that other people are not allowed to perform, but they also limit social workers from other activities that can be performed only by practitioners of another profession. Laws require social workers to report certain information to designated government agencies. Because laws differ from state to state, we avoid mentioning specific ones. Our purpose is merely to indicate the importance of laws for all social workers, no matter what setting they work in.

DIFFERENCES BETWEEN LAW AND ETHICS

What are the similarities and differences between law and ethics? Law has an ethical dimension. Thus Albert (1986) insists that "it is altogether misleading to say ... that legal duties have nothing to do with moral duties" (p. 9), but there are differences. Whereas observance of the law is obligatory and enforced by threat of punishment, compliance with ethical principles is voluntary and reinforced only by a moral respect for values. Professional ethics, however, may also be enforced by professional sanctions; such sanctions may range from a simple censure to cancellation of permission to practice. A professional who is guilty of unethical or unprofessional behavior may be punished by a court of law and also may be disciplined for the same offense by his professional association.

Whereas ethics are often characterized by a sense of ambiguity and indeterminacy, law is said to be definitive. Yet the outcome of legal disputes is far from certain or predictable. Legal rules are pliable; whether a particular legal rule will apply often depends on the arguments presented by one side or the other or on judicial or contextual factors.

Law is enacted by legislatures and can be changed by a subsequent enactment or by legal interpretations. Ethical rules, although they do change over time, are generally resistant to deliberate changes. Yet there is a close relationship between law and ethics because laws are often based on ethical principles. Thus, the legal principle of *privileged communication* is based on the *privacy* value and the ethical principle of *confidentiality* (see Chapter 8 for a discussion of these principles).

CONFLICT BETWEEN LAW AND PROFESSIONAL ETHICS

Treating people wrongly does not become ethically right even when it is required or sanctioned by law. At times, a practitioner may follow the law and still be guilty of unethical professional behavior. In the past, a number of state legislatures enacted laws that mandated the involuntary sterilization of certain groups of felons and developmentally disabled persons. Can we say that a social worker who participated in these "lawful" programs practiced in an ethical manner? Many social workers claim that compliance with the law requiring the reporting and deportation of those who have entered this country illegally is contrary to professional ethics. Other social workers state that the application of the death penalty, even when authorized by law, is always unethical. Some suggest that there is a moral right, even a moral duty, to violate unjust laws (Pemberton, 1965). Social workers, for example, as advocates for civil rights or for humane treatment of persons with mental illness may engage in illegal behaviors—that is, break the law for ethically principled reasons.

There is a general assumption that human service professionals have an ethical duty to obey the law. However, "in some circumstances, competing ethical principles may be so fundamental that they justify disobedience of the law" (Melton,

1988, p. 944). This dilemma is highlighted by the *Tarasoff* decision (*Tarasoff v. Regents of the University of California,* 1976, 551 P.2nd 334 at 340). The wider implications of this decision will be discussed in detail in Chapter 8. Here we will only note that, in *Tarasoff,* the California Supreme Court held that in some situations the welfare and safety of the community may be more important than the confidentiality principle. Some social workers view this legal requirement to break confidentiality as forcing them to choose, in certain cases, between the professional helping relationship, professional ethics, and law. Other social workers hold that a law cannot override professional ethical duties. Most, however, have accepted the principles of this decision. The Code of Ethics has been revised to reflect the *Tarasoff* decision (NASW Code, 2008, 1.07c); most social workers no longer think that they have to choose between professional ethics and law in the duty to warn. In other situations, the dilemmas posed by the *Tarasoff* decision are still acute. For instance, consider a social worker whose clients include HIV-positive persons. What are the ethical and the legal requirements when such a client admits to his social worker that he continues to share needles or engage in unprotected sexual relations without notifying his partner of his condition? Must this social worker break confidentiality and warn the endangered partner?

When an ethical social worker discerns a wrong against an individual or a group, she is obligated to act. For example, the Code (6.04a) suggests social workers "should engage in social and political action that seeks to ensure all people have equal access to the resources, employment, services, and opportunities they require to meet their basic human needs and to develop fully." Thus social workers are concerned not only with what ought to be but also with how to bring what *is* more in line with that ideal outcome. The feminist approach to ethics must include action to achieve equity for women within existing political, social, and economic structures. When such structures are not amenable to equity, they must be altered to be made more just (Brabeck & Ting, 2000, p. 29).

The NASW (2008) Code of Ethics, in a discussion of the Code's purposes, approaches this issue in a different manner:

> Instances may arise when social workers' ethical obligations conflict with ... relevant laws or regulations. When such conflicts occur, social workers must make a responsible effort to resolve the conflict in a manner that is consistent with the values, principles, and standards expressed in this Code. If a reasonable resolution of the conflict does not appear possible, social workers should seek proper consultation before making a decision.

Sometimes the conflict between ethical behavior and the law is at such a high governmental level that the conflict may not be resolvable at a local or individual practitioner level. Nevertheless, individual practitioners may decide ethically to act contrary to a law. This possibility arose recently in relation to undocumented immigrants. The Border Protection, Terrorism, and Illegal Immigration Control Bill was approved by the House of Representatives in 2005 but was never enacted into law. The legislation as proposed would—among other things—subject to five years in prison anyone who "assists" an undocumented immigrant to remain in the United States. Cardinal Archbishop Roger Mahony of Los Angeles stated that he would instruct the priests of the archdiocese to disobey the proposed law because it is part of the mission of the Church to help people in need. Cardinal Mahony stated that he did not mean that the Church encourages or supports illegal immigration; rather, that from an ethical point of view, denying aid to a fellow human being violates a higher authority than that of Congress (Mahony, 2006). In 2010, the State of Arizona passed an immigration law ordering immigrants to carry their alien registration documents at all times and requiring police to question people if there is any reason to suspect they are in the United States illegally. Opponents called the law an open invitation for harassment and discrimination against Hispanics regardless of their citizenship status. Cardinal Mahony spoke out forcefully against the Arizona legislators and law, calling it a retrogressive, mean-spirited, and useless law (Watanabe, 2010).

MALPRACTICE AND UNETHICAL BEHAVIOR

A social worker's activities may be unprofessional, unethical, or both. An activity is unprofessional when it departs from the usual practice that an "ordinary, reasonable, and prudent social worker with similar education and training would have done in the same or similar circumstances" (Reamer, 2009, p. 122). Such unprofessional conduct may be the result of professional negligence, unreasonable lack of knowledge and skill, or infidelity in professional or fiduciary duties. **Unethical behavior** violates the professional principles and standards promulgated by the profession's Code of Ethics in dealing with clients, colleagues, practice settings, the profession, and broader society.

Failure to provide proper professional service (that is, rendering unprofessional service) can make a social worker who is guilty of malpractice liable to civil suits and/or criminal charges. Failure to provide ethical service can make a social worker liable to professional sanctions. In some situations, a social worker faces all three risks. For example, a social worker who has sexual relations with a client may face a civil damage suit, criminal charges, and professional sanctions for unethical behavior (see Chapter 7 for a more extensive discussion of the ethical issues involved in client/social worker relations). Having sexual relations with a former client may also be unethical and illegal, but after a lapse of a period of time, there may no longer be a case for civil liability. The length of the period of time differs in various states and also depends on the termination date of therapy, when sexual contact occurred, and whether the failure to bring an action within the prescribed period was due to the effects of the sexual contact. The basic question, both legally and ethically, is not the elapsed time, but whether such relations still constitute an exploitation of the therapeutic relationship (Perry & Kuruk, 1993). There is little consensus among therapists regarding post-termination sexual involvements. Some therapists call it an "abomination," and others suggest that there needs to be provision for individual situations with mitigating factors (Shavit & Bucky, 2004).

Legal remedies for malpractice can be classified into three categories: civil lawsuits (potential monetary damages), criminal complaints (potential criminal sanctions, such as jail), and licensing board complaints (potential loss of license to practice for varying periods of times) (Sutherland, 2002). The type of proof necessary for conviction differs according to the charge and the law of a particular state. Among the legal considerations for action in sexual exploitation cases are the wording of the state's sexual exploitation and assault statutes, negligent breach of fiduciary duty, malpractice, negligent infliction of emotional distress, battery, intentional infliction of emotional distress, fraudulent misrepresentation, and breach of contract. Spouses may also assert separate and independent claims for the above and loss of consortium and alienation of affection (Advocate Web, 2002).

Strom-Gottfried (2003) analyzed almost 900 ethics cases filed with the NASW between July 1, 1986, and the end of 1997. Of those cases, 267 were found to be substantiated violations after hearings (cases may include more than one violation; the total number of substantiated violations was 781). Of the boundary violations (dual or multiple relationships with clients), 40% were sexual relationship violations. From 2002 through 2005, the most common complaints and law suits against social workers insured by the NASW Insurance Trust were incorrect treatment, sexual misconduct, suicide or suicide attempts of patients, state board complaints, reporting of abuse to authorities, and dual relationships (nonsexual) (NASW, personal communication, December 21, 2009). Daley and Doughty (2006) compared ethics complaints for social workers in rural and urban areas of Texas; contrary to what they expected, social workers in urban areas were more likely to have complaints against them for boundary violations, including dual roles. According to Mittendorf and Schroeder (2004), sexual misbehavior by social workers remains a problem. Because such behavior is a major cause of claims against social workers, the National Association of Social Workers Insurance Trust limited its coverage of social workers found guilty of sexual involvement with clients to $25,000 (Mittendorf & Schroeder, 2004; Shavit & Bucky, 2004).

Research on ethical lapses by social workers is mainly the result of studies of NASW members and their sanctions. However, Boland-Prom (2009) reported on certified and licensed social workers sanctioned by state regulatory boards from 1999 to 2004. She studied (N=874) sanctioned cases in 27 states. Although the results are limited in their generalizability, her findings are of interest. When only one offense (the most serious type of unprofessional conduct) was examined, the most frequent sanctions were: dual relationships (including sexual and nonsexual); license-related problems (including incomplete or undocumented continuing education units (CEUs) and working with an expired or lapsed license); criminal behavior, both convictions and offenses (including thefts, driving or operating under the influence and drug related offenses, and sex crimes); violations of basic practice standards that all social workers would be expected to maintain (including not maintaining notes and records and breaches of confidentiality); and practice below the standard of care for a specific diagnosis (for example, cognitive-behavioral therapy with a client with Alzheimer's). Box 2.1 presents a complete list of the most serious offenses identified.

Civil suits to recover damages resulting from unprofessional actions or inaction are known as malpractice suits. The relatively low premium rates for malpractice insurance that social workers pay (in contrast to the premiums paid by physicians and other high-risk occupations) suggest that successful malpractice suits against social workers are still rare, but their number is increasing every year. In the early 1970s, there were almost no lawsuits against social workers, but since then the number of suits against social workers insured by the NASW Insurance Trust has increased dramatically (Houston-Vega, Nuehring, & Daguio, 1997). Remember that all professions have experienced a growth in lawsuits in recent decades, which is characteristic of our increasingly litigious society. In the past, there might have been relatively few malpractice suits against social workers because most clients believed in their social workers' selfless dedication to client welfare. The relative scarcity also could have been due to a lack of common law to serve as a cause of legal action (Perry & Kuruk, 1993).

BOX 2.1 | **MOST SERIOUS OFFENSES IDENTIFIED**

Dual relationships	Sexual and romantic
	Nonsexual
License-related problems	CEU noncompliance
	Working with lapsed or no license
	Misrepresentation of information on application
	Misrepresentation of license or training
Crimes (convictions and admissions)	Thefts in billing and other
	DUI and drug-related offenses
	Sex crimes (victims adult and minors)
	Miscellaneous crimes (misdemeanors and felony)
	Crime unspecified
Basic Practice	Did not maintain notes and records
	Confidentiality
	Practiced independently without a license
	Abandoned client
	Problems with report or court letter
	Failed to report child abuse
	Incompetence
	Fraudulent records or forged client signature
	Failed to get supervision
	Informed consent
	Failed to release records to client or parent
	Failed to keep files securely
Below standards of care	
Personal financial	Nonpayment of student loans
	Nonpayment of taxes
Billing irregularities (no criminal convictions)	
Impaired (no criminal convictions)	
Supervision below standards	

Social workers who want to protect themselves properly should know what is involved in malpractice. By learning how liability develops, they can take precautions that will reduce the hazards they may face. One need not be a lawyer to understand the principles involved, though in specific situations legal consultation is desirable. Nevertheless, it is important to keep one's perspective about malpractice and not panic, while recognizing the potential risks that social workers face. Box 2.2 summarizes the four conditions necessary for a client to win a malpractice suit.

BOX 2.2 | NECESSARY CONDITIONS TO BE MET TO WIN MALPRACTICE SUITS

A client must prove these four conditions in order to win a malpractice suit:

1.   The defendant (that is, the social worker) must have a legal duty to provide a professional service that was not provided to the plaintiff (client), with an obligation to adhere to a standard of care for the social work profession (NASW Code of Ethics). Ordinarily, a social worker has such a legal duty once a person becomes a client (whether in an agency or in private practice). Social workers, whether members of NASW or not, have an obligation to be knowledgeable about the standards of care and anticipate being judged against those standards.
2.   The social worker's performance must have been negligent or below generally accepted professional standards of competence. What would other social workers have done under the same circumstances? "Good intentions" or "ignorance" are rarely effective defenses.
3.   There must be a breach of duty and the plaintiff (client) must have suffered measurable harm or injury.
4.   The social worker's actions or inaction must have caused the alleged injury or loss.

BOX 2.3 | SOME EXAMPLES OF POSSIBLE BASES FOR MALPRACTICE SUITS

*   Treatment without obtaining and documenting consent
*   Incorrect diagnosis and incorrect treatment
*   Failure to consult with or refer a client to a specialist
*   Failure to prevent or causing a client's suicide
*   Inappropriate release or detainment of a client in a hospital or confinement
*   Breach of confidentiality
*   Defamation
*   Sexual involvement with clients or other sexual conduct
*   Failure to provide adequate care for clients in residential care
*   Failure to be available when needed
*   Abrupt or inappropriate termination of treatment
*   Improper child placement
*   Failure to report suspected child abuse or neglect
*   Use of unestablished practice methods
*   Practicing beyond the scope of one's competence

There appear to be few limits to the reasons for which malpractice suits can be initiated. The list presented in Box 2.3 shows the great range of possible malpractice actions (Besharov & Besharov, 1987; Corey, Corey, & Callanan, 2003). Many social workers are familiar with several of the risks of malpractice listed in Box 2.3 and the general principles of malpractice litigation, but fewer are well informed about risk-reduction methods (Houston-Vega, Nuehring, & Daguio, 1997). In one research study, 105 New Jersey social workers were asked whether a malpractice suit would be successful in the case of a therapist who asked the police to pick up an emotionally disturbed client. This client had threatened to assault his therapist because he imagined that the therapist had revealed confidential information about him. Only 29 respondents (27.6%) gave the correct answer to this vignette—that there was little or no basis for a successful malpractice litigation based on the therapist's actions. However, 61% gave the correct answer to another illustrative example involving a case where a depressed client threatened to commit suicide and also kill her two children. Social workers were asked whether there was a basis for a successful malpractice litigation against the worker if she failed to inform the client's husband of the threat. The correct answer was that her actions were very likely the basis for a successful litigation. The publicity given to the *Tarasoff* decision in professional journals may explain the higher percentage of correct responses in this instance. Nevertheless, even in this case, 40% of the social workers did not seem to know what was involved in malpractice litigation (Gerhart & Brooks, 1985).

PROTECTION AGAINST MALPRACTICE SUITS

The question remains: How can a social worker defend herself against the possibility of a malpractice suit? There are four major issues regarding risk and malpractice: incorrect diagnosis and treatment; issues related to confidentiality; issues related to documentation (clinical, ethical and legal accountability); and boundary violations. Knowledge and good practice are the best defenses against liability when used in a proactive way. A practitioner should become familiar with the policies and procedures of her agency and be educated in the areas of ethics and best professional practices, including familiarity and skills related to transference and counter-transference. Supervision and consultation should be available and utilized. Also, the burden of ensuring preparation to reduce risks can be shared with colleagues (Chase, 2008). In addition, sound risk management can reduce the degree of risk by implementing a plan for practitioners and agencies that includes having (a) familiarity with "wrongful acts" and possible malpractice actions, (b) a risk management audit (see Box 2.4), (c) a consultative relationship with legal counsel, (d) specialist consultants as needed, and (e) continuing education (Kurzman, 1995).

There are additional means of protecting oneself from malpractice actions. One's practice can be limited to clients for whom the social worker is prepared by virtue of education, training, and experience. Other precautions are honesty and fidelity with clients, knowing one's limitations, and using consultation for difficult situations (Corey, Corey, & Callanan, 2003). Box 2.4 provides a list of how a social worker can protect herself from malpractice actions (Kurzman, 1995).

Furthermore, as our society has become more litigious and accountability is more emphasized, documentation of social work practice interventions takes on greater importance. Documentation that has many uses, ranging from assessment to evaluation of services, also is useful for risk management and prevention or able defense of potential malpractice suits or complaints. Reamer (2005) defined guidelines for risk-management documentation and care recording into four categories: content of documentation, language and terminology, credibility, and access to records and documentation. Documentation—properly done—can be helpful to protect both clients and practitioners in legal situations and complaints to state licensing boards or NASW.

BOX 2.4	PROTECTIONS FROM MALPRACTICE ACTIONS

1. Risk management audit, including

   - Licenses and registrations in order
   - Protocols for emergency situations in place
   - Insurance coverage paid
   - Client records maintained and safeguarded
   - Other factors all in order and up to date

2. Consultative relationship with legal counsel
3. Specialist consultants for

   - Diagnosis and treatment
   - Second-opinion referrals
   - Ruling out organic pathology
   - Psychological testing
   - Evaluations regarding appropriateness of psychopharmacological interventions

4. Continuing education

In regard to documentation content, Reamer (2005) suggests too much or too little content can be problematic in regard to liability risks. Similarly, loose and inappropriate language and professional terminology can create problems. Careful writing that is logical and mindful of potential audiences is essential. Credibility requires social workers to carefully document, for example, informed consent, assessments, termination procedures, and so forth; in other words, the entire process should be documented. Proper documentation is supportive of credibility; when it is missing or not well done, questions are raised. Knowledge of legal responsibilities, including statutes and regulations, regarding access to records and documents is necessary for risk management. Certainly, it is important to recognize that not all storage mechanisms are foolproof.

Furthermore, practitioners should be alert to the potential circumstances under which records will be revealed. An ethical practitioner concerned with malpractice and risk management will—if agency employed—be clear about the documentation standards of the agency, including legal responsibilities and liability. Private practitioners have the responsibility to educate themselves through study and consultation to be prepared regarding all aspects of risk management. There are a number of relevant standards in the Code of Ethics that one should review. They notably are included in Privacy and Confidentiality (1.07), Access to Records (1.08), and Client Records (3.04).

WHO NEEDS PROFESSIONAL ETHICS?

Do professional practitioners require special norms and ethical principles to guide their well-intentioned activities? Are not general ethical principles sufficient?

Whenever two ethical principles or two ethical rules provide contradictory directions, social workers need guidelines to help them decide which takes precedence. Professional ethics seek to provide such guidelines. There are those, however, who see no need for professional ethics. They argue that "common sense" or "practice wisdom" is all a social worker needs in order to make the right decision. While no one should underrate the importance of sound judgment and practice wisdom, many recall the occasions when these simply were not sufficient to arrive at an ethically correct and effective practice decision.

Those who argue that professional ethics are not necessary for social workers may cite one or more of the following arguments:

- *Competence is enough.* Correct practice is based on competence and skill, not on the mastery of ethical principles. Many so-called ethical problems merely reflect poor practice. For example, good contracting will avoid many situations that are presented as ethical problems. Social workers will make more appropriate ethical decisions by becoming more competent.
- *Each case is unique.* Every case is different, and every client presents unique problems. No code of ethical principles can provide adequate guidance for every unique situation a social worker faces.
- *Evidence-based social work is value free.* Evidence-based social work must pay more attention to knowledge and technology than to religion and morality. An exaggerated interest in ethics will deflect practitioners from developing further skill and knowledge, two areas that are extremely important for strengthening professional practice.
- *There is no time.* Social work practitioners have no time for lengthy ethical reflections because practice demands that they act quickly. They do what they think is best for their clients. A code of abstract ethical principles will not help. If social workers were to analyze each ethical problem, they would never get anything done.
- *Philosophers' ambiguity.* At least since Aristotle's day, philosophers have been unable to agree whether anyone can determine the truth of an ethical principle. Under these circumstances, it is not possible to know the correctness of any ethical proposition. It is best not to fool ourselves into believing that professional ethics can help us know what is "right."
- *Relativity.* What is thought to be right varies from country to country and even within a country at different times and for different population groups. In one society it is rude to come late for appointments, in another it is rude to come on time. Which is correct? In one culture a social worker is encouraged to recommend sexual abstinence when appropriate, while in another culture this option is taboo. Which is right? Within U.S. society, different ethnic and cultural groups provide conflicting guidelines to what is correct. In the social welfare field, the emphasis has shifted pendulum-like between individual well-being and societal welfare. Which emphasis best reflects professional social work ethics? Some people believe that there are no fixed ethical principles that hold over time or space. Everything is relative, and there is no way of indicating which choice or option is correct.

- *Instinct and gut feeling.* Practitioners usually know what is right in any given practice situation without having to turn to an authoritative ethical guide prescribed by some superior body. It is far better to trust a worker's intuition than to depend on the enforcement of bureaucratic rules.
- *Coercion.* The adoption of a code of professional ethics will result in latent, if not overt, coercion to make practitioners act only in accordance with that document. Such coercion contradicts the basic social work and societal value of self-determination. A code also tends to stifle professional creativity because it places every social worker in the same mold and expects the same routine standard behavior from every practitioner. Personal ethics and regard for client welfare are far more important for ethical behavior than any fear of sanctions imposed by a professional organization.
- *Virtuous persons.* There is yet another argument, made by Aristotle, that all that is required for ethical decisions is that social workers be virtuous persons. When ethical decisions have to be made, people of good moral character will act ethically, based on their virtuous and morally schooled characters (Broadie, 1991).
- *Wasted effort.* There are so few valid complaints about unethical behavior that a code of ethics and enforcement machinery really are wasted efforts. Actually, there is much variability in the number of ethics complaints dealt with by the NASW. In 1987, there were 54 cases nationwide, rising to 99 in 1993; but in 1996, the number was reduced to 70. The apparent decrease may be the result of an actual decrease in the incidence of unethical behavior or the result of the increased scope of state regulation of social work combined with diminished use of NASW processes (Strom-Gottfried, 2003). Is there an acceptable level of ethics complaints? Can any profession be satisfied that it has reduced unethical behavior by its practitioners to a bare minimum number?

These arguments against a code of professional ethics are not entirely persuasive. Some are fallacious, others distort reality. Here a brief response to some of the arguments must suffice. Chapter 3 will deal in greater detail with the philosophical and clinical bases for these arguments.

Anyone who practices social work knows that social workers seldom take time for drawn-out theoretical debates. Large caseloads and constant client demands for service do not leave time for calm contemplation and leisurely thinking. Ethical decisions, however, need not take a long time. Social workers need help in making correct choices, precisely because they have so little time, and in some cases, ethical choices that will need to be made can be anticipated.

Every social worker knows that each case is unique, yet there are commonalties. Ethical codes address these common elements. Principles and rules in a code of ethics are stated on a generalized level in order to permit adjustment to the unique features of each situation. The voluntary acceptance of professional discipline, including a code of ethics, can hardly be viewed as a violation of the self-determination principle. A person becomes a professional social worker as a result of a voluntary decision. Even though a code of professional ethics does not supply all of the answers (nor should that be its function) that contemporary social workers need, there is a real demand for such a code. In time, improvements will make such a code even more useful.

CODES OF PROFESSIONAL ETHICS

Every occupation that strives to achieve professional status attempts to develop a code of professional ethics. Such a code usually contains a compilation of the ethical principles relevant to the practice of that profession, principles to which the members of that profession are expected to adhere. Many codes of professional ethics also describe the sanctions that will be invoked against those who are unable or unwilling to meet these expectations.

The code of almost every contemporary profession has been written with the following functions in mind:

1. Provide practitioners with guidance when faced with practice dilemmas that include ethical issues.
2. Provide statements of the agreed upon standards of ethical practice, useful for those who evaluate professional conduct and misconduct.
3. Inform clients about what they have a right to expect from their professionals and protect the public from charlatans and incompetent practitioners.
4. Inform other professionals about the kind of cooperation they can give.
5. Protect the profession from governmental control; self-regulation is preferable to state regulation.
6. Enable professional colleagues to live in harmony with each other by preventing or minimizing the self-destruction that results from internal bickering.
7. Protect professionals from litigation; practitioners who follow the code are offered some protection if sued for malpractice.

Because a code of professional ethics tries to provide guidance for every conceivable situation, it is written in terms of general principles, not specific rules. Yet when we compare codes written earlier with those written more recently, we note that the contemporary ones tend to be more specific and try to cover a greater variety of specific situations. Thus the original 1960 NASW Code contained 14 standards, by 1990 the Code included 66 standards, and the latest version of the Code (2008) contains 6 principles and approximately 150 standards.

Internal inconsistencies between various paragraphs of the same code are one of the possible consequences of greater specificity. When there is greater specificity, various ethical principles often conflict with one another, even though each may be valid. One of the major problems of the 2008 Code is that it avoided the specification of a hierarchy of values, principles, and standards. In effect, every standard in the Code is equal to all others. This avoidance of any formulation of ethical principles in a hierarchical order provides the ingredients for many of the ethical dilemmas that we will examine in the following chapters. Another problem, suggested by Marcuse (1976), is that codes of professional ethics often fail to provide answers to ethical dilemmas because their orientation is more likely to be system-maintaining rather than system-challenging. At the same time, it must be remembered that codes of ethics "are not intended as a blueprint that would remove all need for the use of judgment or ethical reasoning" (Conte, Plutchik, Picard, & Karasu, 1989, p. 5).

Codes of ethics generally provide guidance only for good/bad decisions. They are far less effective in helping practitioners make decisions of the good/good and bad/bad variety. It is, however, precisely these types of decisions that trouble many social workers. Good/bad decisions are those where one of the two options under consideration is thought to be correct or right, while the alternative is assumed to be incorrect or wrong. In most instances, social workers have no trouble making ethical decisions of the good/bad variety. Common sense and sound ethical judgment are usually sufficient to guide the practitioner's choice. Good/good decisions, on the other hand, are those where all of the options are beneficial, while bad/bad decisions are those for which all options result in some undesirable consequences (Keith-Lucas, 1977). In many of these latter situations, social workers need help to sort out the ethical aspects in order to make a correct decision.

Exemplar 2.2 illustrates a practice situation that includes an ethical dilemma that is not of the good/bad variety.

| 2.2 | John Miller's Return to State Hospital |

EP 2.1.2

John Miller is seriously mentally ill and has been so diagnosed by several psychiatrists. For the past three years, this 21-year-old adult has been living at home with his elderly parents. He can take care of his own minimal needs, but he has no interest whatsoever in any personal contact. He spends most of the day sitting in the living room, staring either into empty space or at the TV. His parents dare not leave him home alone. They have approached you, John's social worker, requesting that you make arrangements to have him returned to the state hospital because they feel they can no longer give him the care he needs. You appreciate their situation, but you also know that returning John to a state hospital may harm him.

As a social worker, you know that it is unethical to deprive anyone—even a mentally ill person—of his freedom, except under certain clearly specified circumstances. What are the circumstances that would warrant you considering involuntary hospitalization? John Miller's behavior has not been dangerous to himself or others, regardless of the strain on his parents. Suppose this case takes place in an isolated area where there are no alternative treatment possibilities; what should you do if John is unwilling to alter his life? Is it ethical for you to interfere in John's life if he does not want to change his situation? Is it ethical to accept his decision, or should you attempt to change his mind? Is the parents' request sufficient? Is the fact they are elderly and tired sufficient for you to attempt to find alternative arrangements for John? How can you choose between the needs of the parents and John's needs? How would your dilemma differ if the psychiatric diagnosis indicated that sooner or later John would inflict serious harm on others or himself, even though he has been entirely harmless until now? Where in the Code can you find guidance as to whose needs take priority?

A BRIEF HISTORY OF CODES OF PROFESSIONAL ETHICS

All modern professions have developed codes of professional ethics. These became common only in the past century, but their long and checkered history goes back to antiquity. More than 2,000 years ago, Hippocrates (c. 460–377 BCE) demanded that all Greek physicians pledge themselves to a high level of professional and ethical conduct. There is no record of similar codes for theologians and lawyers, the only other professions in the ancient world. The Hippocratic oath became a guide informing medical doctors in many parts of the ancient and medieval world of correct professional behavior.

Just as medicine was the first profession in the ancient world to develop a code of ethics, so did it lead the way in modern times. Dr. Thomas Percival of England is credited with writing the first of the modern professional codes of ethics in 1803. The first U.S. code was enacted by the American Medical Association in 1847 and was modeled on Percival's code. Pharmacists followed a few years later with their own code. Contemporary accounts suggest that pharmacists wrote this code because they wanted the public to know that their professional conduct differed from that of physicians, who in those days did not have a good reputation.

For most U.S. occupational groups, the development of a code of ethics coincided, more or less, with the decision to formalize the transformation of the occupation into a profession. Social workers, for example, were aware that a code of ethics was one of the prerequisites for professional recognition long before the appearance of Greenwood's (1957) important article on the attributes of a profession. They tried to draft codes of professional ethics soon after Flexner (1915) told them that social work was not yet a profession. An experimental draft code of ethics for social case workers, printed in 1920, has been attributed to Mary Richmond (Pumphrey, 1959).

The prestigious *Annals of the American Society for Political and Social Sciences* devoted its entire May 1922 issue to ethical codes in the professions and in business. Contemporary observers viewed the appearance of this journal issue as crucial to the emerging interest in such codes. In the *Annals* article on social work ethics, Mary Van Kleeck and Graham R. Taylor, two veteran social workers, wrote that social work did not have a written code of professional ethics, but that social work practice was ethical because practitioners were guided by the ideal of service and not by any thought of financial gain. Several local and national groups developed draft codes during the 1920s. The American Association for Organizing Family Social Work prepared, but did not adopt, a detailed draft code in 1923.

The American Association of Social Workers (AASW), the largest organization of professional social workers during the early part of the 20th century, endorsed the need for a code of professional ethics. An editorial in the April 1924 issue of *The Compass*, the official journal of the AASW, came out in favor of a code of professional ethics and asked, "Hasn't the public a right to know how the ordinary social worker is likely to act under ordinary circumstances?" The Research Committee of the AASW tried to identify common problems of ethical practice. The AASW Executive Committee appointed a National Committee on Professional Ethics even before this study was completed. This action spurred many local chapters to discuss the need for a code. Several chapters tried to produce draft documents. The Toledo, Ohio, chapter reportedly was the first local AASW chapter to publicize a draft code. Though that draft was limited to a few general ethical principles, it inspired other chapters to try their hand at preparing their own draft code of professional ethics. However, despite much interest, the adoption of a nationwide professional code had to await further organizational developments. It was only in 1951 that the AASW Delegate Assembly adopted a code of ethics.

When the historic merger of all major professional social work organizations took place in the mid 1950s, work on drafting a new code of professional ethics was started almost immediately, but the NASW Delegate Assembly did not adopt a code of ethics until 1960. Seven years later, this code was amended to include a nondiscrimination paragraph. The absence of such a provision from earlier codes tells much about the change in the moral climate of the country and in the profession.

Before long, many social workers called for a complete revision of the code in order to produce a document that would provide clearer guidance for practitioners and that would be more in tune with the realities of contemporary practice. A completely new code was adopted by the 1979 NASW Delegate Assembly. Soon it became evident that this code did not yet provide sufficient guidance for social work practitioners who sought help when facing difficult ethical issues. In an early discussion of the draft code, one prominent social worker noted that its usefulness was limited because of "its high level of abstraction and lack of practice utility" (McCann, 1977, p. 18).

The revised 1979 NASW Code of Ethics placed a much greater emphasis on the welfare of individuals than did the earlier 1967 document. This change may be considered problematic because it tends to shift the focus away from the common welfare. At that time, one analysis of different codes of professional ethics found that all other helping professions (with the exception of medicine) placed a greater emphasis on the common welfare than did social work (Howe, 1980).

Since 1979, the NASW Code of Ethics has been updated several more times. The current version was initially approved by the 1996 NASW Delegate Assembly, then revised by the 1999 NASW Delegate Assembly, and then revised again by the 2008 NASW Delegate Assembly to add additional emphasis on cultural competence and social diversity.

U.S. AND INTERNATIONAL CODES OF ETHICS

We have provided a brief history of codes of ethics because alterations in codes typically reflect changes in the values of the profession and the inclusion of these newly recognized values in the code. Codes of ethics are created through a democratic process conducted by professional organizations, and as such they reflect in their standards the values of the organization as negotiated by those who created the code and those who approve it through votes or other processes for its organizational use. To reach consensus, compromises have to be made so that the code can be approved for use.

If we contrast briefly the NASW Code of Ethics (2008) with the social work code used in Great Britain (2002), we can observe some ways in which the two codes are similar and different as a result of different historical developments and of professional and societal values. Both Codes serve very similar purposes: providing information to the public about standards of services provided by practitioners; and providing guidance to professional practitioners about decisions to be made in determining acceptable and unacceptable professional behaviors. And, when used in conjunction with regulatory body standards, they can be used to determine who may be excluded from the profession on account of unacceptable behavior (Reamer & Shardlow, 2009).

In Great Britain, the social work profession itself did not create its own code of ethics. Rather, a mandatory code of conduct for social workers was first published in 2002 by the General Social Care Council, the body appointed by the government to regulate professional social work and professional social work education. In the Care Standards Act (2002), Parliament charged the General Social Care Council to produce and maintain codes that set standards of conduct and practice. One result was that, in 2005, "social worker" became a protected title, and only those who had professional qualifications were registered and could use the title. At that time, social workers were required to accept a Code of Conduct and could be disciplined if their actions were found to have breached the Code. The British Code is a result of governmental direction, unlike the NASW Code, which was initiated and evolved through the efforts of the professional organization without direct governmental influence (Reamer & Shardlow, 2009, p. 12).

Another difference is reflected in the fact the British Code includes an introduction that describes the function of the Codes, standards for the practice of social care (social work) and standards for social workers who assume managerial roles. The standards are presented together as complementary guides for practitioners and social work managers to combine their efforts to deliver high practice standards. Although the NASW Code recognizes some responsibilities of administrators, the burden of the standards focuses on the responsibilities of the individual practitioner. In Britain, social workers, to date, are the only occupational group required to adhere to the codes of practice. It is possible that over time, others—such as social *care* workers (a general term referring to human service workers and to specific groups such as home care, elder care, etc.) of many types that work within the human services—may come to use the Code as well (Reamer & Shardlow, 2009, pp. 13–14).

There are, of course, other similarities and differences. For example, in Great Britain there is the expectation that social care employers must make sure people are suitable to enter the social casework force and understand their roles and responsibilities. Also, social care employers are required to put into place and implement written policies and procedures to deal with dangerous, discriminatory, or exploitative behavior and practice (Reamer & Shardlow, 2009).

The British Code states that social workers have a duty to respect human rights as expressed in the United Nations Universal Declaration of Human Rights and other international conventions derived from that Declaration. As part of its definition of social work, the Code states that principles of human rights and social justice are fundamental to social work. Further, social workers are expected to account for their practice in accordance with their national and international codes of ethics. The British Code specifies what is meant by social justice. Included in this concept are: the fair and equitable distribution of resources to meet basic human needs; fair access to public services and benefits, to achieve human potential; recognition of the rights and duties of individuals, families, groups, and communities; equal treatment and protection under the law; social development and environmental management in the interests of present and future human welfare; and the pursuit of social justice involves identifying, seeking to alleviate and advocating strategies for overcoming structural disadvantage. At no point does the NASW Code use or refer to the work of international or other bodies.

Similarly, nowhere can one find in the British Code anything that exactly matches the NASW (2008) Code standard 6.01:

> Social workers should promote the general welfare of society, *from local to global levels*, and the development of people, their communities, and their environments. Social workers should advocate for living conditions conducive to the fulfillment of basic human needs and should promote social, economic, political, and cultural values and institutions that are compatible with the realization of social justice.

As the reader can observe from the preceding, however, the NASW Code is much less specific in its references to social justice and what it implies than is the British Code. Although social justice is a theme as well in the British Code, nowhere in the British code is there any expectation that practitioners have responsibilities beyond their own society. Thus Codes of Ethics are not simply objective and neutral creations, they advance values of importance for the organization and profession (British Association of Social Workers, nd).

The Educational Policy and Accreditation Standards of the Council on Social Work Education (2008) includes a global perspective and states that social workers make ethical decisions by applying standards of the National Association of Social Workers Code of Ethics and, as applicable, of the International Federation of Social Workers and International Association of Schools of Social Work *Ethics in Social Work: Statement of Principles*. Thus CSWE—the educational wing of social work—has initiated a new emphasis in regard to ethical commitments by social workers.

The International Federation of Social Workers and the International Association of Schools of Social Work together created *Ethics in Social Work: Statement of Principles* in July 2000. These principles stress human rights and social justice as fundamental to social work. The statement explicitly states that international human rights declarations and conventions form common standards accepted by the global community. The list of documents particularly relevant to social work includes the following:

- The United Nations Universal Declaration of Human Rights (available at http://www.un.org/en/documents/udhr/)
- The International Covenant on Civil and Political Rights (available at http://www2.ohchr.org/english/law/ccpr.htm)
- The International Covenant on Economic, Social, and Cultural Rights (available at http://www2.ohchr.org/english/law/cescr.htm)
- The International Convention on the Elimination of all Forms of Racial Discrimination (available at http://www2.ohchr.org/english/law/cerd.htm)
- The Convention on the Elimination of all Forms of Discrimination against Women (available at http://www.un.org/womenwatch/daw/cedaw/)

- The Convention on the Rights of the Child (available at http://www2.ohchr. org/english/law/crc.htm)
- The Indigenous and Tribal Peoples Convention, 1989 (available at http://www. ilo.org/ilolex/cgi-lex/convde.pl?C169)

The first-time inclusion of this emphasis and international thrust by the CSWE 2008 Educational Policy and Accreditation Standards may be a harbinger of the direction in which the NASW Code will evolve. It is difficult to predict whether or not internationalization of the NASW Code of Ethics will also occur. On the one hand, there is the inclusion by CSWE of international aspects in the EAPS. On the other hand, the U.S. Supreme Court has debated the extent to which international rulings and the judicial rulings of courts in other nations will be recognized and used in U.S. jurisprudence.

Finally, in addition to the codes of ethics discussed above, several other groups of social workers have prepared codes. For example, social workers affiliated with the National Association of Black Social Workers prepared a code of ethics that gives expression to their values and belief that individual welfare can be served best by promoting the common welfare of all African American people. Social workers in clinical practice adopted a code of ethics that reflects their special concerns. The Code of Ethics of the Canadian Association of Social Workers reflects some of the special concerns of Canadian society. A Feminist Therapy Code of Ethics is based upon feminist philosophy, psychological theory and practice, as well as political theory.

CRITICAL THINKING EXERCISES

EP 2.1.3

1. In Chapter 1, you read about competing values. You undoubtedly became aware of the importance of a social worker's values in the ethical decision-making process. Can you identify some of your personal values that might play a part in how you might engage in such a process?
2. Compare and contrast the ethical principles that relate to confidentiality in two of the codes of professional ethics cited above or at the end of Chapter 1. Which code do you consider most helpful when a practitioner must make ethical decisions concerning the principle of confidentiality?
3. Ethical principles and rules are derived from societal values. Identify the relevant social work ethical principles for the following societal values:

- Cultural diversity
- Equality
- Freedom
- Integrity
- Knowledge building
- Privacy
- Social justice

4. As a social worker, if you had to choose between a child's right to confidentiality and a parent's right to know things that affect the child, how would you go about making this decision? What factors would influence your decision?
5. Look on the web for the Feminist Therapy Code of Ethics (the link is provided at the end of Chapter 1). When you compare that code or guidelines with the NASW Code, can you identify themes not emphasized in the NASW Code but found in the feminist code?

Are there any standards that conflict? How congruent are the political stances of the NASW Code and the feminist code?

6. Discuss in small groups whether it is preferable for social workers to work only with clients whose values are similar to their own. Are there any potential ethical positives to such a decision? What are the potential ethical negatives of such a decision?

7. Discuss in small groups whether the NASW Code of Ethics should apply to all social workers, as long as they use the title *social worker* and regardless of whether or not they belong to NASW.

8. There are extensive ethics resources available on the web. Go to your favorite search engine (e.g., Google, Yahoo!, etc.) and type in "social work ethics" to check out several sites. How can you decide which sites are reputable?

SUGGESTIONS FOR ADDITIONAL READINGS

Reamer (1998) traces the evolution of social work ethical norms, principles, and standards. Excellent introductions to the place of moral philosophy in social work practice can be found in Goldstein (1987, 1998) and Manning and Gaul (1997). Mackelprang and Mackelprang (2005) illustrate how end-of-life circumstances have changed dramatically in recent years, causing social workers to reconsider ethical values traditionally embraced by the profession. Barker (1988b) raises a question that faces social workers who are members of several professional associations: Which code of ethics should they follow? Clark (2006) argues that social workers, among other human service professionals, model ways of life and counseling on morally problematic issues and that value-neutrality is neither feasible nor desirable, concluding that the social work role includes demonstrating virtuous character. Reamer and Shardlow (2009) juxtapose and analyze the similarities and differences of the ethical codes of the NASW and the British Association of Social Workers and offer tentative explanations of the differences.

WEBSITES OF INTEREST

There are several websites that provide multiple links to ethics resources; see, for example:

- Lawrence M. Hinman's (University of San Diego) Ethics Updates site: http://ethics. sandiego.edu/
- The Association of Baccalaureate Social Work Program Directors (BPD) Information on Technology Subcommittee on Curriculum Resources on Social Work Values and Ethics: http://www.uncp.edu/home/marson/nlink.htm

COMPETENCY NOTES

Identify as a professional social worker and conduct oneself accordingly: In this chapter, we introduced the idea of competing values and how they relate to ethical dilemmas for social workers.

EP 2.1.1

Apply social work ethical principles to guide professional practice: We have discussed values, including competing values, and how they relate to ethics.

EP 2.1.2

Apply critical thinking to inform and communicate professional judgments: We continue to address critical thinking through the exercises at the end of this chapter and by asking questions throughout the chapter and presenting two exemplars for you to consider.

EP 2.1.3

Engage diversity and difference in practice: We have discussed ways in which the NASW Code of Ethics is similar to and different from the British and other codes of ethics, addressing issues of cultural diversity.

EP 2.1.4

CHAPTER 3

GUIDELINES FOR ETHICAL DECISION MAKING: CONCEPTS, APPROACHES, AND VALUES

This chapter is the first of two chapters that present guidelines and a model for ethical decision making in social work practice. It focuses on professional ethics and values and specifically addresses two policies defined by the CSWE 2008 EPAS: Educational Policy 1.1 on values and Educational Policy 2.1.2 on using social work ethical principles to guide professional practice. As part of this discussion, we consider and clarify the conflicting obligations of personal, group, societal, and professional values.

Social workers must make ethical choices every day. A client tells his social worker that he is planning to commit suicide. A group member who has been unemployed for the past nine months asks his social worker not to tell a prospective employer about his criminal past so that he can get the job, which he needs desperately. Another client has been telling his worker that he embezzled funds from his employer in order to pay for his son's graduate school tuition. A young man threatens to harm a fellow worker who he believes has caused his fiancée to lose her job. Each of these situations confronts the social worker with one or more ethical dilemmas because they involve conflicting obligations. What are a social worker's obligations to her clients, to others who may be harmed or benefited by what the client did or will do, to society, and to her own values? In this chapter and the next, we will provide several guidelines for ethical decision making. Guidelines are not meant to provide specific answers; rather they give the social worker the tools by which she can make more effective ethical decisions. This chapter will discuss the philosophical and practical components of ethical decision making, and the following chapter will provide a model and tools for ethical decision making.

We will begin with an analysis of a practice situation, Exemplar 3.1, to illustrate this approach.

EP 2.1.2

3.1	SERENA ADAMS HAS HERPES

At the Jeanette April residential treatment center for teenagers with emotional problems, the staff became aware that 15-year-old Serena Adams had herpes. Herpes is an incurable disease that lies dormant but is easy to transmit when active at the time of sexual intercourse, even at times when no symptoms are evident. Serena has complained from time to time of itching and sores in her groin and burning sensations while urinating. Although not life threatening, genital herpes can affect one's life by making one more susceptible to HIV infection; newborn babies can be infected if herpes is active in the mother at the time of birth; and one may have to explain the disease's presence to future partners. Serena has been sending notes to Donnie, an 18-year-old male resident, suggesting dates for sex. That Serena is infected is known only to the staff members and to Serena.

The treatment team, after discussing this development, asked Jackie LaMartine, Serena's social worker, to explore the situation with her. She was instructed to try to convince Serena to avoid any sexual relations with Donnie, or at the least to make sure they have protected sex. Jackie said she didn't mind speaking to Serena but felt someone should inform Donnie of Serena's herpes. Jackie thought that not telling Donnie prevented him from making an informed choice, even to assure his use of a condom. When Jackie spoke to Serena, she told her that she knows she loves Donnie and that she feels Serena would want to protect him and herself. Serena refused to cooperate, arguing that the information must be kept confidential, that she and Donnie love each other, and that how they have sex is their own business. She insisted that no one tell Donnie of her illness. The team members are split as to what to do now.

The facts seem fairly clear, as are several of the ethical dilemmas that face Jackie and the team. There are many questions that arise out of the social worker's professional knowledge and experience, among them:

1. Should Jackie and the team leave Serena and Donnie to make their own decisions despite the risks to them both? Is the duty to protect Donnie more important than the maintenance of confidentiality for Serena? If Jackie tells Donnie the facts, she will interfere with Serena's self-determination and freedom, but if she doesn't tell him, she exposes him to potential infection. Is the social worker ethically justified to discuss the situation with Donnie without Serena's agreement?

2. What is the social worker's duty to protect in this situation and whom should she try to protect? Donnie? Serena? Both?

3. What are the long-term potential costs for Serena and Donnie if the team accedes to Serena's request? Are the costs to the agency, to these two residents, as well as to other residents, worth an effort to prevent a sexual relationship, which may not be preventable in any case?

Ethical decision making does not involve the automatic application of arbitrary rules. What MacIver wrote in 1922 is still relevant today: "Ethics cannot be summed up in a series of inviolate rules or commandments which can be applied everywhere and always without regard to circumstances, thought of consequences, or comprehension of the ends to be attained" (p. 7). If there were such inviolate rules or commandments, social workers would find it easier to deal with the ethical problems they encounter.

Social work professionals, like other professionals, make many ethical judgments every day with confidence. They do not think that such judgments are difficult or controversial. The professional Code of Ethics and common sense provide them with sufficient guidance to cope with many of these dilemmas (Beyerstein, 1993). Social workers, however, do not always face simple choices between one good option and one bad option. Instead, they are often confronted by several choices, each one of which contains both positive and negative features, as in Exemplar 3.1. In such situations, the skilled worker must assess and weigh all options and outcomes and then select the one that appears to be the most ethical. How does a social worker know which option is "the most ethical?"

FOUNDATIONS FOR ETHICAL DECISION MAKING

Decisions about ethical questions are rarely idiosyncratic and usually follow an individual's consistent behavior patterns. Because such decisions involve questions of right and wrong, they are deeply rooted in the value system that is most important to the decision maker. Though philosophy has had a major impact on the development of ethics, there have also been other influences, including tradition, politics, religion, race, and gender. Contemporary philosophers have identified two major theories that encompass most approaches to ethical decision making: ethical absolutism and ethical relativism.

ETHICAL RELATIVISM

Ethical relativists reject fixed moral rules. They justify ethical decisions on the basis of the context or situation in which they are made or on the basis of the consequences that result. What are the risks and what are the benefits? What decisions will result in the greater balance of good over bad consequences? An option is chosen because it will lead to desired results or is rejected because it will lead to results that are not wanted. The amount of good that is produced or the balance of good over evil (not any absolute standard) serves as the major criterion for reaching an ethical decision. Jeremy Bentham (1748–1832), one of the earliest exponents of English utilitarianism, accepted "the greatest good for the greatest number" as a binding principle that applies in every situation.

Ethical relativists differ when it comes to identifying the target or the intended beneficiary of the planned decision. Ethical egoists believe that one should always maximize what is good for oneself, no matter what the consequences will be for others. Ethical social workers cannot in their practice be ethical egoists because in their professional roles they cannot always do what is best for themselves, nor can they disregard the consequences of their and others' actions. Ethical utilitarians, on the other hand, argue that the most important thing is to seek the greatest good for the largest number of persons. The greatest good in the situation above would be to protect Donnie, Serena, Jackie, and the agency. But, protecting the agency or Jackie in some situations might not be possible while protecting Donnie and Serena. An ethical utilitarian would weigh and balance actions toward the greatest good but also might have to weigh the differential effects on some and not others.

Ethical relativism is not a recent invention but was already known in ancient Greece. Among its early followers were the sophists and Herodotus. In more recent times, John Stuart Mill, Jeremy Bentham, and Sigmund Freud were among those who followed this approach. All three taught that ethical decisions should be made on the basis of maximizing pleasure and avoiding pain.

There are some who fault ethical relativists because they say that the only thing that matters is the result. If the result is the only thing that matters, is there no difference when an armed robber kills a bystander during a bank holdup, a soldier kills an enemy in combat, or a parent kills a child that a social worker has determined not to remove from the home because of alleged abuse? Different motivations and differing activities lead to the "same" results, but are they really the same?

Many persons question and even discredit the search for certainty and for a rational and definable truth. Some believe that there are no universal truths and that absolute rules are unacceptable. Various "isms" (such as postmodernism, deconstructionism, and social constructionism) claim that situations, including those that require ethical decision making, are best viewed from their "more truthful" perspectives. Because postmodernists believe there are no independent standards of objectivity, no universal truths, and no absolute rules (Rothstein, 2002), they are included here as a subset of ethical relativism. According to some, our era is a postmodernist age and postmodernity is "the point at which modern untying (dis-embedding, disencumbering) of tied (embedded, situated) identities reaches its completion; it is now all too easy to choose identity, but no longer possible to hold it" (Ulrich & Beck-Gemsheim, 1996, p. 24). Necessity and certainty are being replaced by contingencies. The certainties of God, nature, truth, science, technology, morality, love, and marriage are being turned into "precarious freedoms" in which "nothing that has been binds the present while the present has but a feeble hold on the future" (Bauman, 1996, p. 51).

In a world of contingencies, one perspective on ethics arises from postmodernism and the refusal to deceive oneself when there is a loss of legitimacy for universal perspectives and everything seems to be plural, contingent, and uncertain. According to this perspective, self-scrutiny is the key because it will lead to becoming a better person and to becoming responsible and responsive to one's self and to the encounters of the self with the larger world. This form of ethics and ethical action depends on "individuals recognizing the responsibilities they have for others and being prepared to standout even if it is against the tide" (Hugman, 2003, p. 1029).

ETHICAL ABSOLUTISM

Ethical absolutism stresses the overriding importance of fixed moral rules. Philosophers who hold this approach teach that an action is inherently right or wrong, apart from any consequences that might result from it. A specific action or practice is morally right or wrong not because of its consequences or the circumstances but "because of some feature intrinsic to the act or practice itself"

(Callahan, 1988, p. 20). Ethical absolutists maintain that ethical rules can be formulated and that these should hold under all circumstances. For example, they will argue that the rule "a social worker shall tell the truth to her client" is always correct and applies in every situation, no matter how much damage may be caused by telling the truth in any particular situation. Philosophers such as Plato and certain religious philosophers who follow this theory are known as **deontologists.** Immanuel Kant (1724–1804) was the first modern philosopher to adopt deontological concepts, which he expressed through the principle of the categorical imperative— that is, one should "act only in accordance with that maxim through which you can at the same time will that it become a universal law" (Johnson, 2008). He insisted that categorical imperatives (anyone in similar circumstances should act in the same way) are morally necessary and obligatory under all circumstances. Based on this perspective, one should never lie; one should always tell the truth whatever the circumstances. Fulfilling one's obligation has a greater priority than weighing the consequences of one's actions. But, of course, conflicts can occur between two equally obligatory categorical imperatives. Because one has a duty to perform both, conflicts may occur.

It is important to note that many ethical absolutists allow for situations where the fixed rules do not apply. For example, many theologians have accepted the argument, first proposed by the Dutch jurist Hugo Grotius (1583–1645), that one must always tell the truth and never lie, but that it is permissible to speak falsely to thieves because no one owes them the truth. However, there is an important difference between not applying a rule in an exceptional situation and deciding each situation as if there were no rules.

Practitioners may not be aware of these efforts by professional philosophers. Neither do they always know which ethical theory they follow when making ethical decisions. This is especially true because the differences between the major theories frequently are not as clear in practice as they are in theory on the printed page. Because these theoretical approaches often seem to merge in practice many believe that it makes no difference which ethical decision-making theory a social worker follows—but the following analysis will illustrate that it does matter.

DIFFERENT APPROACHES OF TWO SOCIAL WORKERS

We will now return to the exemplar from Chapter 1 with Basanti Madurai to examine how these different theoretical approaches may impact on the ethical decision making of the social worker. Recall that a neighbor had informed social worker Ellen Ashton that Basanti was being abused by her husband; however, when Ellen invited Basanti to join a support group for women who have been abused, Basanti reported that everything was fine. What did you identify as the ethical dilemmas when you first read this exemplar and what, if anything, would you have done?

EP 2.1.2

In the days or weeks since you read Chapter 1, the social worker, Ellen, has invited Basanti to meet with her individually, based on Basanti's initially expressed wish to try to make a better life for her family. During the first meeting, Ellen observed a large bruise on Basanti's arm. When she asked Basanti about the bruise, Basanti admitted that her husband had grabbed her during a disagreement, but that she was sure he did not mean to harm her. During the interview, Ellen established that there has been a pattern of these incidents, but that Basanti does not want to leave her husband and she does not believe her husband needs help. As a new social worker, Ellen was not sure how to respond to this and she was afraid that if she pushed too hard Basanti might not continue to meet with her, so Ellen decided to consult with more experienced social workers in her agency.

The two social workers—Ruth, an ethical relativist, and Anne, an ethical absolutist—might provide Ellen with different guidance. Our focus will be on learning how these differences might lead to different considerations and decisions. Anne, the ethical absolutist, believes that domestic violence is wrong, and women who are in abusive situations should immediately leave to protect themselves and their children if they have any. Therefore, she encourages Ellen to convince Basanti to leave her husband and take her children to a shelter for survivors of domestic violence.

Social worker Ruth views the ethical aspects of Basanti's situation in an entirely different light. Being an ethical relativist, she assesses the consequences of respecting Basanti's denial that there is abuse and her wish to make a better life against the possible harm that Basanti may experience from staying in a violent relationship. Furthermore, her assessment is that the abuse is not life threatening, and she decides that for the time being more information is needed about the situation. She provides Ellen with information about domestic violence, including some research on patterns of leaving and returning. She suggests that even when women decide to leave an abusive relationship, many return (often repeatedly), and that it is therefore very important to do further assessment of the situation and consider the consequences of staying versus leaving for Basanti and her family.

The two decision-making scenarios just described illustrate ethical absolutist and ethical relativist decision making. The decisions made by social workers Anne and Ruth are, in each case, only one of many different scenarios they could choose. The scenarios presented illustrate the general decision-making patterns (absolute rules or weighing the results of actions or omitted actions) connected with each philosophy. The decision as to what is the best course of action in this situation depends upon the social worker's philosophy of life, her values, her commitment to ethical relativism or ethical absolutism, and her assessment of the degree of immediate and direct danger to Basanti's life. It also depends on the influences of the worker's peer group, family, professional group, neighborhood, and society. The situation, as with all ethical dilemmas, touches on the question of priorities. What is best for Basanti and her family? Furthermore, the impact of any decision must also take into consideration other participants in this situation, including the agency, the society that pays for the care that would be provided, the social worker, and other persons who may be involved.

Not all deontologists follow identical ethical rules with respect to any given problem. Identification of the relevant rules is, therefore, of the greatest importance for deontologists. For example, some ethical systems consider abortion to be the same as murder and prohibit it altogether, no matter what the circumstances; others permit abortions under specified conditions, such as danger to the mother's life. Still other ethical systems are mute on this issue, leaving any decision to the individual involved. Social worker Anne may face other ethical dilemmas after she has identified the relevant moral rules. One dilemma arises out of a conflict between two categorical imperatives—the professional value and standard that calls for client self-determination and her own value system that may assign the highest priority to the protection of life. Here are situations where the social worker cannot honor both categorical imperatives, but must make a choice about which one to follow.

CONTEMPORARY APPROACHES TO ETHICAL DECISION MAKING

Philosophers have identified ethical absolutism and ethical relativism as two major ethical theories. Yet these theories are usually presented at so generalized or abstract a level that people do not always find them helpful when coping with the ethical issues they face. In the past, *conscience* was often suggested as the key to ethical decision making. Some contemporary philosophers have substituted *guilt feelings*, while others have added *feeling good*, *democracy*, or *empowerment* as current keys. However, conscience or guilt feelings are too idiosyncratic to serve social work professionals as guides for ethical decision making. One person's conscience will not be the same as another's. Professional ethics need to be common to the entire professional group and should, therefore, be relevant to every member of that profession. Every social worker needs tools of analysis that will permit a more systematic and rational consideration of the ethical aspects of social work intervention. The Code of Ethics of the professional association helps social workers handle clear and obvious ethical choices that arise in practice, states the standards of ethical practice by which professional conduct can be evaluated, and promulgates the ethical principles of the profession, on the basis of assuming that there is consensus within the profession about these (Beyerstein, 1993). Such standards must include knowledge elements, but ethical decision making cannot be based on knowledge alone because ethics deal principally with what ought to be and not with what is. Before presenting our ethical decision-making models in the next chapter, we will discuss a number of approaches that other social workers have found useful in making such decisions.

CLINICAL PRAGMATISM

Many social workers indicate that they are neither philosophers nor specialists in solving ethical problems. Instead, they believe that their primary responsibility is to deliver a high level of professional service. Essentially they agree with Jim Casey, who, in John Steinbeck's *The Grapes of Wrath,* said, "There ain't no sin and there ain't no virtue, there is just stuff people do." They are confident that they will not become entangled in ethical problems if they concentrate their efforts on improving practice. They also suggest that the type of service provided, the nature of the problems dealt with, and the modes of intervention used are determined in the first instance by society; therefore, a worker's personal ethical stance is far less important than societal ethics. Social workers who follow this approach focus on implementing the values of the society that sanctions their activities. For example, one of the functions of social workers in contemporary U.S. society is to help individuals and groups who face various kinds of emotional disturbances and crises. These social workers use societal values as a criterion to identity the types of behavior that require professional intervention, behaviors the society believes to be beyond the norm. They try to resolve any value conflicts that may arise in the practice context by considering the value priorities of those being served.

While this approach seems simple, straightforward, and even supportive of scientific practice, it has a conservative tinge. Radical writers, such as Thomas Szasz (1994) and Ivan Illich (2006), have criticized this approach as unethical because these social workers tend to act as agents of social control on behalf of dominating and exploiting societal institutions. Social workers who follow this approach rarely question society's ethics or its norms (as they understand them). Their practice supports the status quo. These social workers rarely encourage the autonomous development of alternate lifestyles, nor will they be found among those who challenge society's values in other ways. These social workers should remember that they have the professional responsibility and the ethical imperative not to "practice, condone, facilitate, or collaborate with any form of discrimination on the basis of race, ethnicity, national origin, color, sex, sexual orientation, gender identity or expression, age, marital status, political belief, religion, immigration status, or mental or physical disability" (NASW Code, 2008, 4.02). Furthermore, social workers "should advocate for living conditions conducive to the fulfillment of basic human needs ... and ... the realization of social justice" (NASW Code, 2008, 6.01). The question is whether those who follow the clinical pragmatism approach are always aware of the implications of what they are doing. They should seriously consider whether they are in compliance with the professional ethics cited.

HUMANISTIC ETHICS

An idealistic view of human nature as essentially positive, together with an optimistic stance toward the future, provides the basis for this approach. The focus is on causal rather than on moralistic explanations of human behavior. Many practitioners have found the humanistic ethical approach attractive because it combines a strong idealism with opportunities for individual choices. This approach stresses that every person has the capacity, opportunity, and responsibility to make choices that make sense to him or her. The individual client or group, rather than any institution or ideology, occupies the center of attention. Such an approach appears to be particularly suited to the multiculturalism of the contemporary United States, with its emphasis on individualism and pluralism.

Self-realization has been at the center of the humanistic theories of Abraham Maslow, a psychologist, and Erich Fromm, a psychoanalyst. Human beings are believed to be innately good and to have the ability to behave ethically. The inner core of the human personality is intrinsically ethical. Individual freedom and responsibility form the basis of social life. Self-expression and self-actualization are postulated as the desired outcome of mature development. Personal identity is defined by each individual according to self-chosen values that are rationally derived. The priority of professional intervention at the individual level and group level will be to help people achieve self-actualization, rather than to help them to learn how to adjust to the existing social order. On the societal level, social workers who follow this approach will intervene to change those social institutions that inhibit the growth and self-realization of individuals.

Practitioners following this approach can be found in the vanguard of many causes that promote freedom and equality. Some propose disrupting the power hierarchies among therapists, clients, family members, and society in ways that oppose stable social authority structures (Parker, 2003); others emphasize hedonistic rather than traditional values (Orovwuje, 2001). All followers of this approach feel that by clearly identifying value priorities, they will better define and reduce the number of ethical dilemmas they face. Doing so, they feel that they can cope with the ethical aspects of most practice problems. More important, by emphasizing individual responsibility, the major burden for ethical decision making is shifted from the practitioner to the client.

The selection of humanistic ethics as the major approach to ethical decision making has been criticized on several grounds, primarily because such a choice tends to increase the occurrence of ethical dilemmas. Clients come with all kinds of requests; not everyone seeks help for self-actualization. The social worker must also keep in mind that one person's individual self-realization may very well interfere with the self-realization of another person.

Another criticism of this perspective is that it encourages individualism and hedonism, which in many ways fragment and undermine the sense of community that social work aims to build by altering societal structures so that these will become more enhancing of people. This raises the reality of ethical conflicts among individuals, professionals and society because few, if any, client or social worker behaviors are devoid of moral questions and considerations. The chief criticisms of self-realization are that not everyone is innately good, that one person's or one group's fulfillment can clash with that of another person or another group, and that self-realization without boundaries and responsibility can lead to destructive as well as constructive results.

RELIGIOUS ETHICS

Religious ethics presuppose a belief in the existence of God. Whereas secularist philosophers teach that men and women are the creators of their own values, religious philosophers maintain that there is a set of divine values that humans must try to discover. Unlike those who deny the existence of absolute truth and absolute ethical rules, those who follow religious ethics declare that there are eternal rules that give direction for correct behaviors at all times. Believers are convinced that religious faith and ethical morality are two sides of the same coin. They cannot conceive of the long-term effectiveness of ethical principles that come from sources other than divine will. The ethical aspects of interpersonal relations can exist only if one accepts the authority of God. They fully agree with what Ivan said in Dostoyevsky's *The Brothers Karamazov*, "If there is no God, everything is permissible." Jacques Maritain, a Christian philosopher, argued that a secular ethics in which the individual becomes the ultimate goal does not deify the person but degrades him or her because "the greatness of man consists in the fact that his sole end is the uncreated Good" (1934, p. 269). For believers, the search for divine meaning is significant, while nonbelievers consider this search futile.

One of the consequences of accepting the religious approach is that ethics and law merge into one comprehensive, interrelated system. Because ethical principles are usually stated on a very generalized and abstract level, the authorized interpreters of religious law deduce specific applications to daily problems. These deductions become precedence or law. When this occurs, law is no longer separated from ethics but rather it implements ethical principles in daily life. This approach provides those who follow it with a powerful tool that helps them cope with many of the ethical issues they encounter in social work practice. At the same time, these social workers face a very serious problem when they try to apply this approach because they practice in what is essentially a secular society and the law/ethic of their religious grouping may be in conflict with that of another group.

If you consider yourself to be a religious or spiritual person, you might want to think about your own beliefs and how they are related to the kinds of client and community situations you might encounter in social work practice. How might your beliefs and values relate to the NASW (2008) Code of Ethics and to the ethical decisions that every social worker must make in her practice? If you identify potential conflicts between your beliefs and values and the standards of the NASW (2008) Code of Ethics, how might you handle these as they relate to potential practice situations? Although this section has discussed religious ethics in general, later in this chapter we will introduce Confucian and Hindu ethics (the ethical backgrounds of a growing number of Americans), both of which emphasize virtue ethics in which discipline, character, and personal virtues are primary factors in ethical actions.

THE ETHICS OF CARING

The ethics of caring as a late 20th century development has a short history within moral philosophy. Interest or caring is an emotional attitude embedded in a relationship with another person. Some see this relationship as structuring an entire moral outlook. Concern indicates that one is pleased and relieved for a person when the person is doing better and is worried and anxious if things are not going well for him. A concerned person understands what the other person needs and what will contribute to his welfare. He will take on the other person's problems and burdens as his own (in a way), even when this may involve acting against one's own desires and interests (Blum, 2001).

According to those who developed the caring ethical perspectives, the experience of women and children in the private world of parents and families is lacking from traditional models of ethics. Traditional ethical systems miss those feminine psychological traits and moral virtues that society associates with maternal feelings and women in general. Feminists, from a different perspective, raise questions about Western ethics and view traditional ethics as reflecting the masculine culture and masculine ways of reasoning. According to this view, traditional ethical decision making emphasizes universality and impartiality over "culturally feminine ways of moral reasoning that emphasize relationships, particularity, and partiality" (Tong, 1998, p. 261). Other feminists criticize traditional ethical theories because they are grounded in rationality, impersonal principle, and/or rights (Blum, 2001). Much emphasis is placed on an ethic of caring that views individuals as "existing and flourishing only within networks of care ... networks of relationships, practices, values, and ways of life" (Manning, 1992, p. 163).

The ethics of caring suggest that people are by their very nature bound up in relationships with others and that tensions and conflicts in those relations are at the heart of all moral dilemmas. According to this perspective, to resolve such conflicts one must focus on the specific situation of the persons involved, on the web of their relationships, and on how to keep those relations intact without the application of a governing law or principle (Spelman, 2004).

The ethics of caring take as their central focus the compelling moral responsibility of "attending to and meeting the needs of the particular others for whom we take responsibility" (Held, 2006, p. 10). According to Held, when we try to understand what it would be best for us to do and to be, the ethics of caring suggests that we value emotions rather than ignore or reject them. Sympathy, empathy, sensitivity, and responsiveness are to be cultivated in order to determine what morality recommends. The caring and maternal ethic aims at preserving life—feeding, clothing, and sheltering—as well as fosters the growth and training of children and others so that they can become committed and concerned citizens (Tong, 2003).

The ethics of caring rejects more abstract reasoning about moral problems. It questions the universalistic and abstract rules or principles of the more traditional ethical theories that are based on the value autonomy of moral agents, on not being swayed by powerful emotions of the moment, and on acting on the basis of consistent and impartial principles. The ethics of caring posits that the "voice of justice" is more typical of men, while, in contrast, the "voice of caring" is viewed as more typical of many women's thinking about morality.

Bilson (2007) also linked the idea of caring (compassionate concern) to social work and ethics. His view is that all our behavior has an ethical dimension because it changes the lives of those with whom we interact. However, he argues that "we only have ethical *concerns* when we perceive a breakdown in human respect ... the basis for ethical concerns is the concern of an observer for the consequences of the actions of some people on other people and it is based on the emotions rather than rationality" (p. 6). Quoting Maturana, Bilson suggests that which "determines whether we see a given behavior as unethical, and that we act accordingly, is an emotion: love, mutual acceptance, empathy—and not reason" (p. 6). Thus, we do not have to make any decision or invent any rules in ethical choice situations. Spontaneous compassion is already present in all human beings. The issue for training in ethics—according to this point of view—becomes one of further developing our spontaneous compassion and expanding it to accommodate other situations through reflection on our rationalities, actions, and emotions. Ethics is found in human relationships, not in principles. These ideas, based on a biology of caring and compassion, suggest that ethical decision making is inherent in human beings. This argument is suggestive of the character and virtue philosophy to be introduced later in this chapter.

The ethics of caring concerns itself with responsiveness and taking responsibility in interpersonal relationships. It is concerned with context-sensitive deliberation that resists abstract formulations of moral problems. An emphasis on rights, duties, and general obligations is downplayed. However, there are several criticisms that have been made of the ethics of caring. Can one type of human relationship serve as the model for all human relationships? Does this theory over-idealize women and exclude men from maternal work? How does one choose between those who need care, especially where their needs are relatively equal? Caring by itself does not take into account the oppressive contexts in which women live and work. Accepting the idea that caring is innate to women can be used to determine women's social possibilities and roles, stereotyping them and steering them toward particular occupations and tasks (Bowden, 1997). Thus women could be guided or guide themselves toward a more limited number of possible professions and roles. There is another potential downside to caring that deserves a word of caution. Banks (2004) introduces the idea that caring is not without its pitfalls and suggests there can be a dark side, "when care can be controlling, parentalist or overwhelming" (p. 54). It may stifle initiative and downgrade the importance of self-determination.

FEMINIST ETHICS

Feminist ethics are also women-centered and focus primarily on women's moral experiences. As a result, they emphasize the oppressive contexts within which women live and work. Feminist ethics are political in that they are committed to the elimination of the subordination of women and of all oppressed persons. Issues of power—domination and subordination—are more important than questions of good and evil, care and justice, or maternal or paternal thinking (Tong, 2003).

Among the aspects of feminist theory that are important for professional ethics are the following:

- The critique of domination and the concomitant articulation of the value of reciprocity, balancing traditional power differences
- The recognition of the distinctive individuality of the other
- A commitment to an ideal of caring
- A rejection of abstract universality and a model of reasoning that is concerned with context

According to Worrell and Remer (2003), "the social construction of gender relocates women's problems from individual and internal to societal and external. The feminist construction of gender redefines the nature of women's and men's relationship in terms of the expression and maintenance of power" (p. 5). Because domination and oppression in any form are considered morally wrong, feminist ethics are concerned with both the particularities of individual situations and social structural conditions such as racism, classism, and sexism. In ethical decision making, private troubles are viewed within the context of public issues. Personal situations and societal contexts should not be viewed separately (Abramson, 1996).

However, there is no one feminist approach to ethical decision making, and different models (liberal, Marxist, radical, multicultural, existential, lesbian, and others) have been developed. Furthermore, as Glassman (1992) suggests, feminists also find that "their feminist beliefs come into serious conflict with other deeply respected social work traditions, values, and principles" (p. 161). Can social workers respect the cultural values and customs of some ethnic groups that practice and perpetuate oppression? What should social workers who are committed to client self-determination do when clients accept patriarchal or other oppressive communal values?

Parton (2003) introduces a political dimension into the discussion of feminist ethics of care and suggests that care work is "usually devalued as a social activity and practice and is also devalued conceptually through its assumed connection with privacy, with emotion and with the 'needy'" (p. 10). According to Parton, care is devalued when compared to "worthy" qualities such as public accomplishment, rationality, and autonomy. He also suggests it is vital to see emotions as central to an adequate account of human rationality. Humans are relational, interdependent beings. Approaching care as a political concept supports the ideal of a more democratic and more pluralistic form of professional practice.

VIRTUE ETHICS

Virtue ethics originated with Aristotle, who argued there are no general rules for good or right action. Only the person in each case can know then and there what is best, the right reason for the particular situation. One does the right thing as a result of virtues that are taught from youth. People are trained and train themselves to be of good character and to act and behave with practical wisdom, thus learning to be good. Moral training is the inculcation of habits, customs, and mores—that is, accepted ways and behavior. A just and honest person is that way because he has become and is that type of person. Human virtues—justice, courage, generosity, temperance, gentleness—are enacted in behaviors as a result of a developed personal character (Broadie, 1991).

Character is the determining factor. Morality cannot be codified in a general model of ethical decision making. The right thing to do in any situation is what a virtuous person would do in those circumstances. For example, what would Moses, Jesus, Buddha, or another role model do in this situation? Excellence of character is developed through practice. When virtuous practices become habitual, they become part of an individual's character or fixed dispositions that determine an individual's identity. The common aim is to encourage habits and external actions conducive to goodness (Tessitore, 1996).

In recent decades, there has been a revival of virtue ethics and an emphasis on related questions. For example, what makes a particular human quality a virtue? How is knowledge of virtues related to the practice of virtues? How are the virtues used in achieving specific human "goods"? The major Western religions, such as Christianity, Islam, and Judaism, all include humility, patience, peacemaking, and charity as virtues (MacIntyre, 2001) because they assume that only through the use of virtues are we able to function as human beings.

Whose list of virtues is the correct one? A number of criticisms of virtue ethics have been put forth. Because virtue ethics seem to be mainly interested in the acquisition of virtues by an individual person, virtue ethics are viewed by some as self-centered because they are primarily concerned with the person's own character. Virtue ethics fail to provide practical action-guiding help. Finally, right education, habits, and influences can promote virtue, but the wrong influences can promote vice. Some people will be lucky and receive the help they need to become mature and virtuous; others will not. Is it fair to praise the virtuous and blame the others for something that was not within their control (Athanassoulis, 2006)?

McBeath and Webb (2002) advocate for virtue ethics as an antidote to a social work "increasingly routinized by accountability, quality control, and risk management ... there is an emphasis on regulation and duties" (p. 1016). According to McBeath and Webb, this emphasis has created a culture of following approved or typical processes that result in defensive forms of social work. They oppose what they view as a mechanical application of deontological and utilitarian ethics and instead advocate an ethic of virtue and caring. This perspective results in their understanding that "virtue ethics... may not tell us what must be done in this or that case to satisfy an image of social work as a moral enterprise, rather virtue ethics can be used to offer an account of moral existence shaping *the being* of a good social worker. More simply then, the basic question is not what is good social work but rather what is a good social worker" (p. 1020). However, they have not made clear how a virtuous social worker will choose between conflicting values and ethical standards without appropriate ethical decision-making tools.

Confucian Ethics

Confucian ethics has been the primary ethical orientation of and influence on traditional Chinese life and thought. Confucian thought was first developed in antiquity (6th–5th century BCE). It lacks any systematic expression of ethics and is minimally concerned with definitions, but instead emphasizes pragmatic assessment of situations in light of changing circumstances. There are no fixed or absolute principles or rules. Among other features, Confucian ethics seeks a just distribution of the burdens and benefits of society. It places a special emphasis on harmonious human relationships in accord with virtues or standards of excellence in order to guide the way to an ethical ideal of a good human life. Thus, character formation and the personal cultivation of virtues are required. Virtues, rather than rules or principles are the main elements of Confucian ethics, including such personal characteristics as courage, faithfulness, wisdom, kindness, courtesy, and respectfulness. Ethical perplexities arise largely from unanticipated and changing circumstances. Hard cases are resolved not by appeal to rules but to reasoned judgment of what is the right or fitting thing to do in each particular situation. The ethical act and decision derive from a judgment as to what is appropriate to the situation at hand and also to the courage to carry it out (Cua, 2001).

Hindu Ethics

Traditional Hindu ethics are derived from Hindu religion and Vedic texts (ancient Indian texts written in Sanskrit) that supply a moral code of good behavior. Right action leads to liberation from the need to be reincarnated. So, an ethical life is the means to spiritual freedom. Proper guidance, religious observance, and social structures are aimed at securing social harmony and God realization; right action leads to experiencing God. Hindu ethics is primarily concerned with right action as a means of religious fulfillment. Because there is order in the universe, human life can also be harmonious and orderly. Individuals can achieve perfection and the whole system can promote spiritual progress. Because divinity is everywhere, everything must be respected. Liberation and doing one's duty are the two goals of life (Francis, 1995).

Contemporary Hindu ethics are influenced by ideas of human equality, national self-determination for India, economic justice, and social service. One traditional theme (*samatanadharma*) expresses norms in order to assure the well-being of the community, especially the national community. These norms apply to all persons regardless of caste or stage of life: be truthful, be generous, refrain from murder or theft, and avoid injuring others in any way. One has a duty to be self-restrained in all matters. A second theme (*karmayoga*) fosters disinterested action taken in accordance with the requirements of duty, which should lead to personal spiritual fulfillment and the maintenance of a properly ordered society.

At the same time, the search for Indian independence led to the development of an ethic of resistance against British rule by all means necessary. However, Mahatma Gandhi, India's revered spiritual and political leader, took a different approach and emphasized a virtue of nonviolence, truth, and love, both as a means to resist British occupation and in an effort to purge Hinduism of various injustices such as self-immolation of widows. Gandhi also fostered programs of social service, economic reform, and mass education (Reynolds, 2001).

SUMMARY OF CONTEMPORARY APPROACHES

As these approaches find means of dealing with various ethical dilemmas, they may in time challenge and alter the more traditional ethical decision-making patterns in social work practice. Recent writings by social workers concerned with ethical decision making, particularly in Great Britain and Australia, along with feminist and virtue ethics, reflect challenges to traditional ethical approaches as they seek alternative ethical perspectives including caring, virtue, and religious stances. One person's "caring" may clearly not be the "caring" of others and, furthermore, it is difficult to ascertain how "caring" itself will help a social worker choose between good/good or bad/bad ethical choices. Just as clinical pragmatism and humanistic ethics, among other perspectives, have had their impact on ethical decision making in social work, so caring, virtue, and feminist ethics may also play a part in the evolving contemporary ethical decision-making process, although their ultimate impact is not yet clear. Meanwhile, traditional models of ethical decision making offer some guidance as to what to do by providing principles and tools by which professional social workers may make ethical choices. In this book we place emphasis on rational, scientific, systematic, and less ambiguous decision-making processes instead of on the personal characteristics of the decision maker.

PERSONAL, GROUP, SOCIETAL, AND PROFESSIONAL VALUES

Values are a key element in the ethical decision-making process. No wonder Levy (1976b) called ethics "values in action." The purpose of clarifying one's personal and group values, as well as societal and professional values, is to increase one's awareness of the potential conflicts among them and the potential impact these conflicts can have on ethical decision making. Identification of one's values is not a simple task but requires careful thought and effort. What we identify as right and wrong depends on our personal backgrounds and has been formed over time by interaction with family members, peers, authority figures, and the groups and institutions in which we have been members. Recognition of our own values and those of clients, agencies, communities, and other people—including professionals—involved in various practice situations is an important step in preparation for more effective ethical decision making. Ethical decision making requires being alert to the impact of values in order to reduce conflicts and to assist social workers in making ethical decisions based on client needs, societal expectations, and the maintenance of one's own ethical integrity.

Before clarifying the relationship between values and ethics, it may be helpful to differentiate between different levels of values:

1. *Individual or personal values* are values held by one person but not necessarily by others.
2. *Group values* are values held by subgroups within a society—such as religious groups, ethnic groups, disability groups, sexual orientation groups, language groups, and so forth.
3. *Societal values* are values that are recognized by major portions of the entire social system or, at least, by the leading members or spokespersons of that system.
4. *Professional values* are values proclaimed by a professional group, such as social workers.

Generally, these four value sets are complementary or reciprocal, although at times they may be in conflict. Most of the time and in most places, discord among the different level value sets is infrequent, though differences in interpretation, priority, and intensity are not uncommon.

Clarifying Personal Values

Some social workers question or denigrate the importance of personal values for professional practice. They suggest that a social worker must suspend or neutralize her personal values when serving clients. Levy (1976a), who chaired the NASW committee that drafted an earlier Code of Ethics, said: "to be a professional practitioner is to give up some of one's autonomy and to relinquish some of one's right as a freely functioning being" (p. 113). However, in day-to-day practice, the divergence between personal and professional values is rarely as simple as this. The desirability of professional social workers suppressing their personal values may be appropriate in many situations, but remains an ambitious, problematic, and very difficult task.

Others suggest that personal values have relatively little influence on ethical professional behaviors. They claim that social workers know instinctively or intuitively what is the right thing to do. Admittedly, feelings and instincts are important and do influence behavioral choices. However, having a strong feeling for something does not necessarily make for an ethical choice. A worker may feel that she wants to have sex with or befriend a client, but this instinctive feeling, strong as it may be, does not make this behavior ethically correct.

Frankena (1980) indicated that a person's cultural experiences and background, including personal values, implicitly direct that person's ethical decision-making process. However, unless these personal values become explicit, there is danger that biases and stereotypes, rather than professional values and ethics, will shape professional behaviors. Such a danger was reported by both Garb (1994) and Flanagan and Blashfield (2005), whose research findings showed the existence of gender biases in personality assessment for both male and female clinicians and student social workers.

Shakespeare gave sound advice when he wrote: "This above all, to thine own self be true. ... Thou canst not then be false to any man" (*Hamlet*, 1, 3, 78–80). This same advice may also help today's social workers when they consider how their personal values are relevant for ethical decision making. No matter what approach social workers use, it is essential that they clarify and make explicit their own personal values. Those who agree with Siporin (1985b) that "there is a moral and ethical imperative that social workers act as moral agents" (p. 20) know the importance of holding clear, unambiguous, and specific personal and professional values. However, the identification of one's values in clear and unambiguous ways is a difficult task and even when successfully accomplished, there are times when professionals and clients may not be fully aware of the values that impact on their actions.

For example, it is not enough for a social worker to say that she favors (or opposes) assisted suicide. She must be able to define her values about assisted suicide clearly. Does she believe a person has a right to doctor-assisted suicide if death is expected in the next six months and the person is found by a psychiatrist not to be depressed? Or does she believe that, with palliative care, all terminally ill persons can take advantage of the dying process to search for important values, to reconcile with families, and make some valued use of the time? Does she dismiss assisted suicide under any circumstances and opt for life despite the difficulty of the last days? For any of these, one also has to consider what is meant by assisted suicide, ranging from removing life support to discontinuing a feeding tube, to leaving a fatal dose of pain killers available, to administering a fatal dose of medication, and whether any of these options are more or less acceptable than others. These questions are raised here to emphasize that social workers must first clarify their own value stance in relation to value-laden issues they meet in practice situations if they want to be true to themselves and to their profession.

Social workers employed in hospice settings in Oregon, where assisted suicide is legal under certain circumstances, provide care for patients who request assistance with suicide (Ganzini, Horvath, Jackson, Gay, Miller, & Delora, 2002). Is this an ethical professional action? What would be your response if you were asked by a patient to help him plan for and legally act on assisted suicide for himself? In a study to assess the *attitudes* of Oregon hospice nurses and social workers regarding legalized assisted suicide (N = 306 nurses and 85 social workers), almost two-thirds of the respondents reported that at least one patient had discussed assisted suicide as a potential option in the past year (Miller, Harvath, Ganzini, Goy, Delorit, & Jackson, 2004). Social workers were generally more supportive of both the Oregon Death with Dignity Act and of patients choosing assisted suicide compared to nurses. Twenty-two percent of all respondents were not comfortable discussing assisted suicide with patients. However, 95% of both groups favored hospice policies that would allow a patient to choose assisted suicide while enrolled in a hospice and allow hospice clinicians to continue to provide care. Guidance for social workers is available in the NASW Standards for Palliative and End of Life Care (NASW, 2003).

Clarifying Group Values

Social workers, like all other people, belong to more than one group and derive their values from those of their family, community, profession, religion, and other groups in which they are members. Part of analyzing one's value system is clarifying the values of those reference groups with which one identifies. Group membership and context are powerful and often decisive value forces. Like everyone else, social workers act in ways that they might not have chosen except for the influence of groups.

Most Americans grow up valuing a sense of independence. There is, however, a growing diversity of group values and cultural standards that social workers encounter and/or hold. Some groups favor strong interdependence among their members (loyalty, dependence, and connection to the group) and others foster independence (move out, do not be dependent, and steer their own course); what is valued may be different for men and women. Some of these values may be contrary to those held by the mainstream in the United States. Independent decision making is valued by Americans in general, but some groups may hold other values. For instance, persons with Pacific Island backgrounds (among other groups) attach a greater value to group-oriented decisions than to individual self-determination (Ewalt & Mokuau, 1995). Nevertheless, the NASW Code (2008, 1.02) prioritizes self-determination among the ethical responsibilities of social workers. It does so when it encourages social workers to respect and promote this right among clients except when clients' actions or potential actions pose a serious, foreseeable, and imminent risk to themselves or others.

Immigrants often share their residence with relatives or other families because their cultures emphasize family closeness and interdependence or for economic reasons. This emphasis on the extended family is foreign to many Americans who were taught the importance of the nuclear family, and were raised and live in one-family apartments and homes, valuing their individual privacy. Many social workers may come from groups that do not value close and interdependent living arrangements. Similarly, a professional may be unhappy when immigrants turn for help to kin and hometown networks rather than to the professional organizations in which social workers are employed, even when research findings support the effectiveness of these informal helpers (Chow, 1999; Padilla, 1997).

Just as assumptions cannot be made by social workers about their own group values, it is often difficult to offer generalizations about the values of particular client groups. Social workers should keep the following in mind:

- When there are conflicts between the social worker's values and client's values, in some instances the difference may be based on the social worker's or client's membership in a particular group.

- There are limits to the generalizations that can be made about groups, and social workers must take care to avoid the use of stereotypes. Clients may have values that differ from others in their *own* group by date of immigration, whether they were born in the United States, education level, geographic origin, social class, and even language (Agbayani-Siewert, 1994; Fellin, 2000). Differences within a group may be greater than differences between two groups.
- Professional social workers should not assume their clients will necessarily reflect or follow the values of their group.

Social workers who understand and clarify their values and the connection of those values to the groups that affect them and their clients may have a better chance of identifying and handling value conflicts in ethical decision making.

CLARIFYING SOCIETAL VALUES

It grows more and more difficult for social workers to identify and use societal values as ethical guidelines as the United States becomes increasingly a multicultural, multi religious, multi values society. The influx of persons and families from so many different cultures and nations has resulted in an ever-expanding pluralism of values. Nevertheless, a social worker must have accurate knowledge of the various societal value stances and take them into consideration when assessing a problem situation in order to make effective ethical decisions. There may be situations when a social worker is justified, even obligated, to act ways that are contrary to perceived societal norms. In every instance, the worker first has an obligation to clarify the relevant societal values.

The application of societal norms may become problematic when a society accepts values that previously were disvalued, especially when the adoption of the new value occurs unevenly among different groups within society. For example, today many (but not all) Americans accept the value that one may choose one's lifestyle freely, particularly if this does not impinge on the lives of others. Other issues, such as gay marriage, school prayer, abortion, and assisted suicide, divide Americans because the acceptance of these values has not been uniform across U.S. society. When such issues impinge on the decision-making process, the social worker cannot rely on "societal values" to reach an ethical decision.

CLARIFYING PROFESSIONAL VALUES

Social work professional ethics are based on "social work's core values of service, social justice, dignity and worth of the person, importance of human relationships, integrity, and competence. The profession expresses its values through its primary mission to enhance human well-being and help meet the basic human needs of all people, with particular attention to the needs and empowerment of people who are vulnerable, oppressed, and living in poverty" (NASW Code, 2008, Preamble). Essentially, the social work value system reflects a democratic *ethos* that provides for individual and group fulfillment. It calls for respect of individuals and their differences, while at the same time recognizing the need for mutual aid and societal supports so that all persons can attain their maximum potential.

Finding the correct balance between the rights of the group or community and the rights of the individual is often not an easy matter and is a challenge not unique to social work. Such choices present serious dilemmas for which there are few guidelines. Within this balance, however, ethical decisions clearly require adherence to a democratic *ethos.*

Social work practice always involves ethical decision making. Assumptions about morals and values are basic to social workers' theories, policies, and practice decisions. Ethical dilemmas may arise when there is a conflict between the social worker's personal, group, societal, and professional values that are relevant in a given situation. The "absence" of conflict for the social worker may indicate either that the social worker is unconscious of the moral nature of the choices she faces or that the social worker is so clear about her values and societal priorities that her choice is prima facie correct. Another explanation may be that making this decision is not problematic for this worker because such decisions are routine (Fleck-Henderson, 1991). This does not guarantee that decisions made in such situations will be ethically correct. When decisions become so routine that they do not cause the social worker second thoughts, the time may have come for taking extra care in regard to ethical decision making.

CRITICAL THINKING EXERCISES

EP 2.1.3

1. Before moving on to Chapter 4 and the ethical decision-making model and tools we will present in that chapter, please rank order from (1), highest importance or priority, to (7), lowest importance or priority, the following decision-making principles:

   a. Guaranteeing the self determination, autonomy, and freedom of your client
   b. Assuring social justice for your client
   c. Ensuring that the decision you make creates the least harm
   d. Guaranteeing your client's privacy and assuring the confidentiality of any information received from him
   e. Protecting your client's life
   f. Assuring your client's quality of life
   g. Making sure that all of your statements are truthful and provide full disclosure

   Please save your rank ordering so that you can use it in Chapter 4 when we discuss the ethical decision-making model.

2. Social workers deal with varied situations that may be congruent or dissonant with their personal values. Can you identify what your personal values are for the following situations: abortion, genetic screening, religious beliefs or their absence, personal and family responsibility, family planning and contraception, sexual intercourse before marriage, and pornography? From where did you derive your personal values? Can you identify how your values play a part in your personal life and how they might play a part in your professional life? What is said regarding social work practice also holds true for ethical decision making: "As important as self-awareness is value awareness. Helpers cannot be effective if they are not aware of their own values and the impact these can have on the helping process. Many decisions we make as helpers are based on the values we hold" (Alle-Corliss & Alle-Corliss, 1999, p. 11).

3. Imagine the legislature of your state has been alarmed by a sharp rise in the number of children born to young adults with developmental disabilities. Even when these infants

are healthy, many of the parents are not able to give their children the care that they need. As a result, most of these children must be placed in foster homes at great expense to the public. A bill has been introduced by a group of powerful state senators calling for mandatory sterilization of all men and women with mental retardation. The senators argue that this is an effective, efficient, and painless way of taking care of this problem. You have been asked by your local NASW chapter to prepare testimony in opposition to this bill. In your testimony you should be mindful that considerations of efficiency and effectiveness cannot be dismissed out of hand in these days of tight budgets. Yet you might argue that ethical considerations are sometimes even more important. In preparing your testimony, remember that you are trying to convince legislators, not social workers.

4. Organize a class debate on the proposition: "A true professional must be willing to give up some of his autonomy and some of his rights as a freely functioning individual, especially when there is a conflict between personal and professional values."

5. Tonight's forecast is for below-freezing temperatures. The mayor has ordered that the police pick up all homeless persons and deliver them to the city shelter. The police have asked the shelter social workers to help them locate the homeless and persuade them to come to the shelter. You are one of the shelter social workers and know that many homeless persons will refuse to go to the shelter. What are the ethical implications of your agreeing to this request? What is the professionally ethical thing for you do?

6. Most professional associations (e.g., physicians, engineers, lawyers) have codes of ethics available on their websites. Do an Internet search for the code of ethics of a profession other than those listed in Chapter 1. Compare that code with the NASW Code in terms of specificity and usefulness.

7. In this chapter, one of the social workers consulted about Basanti's situation suggested that women in domestically violent situations may be reluctant to leave their violent husbands, and if they do leave, they may return, sometimes many times. What do you think of this? If you are not already familiar with the research on this topic, do a literature search to learn more about patterns of leaving and returning in domestic violence situations. How does what you have learned affect the kind of advice you would give a woman who is experiencing intimate partner violence?

8. Abbott's (2003) Professional Opinion Scale is a values assessment scale for social workers. How would you respond to each of the 40 items? Do you think that these items reflect the NASW (2008) Code of Ethics?

SUGGESTIONS FOR ADDITIONAL READINGS

Landau (1999) studied the impact of professional socialization on social workers' ethical judgment and decision-making orientation. She found that social work education has an important role in conveying central social work values. Klosterman and Stratton (2006) examine the values of Jane Addams, a prominent settlement-house worker and social worker, that influenced her emergence as an internationally known social activist and pacifist who sought a more humane and peaceful society. Clifford and Burke (2005) examine the implications for social work and social work education of developing anti-oppressive ethics in social work education curriculum. Manning (1997) in "The social worker as moral citizen: Ethics in action" argues for moral citizenship to guide ethical social work practice. Abbott (1999) examined social work values within cross-cultural and geographic boundaries and the implications of value bases. A few years later, Abbott (2003) conducted a confirmatory factor analysis on the 40 item, four value subscale Professional Opinion Scale that she developed to "reflect the broad spectrum of public social policy issues identified as being of major concern by the membership of NASW" (p. 645). Brill's (2001) "Looking at the social work profession through the eyes of the NASW Code" provides one view of social work practice and the ethics of the profession. Panchanadeswaran and Koverola (2005) present the findings from a study of 90 women in India who were abused. Anderson and Saunders (2003) discuss research and theory related to the process of leaving an abusive partner. Lovat and Gray (2008) argue for a proportionist ethics in "Towards a Proportionist Social Work Ethics: A Hebermasian Perspective."

WEBSITES OF INTEREST

There are many websites devoted to values clarification. We do not recommend any of them in particular, but you may find it interesting to go to your favorite web search engine and search for "values clarification." Note the specific values and types of activities that some organizations use. For information on values for social work, go to the NASW website at www.socialworkers.org and enter "values" as the keyword to search.

COMPETENCY NOTES

Identify as a professional social worker and conduct oneself accordingly: In this chapter, we have discussed clarifying personal, group, societal, and professional EP 2.1.1   values.

Apply social work ethical principles to guide professional practice: In this chapter, we presented several contemporary approaches to ethics and discussed the relation EP 2.1.2   between ethics and values.

Apply critical thinking to inform and communicate professional judgments: An exemplar asked you to consider and decide how you would respond to an ethical EP 2.1.3   dilemma. In addition, critical thinking exercises relevant to the chapter content were presented.

Engage diversity and difference in practice: Cultural diversity is addressed in the context of clarifying values.
EP 2.1.4

CHAPTER 4

GUIDELINES FOR ETHICAL DECISION MAKING: THE DECISION-MAKING PROCESS AND TOOLS

This chapter is the second of two chapters that present guidelines and a model for ethical decision making in social work practice. It addresses the CSWE 2008 EPAS Educational Policy 2.1.2 on using social work ethical principles to guide professional practice. We will provide several opportunities for you to work with this ethical decision-making model. This model is not a "prescription" but rather a guide that lets you apply critical thinking to inform and communicate professional judgments (consistent with the CSWE 2008 EPAS Educational Policy 2.1.3).

In the previous chapter, we examined the various philosophical components, contemporary approaches, and values that serve as a background for ethical decision making. Our perspective is that social workers should strive to achieve personal virtues but that in addition to being of good character, it is necessary that they be trained and skillful in a systematic approach to ethical decision making. In this chapter, we turn to the practical components of decision making itself. Sometimes a social worker can realize instantly that an ethical decision must be made. More typically, decision making is a process or series of thoughts and activities that occurs over time and that results in a person or group acting (or not acting) in a particular manner. Although the process may not be conscious, it always precedes the making of the ethical decision itself. Decisions will be better, more effective, and more ethical to the extent that the process becomes conscious.

Ideally, decisions are approached step by step, so that one moves through a series of stages until, at the end of the process, one makes *the* decision. It is erroneous to assume that only one person, the decision maker, participates in this process. In fact, there may be many participants involved in the decision-making process, but there is ultimately only one responsible decision maker. Many different persons present information, react to assessments, introduce additional options, or make changes in the environment; these events, in turn, change the nature of the data on which the decision is based or the nature of the decision that is made. But again, only one person is ultimately responsible for the decision.

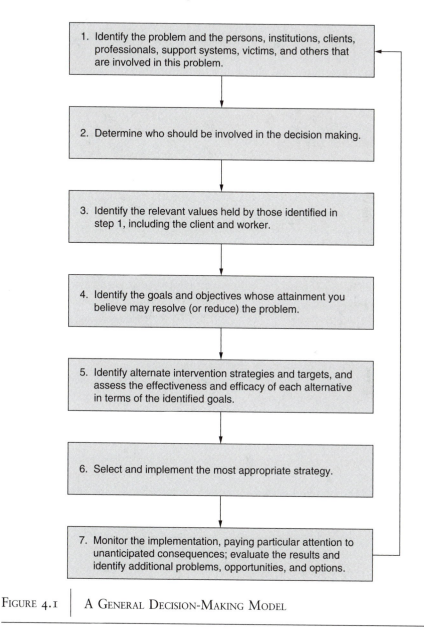

1. Identify the problem and the persons, institutions, clients, professionals, support systems, victims, and others that are involved in this problem.

2. Determine who should be involved in the decision making.

3. Identify the relevant values held by those identified in step 1, including the client and worker.

4. Identify the goals and objectives whose attainment you believe may resolve (or reduce) the problem.

5. Identify alternate intervention strategies and targets, and assess the effectiveness and efficacy of each alternative in terms of the identified goals.

6. Select and implement the most appropriate strategy.

7. Monitor the implementation, paying particular attention to unanticipated consequences; evaluate the results and identify additional problems, opportunities, and options.

FIGURE 4.1 | A GENERAL DECISION-MAKING MODEL

Observing decision making is like watching ocean waves approach the shore. Choices are always influenced by previous decisions that in turn lead to new directions. Ethical decision making is far too complex to permit the development of a simple "how-to" problem-solving model, but we use a model to help social workers understand what is involved in ethical decision making. Like all models in science, such a model will simplify reality by focusing on only one decision. A model is a permissible didactic device as long as it is understood that, in real life, every decision is preceded and followed by other decisions, many of which have a direct bearing on the matter under consideration. In Figure 4.1 above, we present a general model for decision making that is applicable to many different situations and is not limited to ethical decisions. This model is based on the assumption that social workers have the ability and capability to plan rationally what is needed for intervention in human situations and that they want to minimize the irrational, the impulsive, and the unplanned consequences of their actions.

ETHICAL ASSESSMENT SCREEN

The social worker who is alert to the ethical aspects of practice will examine and assess the available options and alternatives somewhat differently than her colleague who is not as concerned with those aspects. This becomes clear when we consider various assessment criteria. In Figure 4.2, we present an ethical assessment screen designed to help social workers further clarify and integrate the ethical aspects of decision making in social work practice.

1. Identify the relevant professional values and ethics, your own relevant values, and any societal values relevant to the ethical decision to be made in relation to this ethical dilemma.
2. What can you do to minimize conflicts between personal, societal, and professional values?
3. Identify alternative ethical options that you may take.
4. Which of the alternative ethical options will minimize conflicts between your client's, others', and society's rights and protect to the greatest extent your client's and others' rights and welfare, and society's rights and interests?
5. Which alternative action will be most efficient, effective, and ethical, as well as result in your doing the least harm possible?
6. Have you considered and weighed both short- and long-term ethical consequences?
7. Final check: Is the planned action impartial, generalizable, and justifiable?

FIGURE 4.2 | ETHICAL ASSESSMENT SCREEN

PROTECTION OF CLIENTS' RIGHTS AND WELFARE

The definition of rights and privileges changes over time, and these changes may create ethical problems. What is at one time thought to be a right may not be so defined in another era—for example, social workers were once expected to protect confidentiality, no matter what the obstacles. Today's social workers continue to value confidentiality, but, for various reasons, they may not be able to keep all information supplied by the client confidential at all times. The reasons for these changes include changes in laws or court decisions; the introduction of new technologies;

managed care and administrative record keeping required by funding and accrediting organizations; participation and consultation with team members, including those from other disciplines; and responsibility to supervisors and courts. In Chapter 8, privacy regulations required by the Health Insurance Portability and Accountability Act (HIPAA, 1996) that was fully implemented in 2003 will be discussed.

Changing definitions of rights are likely to create ethical problems for social workers. Consider the ethical problems faced by social workers in the adoption field as the right of adopted persons to information about their biological parents is becoming recognized in more and more jurisdictions. At one time, the biological and adoptive parents were assured that such information would remain confidential and would never be shared with the adoptee. Since court decisions or legislative enactments in some states now guarantee the right of adopted persons to this information, social workers in these jurisdictions may have little choice but to reveal this information, even though they had earlier, in good faith, assured both the biological and adoptive parents that this information would remain confidential. Is it ethical for social workers in states that have not yet passed such legislation to continue to tell biological and adoptive parents that this information will always remain confidential? This problem goes beyond the field of adoption. Nowadays, no social worker can ever assure a client complete confidentiality because she often cannot control what others (e.g., interdisciplinary team members, insurance companies, etc.) will do with the information that has been appropriately shared. Placing such information in computerized databases, as is now common in many social agencies, only intensifies this predicament.

PROTECTION OF SOCIETY'S INTERESTS

Social workers are caring human service professionals who look simultaneously at individuals, families, and society; therefore, they have to be attentive to both individual and societal needs. But, at times, social workers also are expected to engage in a social control role. Society often grants social workers the power to force marginalized, deviant, and vulnerable clients to conform. This power may be legal, moral, or economic. Threatening to call on the courts or police can be used to coerce clients who fear imprisonment or the risk of losing their children. Social workers may in certain situations control access to services on the basis of clients meeting expected standards of behavior related to dominant social norms. Social workers are also acting as control agents when they set limits on the aggressive or acting out behaviors of adolescents; when they intervene to minimize child, adult, elder, and domestic violence; and when they act to reduce school bullying or to limit drug addictions. Although much has been written in the literature about the caring role, the controlling role has less visibility, but it is, nevertheless, important and potentially powerful. The expectation to actualize both the caring and the social control role inevitably leads to role conflict and ethical dilemmas.

Sometimes it is difficult to balance society's interests with a client's interests. Consider a client who tells his social worker that while he has been unemployed he is spending a lot of time with friends, sometimes spending the family's limited income on beer. He has been enjoying the time with friends so much that he has not been looking for a job and plans to apply for public assistance and Medicaid for his family when his unemployment benefits run out. He is not doing anything criminal, but he is neglecting his obligations as a father and husband and pushing his family's needs onto the State. Although he has not committed a crime, he is not meeting society's or his family's expectations of what a father and husband should be and do. The social worker must weigh her obligations to her client against her obligations to his family and to society. Social control is one of the functions of every social worker, but so is the maintenance of a helping relationship. To which function should the practitioner give priority if she cannot pursue both at the same time? Does it matter whether his behavior harms his wife and children? Can his behavior be overlooked if he is making progress toward attaining identified and constructive intervention goals, such as treatment for alcoholism or drug addiction? Keep these questions in mind as you assess the ethical dilemmas posed in Exemplar 4.1.

4.1	SECURITY OR PROTECTION?

EP 2.1.2

John Newton is a likable young man—22 years old, not steadily employed, but always willing to help. Even before Ray Dunkirk, the community worker, had arrived on the scene, John had organized a number of young adults into a club. This club was well known in the neighborhood for the many helpful services it provided. The community's elderly population was especially appreciative of the security services that the group gave them. Thefts and holdups of older people had ceased ever since this club began to operate in the community. However, Ray became aware that John had intimidated local store owners and obtained regular payoffs from them in return for promising them "protection." What was Ray Dunkirk to do? He considered various options, including the following:

- Overlooking John's protection racket in view of the many positive things he was doing that were benefiting the community
- Reporting John's protection racket to the police, because illegal activities should never be condoned
- Strengthening his relations with John with the view of helping to guide him away from the illegal activity; in the meantime, he would not report the law violation to the police

What are the ethical aspects that Ray should keep in mind while choosing the best option? One ethical dilemma is how to balance the best interests of the various persons and groups involved: older persons, storekeepers, the community, the larger society, and others. Another question concerns the ethics of doing something that might result in the return of violence against the older people of this community. The following discussion is intended to help social workers cope with these conflicts and find answers to these questions.

THE LEAST HARM PRINCIPLE

Sometimes social workers are confronted by problems for which there are no positive choices. Regardless of the option chosen by the client and/or the worker, some harm will come to one person or another, perhaps even to the client or to the social worker. What is the ethical choice in such situations? The **least harm principle** suggests choosing the option that will result in the least harm, the least permanent harm, and the most easily reversible harm. These are not always simple decisions, and, in some cases, there are complex considerations. A social worker has to consider "the least harm to whom?" A given choice may result in the least harm to one person but a more serious harm to another person.

Consider the options facing Ellen Ashton, the social worker who is the decision maker in the Madurai family situation (Exemplar 1.1). Does the least harm principle offer her any guidance in choosing the most ethical alternative? If so, how?

Some have suggested that the routine application of the least harm principle may diminish the possibility of choosing the most effective intervention technique. There may be times when it is justified to use an option that may result in a greater harm but at the same time enhances the likelihood of a successful outcome. However, such a choice should be made only with the full informed consent and agreement of the client.

EFFICIENCY AND EFFECTIVENESS

Many people think that *efficiency* and *effectiveness* are synonyms, but there are crucial differences between these two terms, especially when it comes to ethical decision making. The **efficiency criterion** is concerned with the relative cost (including budget, staff time, agency, and community resources) of achieving a stated objective. Whenever two options will lead to the same result, the one that requires fewer resources is the more efficient one. The **effectiveness criterion**, on the other hand, relates to the degree to which the desired outcome is achieved. When the implementation of one option results in halving the number of child neglect cases in a neighborhood, while the second option reduces the number of neglect cases in the neighborhood by 80%, the latter option is the more effective one—but its cost may be so high that it is considered inefficient.

The choice between two alternate options is easy when the more effective of two alternates is also the more efficient one. But when the more efficient option is the less effective one (or vice versa), the choice becomes more difficult. Furthermore, unethical decisions may be made when only efficiency and effectiveness criteria are considered. At times, the most efficient or the most effective option must be rejected because of its ethical implications. Cuba, for example, as early as 1975, tested all persons who had lived in Africa for diseases. Those Cubans who tested HIV positive were committed to sanatoriums where they were forced to remain, despite human rights complaints by Cuban and other human rights groups. Later, some were allowed to leave these sanatoriums if their condom use and hygiene were approved (Aguilera, 2003). U.S. authorities assessed these actions as highly effective at controlling the transmission of HIV but questioned them from an ethical point of view. Or take another example: In the 19th century, it was common practice to send poor people, or persons with chronic mental illnesses, to another city or deport them to another country; this was an effective and efficient way of eliminating poverty or of eliminating the expense of long-term or repeated hospitalizations, but such actions must be dismissed out of hand by anyone who is concerned with their ethical implications.

More often, the ethical assessment of an option is not as clear as in these examples, and a social worker may find it more difficult to make a decision. For example, what are the ethical implications of forcing poor people to work? Work is highly valued in our society, but *force* means limiting a person's freedom, another important value in our society. The ethical assessment, in this case, demands that we assess work and independence against the loss of freedom. In the past, social work ideology rejected the various "workfare" programs that forced poor people to work. With the implementation of Temporary Assistance for Needy Families (TANF), a change in societal and social work ideology and values has occurred. Although a professional consensus on this issue may still be lacking, there appears to be less agreement on whether "workfare" is unethical than was true in the past (Dolgoff, 2002).

Another kind of ethical quandary arises out of the continuing efforts to deinstitutionalize patients of mental hospitals. When this policy was first proposed some years ago, many professional social workers supported and implemented the program because they thought it would right a wrong. In some instances, the option of releasing mentally ill patients from hospitals was adopted even when it was known that most communities lacked adequate resources for providing care for these people. Many state governments were unable to help communities with the problem because they themselves were facing major budget cuts. How ethical was it to institute a strategy that might result in some long-range improvements, but in the short run might harm many vulnerable people? Was it ethical to do so without first ensuring the availability of adequate community resources? Consider this question by using the ethical assessment screen (Figure 4.2). The ethical assessment screen provides a sequence of questions to be answered systematically that takes a person through the important variables to consider in order to arrive at a thoughtful and careful ethical decision.

RANK ORDERING ETHICAL PRINCIPLES

In the preceding section, we discussed a number of ethical criteria that some social workers have found helpful when assessing decision alternatives. Among these are protection of a client's rights and welfare, protection of society's interests, the least harm principle, and efficiency and effectiveness. These criteria have not been arranged in any order of priority. More specific guides are needed whenever two or more of these criteria point toward different alternatives. Even though some social workers disagree, we believe that the preferred way of resolving such conflicts among ethical principles is a priority ordering of these principles—that is, rank ordering them from the most important to the least important. A priority ordering of principles is especially helpful when two or more ethical standards conflict. Such ordering may be helpful even though "ordering principles is not an easy task" (Christensen, 1986, p. 82) and even when there is not complete agreement on what the order should be. A priority ordering of ethical principles can provide social workers with a guide, but such a guide is not meant to be a magic formula.

Social workers rarely make direct use of theoretical knowledge or philosophical principles when making practice decisions. Instead, they have integrated knowledge and values into a set of practice principles, and these are what social workers use at the critical points in the decision-making process. We have prepared the following two guides or screens that we believe will be helpful in making ethical decisions. We call these guides the **ethical rules screen (ERS)** and the **ethical principles screen (EPS)** (see Figures 4.3 and 4.4). These guides are meant to be only tools—they should never be applied blindly.

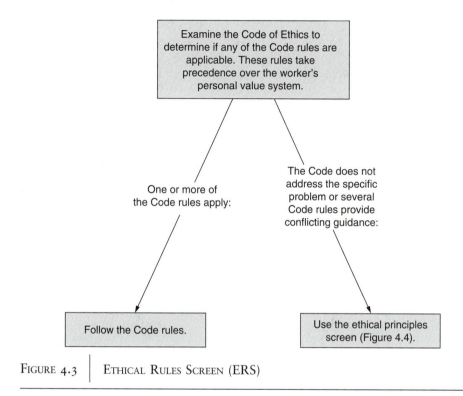

Figure 4.3   Ethical Rules Screen (ERS)

The ERS should always be used first. Only when this screen does not provide sufficient guidance should the social worker turn to the EPS. To be useful, a guide for rank ordering ethical principles must clearly indicate the order of priority of such principles. Once such a priority list has been established, the operating rule is that the satisfaction of a higher-order principle takes precedence over the satisfaction of a lower-order principle. Even though there is not yet agreement on the rank order of professional ethical principles, we have developed the EPS on the basis of our perception of what might be the consensus among social workers. All ethical principles are important. When more than one ethical principle is relevant in the analysis of a set of practice options, and each of these principles leads to a different outcome, the rank order suggested in the EPS can be used to make a decision. In other words, an action based on Ethical Principle 1 is more compelling than one using Ethical Principles 2 or 3. This principle was formulated by Kitchener (1984) and is based on the seminal work of Rawls (1971). Kitchener specifically applied this principle to ethics; she taught that a principle can suggest an obligation, but if there are special circumstances or conflicting obligations, one should always act on the basis of the obligations derived from the higher principle. For example, if both confidentiality (Principle 6) and full disclosure (Principle 7) apply, the ethical principle of confidentiality should receive priority. Because the EPS is the key ethical assessment tool for resolving ethical practice dilemmas, we will comment in detail on each of these principles.

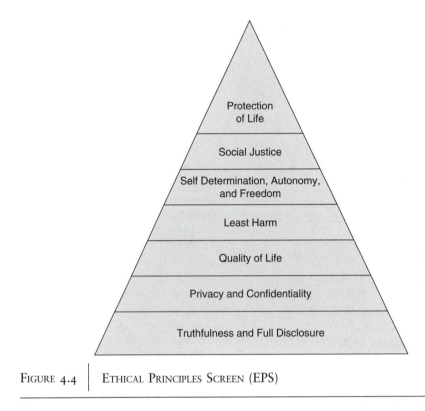

FIGURE 4.4 | ETHICAL PRINCIPLES SCREEN (EPS)

Before we begin our discussion of the individual principles and the ordering that we present for consideration, look at your answer to Critical Thinking Exercise 1 in Chapter 3, where you were asked to rank order seven ethical principles. Why did you rank order the principles in this manner? After reading the previous discussion, are you still comfortable with your ordering? If not, adjust your ordering. EP 2.1.3

ETHICAL PRINCIPLE 1   The *protection of human life* applies to all persons, both to the life of a client and to the lives of all others. In the EPS, this principle takes precedence over every other obligation. "The right to life is the most basic of all rights, for if one's right to life is violated one cannot enjoy any other rights" (Kuhse & Singer, 1985, p. 509).

Most physicians follow this principle of saving and prolonging human life, regardless of the resulting quality of life or the economic costs involved. This life-sustaining principle received wide publicity through the cases of Karen Ann Quinlan and Terri Schiavo, whose physicians refused to withdraw life-support systems even though these patients had been unconscious for many years and there was no further hope for any positive change. Today, physicians keep many Americans alive through the use of high-tech life-sustaining instruments. Social workers, on the other hand, tend to place more emphasis on improving the quality of life for individuals, groups, and communities. Most of the time, social workers are not aware of any conflict between the biophysical principle of sustaining life and the psychosocial principle of improving life. At times, however, there is conflict. One example is the case of a middle-aged man with marked hypertension. The medication that brought down his life-threatening blood pressure also caused sexual impotence (Roberts, 1989). Is it ethical for a social worker to support this client's decision to stop taking the medication so that he can once again enjoy sexual relations? Such a decision may lead to an improvement in the quality of his life (Ethical Principle 5), but it may also contribute to shortening his life span (Ethical Principle 1).

ETHICAL PRINCIPLE 2   The *principle of social justice* suggests that all persons in the same circumstances should be treated in the same way—that is, persons in equivalent situations have the right to be treated equally. At the same time, persons in different situations have the right to be treated differently if the inequality is relevant to the issue in question. Unequal treatment can be justified when other considerations such as beneficence (the duty to do good and not harm others) outweigh the social justice principle or on the grounds that such unequal treatment will promote greater social justice.

For example, this principle applies in situations that involve child abuse or elder abuse because the abused child (or elder) and the abuser are not in an equal position. In these circumstances, the principles of confidentiality and autonomy with respect to the abusing adult are of a lower rank order than the obligation to protect the child or older person, even when it is not a question of life and death. Another situation in which this principle applies occurs when several families apply for limited resources. For example, many families may need emergency housing after a natural disaster, but higher priority should be given to finding housing for families with small children or frail elderly, even while a lower priority is given to families with only healthy adults. Should family composition or prior lifestyles be taken into consideration when assessing alternate options? In situations where one family is demonstrably nearer nutritional or other disaster, the ethical principle permits or even requires the unequal allocation of scarce resources. Can you identify some other situations where the principle of social justice applies?

ETHICAL PRINCIPLE 3   A social worker should make practice decisions that *foster a person's self-determination, autonomy, and freedom,* his right to and ability to make his or her own decisions. Freedom, though highly important, does not override the right to life or survival of the client or of others. No person has the right to decide to harm someone else on the grounds that such a decision is his or her inalienable right. When a person is about to make such a decision, the social worker may be obligated to intervene because Ethical Principle 1 takes precedence.

The risk/benefit ratio may also help determine when the self-determination principle applies and when it is ethical to ignore a client's decision. If the condition facing a client is life threatening and if the risk of intervention is minimal (while the potential benefit of the intervention is great), the social worker may consider proceeding even without a client's consent. In this situation, the client's refusal to comply may or may not be considered an indication of his lack of competency.[1] On the other hand, if the risk is great and the potential benefit minimal, the client's refusal is logical and should be accepted.

ETHICAL PRINCIPLE 4   The *least harm principle* holds that when faced with options that have the potential for causing harm, a social worker should attempt to avoid these. When no matter what a social worker does, harm is unavoidable; a social worker should choose the option that will cause the least harm, the least permanent harm, and/or the most easily reversible harm. If harm has been done, the social worker should attempt where possible to repair the harm done. Removal of a child from an abusive family setting can result in harm to both the child and the family. The least harm principle suggests that the social worker weigh—to the greatest extent possible—how the most good and the least harm will be caused by her decisions.

ETHICAL PRINCIPLE 5   A social worker should choose the option that promotes a better *quality of life* for the client, as well as for the community. Consistent with the Code of Ethics, a social worker's primary responsibility is to promote the well-being of clients (NASW Code, 2008, 1.01). Although "social workers should promote the general welfare of society, from local to global levels, and the development of people, their communities, and their environments" (NASW Code, 2008, 6.01), the priority responsibility is to the client before others.

ETHICAL PRINCIPLE 6   A social worker should make practice decisions that strengthen every person's *right to privacy and confidentiality*. Keeping confidential information inviolate is a direct derivative of this obligation. Professionals have a duty to protect the privacy of clients and groups to the greatest extent possible, consistent with laws and professional ethics. Confidentiality, however, is not sacrosanct when the social worker can prevent violence or harm of a serious nature to others. As will be introduced in Chapter 8, the Tarasoff court decision elevates the prevention of a serious and believable threat of violence over the confidentiality principle.

ETHICAL PRINCIPLE 7   A social worker should make practice decisions that permit her to speak the truth and to *fully disclose all relevant information* to her client and to others. Social and professional relationships require trust in order to function well, and trust, in turn, is based on honest dealing that minimizes surprises so that mutual expectations are generally fulfilled. Social workers are expected to inform clients as appropriate of their relevant training and education, the methods they will be using, fees, confidentiality, the rights of the client, access to files, and so on.

APPLICATION OF ETHICAL DECISION-MAKING SCREENS

Let's try to apply these two ethical decision-making screens to analyze Exemplars 4.2, 4.3, and 4.4.

---

[1] Competency is a legal definition and does not depend on the social worker's diagnosis. The criteria for a court determining that a person is incompetent vary from state to state. Social workers should be aware of the process and requirements for having someone declared incompetent in the state(s) in which they practice.

| 4.2 | What Will Happen to Jimmy Prego? |

Jimmy Prego is a passive, deeply disturbed early adolescent. He lives in a therapeutic home where he has sometimes had to be protected from other residents. Now he is ready to be moved to a less restrictive environment. A therapeutic foster home, something your supervisor originally suggested, seems like the optimum solution. You have contacted such a home and begun plans to move Jimmy in about two weeks. When you inform your supervisor that you have initiated the move and that everything is proceeding routinely, she tells you that space has become available in an even less restricted group home run by your agency and that it would be appropriate to move Jimmy to the group home instead of the therapeutic foster home.

You tell your supervisor that you will check it out, but she seems a little uncomfortable. When you check out the group home, you discover that the residents are older, bigger, and more aggressive than Jimmy. You inform your supervisor that this group home is definitely not appropriate for a boy like Jimmy, who already has had difficulties defending himself where he currently resides. At the same time, you become aware that the agency has placed pressure on all supervisors to boost the group home's census, an action related to agency financial situation. Jimmy's mother is unable to assist in making a decision about his placement because of her overwhelming personal and mental health problems. Jimmy's problems and his age make it unlikely that he is capable of making the decision. Mrs. Prego, his mother, insists that she trusts you and trusts that you will do what is best for Jimmy.

Several issues are involved in this exemplar. Ethical Principles 4 (least harm) and 5 (quality of life) are particularly relevant here. Will the least harm be done by confronting your supervisor and succeeding in obtaining the placement in the therapeutic home, even if it means reducing the agency's needed income? When you examine the Code of Ethics for applicable standards, you find that your "primary responsibility is to promote the well-being of clients" (NASW Code, 2008, 1.01). Who is your client and to whom do you owe loyalty—Jimmy, his mother, your supervisor, your agency, or yourself—as you make your decision about the correct thing to do? Whose best interest takes priority, that of the client, agency, or worker? In addition, some social workers might argue that Ethical Principle 5 is relevant because the worker wants to promote a better quality of life for Jimmy Prego, and the right treatment situation will support that outcome.

Next, who is competent to make decisions? When clients lack "the capacity to provide informed consent, social workers should protect clients' interests by seeking permission from an appropriate third party" (NASW Code, 2008, 1.03c). Jimmy is not capable of making an informed choice. Mrs. Prego trusts you and wants you to make the best decision for her son. Is your supervisor an appropriate third party if she is placing the agency's needs before those of Jimmy? In addition, "social workers should not allow an employing organization's policies, procedures, regulations, or administrative orders to interfere with their ethical practice of social work" (NASW Code, 2008, 3.09d). You, the social worker, and your supervisor may be the only individuals in this situation who are competent to make decisions for the best interest and protection of Jimmy and to advocate for the right treatment plan.

Jimmy's needs take priority over the supervisor's, the agency's, and your own needs. Exemplar 4.3 provides another example.

4.3	STARTING IN PRIVATE PRACTICE

EP 2.1.2

Cliff Baxter is an experienced social worker who recently resigned his agency job in order to devote all of his time to private practice. Before Cliff left the agency, Dennis Norton, a colleague in the agency, told him that he would be willing to refer clients to him for a "finder's fee." As in many private practice beginnings, Cliff is having a difficult time making ends meet. His income last month was not even sufficient to pay the office rent. Should he take Dennis up on his offer?

We will use the ERS and examine the NASW Code of Ethics to determine if there are any rules relevant to this situation. The NASW (2008) Code (2.06c) states: "Social workers are prohibited from giving or receiving payment for a referral when no professional service is provided by the referring social worker." This rule provides such clear and unambiguous guidance that no further screening seems necessary. Cliff should not call Dennis to take advantage of his offer. Would there be ethical issues if Cliff calls Dennis and lets him know he would be happy to accept referrals, but he cannot pay a finder's fee? What if, in exchange for referrals now, Cliff offers to let Dennis use his office space several times a week when Dennis establishes a private practice next year? Would this kind of arrangement be ethical or unethical?

In Exemplar 4.4, we will apply the EPS.

4.4	THE WRONG MAN SITS IN PRISON

EP 2.1.2

Raul Lovaas has been enrolled in a drug rehabilitation program to break his cocaine addiction. The program's treatment routine includes pharmacological treatment, group therapy, and individual therapy. You are his social worker. You have succeeded in establishing a good relationship with Raul in your daily treatment sessions. One morning, Raul tells you that, some years ago, he accidentally injured a bank guard during a holdup. He was never caught by the police, but another man was convicted for this crime and now sits in prison on a lengthy sentence. For several days you have been trying to convince Raul that he should talk to the police in order to free an innocent man from prison. Raul not only refused to listen to your suggestion but said that he expects you to keep what he has told you in complete confidence. What should you do?

These are some of the thoughts that you have:

1. The wrong that you may cause by breaking confidentiality is hardly of the same importance as the wrong inflicted on an innocent person who is now imprisoned.
2. The effectiveness of the entire program may be compromised if it becomes known that social workers do not always keep the information they receive from clients confidential.
3. On the other hand, reporting Raul's participation in the holdup could cause the release of a wrongly convicted person.

Several ethical principles should be considered. Ethical Principle 3, the principle of self-determination, autonomy, and freedom—specifically, the freedom of an innocent man who is now imprisoned; and Ethical Principle 6, the principle of confidentiality—specifically, respecting the confidence of the information that your client, Raul, gave you. Some may also base their decision on Ethical Principle 2, the principle of social justice, because an innocent man in prison is obviously not in an equal situation and requires additional resources in order to regain access to equal opportunities. Because Ethical Principle 6 (confidentiality) is of a lower order than Ethical Principles 2 and 3, the second consideration leads to the decision that you are ethically justified in breaking confidence and reporting to the police what you have learned from Raul.

From a practice point of view, another consideration may be especially important because in most situations we would hesitate to do anything that might impede the effectiveness of an intervention. It might be argued that a program that can improve the quality of life (Ethical Principle 5) of many people who are addicted to drugs should receive preference over the quality of life of one individual, even if that person is falsely imprisoned. It is likely, however, that such reasoning involves a number of fallacies, including the following:

- We have no information on the effectiveness of this rehabilitation program. How effective is it in improving the quality of life of all/most/some participants?
- We do not know what impact, if any, breaking confidentiality will have on the effectiveness of the program. It may well be that other participants will be happy that the worker was instrumental in freeing an innocent person from prison.
- Statistical probabilities are never a permissible substitute for ethical screening.

In other words, the quality of life principle (Ethical Principle 5) is not relevant in this situation, but even if it were, it would be of a lower order than Ethical Principles 2 and 3. Consideration 3 is therefore not relevant and should be ignored in making an ethical decision. We would conclude that you are obligated to inform the police if you are unable to convince Raul to do so himself.

THE IMPORTANCE OF IDENTIFYING ONE'S OWN HIERARCHY OF PRINCIPLES

Although the NASW Code of Ethics (2008) recognizes "the possibility of conflicts among the Code's values, principles, and standards," it does not specify which values, principles, and standards are more important and ought to outweigh others in instances when they conflict. Nevertheless, social workers are frequently faced with conflicting standards and loyalties, and a hierarchy may help when choosing among principles. Ultimately, each social worker, when faced with conflicts in ethical standards or loyalties, must use such a priority ladder in the context of the Code of Ethics, the ethical criteria suggested above, and her own values.

Originally, Loewenberg and Dolgoff (1988) based the hierarchy on their perception of what the common consensus might be, and the hierarchical list of principles was changed in the following edition of their book (Loewenberg & Dolgoff, 1992). Beyerstein (1993) suggested that because a professional code of ethics is created through a democratic process, members of the profession can only agree on the obvious, and they fudge, or dodge, difficult or contentious principles through compromise, leaving the choice of a hierarchy of principles to the individual decision maker.

Over time, the makeup of the profession itself has become more diverse as a result of immigration and other societal and professional factors, including generational and other differences, which may result in more disagreement about the relative importance of ethical principles. We have found that there is little agreement on the rank ordering of the ethical principles, suggesting that perceptions may change over time. Harrington and Dolgoff (2008) found the principle hierarchy suggested corresponded well to the principles of human rights, human dignity, and social justice identified by the International Federation of Social Workers and the International Association of Schools of Social Work. When they offered several workshops on ethical decision making and asked the participants to rank the principles according to their own values, there was no unanimous agreement on the hierarchy of principles. It is no wonder that different hierarchies lead to different decisions when facing ethical dilemmas.

SUMMARY AND CONCLUSIONS

In this chapter, we have examined a series of guidelines and decision-making tools that social workers can use when making ethical decisions. We noted that every social worker is confronted by ethical dilemmas and that these always require choices that must be made before action can be taken. Iserson (1986) suggested that we ask three questions as a final check before moving to the action phase of ethical decision making:

1. *Impartiality* Would you be willing to act the way you have chosen if you were in the other person's situation? This question asks the social worker to consider the effect her action would have if she or a member of her family or other loved ones were the recipients of the action. The purpose of this question is to correct for partiality and self-interest and to minimize or prevent the possibility they will play too dominant a part in the decision.

2. *Generalization* Are you willing to undertake this action in similar circumstances? Generalizing a particular decision may reduce bias and partiality, but it also may blind one to the unique qualities of a situation that demands a unique response, one that would not generally be used in many other situations. When one evaluates a particular action in light of its general applicability to similar situations, one is concerned with both the breadth and range of effects and the short- and long-range consequences. The purpose of this question is to make the social worker think of the consequences of an action beyond the short term and to consider it not as a particular instance but as a justified general practice in similar circumstances.

3. *Justifiability* Can you explain and justify your decision to others? The purpose of this question is to make certain that you have, in the available time, consciously and purposefully considered the options and have made certain the client's rights and best interests are served by your professional actions in the context of the values and standards of the profession.

CRITICAL THINKING EXERCISES

EP 2.1.3

1. In the previous chapter, we asked you to rank order the seven ethical principles. How does your rank ordering compare to the ethical principles screen (EPS)? If your priority ordering differs from ours, how will this affect the decision making in the above exemplars? After further thoughts and reading the preceding discussion, would you make any changes in your ordering? Why or why not? Compare your rank ordering with that of others in your class and discuss why you ordered the principles differently.

2. Identify two ethical decisions in social work practice you recently made or learned about. On the basis of the ethical assessment screen and the ethical principles screen, would you change the ethical decision that you or the other social worker made?

3. Do you believe that the NASW Code of Ethics assumes that one particular ethical standard has the highest priority for social workers' ethical behavior? If yes, which standard do you think it is and why?

4. The director of a drug addiction rehabilitation program faces a difficult budget allocation decision. He has sufficient resources to implement only one of the two programs his agency would like to offer. Program A is geared to elementary school students. It will serve 500 children from some of the city's most troubled neighborhoods. Past experience has shown that 200 children will be addicted to drugs by the time they are 16 years old if the program is not offered. But if the program is implemented, the number can be reduced to no more than 50. Program B focuses on the rehabilitation of adolescents who are addicted to drugs. Fifty teens can be served each year, with a 60% success rate. What ethical considerations should the director examine? What ethical rules and ethical principles can he use to help him make a decision? Should the availability of outcome data affect the decision-making process?

5. Exemplar 4.2 demonstrates a conflict between the needs of the client and the needs of the agency. Social workers who provide direct service may have a different perspective on this dilemma than social workers who are supervisors or agency administrators. Arrange to talk to someone who is in a supervisory or administrative social work position—what is his or her perspective on this issue? Did this discussion influence your perspective?

SUGGESTIONS FOR ADDITIONAL READINGS

Dean (1998) describes her view of "The Primacy of the Ethical Aim in Clinical Social Work: Its Relationship to Social Justice and Mental Health" concepts. Kurri (2005), in "Placement of Responsibility and Moral Reasoning in Couple Therapy," illustrates the importance of moral and ethical judgments in family and couple therapy. Hugman (2003) argues that postmodernism may assist social work to examine the diverse, provisional, and uncertain nature of all aspects of social work, including knowledge and skills, values and ethics. Landau and Osmo (2003) explore "Professional and Personal Hierarchies of Ethical Principles." Smith (2004) argues that social work is more than a series of technical activities based on what works, particular role expectations, and regulatory and legal frameworks. Individual encounters between social workers and those being served are morally charged in regard to their impact on the service users' well-being. Bryan (2006) argues that ethics should concern itself with a common morality, that is "what ought not to be" rather than a preoccupation with what "ought to be." She suggests that a desire to avoid harm is a stance commonly shared by all moral agents and that the moral rules that govern professional behavior should be derived from the moral rules to which all people, regardless of professional role, would agree to abide. We introduce this idea because of its unique perspective. However, given the plurality of values in our society, it is difficult to see any unanimity, even about what ought not to be.

COMPETENCY NOTES

Apply social work ethical principles to guide professional practice: In this chapter, we presented a model for ethical decision making and asked you to apply the model to EP 2.1.2 several exemplars.

Apply critical thinking to inform and communicate professional judgments: Several exemplars asked you to consider and decide how you would respond to an ethical EP 2.1.3 dilemma using the tools presented in this chapter. In addition, we presented critical thinking exercises relevant to the chapter content.

ETHICAL DILEMMAS IN PROFESSIONAL PRACTICE

CLIENT RIGHTS AND
PROFESSIONAL EXPERTISE

This chapter addresses the sometimes conflicting claims of professional expertise and client rights, such as self-determination. We will show how to use social work ethical principles to guide professional practice. We will provide several opportunities, through exemplars and questions, for you to work with the ethical decision-making model presented in the previous chapter, which we hope you will use to apply critical thinking in order to inform and communicate professional judgments. This chapter addresses the issues raised in CSWE 2008 EPAS Educational Policies 2.1.2 and 2.1.3.

WHO IS THE CLIENT?

The question "Who is the client?" may indicate the source of several ethical dilemmas. In the classical professions, such as law and medicine, a client was traditionally defined as the person(s) who engaged the practitioner and paid her a fee. Alternatively, the client is the person (or the system) whose behavior is to be modified or changed by the professional's intervention. However, these definitions may not be entirely appropriate for most social workers, especially for those who are employed by an organization, such as a social agency, a department of government, or an institution. According to the traditional definition, the organization that pays the social worker's salary would be considered the client. But is the school really the client of the school social worker? Is the prison the client of the correctional social worker? Nowadays, the traditional definition may be too narrow, because it was originally devised for clients of independent professional practitioners in private practice.

The alternate definition also is problematic because it is not always accurate to say that the client is the person or system whose behavior needs to be changed. Often social work intervention does not focus on changes in the client system, but rather on changes in other systems, such as a court, employer, social agency, or

local housing authority. The worker may help the client to become his own advocate *or* help the client by advocating with or attempting to change other systems
that impact on the client, so that the client may gain access to needed resources.
In the past, the social worker automatically considered the person(s) who applied
for help as her client(s); however, today the answer to the question "Who is the
client?" is not quite so simple, as Exemplars 5.1 and 5.2 illustrate.

In Exemplar 5.1, who is Robin Osborn's client—Arlene Johnson or the premature infant? Whose interests should be accorded priority? Exemplar 5.2 is quite different, but it raises similar questions.

5.1   ARLENE JOHNSON'S ABORTION

EP 2.1.2

Arlene Johnson, 18 years old and single, is nearly six months pregnant. Yesterday, she
came to the Women's Counseling Center to request help in getting an abortion. At the
time of the abortion procedure, the fetus was considered viable and was placed in the
neonatal intensive care unit as a high-risk premature baby. Arlene was extremely upset when she learned that the "abortion" had resulted in a live infant. She refused to
look at the baby or take care of it. Instead, she threatened to sue the doctor and the
hospital if the infant survived despite her expressed wish for an abortion. Arlene asked
Robin Osborn, the hospital social worker, to make sure that the baby not be given
intensive care, but rather be left alone so that it would die quickly.

5.2   MRS. LINDEN'S CLASSROOM

EP 2.1.2

Mrs. Linden is a fifth-grade teacher in the Abraham Lincoln Elementary School. The
school is located in a neighborhood into which a large number of Central American
families have moved recently. Joan Ramirez is the social worker assigned to this
school, and her caseload includes several children in Mrs. Linden's class. Yesterday,
Mrs. Linden asked Joan for help in keeping her pupils quietly in their seats. She told
Joan that never in her 20 years as a teacher has she had as much trouble as this year.
She thought that her troubles were caused by the many children who do not speak
English well. Surely Joan could advise her how to handle these children so that they
would be quiet and stay in their seats.

Again, who is the client—Mrs. Linden, the pupils, their parents, or the school?
Whose interests should be accorded priority? What if Joan believes the problem
stems from a different source, such as racism or parent, teacher, or school administration inflexibility? How can Joan Ramirez balance the interests of the various individuals involved, several of whom may have conflicting expectations? The two
problem situations in Exemplars 5.1 and 5.2 seem quite different, but in each case

the request made by the applicant for service creates a dilemma that has ethical implications for the social worker. Arlene Johnson does not want to have a baby, but now that a live infant has been born, her expectations of the obstetrician (and the request she made to the social worker) conflict sharply with the rights of the infant and with what society expects from these professionals. Joan Ramirez is approached by Mrs. Linden, but the students are already her clients. Is the problem with the students, Mrs. Linden, or the school setting? What should Joan do about the role conflict? To whom does she owe loyalty? The social worker is not at all sure that the problem is with the pupils; perhaps the teacher is the real problem. What is the ethical thing to do?

One of the reasons why the question "Who is the client?" causes so many ethical dilemmas is that the question itself is based on an oversimplified and not entirely accurate model of the professional relationship. The traditional model included only the practitioner and the client. An updated model might include the applicant, client, target, beneficiary, practitioner, agency, community, and others. Each of the four positions noted in Figure 5.1 can be occupied by one or more persons or institutions. Sometimes the same person is the applicant as well as the client, target, and beneficiary. At other times or in other situations, different persons occupy each of these positions. The applicant may not be the client (e.g., when a mother applies for services for her child) and the client need not be the target (e.g., the target may be an employer or school principal), nor is the client necessarily the beneficiary of the intervention.

Applicant	The person(s) or system that requests help with a defined or felt problem
Client	The applicant who enters into a formal, contractual, goal-focused relationship with a social worker
Target	The person(s) or system(s) that must be modified in order to achieve the desired outcome to which client and worker have agreed
Beneficiary	The person(s) or system(s) that will benefit from successful goal achievement in which the resolution of the ethical issues may not fully coincide with the legal requirements

FIGURE 5.1   SOME PARTICIPANTS IN THE SOCIAL WORK PROCESS

Social workers who engage in genetic counseling are constantly faced by difficult problems that involve ethical issues. Modern medical procedures such as amniocentesis and chorionic villus sampling make it possible to detect hundreds of different genetic disorders *in utero*. When there are positive findings, the social worker must help parents think through all of the implications for the fetus, the parents, their families, and those involved as health practitioners, so the parents can make the best decision. However, some physicians may expect the social worker to persuade the pregnant mother who has received positive indications of a genetically defective fetus to abort, while other doctors may expect the social worker to persuade the mother not to abort. These expectations may be based on the physicians' best professional judgment or on their own religious or other principles. Should the best interest of the as-yet-unborn child play a part in the decision? What is the best interest? Should the social worker stress arguments in favor of abortion, even if it is evident that the parents do not want to terminate the pregnancy? What is the ethical stance that the social worker should adopt? Should the decision of the social worker depend on knowledge of the statistical probability of the predicted consequences of genetic effects—that is, mild or severe effects leading to a degree of independence or to the need for constant care and assistance? How would your decision in such a situation be affected by your own values and religious beliefs?

Social workers in the criminal justice system face similar ethical issues. In the probation service, social workers regularly prepare reports for the court judge. The judge takes these reports into consideration when making a final disposition of the case. The ethical dilemma here is that the social worker has responsibilities both toward the alleged delinquent and toward the court. She is helper and judicial fact finder. The client/worker helping relationship started during the first contact with the offender, long before the social worker has completed her evaluative assessment or presented her report to the judge. To whom does the social worker owe priority consideration—to the detainee or to the judge? Who is her client? Note that, in the criminal justice system, social workers will often face situations in which the legal requirements may not fully coincide with professional ethical principles. Does it help if the social worker explains her court responsibilities to the client? If yes, then what should the social worker tell the client?

EP 2.1.1

PROFESSIONAL EXPERTISE AND SELF-DETERMINATION

An ethical dilemma arises out of a conflict between two professional obligations: (1) to support or guarantee the client's self-determination and autonomy, that is, the person most affected by a decision should make that decision; and (2) to make decisions that will assure a positive outcome and secure the optimum benefit for the client on the basis of the knowledge and skill available to the professional social worker.

Social workers have always believed that every person has a right to make his or her own decisions. Veteran social worker Charlotte Towle (1987) noted decades ago that "a person has a right to manage his own affairs" (p. 15). The NASW Code of Ethics (2008) states, "Social workers respect and promote the right of clients to self-determination and assist clients in their efforts to identify and clarify their goals" (1.02). This rule seems clear and unambiguous. The Code also states "social workers may limit clients' rights to self-determination [only] when, in the social workers' professional judgment, clients' actions or potential actions pose a serious, foreseeable, and imminent risk to themselves or others" (NASW Code, 2008, 1.02).

At one time, this ethical conflict between the client's right to self-determination and the social worker's expertise was less severe because much greater respect was given to professional expertise at that time, even though there was a great deal of uncertainty about the adequacy of social work knowledge and about the effectiveness of social work intervention. Although the application of professional knowledge and appropriate professional skills contributes to positive client outcomes

(Claiborne, 2006; Cummings, Cooper, & Cassie, 2009; Harris, 2009; Lundahl, Nimer, & Parsons, 2006; Nissen, 2006; Rizzo & Rowe, 2006; Roseborough, 2006), the ethical problem with potentially critical implications is how to balance client self-determination with the use of professional knowledge and skill. Is it ethical for a social worker to refrain from using her professional knowledge—known by her to be effective—if the client chooses an option that is not consistent with evidence-based recommendations and that may not result in positive outcomes?

The social worker may know what strategy will best achieve the objectives that the client has chosen. Is it ethical for the social worker to implement this more effective strategy when the client prefers another approach? The social worker may understand what the client needs or wants even before the client is aware of this. May the social worker follow the strategy suggested by her knowledge and insight when the client has made another, less beneficial decision based on ignorance or partial knowledge? Does it make a difference if the client has made the decision on the basis of his cultural values?

Some social workers do not hesitate to give priority to their professional knowledge and skill, even when this means ignoring a client's input. Earlier ideas concerning conflict between self-determination and paternalistic intervention by the professional are being reexamined. Taylor (2006) studied 320 clinical social workers who had an average of 25 years experience in mental health services; he asked them about their views on self-determination and involuntary treatment. All reported a positive attitude about the importance and utility of self-determination. However, they indicated that, over time, their way of thinking changed so that they were relatively untroubled in practice situations that presented a conflict with the value of self-determination, such as when the client was in need of involuntary treatment interventions. They understood that there are situations where patients or clients are unable to make informed decisions and judgments based on reality (i.e., not based on valid information or poor reality assessment) so that beneficent actions by the social worker are necessary. A British study of community care similarly revealed justification for beneficent and paternalistic interventions by social workers in some situations (Clark, 1998).

Kim and colleagues (2008) studied the attitudes and views regarding psychiatric advanced directives and health care powers of attorney in a sample of 193 direct service providers (the majority of whom were licensed and experienced) who worked with patients with psychosis. Psychiatric advance directives are legal documents that describe a competent person's specific instructions and preferences regarding future psychiatric treatment (mental health professionals, programs, facilities, and surrogate decision makers) in the event the person may not be able to communicate treatment choices at that time. Advanced directives enhance self-determination because individuals can make decisions when they are competent to do so. Proponents of advanced directives believe they encourage discussion between the client and provider and facilitate planning for future crises. Proponents also believe that clients' access to their preferred mental health treatment during crises may enhance treatment adherence and a therapeutic alliance. Others have mixed opinions and feel advanced directives have the potential to decrease the tension between client autonomy and coercive interventions and such directives may run into legal problems in practice. Respondents were more favorable to health care powers of attorney than to advanced directives (Kim et al., 2008). Those social workers who viewed health care powers of attorney more favorably did so because the involvement of a proxy decision maker, typically a family member, was perceived as a more reasonable arbiter of treatment decisions than are advance directives. The involvement of a proxy decision maker provides more opportunity for collaborative decision making.

Nevertheless, most social workers believe not only in the right but also in the effectiveness of client participation in as many phases of the social work process as possible. The potential conflict between the value of client self-determination and the worker's use of professional knowledge and skills is often complicated by the question as to who is the client for whom knowledge and skills will be applied. We will turn now to consider the question of self-determination in more detail.

SELF-DETERMINATION

Immanuel Kant, one of the early giants of modern philosophy, insisted that a person's right to determine his or her own destiny is unconditional. He taught that persons are always ends in themselves and should never be treated as means. Self-determination is a first-order principle in U.S. society. Though not specifically mentioned in the Constitution, the U.S. Supreme Court, in a series of due-process cases, equal protection cases, and privacy cases, developed the rule that self-determination is a fundamental right that is protected by the Ninth and Fourteenth Amendments.

The individual's right to make his or her own decisions is the source for the social work value of self-determination. Many hold that self-determination is an absolute right. Yet most social workers would agree with Rothman (1989) that when used as a practice principle, its application is limited. For practitioners, the principle of self-determination can raise as many questions as it answers. No wonder that Rothman (1989) states "self-determination is accorded utmost esteem in the profession [but] its meaning and application are clouded" (p. 598). The right of self-determination can become the source of common and perplexing dilemmas. How can a practitioner respect and uphold client self-determination when working with a client whose concept of what is good for him differs from that of the social worker or is at variance from the needs or desires of those who will be affected by the client's decision? What if the client who has many positive attributes wants to make self-destructive or criminal decisions? Should a mentally ill person (or any person) be allowed to refuse treatment or be permitted to live on the street? What degree of mental instability calls for limiting self-determination?

Hartman (1997) suggests that even though many social workers believe that in their practices they always honor the client's right to self-determination, this is often an illusion because many clients cannot fully exercise this right. Because true self-determination requires "access to resources, access to opportunity, and access to power," there are real limits to self-determination (Hartman, 1997, p. 216). This is especially true because real self-determination requires power and resources, something that many clients lack.

Ethical dilemmas become more frequent and increasingly perplexing as major life decisions involve highly technical and specialized considerations that often are beyond the comprehension of most people. Reliance on professionals who have the necessary expertise has become more common, so that directiveness as a helping technique appears to have become more acceptable. There is an urgent need to re-examine issues of self-determination and autonomy as social workers respond to new mandates and demands in relation to persons with disabilities and to those who are especially vulnerable. In some cases, clients are unable to take care of themselves. In such situations, social workers intervene protectively, often despite the client's objections. For example, is it ethical for a social worker to act when a suicidal client requires psychiatric hospital commitment but does not want to be admitted to the hospital? The use of directive methods raises an ethical question as to whether the ends ever justify the means. Should a client be pressured into do-ing things he does not want to do, even when his social worker is certain that this will contribute to solving or reducing his problem? Is it ethical for a social worker to deceive a client in order to have him participate in a treatment that he would reject if he knew all the facts? Perhaps the key to answering these and similar ques-tions is not whether directiveness by the social worker is permissible, but rather who has the right to decide whether a client can or cannot manage for himself at this particular time, in this particular situation.

Some professionals do not hesitate to use their knowledge and power to move the client in the "right" direction. Some suggest that control of the client by the worker occurs in all professional relationships, no matter what theoretical frame-work is used (Dworkin, 1985). Usually, this control is not manifest but occurs in an implicit or unconscious way. Dworkin suggests that it would be better if this control were acknowledged and exercised in a systematic and explicit way. A pro-fessional should consider whether (a) her intentions are in the best interests of the client, (b) her personal investment in the situation is clear and not motivating her actions, and (c) because of the power differential, there is no conflict between her best interests and those of the client. Berlin (2005) assumes that social workers ex-press their power for basically compassionate reasons and suggests that "recogniz-ing the other person's autonomy and capacity tempers the controlling aspects of compassion, thus enhancing the client's self-determination and autonomy" (p. 485).

Control and manipulation are not acceptable professional methods. Social workers must consciously avoid these and frequently reassess the meaning and practice of client self-determination. What are the ethical considerations that should guide a social worker who is convinced that an older adult client (who can no lon-ger cope alone at home) should enter an assisted-living facility very soon, but who knows from past experience with this client that every worker suggestion elicits a "no" response? If this client has close relatives, should they be asked to make the decision? If there are no close relatives, should the worker make the decision with-out fully involving the client?

Consider an aging person in a nursing home who is physically disabled, con-fined to a wheelchair, incontinent, and eating poorly. This woman, who has been fiercely independent throughout her life, now wants to return to her home, even though she needs special care. Her aging sister says she will be able to provide care for her at home. Although this woman has the law on her side (1990 Patient Self-Determination Act and 1993 Uniform Health Care Decisions Act), her social worker should oppose her voluntary discharge if it appears to be life threatening

(Sasson, 2000). Such interventions in the life of the client can range from one-time to ongoing, with minor or major involvement, and must be related to the degree of rational impairment or incapacity for decision making demonstrated by the client, as well as the amount of risk or danger inherent in the present situation.

Bergeron (2006) explored the issue of self-determination as it relates to victims of elder abuse and neglect. He challenged the idea that self-determination allows victims of abuse and neglect to refuse intervention. Typically, mental incompetence is cited as the reason adult protective workers might disregard the older person's right to self-determination. However, clear directives concerning competency and self-determination are often lacking. This allows adult protective workers to close some cases when the person refuses services, yet sets up a conflict between the right to refuse services (self-determination) and the social worker's duty to protect.

There is some evidence that class-related or age-related criteria are sometimes used to assess the capacity of different client groups to make autonomous decisions. Those who work with older clients are very much aware of this problem, but this ethical quandary is not limited to older adults. Stereotypes also exist about teenagers, racial and ethnic groups, genders, rich and poor, and other groups. A situation involving both the dilemma of "Who is the client?" and the problem of self-determination is illustrated in Exemplar 5.3.

| 5.3 | SHOULD ELEANOR POMER COME HOME? |

EP 2.1.2

Eleanor Pomer is 8 years old, the youngest of six siblings. She has been diagnosed with Down syndrome. For the last three years she has been a resident in a special school. According to her cottage parents, psychologist, teacher, and social worker, she functions on a moderate level but needs assistance with certain daily activities. Both of Eleanor's parents are employed. They rent the downstairs apartment of a two-family home in a working-class neighborhood about one hour's drive from Eleanor's school. For the past year, the Pomers have visited Eleanor once a month, and Eleanor has successfully spent one weekend a month at home. Both Eleanor and her family look forward to these visits.

The school's staff feels that Eleanor now is ready to leave the school and live at home. The social worker has acquainted Eleanor's parents with this staff assessment. She has told them about the community resources that are available in their city and has urged them to take Eleanor home. However, the Pomers disagree with the staff recommendation. They are satisfied with the present arrangement because they feel that it would be too much of a strain on their other children if Eleanor lived at home. The social worker is convinced that it would be best for Eleanor to leave the school and resume a more normal home life. She is aware that Eleanor is excited about the possibility of living with her parents and brothers and sisters.

The ethical problem in this situation arises out of the conflict between applying professional knowledge and respecting the client's right to make decisions. It is further complicated by the question of who is the client. How much weight must the social worker give to the Pomers' and to Eleanor's wishes? Should the most important criterion in reaching a decision be what is best for Eleanor? Who decides what is best for Eleanor? What about the welfare of the other Pomer children? Does the social worker have an ethical right to manipulate the environment (e.g., by raising the tuition fee) in order to "help" the Pomers reach the decision that staff thinks is best for Eleanor? Are there standards in the Code that will help her decide what the correct decision is? Does the ethical principles screen in Chapter 4 provide any guidance?

Another basic ethical dilemma in social work practice arises out of two professional principles—at times contradictory—that all social workers have accepted: (1) the principle to provide professional help when needed or requested by a client in order to assure or improve that person's welfare, and (2) the principle to not interfere with a person's freedom. Ideally, a social worker should not experience any conflict between these two rights (or principles), but what if a person's well-being can be achieved only at the expense of his or her freedom? Who defines well-being? Who defines the need for professional help? Who can legitimately request professional help for another person?

Unless there are serious indications to the contrary, no social worker will want to interfere with another person's freedom, even if that person is her client. It is, however, generally agreed that there are occasions when intervention becomes necessary, even if it is at the expense of freedom. Most people agree that a person's right to self-determination should be limited when its exercise will result in harm to another person, but what if the harm is only to the person himself or herself? Though the conditions that justify intervention may seem clear, a social worker will discover many ambiguities. What is *clear and present danger*? How can it be demonstrated? When is harm sufficiently grave to warrant coercion? Who may coerce? How certain must the social worker be that her intervention will prevent the harm before she is justified in curtailing a person's freedom? Consider the situation in Exemplar 5.4.

EP 2.1.2

| 5.4 | HOW IMMEDIATE IS THE DANGER? |

Social worker Maria Espinosa has been working for one month with Allison Bode, an extremely thin, almost gaunt, reserved 17-year-old college freshman. Allison was referred to the Family Counseling Center by her pastor after she told him of her loneliness and obsessive thoughts. She came for help with the agreement and support of her parents. Allison is doing passing work academically but has been unsuccessful making friends at school, and for five months she has had practically no social life. This afternoon, Allison told Maria that her menstrual cycle has stopped. When Maria explored the situation, she learned that Allison is on an extremely restricted diet and exercises two to three hours a day to lose weight. She is slightly depressed but still able to concentrate on her schoolwork and reports she is seldom irritable. Based on all of this information, Maria is quite certain that Allison has anorexia and suggests she go to the college health service to consult with a physician. As soon as Allison heard the suggestion, she rejected it.

Is anorexia a case of clear and present danger that requires immediate action? What harm would be done if a few more weekly sessions are used to help Allison act to protect her health and her visit to a physician is delayed? Should Maria contact Allison's parents? Or should Maria call on the authority of the college and medical personnel to coerce Allison to attend to her illness? What is the ethically correct choice?

More crucial than the type of problem or the chances of rehabilitation or recovery is the question of the client's capacity to make decisions. As long as she can make informed decisions, the social worker has no mandate to interfere, unless (a) it is a question of life and death for the client, (b) there is serious danger to others (the duty to protect will be discussed in more detail in Chapter 8), or (c) reporting is mandated by law. The social worker's task is to enable the client to make an informed decision to the maximum extent possible.

An additional dimension of the social worker's ethical mandate arises from her professional obligation to do more than merely observe the negative injunction of not interfering with a person's freedom. In addition, every social worker has a professional obligation to undertake positive actions designed to strengthen or promote the client's freedom. If promoting a client's self-determination and not interfering with the client's freedom is to be more than empty rhetoric, social workers must understand that a person is truly autonomous only when all of the following conditions prevail:

- The context provides more than one option from which a person can make a choice.
- There is no coercion by the social worker or by other professionals to choose one or another option.
- The person is aware of all the available options.
- The person has accurate information about the cost and consequences of each option so that he or she can assess them realistically.
- The person has the capacity and/or initiative to make a decision on the basis of this assessment.
- The person has an opportunity to act on the basis of his or her choice.

Taking into consideration these conditions, we must conclude that the freedom of most social work clients is quite limited. Social workers must be concerned when anybody's freedom is limited. Americans enjoy more freedom than the citizens of many other countries, but social and economic conditions limit some of the freedom of most people in almost all contemporary societies. Inequality, racism, sexism, and ageism are especially blatant conditions that limit people's freedom. Stevens (1998) reminds us that the freedom to choose and the right to make decisions are profoundly cherished rights; however, "self-determination is grievously restrained when opportunities for social mobility are blocked" (p. 294). Social workers are committed to using their professional skill and know-how to help not only their clients but all people gain full freedom. This ethical commitment may explain why so many social workers can be found in the forefront of struggles for more freedom and greater equality for all people. But this ethical concern for greater autonomy must also find expression in the day-to-day practice of social workers.

The ability to engage in self-determination also varies with the dependency of the client on the benefits he receives from his social worker. The more essential and valuable the goods or services received, the greater the client's feelings of dependency on the worker and the less likely it is that he will choose an option that he believes his social worker will disapprove of. Thus, public assistance recipients, especially those who believe that they themselves are personally responsible for being on welfare, are less assertive about their rights, less likely to disagree with their caseworker, and less prone to appeal a decision. Stigma, loss of self-esteem, psychological and economic hardship, and a lack of options undermine the ability to be self-determining (Goodban, 1985). Fewer options become available for public assistance clients as the rules demanding work become ever more rigorous (Pear, 2006; Soss, Schram, Vartanian, & O'Brien, 2004). For example, under the Personal Responsibility and Work Opportunity Act (1996), people who do not comply with work rules can lose all or some of their cash assistance, food stamps, and Medicaid; any one of these losses, even a partial one, can have serious consequences for their families (Lens, 2006).

When a person has limited power and becomes dependent on a professional or an institution, his or her vulnerability increases to the point where it will interfere with his freedom. This occurs not only in the public assistance arena (Fawcett, 2009). For example, many older women experience income and health problems; at the same time the availability of support networks becomes much more limited—this, in turn, can result in loss of self-confidence and adverse coping abilities. People with certain disabilities, including those with mental health diagnoses, also may be more vulnerable and therefore become more dependent upon social workers.

The limited knowledge and/or capacity of many clients to engage in autonomous decision making places a crucial ethical obligation on the social worker because she is obliged to help them make reasoned choices that will maximize their benefits, while at the same time preserve and strengthen whatever autonomy and freedom they possess. This ethical dilemma remains even when it is recognized that, in the final analysis, the center of gravity in the helping process remains with the professional. Along these lines, Rothman (1989) concluded, "the prime responsibility for making professional decisions about means of helping the client falls to the practitioners" (p. 608).

At this point, we want to introduce another caution about self-determination that takes on special importance as the population of the United States becomes more diverse. The high value given to self-determination in U.S. society is derived from the importance assigned to the individual and individualism in this culture. Furlong (2003) suggests there are difficulties with these concepts despite the priority given to them in Western cultures because in many other cultures they may be assigned a far lesser value. In other words, the concepts universally accepted in U.S. social work may have different meanings and level of importance in cultures that limit individualism and place greater emphasis on the community and the group.

AMBIGUITY AND UNCERTAINTY

The degree of ambiguity and uncertainty encountered in practice situations can increase the probability of ethical dilemmas. By ambiguity, we mean that the social worker has imperfect or incomplete information about the situation being confronted. Three types of ambiguity and uncertainty make for ethical problems in social work practice: (1) uncertainty about values and goals, (2) uncertainty about scientific knowledge and about the facts relevant to any specific situation, and (3) uncertainty about the consequences of the intervention.

Ambiguity may be a more critical problem for social workers than for many other professional practitioners because the issues with which social workers deal are often nonspecific, and because social workers generally have less control over the outcome of their intervention than do practitioners in many other professional fields. There may be ambiguity about the nature and assessment of the problems that persons bring to a social worker. Frequently, despite their experience of pain and discomfort, clients do not really know what their problem is, what their goals are, or how to achieve them. Neither they nor their social workers may recognize the precise nature of their troubles, or there may not be any way to help the client. In addition, there may be many different participants in the situation, such as clients, family members, neighbors, other mental health professionals, and insurance companies, all of whom may have different ideas about the desired outcome (Kirk & Kutchins, 1992).

So many different factors impinge simultaneously on a person that it is often difficult for a social worker to assess the specific impact of her intervention. An unsuccessful outcome may be (but need not be) due to something that the social worker did or did not do—or it may be the result of factors over which the social worker had no control. The same intervention activity in two seemingly identical problem situations may lead to two entirely different outcomes because of factors over which the social worker has no power. Nor will anyone ever know what might have happened had she not intervened or had she used a different intervention strategy. For example, in a case of suspected child abuse, a social worker cannot predict with any certainty what might happen if the child stays with his parents, nor will the worker know for certain what might happen if the child is forcibly placed in out-of-home care. One such situation with many ambiguities is explored in Exemplar 5.5.

| 5.5 | A VICTIM OF CHILD ABUSE |

EP 2.1.2

Several months ago, Wendy Gillis told her public welfare social worker that she suspected that an upstairs neighbor, George Hill, regularly and brutally beat his 2-year-old son, Leroy. She heard the most frightful noises several evenings each week. When she saw the boy at rare intervals, he always wore bandages and looked so sad. The worker noted these remarks in her case report, but took no further action.

Last month, George's wife, Anne, brought Leroy to Lakeside General Hospital emergency room. Leroy suffered from multiple fractures, which, according to his mother, occurred when he fell down the front stairs. The attending physician did not believe her story because the X-ray revealed a large number of previous fractures in addition to the current ones. As required by law, he notified child protective services (CPS) that he suspected child abuse. Andre Conti, an experienced CPS social worker, was sent to the Hill home to investigate. He talked at length with both parents, who admitted beating Leroy occasionally when he misbehaved, as their way of disciplining him. Andre suggested that there were other ways to teach a boy to behave properly but concluded that the boy was in no immediate danger.

Two weeks later, another social worker made a follow-up visit to the Hill home. This worker, Millie Walker, agreed with Andre's assessment that for the time being there was no need to remove Leroy from his home. Ten days after Millie's visit, Anne Hill called for an ambulance, saying that her son was having difficulty breathing. When the ambulance crew arrived, they found Leroy unconscious. Twelve hours after he was brought to the hospital, he was pronounced dead. The postmortem confirmed that death was caused by a severe beating with a blunt instrument.

This exemplar gives rise to a number of questions with ethical implications, including the following: Did Wendy Gillis's social worker pay sufficient attention to the report of suspected child abuse and was Wendy's concern sufficient reason to warrant interfering in the Hill family? How can Andre Conti or any social worker know for certain that a clear and present danger existed for Leroy's life? When does parental discipline become child abuse? Under what conditions is the removal of a child from his family justified? How certain must a social worker be of the consequences before deciding to leave an endangered child with his family?

It should be noted that there are three sets of ambiguities in the Leroy Hill exemplar:

- Ambiguities resulting from a lack of clarity of societal norms (e.g., what are the limits of parental discipline?)
- Ambiguities resulting from a lack of knowledge (e.g., what evidence is sufficient to warrant intervention?)
- Ambiguities resulting from an inability to know what the future will bring (e.g., what will be the consequences of intervention?)

The social workers involved in this case made professional judgments that Leroy was not at risk. As a consequence of their mistaken judgment, Leroy is now dead. The mistake could also have gone the other way—identifying a risk when there was no danger to the child's welfare and thus removing the boy from his home and family needlessly. Every social worker in this situation faces a critical ethical dilemma because both types of mistakes cannot be avoided at the same time. Ambiguities and uncertainties are endemic conditions in social work practice. Neither the social worker nor anyone else can know for certain that a given parental behavior will lead to the child's death. The test of an effective social worker is that she should retain the ability to function even while coping with the ethical dilemmas that result from ambiguity and uncertainty.

Practice dilemmas create role conflict, uncertainty, ambiguity, and insecurity for social workers, who cannot be aware of all the forces that are operating in the context of any particular ethical decision-making situation. Braye and Preston-Shoot (1990) identified a myriad of dilemmas that are involved in decision making in child welfare. We list only a few of these as examples:

- rights of those involved versus risks
- needs required versus available resources

- duty (what do we have to do?) versus power (what we may do if we want to)
- legalism (decisions based purely on laws) versus professionalism (what weight does professional opinion have?)
- humanitarianism versus economics
- professionalism (how much autonomy?) versus the agency (guidance and direction)
- social work professionalism versus another discipline's professionalism
- professionals versus consumers (how much weight to attach to their views and those of their allies?)

Social workers help individuals but also represent society, and each of the above dilemmas has to be considered. The social worker must navigate between helping individuals and acting for society, being an agent of the client and an agent of the agency. Each ethical dilemma presents ambiguities that must be dealt with by the social worker on the basis of assessments and social work skill. It may not be comforting, but, there are no right answers when there are few—if any—clear definitions of acceptable or unacceptable risks.

CRITICAL THINKING EXERCISES

EP 2.1.3

1. Role-play the situation described earlier in this chapter, in which the social worker has determined that her older adult client is no longer able to live alone in his home. We know that this client responds negatively to every worker suggestion. Try various approaches to this problem situation. Keep in mind the ethical aspects.
2. Rothman (1989) and others have stated that the primary responsibility for making professional decisions falls on the social work practitioner. On the other hand, many social workers argue that the client has the exclusive right to make decisions about his life. Interview a social worker about these two professional perspectives. Ask them what ethical factors they consider when they decide to take the primary responsibility for making professional decisions about the client's personal life situation.
3. Assume that you are the child protection social worker sent to investigate the report of Leroy Hill's abuse (Exemplar 5.5). What criteria would you use to arrive at a decision to remove or not to remove Leroy from his parental home? Keep in mind the ethical aspects.

SUGGESTIONS FOR ADDITIONAL READINGS

Healy (2004) explores the degree to which practitioners try to influence clients to accept a course of action preferred by the practitioner and the means they use to do so. Moody (2004) describes how social workers employed in hospital discharge planning face frequent conflicts between patients' rights and the pressures of managed care. Dwyer (2005) examines the complexities of social work and difficult work environments that can engender situations in which it is difficult to protect the self-determination of older people.

WEBSITES OF INTEREST

- The Center for Self-Determination: http://www.centerforself-determination.com/index.html
- Extensive information on Self-Determination Theory as well as citations and links for numerous articles on self-determination: http://www.psych.rochester.edu/SDT/index.php
- The Center on Mental Health Services Research and Policy at the University of Illinois at Chicago provides several tools to advance self-determination for people with psychiatric disabilities: http://www.cmhsrp.uic.edu/nrtc/tools.asp

COMPETENCY NOTES

Apply social work ethical principles to guide professional practice: In this chapter, we discussed client rights, self-determination, professional expertise, and ambiguity as EP 2.1.2 they relate to ethical dilemmas and decision making for professional practice.

Apply critical thinking to inform and communicate professional judgments: Several exemplars and critical thinking exercises ask you to consider and decide how you EP 2.1.3 would respond to ethical dilemmas.

CHAPTER 6 | VALUE NEUTRALITY AND IMPOSING VALUES

This chapter addresses the CSWE 2008 EPAS Educational Policy 2.1.1 on becoming a professional social worker, specifically focusing on values. We also continue to present content on Educational Policy 2.1.2 about using social work ethical principles to guide professional practice. We will provide several opportunities through exemplars and questions for you to examine your personal and professional values and to work with the ethical decision-making model, which we hope you will use to apply critical thinking to inform and communicate professional judgments (Educational Policy 2.1.3).

In today's world, some scientists try to avoid all questions of values and morals because they have a deep commitment to the principle that knowledge can be derived only from empirical data. In the same way, many social workers also aim to base their practice exclusively on scientific principles; therefore they try to avoid all value considerations. One of the traditional expectations of professional social workers is that they not impose their personal values on clients and that they suspend judgment about clients' behavior and actions, even when their own values or societal values demand a judgment. In the real world of social work practice, however, things are not always so simple. The Code of Ethics (NASW, 2008, Purpose) recognizes that social workers "should be aware of the impact on ethical decision making of their clients' and their own personal values and cultural and religious beliefs and practices. They must be aware of any conflicts between personal and professional values and deal with them responsibly." It is never possible to avoid values because crucial professional decisions always involve value choices—if not worker values, then values of clients or of society. Professional decisions by social workers about means and ends are not simply technical choices but arise out of the historical situation, culture, and values in which both the social worker and all other participants are rooted (Iversen, Gergen, & Fairbanks, 2005).

As noted in Chapter 2, values play a central role in social work. In addition to considering individual and societal values, the social worker must also consider the impact of professional values on ethical decision making. The core values of the profession include: service, social justice, dignity and worth of the person, the importance of human relationships, integrity, and competence (NASW Code of Ethics, 2008, Ethical Principles).

CLIENT/WORKER VALUE GAP

A large gap between a worker's personal values and those of social work clients is not uncommon. The personal value systems of social workers differ from those of the general population. The importance social workers assign to personal relationships, service to others, and open-mindedness, as well as to equality (equal opportunity for all), helpfulness (working for the welfare of others), being broadminded (open-mindedness), social justice, human rights, client self-determination, and respect for diversity differ from the values held by the general population (Abbott, 2003; Horner & Whitbeck, 1991). This gap provides the basis for several potential ethical problems and dilemmas. Another source of ethical dilemmas may be the discrepancy that exists between the religious beliefs and practices of many clients and the nonreligious values of many mental health professionals. Hodge (2002) contrasts the belief in a personal God held by large proportions of the U.S. population and the large percentage of social workers who reject this belief. He points out that members of all religious groups hold many values that are different from the majority of social work practitioners.

Hodge (2004) conducted one of the few studies of how the espoused values of social workers may differ from those of working and middle class persons in general. Hodge used the General Social Surveys (1972 to 1998), which include a representative sample of the entire noninstitutionalized population of the English-speaking households in the continental United States. Although only a few social workers are included each year, because the exact same wording of questions is used each year, the answers of social workers over time can be pooled. The affirmed values of graduate social workers differed in many ways from those of working and middle class Americans.

Hodge (2004) found that social workers were more likely to identify as Democrats; were more liberal; and thought too much money was being spent on the military whereas too little money was being spent on welfare, solving problems in big cities, and improving the conditions of African Americans. Social workers were also more likely to endorse the legalization of marijuana than members of the working and middle classes; and social workers were twice as likely to oppose the death penalty for convicted murderers. A large gap also exists in regard to gun ownership (fewer than 20% of social workers, almost 50% of the working class, and more than 40% of the middle class own guns). Graduate level social workers were significantly more likely (almost 50% affiliated) than members of the working and middle classes to belong to a liberal religious denomination. And, in regard to the issue of abortion, more than three-quarters of graduate level social workers reported pro-choice positions, whereas roughly two-thirds of the working class were pro-life. Social workers were more likely to view adultery as morally acceptable behavior than members of the working and middle classes. Similarly, social workers were significantly more likely to view homosexual activity as morally appropriate behavior than were members of the working and middle classes (Hodge, 2003). It is important to note that the data for this study were collected from 1972 through 1998; there is no way of knowing whether these differences have become more or less pronounced since that time.

Clients' degree of religiosity and the depth of knowledge of and commitment to specific religious values should always be a consideration in the social work encounter—because there may be value conflicts between the worker's values and those of the client. These differences in religious values are only one area of value discrepancy, reflective of the discrepancies that may exist in other areas, such as economics, socioeconomic status, and politics. Knowledge, skill, experience, self-management, and conscious use of self can enable a social worker to make appropriate judgments and decisions despite such differences.

Shared values may optimize the chances for successful outcomes. However, the basis for continuing work is the recognition that the client's values should have priority in making decisions. The worker needs to make sure that the client is aware of all that is involved—risks, outcomes, and so forth—but in the end it is the client who must make the decision, even if such a choice is contrary to the worker's values. When the question of congruence between the values held by patients and therapists and the outcomes of therapy have been examined, the best outcome arises when the "values ... shared between patient and therapist are moderately similar, neither too close nor too divergent" (Holmes, 1989).

Matching client and worker values may be desirable, but is not always possible in the world of practice. A variety of problems can arise when there is a significant client/worker value gap, but here our concern will be limited to the ethical aspects. These relate primarily to the possibility of value imposition when there is a major divergence between client and worker values. Because of the power imbalance between client and worker, this ethical problem is often acute. A typical client/worker value gap is described in Exemplar 6.1.

6.1	HAVING A BABY AND SUBSTANCE ABUSE

EP 2.1.2

Jeff Butz, a child protection services worker, received a call from the Community Hospital social worker. Mona Koss, a single mother with a substance abuse problem, gave birth to a baby girl two days ago. Mother and baby are due to be discharged tomorrow, but the hospital social worker does not think that the infant will be safe if she goes home with her mother. Mona, who has no permanent home, is currently living with a drug dealer who in the past has been involved in physical and sexual abuse situations.

The world of Jeff Butz is as far from Mona Koss's world as the North Pole is from the South Pole. Their lifestyles and value systems are diametrically opposed. One way for social worker Jeff to respond to the telephone call he received is to initiate legal proceedings (which may be required by law in the state where he practices) in order to remove the infant from her mother. Such a move may be congruent with his own personal values and with what he believes to be societal expectations. However, can he ignore Mona's wish to keep her baby? What is best for the newborn infant? Should Jeff explore these questions with Mona before making any decisions?

A client/worker value gap is often unavoidable. The social worker and the client have different positions in the helping system—one is a client, the other is a professional; the client has a problem, the social worker does not. Social workers must, therefore, develop ways to deal with the value discrepancies that arise out of these status differences. Some have found the following approach useful:

1. Identify the differences and how they might affect both client and worker.
2. If possible, identify the problem in ways that avoid the conflicting values.
3. During the intake/assessment/diagnostic stage, the social worker should determine what may be the relationship between these value differences and the presenting problem.
4. Work first on parts of the problem that do not present value differences.
5. The social worker should discuss her findings with the clients so that together they can participate in determining whether these differences might complicate the social work process. No prior assumption should be made that a client is not ready and able to participate in such joint decision making.
6. A joint decision should be made whether to continue the social work process or whether the gap is so vast that it is preferable to continue the social work process with another social worker with more congruent values, if such a worker is available.

VALUE NEUTRALITY

Weick (1999) suggested that professional practice requires listening to what the client is really saying "without imposing one's own values, beliefs or judgments" (p. 331). Some clinicians consider neutrality a fundamental clinical principle and ethical requirement (Simon & Gutheil, 1997). For example, Cervera (1993) urged social workers who work with pregnant teenagers to maintain a neutral position about the girls' behavior in order to be really helpful. One reason for suspending value judgments about such matters as drug use, lifestyle choices, or personal relationships is that it is not the social worker's role to impose her own values. Others believe that in our pluralistic society there is no longer any absolute right or wrong. What might seem wrong to one person will seem right to another. What is right today may be wrong tomorrow. Sophie Freud (1999) observed that even the concept of normality "has become so fuzzy to the point of making the very word *normal* a problematic word.... We can no longer agree on our values" (p. 338).

There are critical questions about this value-neutral stance that must be considered. One of these is whether value neutrality or value suspension is a realistic option for social workers. Turner (2002) suggests that "it is impossible to interact with another human being... without making a series of judgments and observations about them that shape our responses to them" (p. 61). What are social workers to do with the values they hold when working with clients who hold contrary values? Can social workers really avoid communicating their own values—if not deliberately, then through subtle or nonverbal exchanges?

There are no easy answers to these questions, but these considerations must be faced by every practitioner. Many believe that suspension of judgment, a basic concept in social work, has been so misinterpreted that it has become the cause of much unethical professional behavior. Siporin (1985a) thought that avoiding moral judgments does not help the client achieve his goals; he writes that "in being of help to people, there is need to make moral ethical judgments, and to help clients do so as well" (p. 202). Goldstein (1998) suggests that the social work practitioner cannot be concerned only with what works but also must develop a moral orientation. Because the situations and problems of social work practice present difficult moral dilemmas, Goldstein believes that social workers have an ethical obligation to act as moral agents—they cannot ignore what is good and ethically correct, what is "right" and "wrong." It is impossible to avoid moral and ethical issues that exist at each step of the social work processes. Maslow (1969) suggested that "a value-free philosophy of science is unsuitable for human questions, when personal value, purposes, and goals, intentions and plans are absolutely crucial for the understanding of any person, a value neutral, value avoiding model of science (is) quite unsuitable for the study of life" (p. 725). The study of human behavior cannot be value free; such a morally neutral, value-free science not only can be wrong but it also may be potentially dangerous to assume that value neutrality is a desirable characteristic of social work.

Value neutrality may cause damage in the following situations:

- Attention is not paid to potentially self-destructive or other-destructive acts.
- Social workers fail to distinguish between what is functional or dysfunctional behavior and what is normative or pathological conduct.
- Although the worker may intend her silence to be an expression of value neutrality, the client may think that the social worker approves of what he does when she fails to challenge the behavior.

Value neutrality is itself a value. Sometimes social workers do not acknowledge their own moral judgments. The contemporary social worker who bases her practice on value neutrality may be avoiding all moral dilemmas by accepting the client's absolute right for self-determination. Historically, value suspension became a professional response to the moralistic paternalism that was practiced by the Friendly Visitors (the volunteers who preceded professional social workers in the last decades of the nineteenth century); such an approach was modeled after the early psychoanalytic view that therapy should be a value-free scientific activity. Originally, suspension of judgment meant that the social worker related to the client's whole person and to his strengths, instead of only to his weaknesses and problems. It meant trying to understand this person in terms of his total personal history, environment, culture, and community. If the client's behavior was problematic, then the social worker was ready to help him change that behavior without condemning him. This was often expressed as, "I accept you, but not your behavior." Can we honestly say that we do not care what a client does? Can we accept child molestation, neglect, violence, cheating, stealing, or lying? Dare social workers not condemn physical and sexual abuse, rape, beatings, irresponsible sexual activities, and similar antisocial behaviors?

According to Clark (2006), "key values such as respect and self-determination have to be actualized in practical contexts that inevitably favor one credible interpretation over another ... the expression of key values cannot be independent of personal sympathies" (p. 76). Bergin (1980, 1991) argues that therapeutic neutrality is a myth, that even the most "nondirective" of therapists maintain strongly held values that are communicated in one way or another to clients.

Clark (2006) proposes that social workers recognize the inevitability of values intruding into professional relationships and suggests that greater openness about this is correct and effective in achieving client goals. The following ideas make clear his position on the absurdity of value neutrality:

- The claim of social workers' value neutrality is, in practice, a sham. It is not humanly possible to maintain a truthful engagement, expressed in an authentic interpersonal professional relationship, when the professional holds in abeyance his own personal feelings of dismay or censure of aspects of the client's life that are pertinent to the work at hand....
- Social workers and their agencies cannot in practice avoid setting standards of the good or adequate life, even if they wished to do so. Instead of shirking these choices, they should make them positively and openly rather than implicitly and covertly. (p. 79)

The social work role entails modeling ways of life and counseling about morally problematic issues, as well as the competent delivery of services. In today's practice context, social workers have to balance the notion of the client's right to self-determination with being directive. There is more clarity about the social worker being directive when clients do not have the capacity to make informed decisions and when there is the likelihood of potential harm and danger to the client or to others. Emphasis on practitioners providing direction may result from demands by managed care, pressures to maintain agency funding or income, and the implementation of productivity measures.

Rothman and colleagues (1996) found that all social workers, even those using psychodynamic as well as cognitive-behavioral, task-centered, and brief treatment focuses, used a broad range of directiveness modalities in their practices. Although the directiveness modalities they used were influenced by specific contextual factors, they avoided either extreme—directiveness/paternalism or client self-determination—as their only practice pattern. However, this flexibility and consistency reflects one of the practical limitations to social worker value neutrality. In some cases, value neutrality may actually minimize or avoid the social worker's ethical and legal responsibility to "promote the well-being of clients" (NASW Code, 2008, 1.01) when intervention is called for by the situation. On the other hand, however, if the social worker is directive, her directiveness may lead to issues of value imposition on clients who are vulnerable.

VALUE IMPOSITION

Much of what social workers do involves helping people choose between available options. Both the worker's and the client's values are important considerations in making this choice. Can a social worker provide this help without imposing her own values? This question takes on special urgency because social workers often grapple with strategies that are designed to modify or change the behaviors, beliefs, and values of clients.

Some approaches to helping people with problems assume that it is desirable to systematically change their values and thought patterns by substituting more sensible and rational thoughts and values, such as those held by social workers. Rational emotive therapy (RET), developed by Albert Ellis, is one school of therapy that recommends this view. The therapist's values always should influence client values. For example, RET "shares the views of ethical humanism by *encouraging* people to emphasize human interest (self and social) over the interests of deities, material objects, and lower animals" (Dryden & Ellis, 1988, p. 232, emphasis added). Those following this school suggest that these values be used in a conscious and controlled manner (Frank, 1991). But many disagree with any attempt to impose values.

Even when a social worker does not want to impose her own values, she may do so unintentionally. Covert messages about values, such as body language, facial expressions, and tone of voice, are often more powerful than overt ones. The social worker may be unaware that she is subtly communicating her preferences or values commitments in these ways. A social worker may also define the goals and outcomes of the treatment without once saying what she deems appropriate, but by not presenting options she considers inappropriate, she has effectively imposed her values. How can one ethically justify such worker control? Some have suggested that an explicit communication of the social worker's values would safeguard the client against such potential misuse of power by the worker. Sophie Freud (1999) went so far as to suggest "it might even be best to admit our own biases to our clients and engage in honest debates with them ..." (p. 338). Such self-disclosure of the worker's values may enhance the client's comfort with and sense of trust in the practitioner. However, value self-disclosure may be harmful when used inappropriately or at the wrong time, especially early in the professional relationship. Spero (1990) and Strean (1997) concluded that any short-term advantages of a worker's value disclosure may be cancelled by long-term harmful effects.

The problem facing the social worker working with Bess and Todd Moore, described in Exemplar 6.2, illustrates the range of ethical dilemmas around the issue of imposing values.

6.2	SAVING A MARRIAGE

EP 2.1.2

Bess and Todd Moore have agreed to seek help to rescue their marriage. Bess recently discovered that Todd has been having sex with several other women over the past few years. Todd has told the social worker that his sexual relations with other women are merely physical. He has greater sexual needs than Bess and therefore cannot give up these relations. Yet he loves his wife and wants to continue this marriage. Bess is ready to forgive the past, but cannot bring herself to live with Todd knowing that he will continue to have sex with other women.

Different social workers hold different values about marriage and extramarital relations. Should the social worker keep her own values to herself so that she will not influence the Moores' decision? Is this possible? Or should the social worker openly state her own values and then let Bess and Todd work on a solution to their problem? Which is the more ethical approach?

A recently developed school of thought suggests a third approach, challenging the assumptions of objectivity, value neutrality, and scientific expertise. Using assessment as their focus, Iversen, Gergen, and Fairbanks (2005) suggest the importance and validity of engaging in dialogue and collaboration with clients. The social worker should engage in active negotiation with the client to define the problem rather than assume that she knows what the problem is. From this perspective, they propose understanding assessment as a collaborative deliberation concerning various possibilities for the client's life, relationships, and the future. However, the social worker cannot evade making decisions about assessments and any conflicts of values by simply engaging clients in collaborative assessments.

Do social workers have a responsibility to examine, together with the client, the ethical nature and quality of the problems that people bring to them? Or is it more helpful to overlook the moral aspects of the situation? Society, with near unanimity, condemns child sexual abuse and incest. Should a social worker assume a value-free stance and listen to her client's report of what could be incestuous behavior with the same equanimity as she would listen to any other problem he may raise? Should she communicate to this client the community's valuation of incest? Does it make a difference whether the abuser or the victim is the worker's client? Are there cultural factors that might make a difference in assessing the ethical implications of this type of behavior? What if the client's ethnic culture does not proscribe father/daughter relations that do not involve penetration? What if the incestuous relations occur between consenting adults? What if the abusive behavior occurred twenty years ago? What about legal requirements to report abuse? To what extent would keeping quiet translate into condoning such behavior? What is the social worker's role in these and similar situations as a societal agent?

Our discussion above is based on assumptions prevalent in social work regarding the right to differences and an emphasis on diversity. Not everyone agrees with this preoccupation of social work with difference and diversity. Webb (2009) argues that from an ethical point of view this is a bankrupt perspective in which social work ethics rests on human rights ethics that rely on local, specific, and culturally diverse ideology. By accepting this assumption, the profession fails to generate real political change. The emphasis on differences and diversity results in a displacement of class as the signifier of inequality and injustice, which, according to Webb (2009), results in difference becoming a conservative principle supporting inequality, division, and separatism.

Webb (2009) also points out that the Code of Ethics of the International Federation of Social Workers contains explicit sections on human rights and social justice that serve as justification for social work action. He suggests that human rights are more ambiguous than they may appear. Furthermore, human rights are always potentially in tension with other sets of rights (parents' rights versus children's rights, older adults versus children, one group's rights versus another group's rights). He suggests that to focus on identity differences (and their accompanying politics and ethics) can lead to ignoring issues of unequal distribution of resources in a society.

MAKING JUDGMENTS ABOUT VALUES

The three types of value situations that have been discussed in this chapter—client/ worker value gap, value neutrality, and value imposition—form a matrix of ethical considerations. Even those social workers who are committed to maintaining a value-free stance will abandon this behavior beyond a certain point. To give an obvious example, no social worker will sit by quietly when a father describes how he threw his 1-year-old child from a third-floor balcony. But the ethical dilemma is more serious than such atypical examples suggest because, in fact, ethical quandaries involving the social worker's values and judgment occur at every step of the social work process. The social worker who suspends her judgment when a client relates a promiscuous episode or an aggressive behavior incident may be as judgmental as her colleague who does not hesitate to indicate disapproval. When a client expresses guilt about a certain behavior but continues to engage in that behavior, he may conclude that the worker considers such behavior acceptable if she addresses only the problem of guilt. Is such a stance ethical for a social worker?

It has been suggested that in these and similar situations a social worker can avoid making judgments by letting the client decide what he wants—whether he wants help with his "guilt" or with the "deviant" behavior. At first glance this appeal to the principle of client self-determination seems to solve all ethical problems. On second thought it may turn out that this is an irresponsible and perhaps even an unethical response to a client who desperately seeks help or a client who is involuntarily receiving services. Even when the client's request for help is specific, the worker may have a societal responsibility that she dare not shirk. For example, is it ethical for a social worker to help a client manage and reduce his feelings of guilt so that he can continue an extramarital affair, continue abusing his wife, or continue stealing money from his employer?

This ethical dilemma may increase as the population of the United States grows more diverse through changing patterns of immigration and social workers are faced more frequently with behaviors that lie outside their own cultural experiences. Consider Exemplar 6.3.

6.3 | LOYALTY TO SELF OR FAMILY?

EP 2.1.2

Rosa Arriga, a social worker at a family service agency, has seen Adira Salima for three sessions. Adira has been depressed, has experienced much conflict at home with her parents and other relatives, and has been subject to much anxiety on her job, where she works as a packer for minimum wage. All family members, including Adira, are recent immigrants to the United States. All must work because without everyone's paycheck they will not be able to maintain even a marginal existence. Her supervisor, who likes her, referred her to the agency for help. Adira told Rosa that her family continues to maintain the traditional culture of their country of origin. Thus, her parents will not allow her to have a normal U.S. social life because they are planning to arrange a marriage for her. She is not allowed to date. She cannot leave her family home because her earnings are insufficient to support herself elsewhere. Her knowledge of English and her other skills are not sufficient to qualify her for a better job. Adira vacillates between feeling pride at doing what is expected in her family's culture and wanting to become more Americanized by dating and deciding for herself whom she should marry.

What should be Rosa's approach? Should she support Adira's loyalty to her family, knowing that they are all dependent on each other and that they are her only relatives in the United States? Should she support Adira's struggle toward more independence? If Adira has the possibility of living with extended family members or friends, should she be encouraged to leave home and live with them? How should Rosa, who is a feminist, respond to this situation? Would it be possible or appropriate for her to be value neutral when discussing options with Adira? Would it make a difference if Rosa were from the same culture as Adira's family and a member of their community?

Some social workers try to avoid the ethical dilemma by suggesting to a client that they approve or disapprove only of a specific behavior, not of the client. This is a fine, almost legalistic distinction that may seem to avoid the ethical issues posed here. Such a solution, however, creates other practice problems and does not really avoid the ethical issues raised. Perhaps a more realistic way of phrasing this ethical obligation is to demand that the social worker's own value judgment never become the sole or major criterion for making a decision. There is no relationship that is free of values. At the same time, we must remember that it is the client's responsibility to identify the values that will guide his behavioral choices; the social worker can never assume this responsibility (Frankl, 1968).

THE INEVITABILITY OF VALUES

In this chapter, we have included sections on value neutrality, the imposition of values, and client/worker value gaps. One must remember that practice should reflect the value principles of the social work profession as they are expressed in the Code of Ethics of the professional association. Goldstein (1998) describes the ethically grounded social worker as "alert and responsive to questions of moral choice, social justice, prevailing moral codes of conduct, and, not the least, personal accountability whether she is doing research, applying theory, planning, or engaging in practice—any professional activity that impinges on the life and well-being of others" (p. 246). Ethical decisions by social workers have importance at every level of practice—direct practitioner, supervisor, administrator—regardless whether the service focus is on the individual case or on societal and political action. One means of selecting from the multitude of ethical issues for social workers in practice is through a screening device. Behavior can be considered along a continuum. Knowing where one falls on this continuum can help in deciding when one can anticipate value conflicts. One can observe in the continuum of worker values shown in Figure 6.1 that a social worker may find it inadvisable in some situations to work with clients whose values are significantly contrary to her own. This continuum is intended to assist social workers in a systematic way as they consider differences in values concerning themselves, clients, and agencies.

Applicant	The person(s) or system that requests help with a defined or felt problem
Client	The applicant who enters into a formal, contractual, goal-focused relationship with a social worker
Target	The person(s) or system(s) that must be modified in order to achieve the desired outcome to which client and worker have agreed
Beneficiary	The person(s) or system(s) that will benefit from successful goal achievement in which the resolution of the ethical issues may not fully coincide with the legal requirements

FIGURE 6.1 | SOME PARTICIPANTS IN THE SOCIAL WORK PROCESS

In Exemplar 6.3, conflicting cultural values are in play. The question was raised as to how a social worker who is committed to strong feminist values might deal with the value conflicts in the situation. What should an ethical social worker do?

There are, however, prior implications for the social worker, derived from the continuum of worker values. If information is known to them about the values of a potential employing agency, should social workers (given their own conflicting values) seek employment or accept jobs with employers who only will or will not oppose family planning or are pro-choice, overtly or covertly discriminate against particular groups, and view stern discipline of children as appropriate? Thus, even before engaging in the work of the agency, social workers have to consider whose values take priority.

Situations such as those described in this chapter may present painful dilemmas for both clients and social workers. Incidents of neglect, abuse, and violence also raise questions as to whom the social worker represents, whose welfare takes priority, and what the social worker's roles are as a moral agent. The Code of Ethics (2008) states that "social workers should promote the general welfare of society" (6.01); "social workers should act to expand choice and opportunity for all people, with special regard for vulnerable, disadvantaged, oppressed, and exploited people and groups" (6.04b); and "social workers should act to prevent and eliminate domination of, exploitation of, and discrimination against any person, group, or class on the basis of race, ethnicity, national origin, color, sex, sexual orientation, gender identity or expression, age, marital status, political belief, religion, immigration status, or mental or physical disability (6.04d). Do these code provisions give clear direction to the social worker when she faces the type of ethical dilemmas discussed in this chapter?

CRITICAL THINKING EXERCISES

EP 2.1.3

1. The NASW Code of Ethics has a strong values base. Should someone become a social worker if they do not agree with the values presented in the Code of Ethics? Organize a class debate on this issue.
2. It has been said that even when a social worker does not declare her values publicly, her lifestyle and her nonverbal communications will usually indicate the values she holds.

Identify how your own lifestyle and your nonverbal messages might inform client Adira Salima (Exemplar 6.3) of the values you hold. What problems might this create for maintaining a professional relationship?

3. Some have compared the risk of acquiring HIV from sexual activities with the risk of a fatal automobile accident. If someone uses this comparison, does he or she communicate a value, or is this an example of value neutrality? Defend your answer.

4. Your client feels very guilty about engaging in certain behavior. Assume that this behavior is not illegal. He asks your help, but he does not specify whether he wants help in dealing with his guilt or in extinguishing the behavior. Discuss the ethical implications of choosing either approach. Will the specific behavior make a difference in your ethical assessment? Try to assess the two approaches with the following types of behavior: overeating, smoking, gambling, masturbation, eating foods his physician suggested he avoid, having an extramarital affair, or working out for an hour five times a week.

5. How would you have responded if you had received the telephone call that Jeff Butz received (Exemplar 6.1)?

6. Can a social worker be neutral and value free concerning such issues as suicide, adultery, use of drugs, or engaging in illegal behaviors? There are social workers who might support a person's right to engage in these behaviors because they believe they should take a value-free approach. In a group discussion, decide which view is right. Identify the implications of each approach for ethical decision making. What options are available for a social worker in dealing with issues such as these? Who will decide and what values will prevail?

7. Some students believe that premarital sex, same-sex relations, and abortion are sinful. A social work instructor and the NASW (2008) Code of Ethics indicate that such behaviors among adults are acceptable. How should this value gap be handled in the classroom?

8. Select a topic that you have a strong values perspective about (e.g., abortion, assisted suicide, corporeal punishment) and role play working with a client with an opposite values perspective. Ask observers to note whether your nonverbal communication is consistent with your verbal communication and whether either or both indicate your values on this topic.

9. Interview a human services professional about whether it is possible and desirable for a social worker to remain neutral and keep her own values from influencing clients.

SUGGESTIONS FOR ADDITIONAL READINGS

Clark (2006) suggests that the place of values in social work practice is crucial, and social workers have to be moral agents. Simon and Gutheil (1997) defend the duty of neutrality for therapists. Bisman (2004) discusses social work values as "the moral core of the profession." Iversen, Gergen, and Fairbanks (2005) trace the assessment procedures in social work to empiricism, suggesting they are based on assumptions of objectivity, measurement accuracy, value neutrality, and scientific expertise.

WEBSITES OF INTEREST

Try using any Internet search engine to search for "social work values" or "value neutrality in social work," and you are likely to get thousands of hits. If you are interested in this topic, try doing this kind of search to get a sense of the incredible amount of information available on the web. If you don't want to start that broadly, you might want to visit the following sites.

- Scottish Executive Publications for an article on "The Role of the Social Worker in the 21st Century: A Literature Review, Part 4 Social Work Professional Values and Ethics": http://www.scotland.gov.uk/Publications/2005/12/1994633/46349
- The Association of Baccalaureate Social Work Program Directors (BPD) has an Information Technology Subcommittee on Curriculum Resources for Social Work Values and Ethics: http://www.uncp.edu/home/marson/nhome.htm
- The Center for the Study of Ethics in the Professions at the Illinois Institute of Technology provides links to hundreds of professional codes of ethics and information on the function of codes of ethics, including a case study for using a code of ethics: http://ethics.iit.edu/%20codes/
- The International Federation of Social Workers presents their social work values: http://www.ifsw.org/en/p38000208.html
- The Bureau of Labor Statistics (BLS), U.S. Department of Labor, *Occupational Outlook Handbook, 2010-11 Edition*, Social Workers, provides the occupational outlook for social work and other disciplines; note that the discussion of social work includes values: http://www.bls.gov/oco/ocos060.htm

COMPETENCY NOTES

Identify as a professional social worker and conduct oneself accordingly: In this chapter, we discuss values and how they relate to ethical dilemmas for social workers.

EP 2.1.1

Apply social work ethical principles to guide professional practice: In this chapter, we discuss how values are related to ethical decision making and ethical social work practice.

EP 2.1.2

Apply critical thinking to inform and communicate professional judgments: Several exemplars asked you to consider and decide how you would respond to ethical dilemmas, and exercises at the end of the chapter address critical thinking.

EP 2.1.3

Engage diversity and difference in practice: In this chapter, we discuss cultural diversity in relation to values.

EP 2.1.4

THE PROFESSIONAL RELATIONSHIP: LIMITS, DILEMMAS, AND PROBLEMS

This chapter addresses the CSWE 2008 EPAS Educational Policy 2.1.1 on becoming a professional social worker, and we also continue content on Educational Policy 2.1.2 on using social work ethical principles to guide professional practice. Because the issues in this chapter may be personally challenging, we provide nine exemplars and many questions to help you examine these issues surrounding the professional relationship, which we hope you will use to apply critical thinking to inform and communicate professional judgments (Educational Policy 2.1.3).

The essence of social work practice can be found in the relationship between the social worker and her clients. Trust is a central element in this relationship because a helping relationship requires that the client will be able to trust his social worker (which may be difficult for involuntary clients), and the social worker must be able to at least put aside or neutralize her doubts about her clients. However, it is important that the social worker recognizes that for the client "to trust is to become vulnerable and dependent on the good will and motivations of those we trust" (Pellegrino, 1991, p. 69). Going to a social worker or to any other professional for help requires that the help seeker or client believes that the professional will act morally, will perform professional functions competently, and will be concerned about the problems the client brings to the situation. The client is dependent upon the prudence of the professional. In order for the client to receive any service, it is often necessary that he remove the protective cover that his privacy normally gives him. The client will do so only when he believes that the professional will use her good judgment and skill for his welfare.

PROFESSIONAL RELATIONSHIPS AND SPECIAL DUTIES

The "link between the professional and the client is a professional relationship. The client who trusts the professional entrusts his total self (not just his possessions) to the professional" (Sokolowski, 1991, p. 31). The professional presents herself as trustworthy because she is certified as a professional. This means that she is obligated both to the client and to the profession. Actually, most clients cannot evaluate the trustworthiness of the social worker to whom they have been assigned or to whom they turn; instead they place their trust in the reputation of the employing agency, governmental licensing, and professional certifications. We do not personally check out every airplane pilot or railroad engineer with whom we travel; we depend on the employer to select qualified professionals and government licensing to confirm the professional's preparation. Similarly, clients trust that their vulnerability will not be exploited by the social work professional for her own purposes such as power, profit, or pleasure.

The social work professional's relationship with the client assumes special duties that arise because of the trust or confidence the client places in the social worker. The professional role introduces a power imbalance—in this relationship the client has certain needs, and the social worker has various powers. The professional's knowledge, as well as her power, can dominate and influence the client. It is crucial, therefore, that the social worker act in the best interest of the client and not take advantage of him in order to promote her own (or her agency's) interests. The confidentiality and informed consent obligations are intended to prevent the abuse of power by the professional practitioner. Basic to this relationship is the requirement that the social worker be honest. Likewise, it is important that social workers recognize the ethical nature of the professional relationship and the limits it places on social workers in their dealings with clients. These ethical duties are found in the Code of Ethics, but social workers should be aware that recognizing the ethical nature of practice does not avoid all conflicts of interest.

Many of the responsibilities of social workers introduced above are based on their ethical *fiduciary* relationships with clients. A fiduciary relationship involves a confidence or trust (Webster's, 1989). For social workers, a fiduciary responsibility means that the social worker is responsible for acting primarily for the benefit of each client. Clients place their trust in the fiduciary characteristics of social work professionals' relations with clients and with legal and ethical standards for professional conduct (Kutchins, 1991).

Many social workers assume clients trust them and the social agencies that employ them, even though the distrust of all professionals and of many social agencies is widespread. Many people are wary about placing their trust in any professional, including social workers. Trust, while necessary, is not enforceable. Clients cannot be compelled to trust a worker or a social agency, even when they have no choice about the service they need. Likewise, social workers cannot be required to trust their clients, even when practice theory demands that they do so. Today, the caution of clients may reflect not only their own questions but also the skepticism and climate of distrust found throughout society. Several additional factors have affected the trust relationship, including limitations on professional judgments, democratization and the rights revolution, and the growing lack of privacy.

LIMITATIONS ON PROFESSIONAL JUDGMENTS

The advent of managed care of health and mental health services, where specialized skills and professional judgment are required, has tended to undermine the professional authority and powers of clinicians and others by limiting their control over treatment choices, instituting productivity reporting systems that intrude upon professional decision making, and skewing treatment choices and options. Hall and Keefe (2006), in a national study of social workers, psychologists, and psychiatrists, found that these professionals did not see themselves as having adequate skills to interact effectively with managed care organizations to ensure the care they are providing is certified and follows best practice guidelines. Professionals can have difficulty defending their intervention choices. Furthermore, because of managed care, social workers often cannot make decisions about what services they can provide, thus conveying to the client the existence of a hidden, unapproachable, and unaccountable presence of another who affects his life. On the other hand, managed care may protect the client and society from exaggerated or distorted professional decisions, from providing treatment that may be profitable to the practitioner but not effective for the client. However, clients may not know who is making decisions—the clinician or someone at the insurance company. This raises the issue of honesty. When the social worker does not make the decision, is she obligated to tell this to the client? How does doing so affect the professional relationship?

Bennett, Naylor, Perri, Shirilla, and Kilbane (2008) studied the attitudes of NASW members in the State of Illinois toward managed care and its impact on their practices. They found that managed care negatively impacted clinicians in terms of their preferred practice, earnings, and job satisfaction. The researchers also found that the decisions that were more likely to be influenced by managed care were the number of sessions, reducing fees, and advocating for clients. The authors recommend advocating for change in policies, procedures, and practices; and educating and training social workers to more efficiently, effectively, and ethically navigate the managed care system. These suggestions mirror the comments of Hall and Keefe (2006) introduced previously that reflect social workers' unpreparedness for dealing with managed care organizations.

Democratization and the Rights Revolution

The consumer rights revolution followed in the footsteps and flowed out of the civil rights movement and legislation, the development of self-help organizations, demedicalization and growing emphasis on personal self-care, deinstitutionalization of the mentally ill population, and the independent living movement of physically disabled people (Tower, 1994). These consumer movements often criticized professionals. Two aspects of these criticisms are (1) a desire by clients to affect the quality of services they receive and (2) their desire to participate in gaining greater control over standards. As a result of these developments, professionals have to explain to clients how they can help, how long it will take, and what the expected outcomes will be, with an emphasis on effectiveness of treatment and accountability. Decisions and notes previously not shared with clients are now open to inspection by clients and others. These changes empower clients and democratize the delivery of services to a greater extent. For every change, however, there is a cost. The question is how this greater accountability affects the client, the worker, and the effectiveness of the helping system. These accountability systems may be interpreted by professionals as indicating a lack of trust in their judgment, while the social worker's caution about what to place in a record may potentially reduce the record's usefulness as a tool to help the social worker analyze and plan.

A DISAPPEARING SENSE OF PRIVACY

At one time personal privacy seemed absolute. Nowadays, almost everyone is aware that personal privacy is limited. Supermarkets and other businesses track purchases made by individuals; identities are stolen (e.g., social security numbers are used, purchases are made with credit card information obtained illegally, hackers invade hospital individual health files); Internet surfing is recorded; electronic messages are retrieved by persons other than the intended recipients; and mishaps are reported where information being sent to one recipient (such as an insurance company) can be received by others. This is the background in which citizens in general no longer trust the professional's claims that privacy and confidentiality will be respected. Nowadays, no professional can guarantee privacy or confidentiality. Both clients and professionals recognize that the professional no longer controls the data provided by the client.

LIMITS OF THE PROFESSIONAL RELATIONSHIP

Primary relationships, especially those within the family or between friends, have few limits. The professional relationship between the client and social worker, on the other hand, is not a primary relationship because it is limited and focused on the problem for which help is sought. The professional assumes responsibility for helping the client with his problem(s), and traditionally, the relationship terminates once these objectives have been achieved. Thus, it is a limited relationship in contrast to the broad primary relations that most people treasure. We will focus on the ethical problems and dilemmas that social workers face because of their commitment to certain values within the professional relationship. One of the major causes for ethical problems in this area arises whenever a social worker determines that her client needs help that goes beyond the limits that the traditional professional relationship allows. But there are other, equally perplexing ethical dilemmas, as the discussion in this chapter will show.

The limits of the professional relationship can raise a number of ethical issues. Some social workers prefer to hide behind the limited professional relationship because they are uncomfortable with their clients' lifestyles and cultures. At the same time, many social workers want to identify with their clients by expressing empathy with their fate. Without wanting to imitate a lifestyle that is not authentic for them, they want to learn about and participate more fully in their clients' lives because they know that they cannot be effective and helpful without such knowledge. But this type of knowledge is not available if the relationship is limited to 9 A.M. to 5 P.M., Monday through Friday.

Many conscientious social workers are not entirely clear about what the correct professional conduct is. Is it ethical for a social worker to accept an invitation for Sunday dinner in the client's home or to join the client on Friday evening in the local bar? May a social worker reciprocate and invite a client for supper at her home or in a restaurant? Is it appropriate for a social worker who wants to learn about a particular culture to accept an invitation from a client to explore the client's ethnic neighborhood with him so as to understand better the culture from which he has come? Until recently, practice wisdom has given fairly clear and generally negative answers to all of these questions, but, increasingly, social workers express discomfort with the barriers that have been erected between them and their clients.

The NASW (2008) Code of Ethics (1.06 a, b, c, d) suggests that dual relationships and conflicts of interests can be accommodated within sound social work practice if professional discretion is used and there is no risk of exploitation or potential harm to the client. Dual relationships occur when a social worker "assumes a second relationship with a client that may cause actual or potential conflicts between their professional duties and their social, religious, or business relationships" (Johner, 2006, p. 2). Boland-Prom and Anderson (2005) explored this issue and suggest that proper decision making can—in certain cases—provide for such dual relationships. Aside from prohibiting any sexual relationships with clients, they suggest much depends on the legal and other contextual factors, type of social work practice, history of the relationship, and degrees of dependence and vulnerability.

Although the relationship is supposed to be a limited one, social workers often have an emotional reaction to their clients. Such feelings may be natural, but the consequent worker behavior may cause ethical problems. When a worker's own needs become entangled with the professional relationship, emotional feelings may become destructive. In such situations, the social worker may lose her sense of objectivity; instead of helping the client, she may cause harm.

Maidment (2006), an Australian social work educator, points out that dealing with the ambiguities of proper boundaries between client and social worker must be done within a context that includes organizational and managed care risk management and accountability. Our increasingly litigious society tends to encourage caution regarding professional relationships that go beyond the generally accepted conventional boundaries. Together, these factors encourage social workers to carefully consider what is personal and what is professional in their relationships. Meanwhile, social workers should be cautious about over-involvement with clients; for example, they should "keep a distance": no hugs and no acceptance of gifts or invitations to parties or dinner. However, social workers need to keep in mind the cultural setting in which the relationship occurs. In many cultures, if the social worker refuses a cup of tea and a cookie during a home visit, she may be considered rude or even insulting.

Maidment (2006), possibly reflecting a more general redefinition of dual relations in practice, however, argues that clients have strong needs for belonging and meaningful relationships with others, including social workers. She does not rule out the use of touch, the importance of reciprocity between client and social worker, including love and relational spirituality that emphasize the interconnectedness and interdependence that exists between all people. She asks whose needs are being met by strict professional dual role boundaries. Her response suggests effective client/social worker partnerships and the services to be provided can be undermined by too strict observance of dual role relationships. Keeping a distance can result in serving the needs of the social worker and not those of the client. Finally, she contends that the rapid changes in our environments and the ways services are delivered require reconsideration by social workers of the dual relationship and boundary guidelines. She opts for much broader definitions of appropriate dual re-lations, than conventional definitions suggest, based—of course—on professional assessments of the client situation, including physical touch, mutual storytelling, and social worker self-disclosure.

CLIENT INTERESTS VERSUS WORKER INTERESTS

Giving priority to a client's interests is one of the cornerstones of professional social work codes of ethics. The NASW (2008) Code of Ethics expresses this professional obligation as follows: "Social workers elevate service to others above self-interest" (Ethical Principles) and "Commitment to Clients: Social workers' primary responsibil-ity is to promote the well-being of clients. In general, clients' interests are primary" (NASW Code, 2008, 1.01).

This ethical principle is meant to safeguard the client from exploitation because most clients can neither control nor evaluate practitioner activities. Providing un-necessary treatment is one example of a violation of this ethical principle. From time to time, professionals (psychiatrists, social workers, and others) as well as so-cial agencies and institutions are charged with needlessly extending the period of service or providing unnecessary services for financial or other reasons. Some hold that this practice hardly presents an ethical problem for the majority of social workers who are employed by social agencies because the workers themselves do not gain any economic advantage when they offer these unnecessary services. This may be an ethical problem for an occasional social worker in private practice who may be tempted to place financial gain above client interests, but even agency-employed social workers might face this ethical dilemma if urged by their supervi-sor to keep a child in a more restrictive treatment setting than needed so that treatment facility will have enough clients to remain open or if the agency is experiencing budget difficulties.

There are other ethical dilemmas of this type that do not involve financial gain for the individual or the agency. For example, a social worker is in the middle of preparing supper for her family when she receives an emergency call for help from one of her clients. Should she drop everything and rush out to help her client, even if this means that her family will once again have to make their own supper? An-other social worker has a very important date she is to meet within the hour when she is notified that one of her foster children has run away. What should she do? What is the ethical thing to do?

Social workers face critical ethical problems when there is a threat to life. For example, must a social worker give priority to client interests, even when this may result in physical injury to the worker or her family? Do considerations of self-preservation and survival legitimize actions that ordinarily might be considered unethical?

Gewirth's (1978) Principle of Generic Consistency may be helpful when consid-ering these problems. He stated, "Act in accord with the generic right of your reci-pients (that is your clients) *as well as yourself*" (p. 135, emphasis added). Gewirth suggests that there is no need for the worker to abdicate the right to her own wel-fare, even when this right conflicts with the client's right to professional services. Because Gewirth's principle was not developed to guide professional activities, some people argue that it does not apply to professional practitioners. Instead, they hold that a professional should always be guided by the ethical obligation to give priority to a client's interests, no matter what the consequences to herself. They take this position because the Code (2008, Ethical Principles) requires that "Social workers elevate service to others above self-interest."

EP 2.1.2

Those who would follow Gewirth's lead must consider whether ethics are relative (see Chapter 3 for a discussion of ethical relativism versus absolutism). Do ethical obligations change according to their consequences? What must be the degree of potential harm before it is permissible to disregard the ethical rule that demands giving priority to a client's interests? Or must social workers serve their clients' interests at all times, regardless of the consequences? Is it ethical for them to declare that under certain unusual circumstances the professional obligation to serve their clients' interests is no longer primary? How did you respond to Exemplar 1.3, where the social worker is asked to leave her family in a potentially dangerous situation so she can respond to clients' needs? Would you still give the same response now that you gave when you first read Chapter 1? If not, why has your response changed?

Consider Diggs's (1970) observation that "there is an important difference between interpreting a rule or violating it in *special circumstances*, and deciding each individual case just as if there were no rules" (p. 267). This formulation permits retention of the client-priority ethical rule except in special circumstances, such as when the life of the worker is threatened, because in such a case absolute adherence to the rule (client's interests above all) would be unrealistic and unwise.

DUAL ROLES WITHIN THE PROFESSIONAL RELATIONSHIP

In this section, we will examine issues related to dual-role relationships. By **dual-role relationships,** we mean the social worker interacts with a client in a role in addition to that of the social worker's professional role. Examples include such roles as a teacher, a member of a church committee, or a sexual or business partner. Please keep in mind that there are differences between conflicts of interest and dual roles. A **conflict of interest** occurs when a social worker advances her own interests or the interests of others in ways detrimental to clients' or others' interests. Social workers may be parents, members of religious groups or political parties, or members of other groups. Conflicts of interest can occur when the social worker has conflicting personal interests—her interests as a parent, as a member of a religious group, or as a business person. Consequently, social workers can be faced with personal conflicts of interest. In addition, social workers face conflicts of interests when they seek the attainment of their own interests ahead of those of their clients. The NASW (2008) Code (1.06 b) cautions against taking unfair advantage of any professional relationship to exploit others in order to further one's personal, religious, political, or business interests.

Social workers reside and practice in communities, and they have social, business, financial, religious, or other roles in addition to their professional roles with clients. There are a number of situations where it is clear the avoidance of dual relationships is difficult. The possibility of dual relationships may be minimized in large urban areas and it is possible that dual relationships are encountered more frequently in small towns and rural areas. However, even in urban areas, dual relationships may be difficult to avoid, particularly in smaller subcommunities such as religious, political, sexual orientation, new immigrant groups, and self-help groups associated with physical illnesses and chemical dependency. Here are some examples of dual-role relationships:

- You discover that your client, Bertha Martins, is your dentist's mother.
- Kathleen Olds, your daughter's new teacher, is the mother of Tom Olds, a troubled teenager whom you have been treating for the last year.
- Lorraine Simkins, the wife of Al Simkins, stockbroker, is your client and inadvertently discloses insider information about local businesses in which you own stock.
- Your client, Cynthia Goddard, joins a recreational basketball league, and her assigned team plays regularly against the team to which you belong.

In such dual-role situations, it is always possible for a client to be confused by the existence of the dual roles, for the professional to exploit or harm the client in some manner, or for the additional role to interfere with the professional relationship by creating conflicts of interest for the practitioner and ambiguities and confusion for the client. The NASW (2008) Code of Ethics states "social workers should not engage in dual or multiple relationships with clients or former clients in which there is a risk of exploitation or potential harm to the client. In instances when dual or multiple relationships are unavoidable, social workers should take steps to protect clients and are responsible for setting clear, appropriate, and culturally sensitive boundaries" (1.06c). These same guidelines apply to social workers who are supervisors (Code, 2008, 3.01b, c), or educators and field instructors of students (Code, 2008, 3.02d). These standards highlight the issue of dual-role relationships and require that social workers take steps to limit such relationships or to avoid them altogether whenever this is possible, thus avoiding actions that are detrimental to clients, supervisees, and students. The major focus of these standards is to avoid exploitation or harm to clients, former clients, supervisees, and students.

Must dual-role relationships necessarily interfere with professional relationships? Do they always result in conflict? In modern society, where everyone fills multiple roles, there are many situations where social workers and clients participate in dual or multiple relationships. Both may be members of the same political party, church, mosque, or synagogue, or their children may attend the same school or be classmates. There is no reason for a social worker to withdraw from these activities simply because a client also engages in them. The issue is to separate the professional relationship from other relationships. Among the relationships with clients that should be avoided are dating, bartering services, buying products, investing work or money in businesses, and endorsing or recommending a client's business to potential buyers. For example, how should you respond if the used-car salesman who is a client offers to sell you a car at a discount? Why should these relationships be avoided or—if unavoidable—minimized? What are the ethical implications for the social worker?

RECONSIDERING AND FURTHER DEFINING DUAL RELATIONSHIPS

Essentially, dual relationships are problematic because they can be harmful. Recently, questions have been raised about whether it is necessary to forbid all dual relationships.

Zur and Lazarus (2002) offered arguments for and against dual relationships with clients or patients, thus implying that dual relationships are often inevitable, especially when the social worker is in private practice or in a denominational or special-group agency. They argue that boundary violations sometimes are harmful and exploitative but at other times or in other situations they may be constructive (e.g., a home visit to a bedridden client or attending a family event such as a wedding). Rigid boundaries can reflect distance and coldness. Furthermore, there is no reason to assume that a hug, home visit, or acceptance of a gift will inevitably lead to exploitation. These may strengthen the professional relationship if they occur within that framework. Clients, particularly in mental health settings but not only there, can profit from a "sense of belonging, connectedness, and meaningful relationships with others, including workers" (Maidment, 2006, p. 117).

Dual relationships can occur in both clinical and other social work practice settings. Boland-Prom and Anderson (2005) suggest that as the size of the community decreases, the possibility for contact other than the professional relationship increases. In addition, there are communities (e.g., rural, religious, feminist, gay, and ethnic minorities) in which it may not be desirable to maintain rigid separations from dual relationships. Further, social workers recovering from chemical dependency may find themselves at self-help meetings with present or former clients.

Dual relationships are a reality in many situations, potentially involving many clients. In fact, there are treatment situations that can call for practitioners to have informal encounters with a client, such as eating a meal, visiting a community center or library with a client, or attending a dramatic performance or sport event that helps the client make progress. Where a social worker voluntarily enters dual relationships, such relationships should "be based on a thoughtful analysis that can be articulated, documented, and ultimately justified as being within a sound practice model" (Boland-Prom & Anderson, 2005, p. 505). A careful assessment of the contextual issues is crucial, including the mental health of the person involved, vulnerability, role of minority and self-help communities, and type of practice (clinical, community organizing, policy and planning, evaluation, and administration). Where possible, careful consideration of the ethical, legal, and risk prevention issues prior to entering the dual relationship is essential.

Social workers in certain situations may not have a choice about dual role relationships. Zur (2009) describes a number of legal imperatives that result in changing the social worker's relationship with others. Most commonly, dual roles may be mandated by the military and correctional institutions. Dual roles occur when psychotherapists have a therapeutic relationship with their patient and, at the same time, have a legal and ethical responsibility to other people who are not patients. Military law mandates that psychotherapists in the military give higher priority to national defense, unit integrity, and combat readiness than to concerns with the individual psychotherapy client. This priority is made clear by the "need to know" clause that gives a commanding officer the right to view or be privy to specific client information that is relevant to national security or combat readiness. Psychotherapists who work in prisons must give higher priority to matters of security, escape risk and violence, than to their individual client's welfare. Similarly when working with police, psychotherapists may also be involved in other roles where they may have to evaluate and make decisions about those they are working with, for example, training, consultation, and other activities. These are all situations in which social workers must serve two masters, the client and the institution, unit, or nation. Are social workers protected in such situations by the NASW (2008) Code Standard 1.01 "In general clients' interests are primary. However, social workers' responsibility to the larger society or specific legal obligations may on limited occasions supersede the loyalty owed clients, and clients should be so advised." Also, Standard 1.07c permits breaching confidentiality for compelling professional reasons.

SEXUAL RELATIONS WITH CLIENTS

The NASW (2008) Code of Ethics is quite clear that "social workers should under no circumstances engage in sexual activities or sexual contact with current clients, whether such contact is consensual or forced" (1.09a). This ethical rule is found in the codes of ethics of most professions. In addition, similar standards prohibit such sexual activities "with clients' relatives or other individuals with whom clients maintain a close personal relationship when there is a risk of exploitation or potential harm to the client" (1.09b) or "with former clients because of the potential for harm to the client" (1.09c). In addition, social workers "should not provide clinical services to individuals with whom they have had a prior sexual relationship" (1.09d).

Nevertheless, sexual misconduct with clients is the second highest allegation for claims against social workers covered by the NASW Insurance Trust, preceded only by incorrect treatment, and followed by attempted or completed suicide. For the period from 2002 to 2005, allegations of nonsexual dual relationships with patients made up the second largest group of claims after claims for sexual misconduct (Imbert, 2006). A more recent cumulative compilation of claims over an approximately 40-year period found the relative frequency of incorrect treatment, sexual misconduct, and attempt at or suicide by clients remained constant. Sexual misconduct accounted for more than 17% of claims against NASW members from 2002 through 2005 (NASW, 2006) and also throughout the 40-year period (NASW, 2009). These numbers should be interpreted with caution because they only represent complaints against NASW members, and this may underestimate the problem because complaints to licensing boards and malpractice insurers are not included here. In addition, the number of persons who do not report social worker/client sexual contact is unknown (Freud & Krug, 2002), nor is it known whether all of the claims were justified.

Mittendorf and Schroeder (2004) conducted an exploratory study of 144 social workers in private practice settings to examine their attitudes and beliefs about sexual involvement with clients and their knowledge of the prevalence of this behavior. When respondents were asked if they ever had a client who reported having sexual contact with a previous therapist, 54% answered affirmatively. These 77 respondents acknowledged having had a total of 245 clients who reported having sex with previous therapists, including social workers, psychiatrists, psychologists, clergy, and counselors. Ninety percent of the sexually exploited clients were female.

Fewer than one third of the respondents reported the exploitive therapist to a licensing board or other authorities.

Sexual misconduct with current clients or patients can be harmful in several ways: (1) it can cause emotional and mental harm; (2) it risks impairing the social worker's judgment and harming the effectiveness of the therapy; and (3) doing so risks harming the reputation (and the general success) of the profession (Gorman, 2009). Patients of psychotherapists often cannot adequately appreciate the risks of engaging in sexual relationships with their psychotherapists because they have diminished capacity to make autonomous decisions about the risks. A psychotherapist who engages in a sexual relationship with a current client risks creating a conflict of interest that may reduce the effectiveness of the therapy. Thus, sexual misconduct with a patient can harm the patient's health, the therapy's effectiveness, and the profession's reputation (Gorman, 2009).

In regard to sexual relations with a former client, it is at least arguable that an act that is unethical today continues to be unethical at a later date. Those social workers who engage in sexual relationships with former clients or claim that an exception to the prohibition is warranted must demonstrate "that the former client has not been exploited, coerced, or manipulated, intentionally or unintentionally" (NASW Code, 2008, 1.09c). A study of 654 NASW members' definitions of who is a client found that approximately half of them believe that "clienthood" ends when service is terminated, while the other half believe "once a client, always a client." Others believed that various time periods following service defined whether a former client retains the status of client. No agreement was found among MSWs regarding the definition of who is a former client and what is appropriate behavior at different times after the termination of direct service regarding various dual relationships (Mattison, Jayaratne, & Croxton, 2002). This lack of consensus suggests a need for caution when practitioners make decisions in these areas. State laws as well as a practitioner's decisions about clienthood affect these situations. Clearly, the lack of agreement suggests the need for further discussion of this issue. In some states, legal action against the practitioner is not avoided by the formal termination of the treatment relationship, while in other states sexual contact following the termination of client status may be illegal for various periods (Gorman, 2009; Perry & Kuruk, 1993).

Sexual intimacy between professional social workers and clients is not simply an ethical breach. Such intimacy with clients is also grounds for legal action in all 50 states, where the social worker may be sued for battery, malpractice, intentional and negligent infliction of emotional distress, and sexual abuse. Abuse of clients can result in symptoms, akin to those of post-traumatic stress disorder, that are disturbing, harmful, and emotionally long lasting and can have effects on family, friend, and work relationships. Sexual relations with clients, current as well as past, is unethical, illegal, and unprofessional because clients are dependent on their social worker; exploiting this dependency for personal gain, sexual or nonsexual, is prohibited, regardless of whether the social worker's action affects the therapeutic outcome.

Knowledge of sexual contact by other social workers also raises significant ethical issues for the social worker who was informed of these actions. What should a social worker do if she learns that sexual behavior between her current client and another social worker occurred in the past? Does it matter how old the client was when the sexual contact occurred (e.g., if the client was under the age of 18)? What should she do if the sexual behavior with another social worker is ongoing, and what is her responsibility if the professional engaging in sexual behavior with a client is a member of another (non–social work) discipline?

Despite the unambiguous professional admonition against sexual contacts with clients, these continue to occur. However, there are some who suggest there may be other ways of viewing such relationships. Maidment (2006) argues that alternative perspectives should be considered within the framework of ethical behaviors. She recognizes that "client-worker relationships [have] focused on the deleterious nature of sexual contact in professional practice." She states that she does not support "the existence of sexual relationships between workers and clients," but adds that "the vociferous nature of moral condemnation regarding such cases has effectively silenced *any* debate about alternative models for managing this aspect of ethical practice" (p. 118).

Those who say there is no problem when sex takes place between social work professionals and their clients are underestimating the impact of such behavior both on professional relationships and on the lives of their clients. These relationships between social workers and clients are serious because of the consequences for the persons involved. The consequences for the therapist are malpractice and possible legal suits; in addition, the behavior distorts the professional relationship, affects the practitioner's thought processes, and puts objectivity at risk so that professional treatment is undermined. The consequences for the client include ambivalence, guilt, emptiness and isolation, sexual confusion, impaired ability to trust, confused roles and boundaries, emotional lability, suppressed rage, increased suicidal risk, and problems in cognitive functioning, including concentration and memory, flashbacks, intrusive thoughts, unbidden images, and nightmares (Pope & Vasquez, 1998; Pope, 2000).

Jayaratne, Croxton, and Mattison (1997) studied six domains of social work practice: intimate relationships, dual-role relationships, mixed modalities, advice giving, boundary behaviors, and financial transactions. The study was based on a large sample of the membership of the Michigan Chapter of NASW. Some of their findings are summarized in Table 7.1. Although only a small number of practitioners report they have dated a former client, more than 6% think it appropriate to do so. Similarly, a small number report they have had sex with a former client, whereas almost 5% believe that such behavior is appropriate. Very large percentages report they have dual-role relationships with clients (e.g., friendship, serving on the same boards or committees). Only a few social workers use massage in their practices, however, more than one in eight believe to do so is appropriate; almost 40% believe it is appropriate to touch a client as a regular part of the therapy process. Maidment (2006) argues that alternative views of ethical standards need to be considered and suggests that "respectful and appropriate physical contact between the client and worker conveys a sense of connectedness unparalleled by verbal assurance and empathy" (p. 118).

Exemplar 7.1 raises an ethical issue that all social workers need to consider before they potentially meet the situation in practice.

| TABLE 7.1 | FREQUENCY AND PERCENTAGES OF INCIDENTS AND PERCEIVED APPROPRIATENESS OF BEHAVIOR OF SOCIAL WORK PROFESSIONALS |

Behavior	Respondents Have Done		Perceived as Appropriate	
	N	%	N	%
Go on a date with a former client	7	.8	53	6.4
Have sex with a former client	9	1.1	37	4.6
Develop a friendship with a client	174	21.2	170	21.0
Have clients with whom you have another relationship	185	22.5	270	33.5
Serve on community boards or committees with clients	187	22.6	471	58.7
Use massage	15	1.8	107	13.7
Touch a client as a regular part of therapy process	253	31.2	319	39.9
Give financial investment advice	37	4.5	64	7.7
Advise clients to do something that may be illegal	25	3.1	30	3.7

Source: Adapted from S. Jayaratne, T. Croxton, and D. Mattison (1997), "Social Work Professional Standards An Exploratory Study," *Social Work, 42,* 187–198.

EP 2.1.2

| 7.1 | TREATMENT OF AN INFERIORITY COMPLEX |

Jill Jordan, a 35-year-old divorcée, has been a client of the Family Consultation Center for a number of months. Her presenting problem is that she feels inadequate, unattractive, and stymied in her career. She feels that her negative self-image contributed to her divorce and has become a barrier to advancement on the job. Finding fulfillment in her career and developing more rewarding relationships depend on her becoming more positive about herself and being more optimistic.

Bob Temple, an experienced social worker, was assigned as her therapist. A contract was established with the presenting problem as the focus. During the course of treatment, Bob was very understanding and warmly responsive to Jill. His objective was to restore Jill's faith in herself. As treatment proceeded, Jill did not hesitate to express her admiration of Bob. At the end of one session, she spontaneously hugged him and said how appreciative she was for all his help. As she experienced more successes in her life, she would ask for a hug as a sign of his support for her. Still later, she made it evident that she was attracted to Bob and would not reject his interest in her. Bob was also attracted to Jill. He wanted to pursue a personal relationship with her, but he knew that the professional ethics demanded that he not do so.

What is the most ethical way of handling this problem?

1. He can deny his feelings and continue treatment but discontinue the hugs; chances are that these emotions, if controlled, will not interfere with the treatment.

2. He can maintain a professional relationship in the office and join her church, where there will be opportunities for them to meet after hours, outside the office.

3. He can accept his emotional attraction to Jill, but at the same time realize that a professional social worker cannot have a personal relationship with a client. Next time Jill broaches the subject, he should tell her that he likes her and that if he were not her social worker he might become involved with her. However, because he is her social worker, his task is to help her professionally; no other relationship is possible.

4. He realizes that he cannot control his emotions. Therefore, it is best to terminate the relationship and refer Jill to another social worker.

5. He realizes that he cannot control his emotions. Therefore, it is best not to deny his attraction for Jill and instead ask her on a date; at the same time, he can continue to be her social worker.

6. He considers having sex with Jill as a therapeutic activity, just as hugging her at times provides support, doing so will help her regain her self-confidence.

Options 5 and 6 are clearly not acceptable. In most jurisdictions, this behavior is judged as illegal, even criminal. The NASW (2008) Code of Ethics prohibits it, as do the ethical codes of other professions. Though there is no ethical or professional justification for this choice, we mention it because we are aware that a small number of our colleagues do engage in such behavior, a behavior that is blatantly unprofessional and unethical. But some of the other options are also unethical and/or go against the NASW Code. Use the two ethical decision screens presented in Chapter 4 to determine which might be the preferred approach in the situation facing Bob Temple.

STUDENTS AND SEXUAL RELATIONS

Sexual relationships between social work students and their field or other instructors also cause damage and have the potential for later imitative behavior by the student. Such sexual relationships can be replicated and reinforced in subsequent practice with clients. Barnett-Queen (1999) studied sexually oriented relationships between educators/field instructors and their student/supervisees. Those studied were 1,104 members of the mental health division of NASW ($N = 568$) and members of the American Mental Health Counselor Association, a division of the American Counseling Association ($N = 536$). Barnett-Queen (1999) found that in the sample studied, the social work profession may be more careful about sexually appropriate behavior between its educators and trainees than the counselors. The majority of the three impact-vulnerable groups (sexual contact participants, sexual advances participants, and aware nonparticipants) negatively judged the ethical impact and coercive nature of these experiences. Bonosky (1995), in a study of female psychologists who reported having had sexual relationships with supervisors, found that almost one in four (23%) reported subsequent engagement in sex with a client compared to only 6% of those who, while they were students, had no sexual experiences with their educators.

There is an additional aspect to sexual relationships that involve students. In a study of 349 social work students' attitudes about sexual contact with clients and their training and education in this area, Berkman, Turner, Cooper, Polnerow, and Swartz (2000) found relatively high levels of approval of sexual contact between social workers and clients in certain circumstances (e.g., when the social worker's role was to assist the client with concrete services only; the clinical relationship has been terminated and lasted only two sessions). Students with less social work experience and who thought class content on sexual ethics was inadequate were more likely to approve of sexual contact between social worker and client. Parenthetically, the students felt they had not received adequate education or training on sexual ethics and many felt unprepared to handle sexual feelings from or toward a client. Do you think it is ever appropriate to have sexual relations with a client or an instructor? If so, when and under what circumstances is it appropriate? How would you respond if an instructor or a client tried to initiate a sexual relationship with you?

TOUCHING

Touching became a widespread practice technique during the late 1960s and early 1970s as a result of the popularity of the encounter movement. Some have questioned the ethical propriety of touching, believing that such behavior is only a first step that will inevitably lead to full sexual relations. Others reject this assumption, suggesting there are many types of touching, including therapeutic touching (Durana, 1998). Durana, in a comprehensive review of empirical studies of nonerotic touch in psychotherapy, found there were few such studies, most of the emphasis having been placed on erotic contact. Although Durana concluded that touch has become "an integral part of the clinical practice of many psychotherapists" (p. 15) and that it has beneficial uses in certain circumstances, nevertheless he suggested that legal and ethical considerations combined with transference and counter transference issues make touching in psychotherapy a sensitive subject. The Code recognizes physical contact as a practice modality but cautions that "social workers should not engage in physical contact with clients when there is a possibility of psychological harm to the client as a result of the contact (such as cradling or caressing clients). Social workers who engage in appropriate physical contact with clients are responsible for setting clear, appropriate, and culturally sensitive boundaries that govern such physical contact" (NASW Code, 2008, 1.10).

OTHER SOCIAL RELATIONS

Although almost all social workers agree with the ethical prohibition against engaging in sexual activities with clients, there is less agreement about the ethical propriety of engaging in other social relations. The findings presented in Table 7.1 clearly indicate the disagreement that exists among professional social workers as to what are appropriate professional behaviors. Some of the results highlight the lack of consensus about which social relations should be considered unethical. Although not included in Table 7.1, Jayaratne, Croxton, and Mattison (1997) found that large percentages think it appropriate to hug or embrace a client (see NASW Code, 2008, 1.10), pray with a client, recommend a religious form of healing, comment to clients about their physical attractiveness, discuss one's religious beliefs, or accept goods or services from clients instead of money (see NASW Code, 2008, 1.13).

TRUTH TELLING AND MISREPRESENTATION

The NASW (2008) Code of Ethics states that "social workers should not participate in, condone, or be associated with dishonesty, fraud, or deception" (4.04). Telling the truth and avoiding deceptions are basic ethical obligations. Every human interaction is based on the premise that each side in the interaction intends to tell the truth. Deceiving—that is, deliberately misrepresenting facts in order to make another person believe what is not true—violates the respect to which everyone is entitled. Telling the truth to a client is an even stronger professional obligation than the generalized obligation of truth telling because of the professional's fiduciary responsibilities. This professional ethic is anchored in the specialized client/practitioner relationship and in the obligations that a practitioner owes to her clients.

Some practitioners may believe that it is ethical to use dishonesty when it is in the client's interest, but such a stance requires further thought before it can be accepted. For example, is it ethical for a social worker to present a wrong diagnosis in order to provide a service that otherwise would be not be available? Bayles (1981) concluded that the obligation to be honest with clients does not require honesty toward a third party, especially when the professional is acting on a client's behalf. Do you agree with Bayles' conclusion? Why or why not? Is honesty always the best policy for a social worker? Haley (1976) raised a number of questions about the efficacy of always being honest, including the following:

- Do therapists have an ethical obligation to be honest in their professional relationship when the professional situation is not an honest human experience, but a paid relationship?
- Can any therapist, no matter what her orientation, claim that she is willing to share with a client all of her observations and understandings?
- Must a therapist answer all questions that a client has about the treatment or intervention that the practitioner plans to use? How will understanding the theory used by the therapist help this patient to achieve autonomy?
- Will an "honest sharing" of understanding solve the problems for which the patient is paying his money to get help? (p. 208)

Although Haley (1976) was discussing therapists in particular, his comments could apply to any social worker. Haley (1976) presents one point of view, but not everyone agrees. In addition to Haley's questions, there are a number of ethical dilemmas that the attempt to tell the truth may provoke. Consider the ethical problems facing Gail's social worker in Exemplar 7.2.

EP 2.1.2

| 7.2 | Gail Finds a Job |

Gail Silva is a single parent raising two daughters, ages 6 and 7. She has been trying to find a part-time job to supplement her meager child support income ever since her younger daughter started kindergarten two years ago. She has been repeatedly refused a job because she has had no prior work experience. By now she has become very frustrated and has developed a very negative self-image.

She believes that nobody wants her—neither as a spouse nor as a worker. This morning, she told you excitedly that she thinks she has found a job. As she describes the job, you realize that she is telling you about an employer who is known to exploit his workers and who pays below minimum wage, when he pays at all. Should you tell Gail the truth about her prospective employer? Or should you share her enthusiasm, hoping that things will work out? What is the ethical thing to do?

Several options might be considered:

- Don't say anything.
- Tell her everything and urge her not to take this job.
- Point out the advantages (a job, an employment history) and disadvantages (low pay, exploitation) and let her make the decision.

Which option would you choose and why?

Deception has become so common in our world that we hardly pay attention to the little lies and half-truths that everyone uses and knows how to justify. Nyberg (1996) suggested that deception is a necessary part of our world: "... deception is not merely to be tolerated as an occasionally prudent aberration in a world of truth telling; it is rather an essential component of our ability to organize and shape the world, to resolve problems of coordination among individuals who differ, to cope with uncertainty and pain, to be civil and to achieve privacy as needed, to survive as a species, and to flourish as persons" (p. 187). Or, as he suggests: "to live decently with one another we do not need moral purity, we need discretion—which means tact in regard to truth" (p. 202).

What are the ethical implications for a social worker who lies? What is the ethical question involved in telling another person a bit less than the full truth? When a social worker decides to withhold the truth from a client or to deceive him, she usually thinks that she is doing so for the client's benefit. Whether her decision was ethically justified cannot be assessed empirically. Do the following reasons provide sufficient justification for a social worker to deceive her client or not tell him the full truth?

- To make a client-selected goal less desirable
- To create new goals
- To obscure options
- To increase options
- To change the cost/benefit estimate for one or more options
- To increase or decrease client uncertainty

- To increase or decrease client anxiety
- To protect the client from a "damaging" truth
- To protect the effectiveness of the current intervention strategy
- To obtain the client's "informed" consent
- To protect confidential information received from a third party
- To strengthen the relationship with a client by lying at his request to a third party
- To increase the worker's power over a client by withholding information
- To make the worker look good by papering over mistakes she has made

Are any of these reasons applicable in Exemplars 7.3 and 7.4 ? If applicable, does this make dishonesty ethical?

7.3	A GROWTH ON THE FOOT

EP 2.1.2

Art Elder, age 34, is a high school teacher. At present he is a patient at University Hospital because he has a growth on his foot. His physician told him that there are two ways of treating this problem. Both involve some risks. When Art asked what he would advise, the physician suggested surgery. Sally Brown is the social worker in the surgical department. From her discussion with the resident, she learned that Dr. Kutner, the physician, did not tell the patient all the available choices and that he withheld information about the option with the least risk. Evidently, he weighted his presentation in favor of the experimental surgical treatment method that he is just now developing.

Here we are not concerned with Dr. Kutner, but with Sally Brown. Should she discuss the issue with Dr. Kutner, tell Art the truth, mind her own business and leave the giving of medical information to the medical staff, or suggest that Art get a second opinion? It may be that such behaviors by physicians are uncommon, but Sally still faces an ethical dilemma. On what basis can she decide the ethical course of action? Is failing to tell Art about this situation the same as if Sally directly told him a lie or provided misinformation?

Social workers in direct practice are not the only ones who may have ethical problems with truth telling. Exemplar 7.4, from the field of social work administration, also raises questions about the ethics of truth telling.

7.4	THE FRANS MUSIC APPRECIATION ROOM

EP 2.1.2

The Frans family contributed a considerable sum of money to the Uptown Community Center to furnish and equip a music appreciation room in memory of their mother. An appropriate plaque marks the room. Since the center accepted the contribution, the neighborhood has experienced a large influx of immigrants from Southeast

Asia. Because of their needs, the room is now used for purposes other than those designated by the donors.

You are the center's associate director. You know how important the music appreciation room is to the family. There is a good possibility of obtaining additional donations for other projects from this family, but if the family discovers that their room is no longer used for music appreciation activities, they may lose interest in the Uptown Community Center. At the monthly meeting of the board of directors, you meet Gerald Frans. He asks you how the music appreciation room is doing.

How should you reply? Do you tell the truth? Do you try to avoid the issue by shifting the conversation to another area? Do you tell a little untruth, such as "the immigrants love music"? Or not? What is the ethically correct response? How do you decide?

Social workers at every level sometimes have to choose between loyalty to a friend or colleague and telling the truth. In Exemplar 7.5, a supervisor has to make a choice concerning truthfulness.

EP 2.1.2

7.5 | A SUPERVISOR DECIDES

Karl Samil is a supervisor in a large department of social services. Roger Lewis, a colleague, applied for promotion, and Karl has been asked to provide a reference. He is aware of instances when Roger acted in ways that were harmful to the agency, including inappropriately criticizing the agency at several interagency committee meetings, which may have injured the reputation of the agency's elder abuse team. For over a year, Karl has noted that Roger has been distracted and jumpy about his current job responsibilities. Most of his local colleagues have been aware of his behavior but out of loyalty have kept quiet and have often covered for him. To confuse matters further, Karl and Roger have played cards together in a weekly game since they graduated from college. Even there, Roger's behavior has been somewhat erratic. When Karl spoke to Roger to say Roger seemed unusually upset and distracted, Roger brushed it off. If promoted, Roger will move to another part of the agency.

Should Karl give a positive reference because of personal loyalty, thereby passing Roger Lewis on to another setting without letting them know of his limitations? Should he risk his own reputation if the promotion is gained but Roger does poorly at the job? What about loyalty to himself and his family? Should he turn his back on the agency and the profession? Or should he speak to Roger again and suggest that Roger defer promotion and take care of his own problems?

The question of truth or deception involves the intention of the speaker and not the factual accuracy of the statement. Knowing the truth does not necessarily result in telling the truth, while not knowing the truth does not always result in a deception. The relations between the objective situation and a speaker's intentions are summarized in Table 7.2.

TABLE 7.2	INTENTIONS AND FACTS	
The statement is factually	The speaker intends to be truthful	The speaker intends to be deceptive
True	The speaker intended to tell the truth and did so.	The speaker intended to deceive, but unknowingly spoke the truth. While her intentions were not ethical, her actual behavior does not raise any ethical issues.
False	The speaker intended to tell the truth, but failed to do so because she did not have the correct information. The problem here may be lack of competence or lack of skill, or both, which, *although unintentional, may be unethical.*	The speaker intended to deceive and did lie. *This situation involves questions of unethical behavior.*

It is also possible to deceive without directly lying by exaggerating or manipulating. One social worker, for example, wanted to dissuade a client from placing his daughter with mental retardation in an institution. She arranged for the father to visit the worst possible institution but did not mention the availability of other alternatives. This social worker would never lie, but did she tell the truth? A social work administrator exaggerates the benefits that may result from a new program so that the agency will receive a larger budget allocation next year. Are these social workers acting ethically? Or is this yet another version of the ends-justifying-the-means quandary?

Kagle (1998) maintains that deception—usually considered a deviation from the ethical norm and a violation of trust—is in reality a common and accepted way for social workers to establish personal boundaries and manage interpersonal relationships. She defines deception as a tool that can help clients who feel particularly vulnerable—among other things—seek to preserve their self-esteem, privacy, and control or keep private sensitive information that could lead to punishment. She claims that social workers also may, and do, withhold information or use other forms of deception in the interest of expedience, control, and paternalism. In fact, her view is that "social workers may use deception not only to regulate their relationships with clients but also to manage their jobs" (Kagle, 1998, p. 241).

DIAGNOSIS AND MISDIAGNOSIS

The controversy about the place of diagnosis in social work practice has a number of ethical aspects. Many social workers believe that diagnosis is an essential element in every professional intervention, but others reject its use because they consider it an inappropriate application of the medical model to social work practice. For many, the problem of diagnostics has become even more critical as use of the *Diagnostic and Statistical Manual of Mental Disorders* (DSM-IV-TR) of the American Psychiatric Association (APA, 2000) has spread rapidly among social workers.

Many social workers are required to use the DSM-IV-TR because many government programs authorize service or reimburse for service rendered only on the basis of an appropriate DSM-IV-TR diagnosis; likewise most insurance companies require such a diagnosis before they will authorize third-party payments (Schamess, 1996). Often, authorization and reimbursements are limited to certain diagnostic categories; in other instances, the amount of reimbursement (or the length of the treatment authorized) depends on the diagnosis submitted. These requirements put pressure on social workers to use this diagnostic instrument even though they may not think it is an appropriate diagnostic instrument for social work practice. Some may engage in deliberate misdiagnosis in order to meet the stated requirements for reimbursable social work treatment. Exemplar 7.6 illustrates one of the ethical problems that this creates.

EP 2.1.2

| 7.6 | Let the Insurance Company Pay the Bill |

Christine Sales is seeing a private practice social worker. At their initial session last week, she mentioned that she hoped her insurance company would reimburse her for these sessions. Today, Christine brought in the insurance forms and asked her social worker to complete them. The social worker, who was familiar with the requirements of this insurance company, realized right away that she would have to report a more serious diagnosis than was clinically indicated if she were to qualify the client for reimbursement.

Under what circumstances is it ethical for a social worker to lie about a diagnosis? What are the potential risks for both the client and the social worker? What is the ethical thing to do if the only way the person will receive services is for the social worker to fudge the diagnosis? Earlier, we noted that Bayles (1981) suggests that the obligation to be honest with clients does not require honesty when acting on a client's behalf. Do you accept his point of view?

While some social workers will report a more serious diagnosis to obtain third-party payments, others may report less serious diagnoses and justify it as harmless or in the client's best interest. Generally, social workers use the least potentially harmful diagnosis (also known as the mercy diagnosis) because:

- It minimizes the communication of damaging and confidential information to nonsocial workers, especially to insurance companies and others.
- It avoids the labeling effects of a more serious diagnosis.
- It limits the adverse impact on a client's self-esteem if the client should become aware of the diagnosis.
- It can protect the future employment prospects (and possibly protect a current job) for the client, as well as the potential for future insurance coverage.

These reasons are used to justify under diagnosis by suggesting that this is in the client's interest. Some social workers admit that sometimes they deliberately report an under diagnosis. For example, they might use the category adjustment disorders when a more serious diagnosis would have been more accurate. On the other hand, there are social workers who at times over diagnose. They may use an Axis 1 diagnosis when this is not warranted, in order to qualify a client for reimbursement. Though claiming that over diagnosis is done for the client's benefit, the real beneficiary may be the social worker or agency whose payments are now guaranteed by a third party.

Not all misdiagnoses result from an attempt to gain benefits for the client; some misdiagnoses are the result of practitioner incompetence, influenced by the ambiguity of some diagnostic categories, failure to consider biological and physical factors, or failure to ensure medical review when indicated. Competent social work practice is an expected ethical norm. Another ethical problem arises when a social worker reports a diagnosis for one individual when the primary problem is located in the family system. Because DSM-IV-TR allows only the diagnosis of the problems of an individual, this deliberate misdiagnosis is usually used to qualify for insurance reimbursement. (This situation may also raise questions about who the client is, which was discussed in Chapter 5.)

Even under the best of circumstances, social workers, like all other professionals, will at times make mistakes and err in their diagnosis. Mistakes, though unfortunate and regrettable, but probably inevitable, often have ethical implications. Among these mistakes in diagnostics are the following:

- Lack of sufficient knowledge in using diagnostic instruments such as DSM-IV-TR
- Poor professional judgment
- Deliberate misdiagnosis, often in connection with third-party insurance reimbursement claims and/or reimbursements by government programs

These mistakes may involve both illegal and unethical behaviors. Examine Exemplar 7.7 and consider the ethical aspects involved in arriving at a diagnosis.

7.7	BARRY HAS A LEARNING PROBLEM

EP 2.1.2

Barry is a first grader. He has two older brothers, ages 8 and 10. His oldest brother is doing very well in school, but the middle brother has been identified as a "slow learner" and is in a special education class. Barry's teacher reports that Barry also has some learning problems and finds it difficult to keep up with the rest of his class. The school social worker and the educational psychologist have been discussing what to do with Barry. His tests indicate a relatively low score, but just within the normal range. The social worker knows that Barry would benefit from special attention that his regular classroom teacher cannot give him. However, sending Barry to an ungraded class might label him for the rest of his life, result in his being stigmatized, perhaps being insufficiently challenged, and potentially placing real limits on what is possible for his future.

In this situation, as in many others, the technical task of diagnosis has a number of ethical aspects that every thoughtful social worker must consider seriously before arriving at a decision. Consideration has to be given to the potential short- and long-term effects on the persons immediately involved, including Barry and his brothers, as well as other members of their family, the school, the social worker, and teachers. Furthermore, a decision seemingly affecting only those immediately involved may have potential effects for others who are not so closely involved.

COMPASSION FATIGUE, SECONDARY TRAUMATIC STRESS, AND PSYCHOLOGICAL INDIFFERENCE AS ETHICAL LIMITATIONS

Today, almost everyone experiences sensory overload. Information comes at us constantly by word of mouth, pagers, cell phones, computers, television, radio, and other advanced technologies. We live in an era of sound bites and brief messages intended to convey complex information. Social workers, along with all other human service workers, also experience immense stress on the job, critical stress in their personal lives, and constant pressures to be even more productive, along with a myriad of other stressors. In many cases, this invasion of our personal and professional spaces results in burnout, both as personal alienation and as a coping mechanism in response to these stresses. Social workers upon occasion will tune out; deal only with the surfaces of things; experience a sense of impotence; and distance themselves from clients, colleagues, and their work (Powell, 1994; Soderfeldt, Soderfeldt, & Warg, 1995).

There are costs that come from working in caring professions. Offering professional help to people in crisis can demand a heavy toll in emotional, physical, and social costs. When social workers, in their roles as helpers, hear about traumas, compassion fatigue or secondary traumatic stress may be one "consequence of working with suffering people" (Figley, 1999, p. 4). People can be traumatized without actually being harmed or threatened with harm. Just learning about the traumatic events endured by others can affect helping professionals. Learning about violent personal assaults, serious accidents and injuries, sudden deaths, or the deaths of young children, all can wreak havoc emotionally on helping professionals (Figley, 1999).

Bride (2007) found that "nearly all (97.8 percent) of the respondents [in his study] indicated that their client population experienced trauma, and most (88.9 percent) indicated that their work with clients addresses issues related to those client traumas" (p. 67). Over half (55%) of the participants in Bride's study met at least one of the core diagnostic criteria for post traumatic stress disorder (PTSD) due to their exposure to clients' trauma, which he calls secondary traumatic stress. Bride concluded that "independent of any other traumas that social workers may directly experience, the rate of PTSD in social workers due only to indirect exposure [15.2%] is twice that of the general population [7.8%]" (p. 68). Sprang, Clark, and Whitt-Woosley (2007) found a similar rate, with approximately 13% of their sample at high risk for compassion fatigue or burnout, with women at higher risk than men. In addition, clinicians working in rural locations were more likely to experience burnout than clinicians working in highly metropolitan locations (p. 273).

Contrary to these findings, Devilly, Wright, and Varker (2009) did not find a relationship between work with clients who had experienced trauma and either vicarious traumatization or secondary traumatic stress. However, being new to the profession, safety concerns, and burnout were related to affective distress (Devilly et al., 2009, p. 384). Although it is unclear whether work with clients who have experienced trauma is directly related to compassion fatigue, vicarious trauma, or secondary traumatic stress, it is clear that social workers are at risk for these conditions, which impact their ability to work with clients. How would you respond to the situation in Exemplar 7.8?

| 7.8 | HOW STRESSED IS TOO STRESSED? |

EP 2.1.2

Allison Webster is a social worker who has been working in Haiti since a few months after the earthquake on January 12, 2010. Allison is single, recently completed her MSW, and loves to travel, so she was very excited when she was offered a position working in Port-au-Prince. It has now been over a year since she arrived in Haiti, and she is working with families who lost everything in the earthquake and are still struggling to put their lives back together. Every client she sees has vivid memories of the earthquake and many of them want to share their experience. Recently, thoughts of her clients' stories have been intruding on Allison's thoughts and dreams, and she feels as if she will scream if she hears one more earthquake story. Allison knows that her work is important, but lately she is wondering if she is really cut out to be a social worker because she often feels impatient and unsympathetic with her clients. Mattie James and Allison belong to the same social work support online chat room and as they chat, Mattie begins to wonder if Allison is experiencing compassion fatigue, vicarious trauma, or secondary traumatic stress.

What are the ethical dilemmas in this situation? How should Mattie respond to Allison's request for help? Can (or should) Mattie diagnose Allison's problem based on an online chat? If Mattie suspects that Allison can no longer effectively and ethically provide social work services to her clients, does Mattie have a responsibility to report her suspicions to the agency that employs Allison?

One result of psychological distancing may be paying less exact attention to the ethical dilemmas that one encounters in practice. Hannah Arendt, in *Eichmann in Jerusalem* (1977), characterized this human ability as leading to "the banality of evil." Americans learned about the potential insidious impact of this kind of banality at My Lai in Vietnam and once again at Abu Ghraib in Iraq. Such psychological distancing can lead a social worker to avoid responsibility by distancing herself from clients, to treat clients with less individualization and dignity, or to serve the organization or society when the right action is to serve the individual. What should the administrator in Exemplar 7.9 do?

Is Joseph's decision not to act the result of protecting himself and his family, burnout, or a pragmatic decision? What should Joseph have done? After all, he doesn't have accurate data on the people whose problems are being reported to him by his drivers, nor is it his agency's responsibility to help support all of the city's poor. He is convinced that anyone in his position would do the same thing. Was his decision correct? Was it ethical? Joseph was confronted with a problem situation in which he decided to tolerate the inadequate condition of young women and their families and of the homeless while concentrating on maintaining the Meals-on-Wheels program and, incidentally or otherwise, protecting his family. To whom does he owe first loyalty? His agency? The president and board members? The soup kitchens? The homeless? The young women and their families? Himself? His family?

7.9 | AN ADMINISTRATOR DECIDES WHAT TO DO

Joseph Parocha is the overworked and stressed-out executive director of a Meals-on-Wheels program. Drivers recently have begun reporting seeing longer and longer lines at several soup kitchens as they travel to deliver meals to shut-in older adults. Also, drivers have discovered mothers with young children without sufficient food at several of the houses where they deliver meals. In speaking to the president of the board, Haakon Query, Joseph suggested that the agency also has a responsibility to try to help these other people. After all, their job is helping feed people who are hungry, no matter what their age. Haakon responded sharply that the agency has trouble enough maintaining itself and that he and others on the board would oppose any attempt to assist either the soup kitchens or the young families. The homeless and the young parents are the responsibility of other agencies. The agency should focus on its primary mission of feeding the elderly. Joseph was torn by his feeling that something should be done to help all hungry people. He knew that the staff could be doing more, although he personally didn't need any further pressures. When he talked this problem over with his wife, she reminded him that his health is also important, that their son is to start college this fall, and that their daughter needs braces. Joseph was upset but eventually decided that at this time it was better not to attempt to redefine the mission of the agency by trying to move it in new directions.

SOURCES OF HELP

Social Workers Helping Social Workers (SWHSW), founded in 1980, is a national association that provides assistance to colleagues dealing with issues related to substance use, eating disorders, work addiction, and other issues; for more information, visit http://www.socialworkershelping.org/ or http://www.socialworkershelping.org/index.php/resources for a list of resources.

EP 2.1.3

CRITICAL THINKING EXERCISES

1. If there is an NASW chapter in your area, invite the chair of the Chapter Committee on Inquiry to discuss with your class how they handle complaints about ethical misconduct. You might want to examine with the chair how effective these procedures are.
2. Sexual activities with clients are prohibited by the NASW (2008) Code of Ethics (1.09). Some social workers have argued that there is no scientific evidence that such activities

are necessarily harmful. They say that a rule of this kind is no longer relevant in a society that permits a wide variety of lifestyles. Present arguments both for changing and for retaining this rule.

3. When do you think clienthood ends? What, if any, roles other than that of social worker are appropriate to engage in with a former client? Is there a time period after which some or all of these non-professional roles are acceptable?

4. The limited professional relationship characteristic of the client/social worker relationship baffles many clients. It is a relationship that is quite unlike the formal, bureaucratic relationships with which they are familiar, yet it is also different from the informal primary relations they maintain with friends and relatives. How important is this principle from an ethical point of view?

5. In teams of two, develop two lists: (1) social relations with clients that are ethical and permissible, and (2) social relations with clients that are definitely unethical and therefore prohibited. Compare your lists with those of other teams. Discuss those areas where you find disagreement.

6. Are there cultural issues that influence the profession's definition of what is considered acceptable and what is considered unethical?

Suggestions for Additional Readings

Koenig and Spano (2003) explore sexual boundary violations (which are unethical, harmful, and often emotionally devastating to the parties involved) between educators and students and supervisors and supervisees. Strozier, Kmzek, and Sale (2003) examine the use of touch in social work practice and suggest that its use is not without potential harm. Johner (2006) discusses the legitimization of nonsexual dual relationships in social work practice. Jayaratne et al. (1997) report on research on dual-role and intimate relationships and on boundary behaviors. Adams, Boscarino, and Figley (2006) examine caring professionals and their emotional exhaustion (compassion fatigue) from working with traumatized clients. Bride and Figley (2007) wrote an introduction to the July 2007 special issue of the *Clinical Social Work Journal* that features seven articles on compassion fatigue. Bush (2009) presents a detailed case study and compares compassion fatigue with burnout and secondary traumatic stress.

Websites of Interest

- For an extensive set of resources on burnout and compassion fatigue, including self tests and ideas for combating burnout, see: www.friedsocialworker.com
- Sexual issues in psychology training and practice have parallels in social work. Much information related to sex with clients is examined at: www.kspope.com/sexiss/
- For a wide variety of topics related to social work see: www.nyu.edu/socialwork/ip/

Competency Notes

Identify as a professional social worker and conduct oneself accordingly: In this chapter, we discuss a number of issues related to professional relationships and how they
EP 2.1.1   relate to ethical dilemmas for social workers.

Apply social work ethical principles to guide professional practice: In this chapter, we discuss how professional issues are related to ethical social work practice.
EP 2.1.2

Apply critical thinking to inform and communicate professional judgments: Several exemplars asked you to consider and decide how you would respond to ethical dilemmas and exercises at the end of the chapter address critical thinking.
EP 2.1.3

CHAPTER 8 | CONFIDENTIALITY, INFORMED CONSENT, AND THE DUTY TO PROTECT

> This chapter addresses the CSWE 2008 EPAS Educational Policy 2.1.1 on becoming a professional social worker. In addition, we continue content on Educational Policy 2.1.2 about using social work ethical principles to guide professional practice, specifically related to issues of confidentiality, privacy, informed consent, and the duty to protect. We continue to provide exemplars, questions, and critical thinking exercises that we hope you will use to apply critical thinking to inform and communicate professional judgments (Educational Policy 2.1.3).

A person's right to privacy is a first-order value in the U.S. Every person has a right to determine *when, how,* and *to what extent* he or she wants to share (or have shared) personal information with others. Even though the U.S. Constitution does not explicitly mention a right to privacy, Chief Justice Richard B. Hughes of the New Jersey Supreme Court wrote, "Supreme Court decisions have recognized that a right of personal privacy exists and that certain areas of privacy are guaranteed under the Constitution" (*In re Quinlan,* 170 NJ 10, 1976). Privacy is protected under the Constitution in certain circumstances. The Supreme Court in the landmark case *Griswold v. Connecticut* (1965) ruled that the Constitution protected a right to privacy. The case involved a Connecticut law that prohibited the use of contraceptives. The Supreme Court invalidated the law on the grounds that it violated the right to marital privacy. Although the right to privacy does not appear in the Bill of Rights, a number of Supreme Court rulings support this right. Thus privacy is a protected value—but with some limitations. For example, privacy of school records is limited, and individuals have no right to sue a school for releasing records covered by the Family Educational Rights and Privacy Act (*Gonzaga v. Doe,* 2002). The USA Patriot Act (2001) served to further diminish privacy rights as antiterrorist legislation made it easier for law enforcement persons to conduct electronic surveillance.

The professional ethical principle of confidentiality is derived from the privacy societal value, and confidentiality is highly valued in all countries that emphasize individual rights, such as the United States (Congress & McAuliffe, 2006). This principle is not a modern invention but was already recognized by some in ancient times. For example, in the physician's oath that has been attributed to Hippocrates (460–370 BCE) we read: "What I may see or hear in the course of treatment.... I will keep to myself, holding such things shameful to be spoken about" In the NASW (2008) Code of Ethics this principle appears as a standard:

> Social workers should respect clients' right to privacy. Social workers should not solicit private information from clients unless it is essential to providing services or conducting social work evaluation or research. Once private information is shared, standards of confidentiality apply (1.07a).

Seventeen other paragraphs (1.07b through 1.07r) provide additional explanations and limitations. For example, valid consent is required before social workers can disclose confidential information (1.07b), and clients should be informed to the extent possible of disclosure of confidential information and the potential consequences of such disclosure (1.07d). However, information may be disclosed if compelling professional reasons exist, such as imminent harm to a client or another person. Where disclosure is required, only the minimal amount of information necessary to achieve the goals should be shared (1.07c). Social workers should discuss with clients and other interested parties the nature and limitations of their right to confidentiality (1.07e).

In addition, social workers who provide services to couples, families, or other groups "should seek agreement among the parties involved concerning each individual's right to confidentiality and obligation to preserve the confidentiality of information shared by others" (1.07f); they should also inform clients of policies "concerning . . . disclosure of confidential information among the parties involved in the counseling" (1.07g). Social workers "should not disclose identifying information when discussing clients for teaching or training purposes unless the client has consented to disclosure of confidential information" (1.07p) or with consultants unless the client has consented to disclosure or there is a compelling need for such disclosure (1.07q). Confidential information should not be discussed in public areas (1.07i), and client records, including electronic files, should be stored in a secure location (1.07l). In addition, "reasonable precautions [should be taken] to protect client confidentiality in the event of the social worker's termination of practice, incapacitation, or death" (1.07o).

PRIVACY AND CONFIDENTIALITY

Privacy and confidentiality are often confused (Congress & McAuliffe, 2006). **Privacy** refers to the inherent right of every person to decide what, if any, information about them is shared with others. **Confidentiality** refers to the professional obligation of the social worker or other professional (or bureaucrat) not to reveal to anyone information that she has received from a client without the client's informed consent. However, it is not always easy or possible for a social worker to implement this rule. The Code itself recognizes the possibility that "compelling professional reasons" may require a social worker to reveal information received in confidence "when disclosure is necessary to prevent serious, foreseeable, and imminent harm to a client or other identifiable person" (NASW, 2008, 1.07c). The nature of some of these compelling reasons will be discussed later in this chapter under the section entitled "Duty to Protect." Even those who are committed to practice in an ethical manner and who want to observe confidentiality will face many ethical dilemmas in this area. Social workers may find it difficult to maintain confidentiality when they have a duty to protect the privacy of a client, participate in interdisciplinary teams that require sharing of information, are required to provide accountability data, or must respond to requests for information from third-party payers. Furthermore, there are situations in which courts order disclosure of confidential information, or this may be required by law in some settings, such as probation and parole.

Confidentiality is a principle that affirms the explicit promise or contract not to reveal anything about an individual except under conditions known and agreed to by the client. Although there may not be any exceptions to the *principle* of confidentiality itself, any limitations for compelling professional reasons, are due to the demands of a higher principle (e.g., preservation of life), the power of law, and/or what is needed to insure the best interests of the client. An ethical dilemma occurs whenever a practitioner has to choose among conflicting claims that may be equally valid, such as choosing between a client's right to confidentiality and the right of other people and of society to certain information.

Social workers generally assume that a client's reliance on confidentiality promotes trust in the professional practitioner. Many think that this relationship with the professional would be harmed if clients were aware that there are limits to confidentiality. However, empirical studies do not support the assumption that limiting confidentiality necessarily endangers the client/social worker relationship. Steinberg, Levine, and Doueck (1997) found that only 27% of clients of psychotherapists withdrew from treatment immediately or shortly after they became aware that the therapist had made a mandated child abuse report. Retention in treatment was higher when the informed consent procedure was more explicit and when the reported perpetrator was a third party not involved in the treatment. Similarly, Weinstein and colleagues (2000) found that when mental health professionals reported suspected child abuse and maltreatment, three-quarters of the clients did not terminate their treatment and, in many cases, the therapeutic process was enhanced.

Confidentiality is an especially problematic issue because this ethical principle is based on an oversimplified practice model that includes only the social worker and the client. The reality, however, is much more complex. For example, a child maltreatment case typically involves not only the child who has been maltreated and the adult perpetrator, but also the child's parents, other siblings, and relatives, as well as society and its agents (such as police and courts), child protective services workers, other social workers, colleagues from other fields, administrative personnel, insurance companies, and third-party payers. Each of these may make conflicting demands for confidential information. The ethical considerations for sharing confidential information with each of these participants will differ from context to context because there are varying legal and ethical obligations to share. Marshall and Solomon (2004) stated that "although the importance of confidentiality policies is clear, the implementation of these policies often impedes communication between providers, consumers, and families." In the discussion to follow, we consider confidentiality issues as they relate to working with various other professional practitioners and various service systems, including e-therapy.

OTHER SOCIAL WORKERS

Often, we do not give sufficient thought to the ethical implications of sharing confidential information with other social workers. We are not referring here to small talk at a cocktail party (which is clearly a violation of confidentiality), but to formal or informal consultations with colleagues or supervisors, as well as to the transmission of such information to other social workers who have a professional interest in the information (such as a social worker who is working with other members of the same family, the social worker who will take over the case while the worker is on vacation, and so on). This type of information transmission is intended for the client's benefit because it is meant to assure more effective service, but is it ethical to share this information with others without the client's consent? In many cases, a general informed consent agreement may be helpful, but many clients will sign it as a routine matter, perhaps without really understanding its meanings or implications. Taking special care to make certain a client understands the intention of the form and periodically revisiting the issue of confidentiality and informed consent may be required (we will discuss informed consent later in this chapter).

The NASW (2008) Code of Ethics provides some guidance on this issue. The limitations of confidentiality should be discussed with clients early in the professional relationship (1.07e). When a client has been previously served by another agency or colleague, "social workers should discuss with the client whether consultation with the previous service provider is in the client's best interest" (3.06b). These sections of the Code advise that it is generally not ethical to share information about the client with other social workers without the client's prior consent. However, the social worker should also consider the possible harm that may be caused by not providing vital information to colleagues who are now working with that client. It is this consideration that led Taylor and Adelman (1989) to conclude that "keeping information confidential can seriously hamper an intervener's efforts to help" (p. 80). How can social workers balance the need to protect clients' confidentiality with the need to share information so that the best service can be provided?

COLLEAGUES FROM OTHER FIELDS

Many social workers practice on multidisciplinary teams or in settings where information must be shared with colleagues from other professions whose confidentiality practices may differ from those of social workers. All social workers are aware that "timely and effective interagency collaboration can have many benefits for both clients and workers" (Darlington, Feeney, & Rixon, 2005, p. 1086). Even though it is important to protect confidentiality, it is also important to seek consultation from and collaboration with others when needed. Differences in agency confidentiality policies can be a barrier to effective collaboration, but two or more agencies can formalize and coordinate the consent process and establish specific methods for information exchange, perhaps reducing this potential barrier (Darlington et al., 2005, p. 1094). Frost, Robinson, and Anning (2005) found that issues of confidentiality and information sharing policies were key concerns for social workers who participate in multidisciplinary teams. Problems arose both in relation to social workers being unable to access information from other agencies (e.g., health records) and from their inability to share information from their databases with professionals from other agencies.

Some social workers are required to share information with others because of the type of position they occupy. For example, those who provide case management services are obligated to share information about the client. However, the client must consent to what information will be shared with which agencies before the social worker can share confidential information. Before giving consent, the client must be made aware of what information will be shared with whom—otherwise his consent is almost meaningless.

THE COMMUNITY

Green (2003) suggests that confidentiality and privacy raise critical dilemmas especially for social workers in rural communities. In these small communities, it may be difficult to protect a client's privacy because neighbors may see him enter the social worker's office. Community members may feel entitled to certain information and may pressure the social worker to share information in order to protect community members. For example, community members may feel that they have the right to be notified about sexual offenses, particularly against children. Under Megan's Law and the Adam Walsh Child Protection Act of 2006 (H.R. 4472) communities are notified of convicted sexual offenders through the National Sex Offender Registry and state registries. However, this protection exists only after a person has been convicted of a sexual offense. What is the social worker's responsibility if she knows her client has committed a sexual offense, but has not been convicted?

ADMINISTRATIVE AND ELECTRONIC RECORDS

Social agencies and other employing organizations require that all social workers report information about their clients and client contacts because they need such data for administrative and accountability reasons. The initial request to supply these data may be entirely proper, but once the requested information has been transmitted, the practitioner is no longer able to protect its confidentiality. As the use of computerized records becomes more common in social agencies, this aspect of the confidentiality issue has become even more crucial. The Code of Ethics specifically addresses these issues, requiring social workers to "take precautions to ensure and maintain the confidentiality of information transmitted to other parties through the use of computers, electronic mail, facsimile machines, telephones and telephone answering machines, and other electronic or computer technology. Disclosure of identifying information should be avoided wherever possible" (1.07 m).

The Health Insurance Portability and Accountability Act (HIPAA) (1996) requirements may be helpful in this area, as health care agencies are required to develop procedures to protect the confidentiality of client information (HIPAA will be discussed in more detail later in this chapter). It is not simply the electronic transmission of data, however, that requires precautions. Today, when computers are used frequently to store case and process records, serious thought must be given to ensuring their security against inadvertent errors, hackers, and those who can make business use of the information gathered.

Morin and colleagues (2005) examined older adults' comfort with electronic health records, and found that most were comfortable with having their health data available electronically. Only a few were concerned about errors and confidentiality. Almost all of these patients provided appropriate informed consent for permitting access to their electronic health records, but many did not remember that they could withdraw their consent at any time, suggesting that they may not have fully understood the consent information.

Interestingly, some people like the anonymity provided by the Internet and believe that it actually protects confidentiality. In addition, "the Internet improves access to service for those who may not gain access otherwise. Individuals who are stigmatized, shy, or embarrassed to share personal problems are 'faceless' on the World Wide Web and have been found to be more willing to participate in groups dealing with delicate issues" (Parker-Oliver & Demiris, 2006, p. 130, citing Vernberg & Schuh, 2002). However, it is unclear whether people who feel more anonymous and safe do so because they do not fully understand the potential for being identified in these circumstances.

E-THERAPY

There are a growing number of e-therapy websites, including those involving social workers, where interventions are performed for several mental and emotional disorders such as depression, stress, substance abuse, and eating disorders. Santhiveeran (2009) studied 69 e-therapy sites of social workers. Two-thirds (68%) of the sites with social workers informed their clients of the nature and extent of the e-therapy process. A slightly lower percentage (62%) informed clients of the potential risks. Three types of risks were identified by the websites: technical difficulties (e.g., computer crashes, lack of trust in Internet security); third-party damages (e.g., problems associated with PayPal services and web-hosting services); and shortcomings of e-therapy, which is considered experimental and cannot replace face-to-face therapy that includes the observation of body language and other gestures. Less than half (44%) of the e-therapy websites informed clients of the safeguards to be taken while using computers in therapy such as firewalls and not saving login information on their computers. Only a third of the therapists indicated they would only serve clients from the states in which they had a license to practice. Sixty percent of the websites had procedures in place to deal with emergency situations, thus leaving 40% of the sites unprepared to do so. Santhiveeran (2009) concluded that the websites did not provide adequate information concerning ethical principles.

Earlier, we explored the problem of insuring confidentiality for electronic data kept by the social worker. In addition, although it is known that the use of

e-therapy is a growing phenomenon, the extent to which e-therapy is being offered and the educational backgrounds, certifications, and professional experiences of those providing it are largely unknown. The exact nature of the laws
and regulations of states and how they interact when two or more states are
involved in a situation, the types of interventions used, and the effectiveness of
treatments remain to be fully investigated. The basic question remains: Is
e-therapy ethical?

Insurance Companies and Third-Party Payers

New dimensions have been added to the problem of confidentiality as a growing
number of social workers employed in agencies and in private practice are required
to report diagnoses to insurance companies or other third-party payers in order to
qualify clients for reimbursement. Although clients may consent to sharing this
information because they are interested in having a third party pay for part or all
of the services they receive from a social worker, they are not always aware of the
diagnosis reported or who will be privy to this information. In addition to the issue
of confidentiality, the severity of the diagnosis may be overstated in order to qualify
clients for reimbursement (see Chapter 7 for further discussion of ethical issues
related to diagnosis and misdiagnosis). If clients are aware that third-party payers
may share confidential information with others, including their employers and
future service providers, they may prefer to pay for the services of the social worker
out of their own pocket. The Code of Ethics (2008) specifically states that "social
workers should not disclose confidential information to third-party payers unless
clients have authorized such disclosure" (1.07h).

Police

In many states, the law requires that social workers, as well as other professional
practitioners, inform the police whenever they acquire information about criminal activities that have taken place or are being planned. For example, if a social
worker is present when an adolescent street gang discusses plans for a holdup,
what is expected of her? Should she have any ethical qualms about reporting the
gang's intentions to the police? What is her obligation when a third party (such
as a parent or neighbor) tells her about such a plan? At the very least, she must
ask herself several questions: How reliable is the report? Can the information
be provided without revealing the source? How might such revelation affect the
helping relationship? What harm can be prevented or result by informing
the police?

The situation has a number of legal and ethical elements. To whom does the
social worker owe her primary loyalty—to the gang, parents, neighbors, the police,
or society? What harm could be prevented by her report? All of these and other
questions have legal, professional, and ethical implications. Many social workers
are perplexed by ethical dilemmas arising out of various other kinds of law violations, particularly delinquent acts that do not seem to harm others. Exemplar 8.1
describes one such situation that raises a number of ethical questions about reporting possibly illegal behavior.

EP 2.1.2

8.1 | FRAUD AND AN AGING MOTHER

Social worker Jean Fisher is a marriage counselor and family therapist in the Old Town Family Consultation Center, a nonsectarian agency. Sue and Dean Kern have been coming to her for marital therapy once a week for the past two months. Though their problem is not critical, they came to seek help while their marriage was still salvageable. They have made good progress toward reaching their goal. During today's session, Dean mentioned that he has continued to receive supplemental security income (SSI) payments for his aged mother, who lived with them until she moved overseas two years ago. She now makes her home with his sister, who lives in England.

Should Jean report this case as possible fraud? Does client/worker confidentiality cover this communication? According to the NASW Code (2008), disclosure required by law or regulations is a compelling reason to break confidentiality (1.07e); therefore, it is important for social workers to know the reporting regulations in their jurisdiction and act accordingly. At the same time, Jean must consider what might happen to the client/therapist relationship if she does report what she has learned. Should she discuss the possible consequences of their activities with the clients in an attempt to persuade them to change their behavior so that she will not have to report them? What would Jean's obligation be if she had learned that Dean had escaped from prison 10 years ago? Or that Sue was selling illegal drugs? Does the seriousness of the offense change the ethical considerations? Does the degree of harm to the client or someone else make a difference?

RELATIVES

Are the relatives of a client entitled to confidential information that might affect them? What should the social worker do if a son asks whether his father is dying when the father, who is terminally ill, has specifically asked that none of his relatives be told how ill he is? How does the social worker decide whether to keep the confidence or tell the truth? Do the relatives of a person living with HIV have the right to know about the person's health status? Does the type of relationship matter (e.g., a spouse or a sibling)? This is a type of ethical dilemma that may be especially acute for social workers who are engaged in settings such as health care and genetic counseling and who are privy to medical and or genetic information that may affect the health of relatives (Freedman, 1998).

Are parents entitled to confidential information about their children? Does the age of the child make a difference? For example, Planned Parenthood researchers in Wisconsin found that most girls under 18 would stop or limit their use of health services at family planning clinics if their parents had to be told they were seeking prescriptions for contraceptives (Flaherty, 2002). Consider Exemplar 8.2, which discusses confidentiality in a school setting.

8.2 | Debbie Roberts Is Pregnant

EP 2.1.2

Debbie Roberts is a 12-year-old eighth-grader who is 10 weeks pregnant. She has been a good student, and her teacher reports that she has never had any problems with Debbie. The school nurse referred Debbie to the school social worker because Debbie refused to discuss her condition with the nurse. At first, Debbie also refused to speak to the social worker, but later she told her that she did not want to have an abortion. She repeatedly emphasized that she did not want her parents to know that she was pregnant. Debbie will not reveal who the father is, and the social worker suspects that Debbie may have been sexually abused.

Should Debbie's parents be told about their daughter's pregnancy? Should the social worker know who father of the baby is before speaking to her parents? Should child protective services be told about the situation? What is the ethical approach to this ambiguous situation?

Clients

What are a social worker's obligations when a client wants information about himself, such as wanting to read his own case record? According to the NASW (2008) Code of Ethics, "social workers should provide clients with reasonable access to records concerning the clients.... Social workers should limit clients' access to their records, or portions of their records, only in exceptional circumstances when there is compelling evidence that such access would cause serious harm to the client" (1.08a). Ambiguities about what constitutes "reasonable access," "exceptional circumstances," or "serious harm" make it difficult to implement this standard.

There are a number of arguments against sharing confidential information with the client, especially against granting him unlimited access to his own record:

- The case record may contain information supplied on a confidential basis by a third party, such as another social worker, teacher, neighbor, or relative. According to the NASW (2008) Code of Ethics, "when providing clients with access to their records, social workers should take steps to protect the confidentiality of other individuals identified or discussed in such records" (1.08b). This suggests that while the social worker needs to protect the confidentiality of others mentioned in the client's record, this is not a sufficient reason to deny the client access to his records.

- The case record may contain raw data that have not yet been checked or evaluated, or test results or other data that may be misinterpreted by a lay person. The NASW (2008) Code of Ethics requires social workers to "provide assistance in interpreting the records and consultation with the client regarding the records" (1.08a). Therefore, this may not be a sufficient argument for denying access to client records.

- The social worker may use the case record to explore various options or to ask herself questions that need further clarification; when the client reads such material, his trust in the worker may be impaired. In this situation, the social worker will need to assess the potential for serious harm to the client that may be caused by his reading the record. If this is the case, then access may be limited or denied (NASW, 2008, 1.08a).

- Reading or hearing negative information about himself may hurt the client. Again, if the potential for serious harm exists, then access may be denied.

Whenever the social worker denies access to the record, "clients' requests and the rationale for withholding some or all of the record(s) should be documented in clients' files" (NASW, 2008, 1.08b).

On the other hand, there are also several arguments in favor of giving clients access to their own case records:

- Reading the information gives the client an opportunity to correct mistakes.
- A client can give informed consent to share information with others only if he knows what this information is.
- Knowledge of information may lead to change, whereas ignorance will result in only maintaining the present unsatisfactory situation.
- Opening the case record will demonstrate the efficacy of client/worker cooperation and may be followed by even greater client participation in the social work process.

We have presented a number of (but not all) arguments for and against opening case records to clients in order to help social workers arrive at an ethical decision. Admittedly, this is a decision that few social workers employed in agencies have to make alone because, generally, agency policy and directives on this point are specific and clear. However, if you were asked to present to an agency board of directors on the issue of client access to records, what would your recommendations be? If you were in private practice, what policies would you decide on regarding client access to records?

LIMITS TO CONFIDENTIALITY

Clearly, there are limits to confidentiality. In the first meetings between the client and the social worker, the nature of confidentiality should be explained to clients and other interested parties, including the limitations of the clients' right to confidentiality. This information may need to be reviewed periodically throughout the professional relationship (NASW, 2008, 1.07e). However, in what detail should these limitations be discussed? Weinstein et al. (2000) found that about 40% of experienced mental health practitioners *did not* inform clients about the limits of confidentiality until information came up that they were required by law to report to the authorities. At the same time, Weinstein et al. found that informing clients about the limits of confidentiality did not deter them from entering treatment. We will discuss the concept of informed consent in greater detail later in this chapter.

Social workers have legal obligations to breach confidentiality under certain circumstances. Because the limitations and circumstances vary by jurisdiction or location, this is an area that social workers should carefully investigate to ascertain their responsibilities. Bond and Mitchels (2008) reviewed the types of cases in Great

Britain where mandated reporting was a legal obligation. Among these were court orders, preventing or assisting in the detection of terrorist activities, prevention of serious crime, drug trafficking and money laundering, protection of children from abuse, protecting clients from self-harm and suicidal intent, and prevention of serious physical harm likely to be inflicted by a client on another adult.

HEALTH INSURANCE PORTABILITY AND ACCOUNTABILITY ACT (HIPAA, 1996)

The privacy rule provided by HIPAA protects all individually identifiable health information held or transmitted by a covered entity or its business associates, in any form or media, whether electronic, paper, or oral. This information is referred to as protected health information. Included in individually identifiable health information is demographic data related to individual's past, present, or future physical or mental health or condition; the provision of health care to the individual; and the past, present, or future payment for the provision of health care to the individual that identifies the individual or for which there is a reasonable basis to believe it can be used to identify the individual.

Social workers and others (health plans, health care clearinghouses, and health care providers who transmit health information electronically) are expected to be in compliance with HIPAA requirements. The Department of Health and Human Services (DHHS) established a standardized electronic format for eight common health care transactions: claims payment and remittance advice, coordination of benefits, eligibility for a health plan, enrollment and disenrollment in a health plan, health care claim status, premium payments, and referral certification and authorization. The 2002 HIPAA privacy regulations (P.L. 104-191; Standards for Privacy, 2002) amended the original act by replacing the requirement for patient authorization with only a notice of the provider's privacy policy for information about treatment, payment, or health care operations. HIPAA was passed in 1996, but it was not fully implemented until April 2003.

Yang and Kombarakaran (2006) suggest that the 2002 HIPAA provisions provide less protection than the original 1996 provisions and allow greater opportunities for breaches of confidentiality. But this amended rule does not preclude social workers from obtaining a written consent prior to release of information for treatment and payment. Providers are still required to have a separate written authorization from the client for each *non-routine* use and disclosure of health information (Yang & Kombarakaran, 2006), and there are special HIPAA privacy protections for psychotherapy notes.

In states where minors can give consent to health care treatments, they also have the right to make their own decisions about the release of protected health information. In those states, their parents are not considered to be their personal representatives for this purpose. In some states, minors are permitted to consent to drug and alcohol counseling, mental health treatment, or health care regarding pregnancy without parental consent. In these states, social workers may exercise their discretion to deny or provide access to the records by a parent. If a parent voluntarily consents to a confidentiality agreement between the minor and the social worker, the minor can also make individual decisions about the use and disclosure of their own protected health information. If a state law has specific provisions that grant or deny access by the parents to minors' health information, the state law applies (NASW, October 1, 2002).

HEALTH INFORMATION TECHNOLOGY AND CLINICAL HEALTH ACT (HITECH, 2009)

On February 17, 2009, President Barak Obama signed into law the Health Information Technology and Clinical Health Act (HITECH) as part of the American Recovery and Reinvestment Act, an economic stimulus program. HITECH provides $19 billion over a four year period under Medicare and Medicaid for providers who adopt and use health information technology. The law also expanded security and privacy provisions and penalties to HIPAA business associates of covered entities. NASW (2009) in "HITECH HIPAA for Social Workers" identified certain aspects of the legislation affecting social workers:

1. HITECH specifies that none of its provisions are intended to affect established patient privilege laws such as the psychotherapist-patient privilege established by the U.S. Supreme Court in *Jaffee v. Redmond* (1996), and that state laws that are more protective of privacy will be not be preempted.
2. The act requires a notice of privacy breaches, including disclosure of any protected health information, not only demographic information. The HITECH privacy and security breach notice provisions substantially alter the HIPAA requirements in cases where a breach involves more than 500 people. Covered entities must report breaches to the Department of Health and Human Services and in some cases covered entities must also report the breach to the media.
3. The breach notice requires that a covered entity notify each individual affected by a breach and that business associates that discover a breach are to notify the covered entity of the identity of the individuals affected by a breach.
4. The content of the breach notice must include: A brief description of the incident, including dates; types of information involved (e.g., social security number, name, address, etc.); steps individuals should take to protect themselves from potential harm due to the breach; a brief description of the covered entities' actions to investigate, mitigate harm, and prevent future occurrences; and contact procedures for questions or additional information, including a toll free number, e-mail address, and website or postal address.

NASW suggests those who are subject to HIPAA standards invest in data encryption for their electronic client records (Pace, 2009). Although there is no requirement that client data be encrypted, there is a requirement to put policies in place to prevent and identify a potential breach of client information and respond promptly with required notifications and mitigation. If the data breached are encrypted and unusable after its release, there is no HIPAA requirement for a breach notification.

Where third-party vendors handle client information such as billing, that information is also subject HIPAA standards. So, any contracts with third-party vendors need to outline the vendor's responsibility to send out notifications in case of a breach. Social workers are also encouraged to develop a system to detect breaches and procedures for handling violations if they occur; have a breach response plan in place; and include specific breach notification responsibilities when revising business associate agreements. As with any new law or policy that has the potential to have a major impact on social work practice, social workers are encouraged to stay updated on this issue in terms of federal and state law, as well as agency administrative policies in regard to HITECH and HIPAA.

CHILD WELFARE AND CONFIDENTIALITY

Social workers and other professionals are required by law to report all cases of suspected child abuse and neglect to the child protective services (CPS) agency or other designated authority. Although details vary from state to state, such reporting is required in every jurisdiction in the United States and in many other countries. There is less concern with the ethics of breaking confidentiality in cases of child abuse and neglect because of the greater ethical imperatives on finding ways to assure the safety of the child.

Surveys have found that one in three professionals have had contact with at least one case of suspected child abuse that they have declined to report, and they reported only about one third of the abuse cases they suspected (Kalichman, 1999, p. 4). When a report is made to child protective services, the CPS worker is required to investigate the reported maltreatment and is required to take any necessary action to protect the child. Social workers who continue to be uneasy about the ethical and practice implications of reporting suspected child abuse that involves one of their clients might want to consider the following options when the need to report arises:

1. Work with the client to help him (if sufficiently able) to make the report himself; the social worker should follow up with the client to make sure that the report was made.
2. Discuss with the family why a report needs to be made, what the potential benefits and risks to the family are, what procedures will be followed during the investigation, and if the report is substantiated or indicated, what some of the treatment options are likely to be. The social worker should be aware of the procedures followed in her area so that she can accurately inform clients about what to expect.
3. Report without notifying the family if failing to report would place the child at immediate risk.

It is important to note that not all parents with mental illness or substance abuse problems will maltreat their children, yet children of such parents are at higher risk for child abuse and neglect (see Darlington et al., 2005; Kroll, 2004). Consequently, professionals working in these areas may be more likely to become involved in reporting suspected child abuse or may be asked to share information about a parent's mental health or substance use with child protective services workers. Kroll (2004) also notes that children may feel uncomfortable or disloyal discussing parents' substance use, and that professionals need to be "clear about issues of confidentiality, so that children [know] what would happen to the information they gave and that they would not be punished, judged or blamed for talking about parents' behavior" (p. 137).

Vulnerable children in their own families are not the only children who need to be protected from abuse and neglect. The protection of those in families and another group of vulnerable children depends on communication among professionals. For example, collaboration between child welfare, education, health, mental health, juvenile justice, and other systems is also important because children and youth in foster care "are one of the most educationally vulnerable populations ... [and] no one agency has [all] the resources or expertise to provide the services and supports required to better serve these young people" (Zetlin, Weinberg, & Shea, 2006, p. 166). Zetlin et al. (2006) conducted focus groups to examine ways to support education of foster care youth. Among the themes that emerged were concerns about the adequacy of educational records (such as not being able to keep track of all the schools the youth attended and what courses they had taken at each), the difficulties of interagency collaboration, and issues of confidentiality. Because each agency often has its own confidentiality and data sharing policies, information about youth is more limited than if all records were kept by one agency (Zetlin et al., 2006). Should confidentiality of records be maintained to such an extent that it interferes with providing effective interventions? How should social workers balance these two goals?

PRIVILEGED COMMUNICATION

Privileged communication is a legal right granted by legislative statute; guarantees that certain information need not be revealed in court without the consent of the person who originated the communication. Privileged communication is a rule of evidence that allows one party in a legal proceeding (in this case, the client) to limit the admissibility of statements originally communicated in confidence, thus rendering the witness (that is, the social worker) "incompetent" to testify regarding a particular matter. The common law principle that the public has a right to every person's evidence is followed in the absence of a statute of privilege. No person can refuse to testify in court when called to do so. Persons reluctant to testify can be subpoenaed or commanded to testify by the court; failure to appear and testify in response to a subpoena can result in a citation for contempt of court. Historically, privileged relationships have been limited to husband/wife, attorney/client, and priest-confessor/worshipper. Any other relationship is privileged only when so defined by a statute enacted by a state legislature. All 50 states and the District of Columbia have enacted laws concerning privileged communications. Special attention must be paid to this issue by social workers because the specifics of the privilege differ from state to state.

"Every U.S. jurisdiction has recognized some form of evidentiary privilege for statements made by a patient to a psychotherapist for the purpose of obtaining treatment" (Harris, 1999, p. 36). On the federal level, the U.S. Supreme Court established the psychotherapist/patient privilege in the federal courts with its ruling in *Jaffee v. Redmond* (1996). The Court had not previously addressed this issue, but did so in a case involving a licensed clinical social worker, simultaneously establishing the principle for psychiatrists and psychologists. For practical purposes, the Supreme Court ruling extends the privilege to civil actions in federal courts, thus institutionalizing the recognition of psychotherapist/patient privilege. The exact dimensions of the privilege will evolve through case decisions as they unfold. For example, in *United States v. Chase*, the United States 9th Circuit Court of Appeals ruled in August 2002 that there *is* a dangerous patient exception to the *Jaffee* privilege, a ruling opposite to a position taken by the 6th Circuit in *United States v. Hayes*. During 2001, the 9th Circuit ruled that communications between an unlicensed EAP counselor and a patient are protected from compelled disclosure by the privilege established by *Jaffee*. The privilege belongs to the client, not to the social worker. When a client waives the privilege, the social worker must testify in court, even if the client does not know or is not certain what information is included in his case record and even if this testimony may harm him. Other interested persons do not control the privilege. For example, a father or husband cannot suppress or waive testimony of a social worker who is treating his child or wife, even when he pays for the treatment (VandeCreek et al., 1988).

In many states, the privilege ceases to exist if a third party was present at the time that the client communicated the confidential information to the social worker. However, some state laws specifically extend the privilege of communications to situations that involve group, marital, and family therapy—that is, to situations where third parties are present (VandeCreek et al., 1988). In other states, the courts decide whether the rule of privilege applies, but no clear trend has evolved regarding communications in the presence of third parties. The Minnesota Superior Court addressed this question in *Minnesota v. Andring* (10 FLR 1206, 1984) and ruled:

> The participants in group psychotherapy sessions are not casual persons who are strangers.... Rather, every participant has such a relationship with the attending professional, and in the group setting, the participants actually become part of the diagnostic and therapeutic process for coparticipants.
>
> An interpretation that excluded group therapy from the scope of the psychotherapist-patient [privileged communication rule] would seriously limit the effectiveness of group psychotherapy as a therapeutic device.... [T]he confidentiality of communications made during group therapy is essential in maintaining its effectiveness as a therapeutic tool.

In the absence of a privilege statute, a social worker who testifies about confidential information that she has received from a client may face a double bind—if she testifies, she may be sued by the client for revealing confidential information; if she refuses to testify, she may be cited for contempt of court. Privileged communication is a legal and not an ethical concept. Questions arising out of privileged communications require legal consultation.

INFORMED CONSENT

The professional ethics rule of **informed consent** is derived from the moral principle of autonomy, which states that all persons have the capacity for self-government and self-decision making. This capacity must be respected at all times by all helpers. Informed consent means that a social worker or another professional will not intervene in a client's life or release confidential information about him unless that client has freely consented. It cannot be assumed that because a client consented in the past he will again consent now. It is therefore important that consent be obtained every time a client starts a new treatment procedure, every time he starts with a new social worker, and every time that confidential data will be released to a third party (Manning & Gaul, 1997). The NASW (2008) Code of Ethics states clearly that:

> social workers should provide services to clients only in the context of a professional relationship based, when appropriate, on valid informed consent. Social workers should use clear and understandable language to inform clients of the purpose of the services, risks related to the services, limits to services because of requirements of a third-party payer, relevant costs, reasonable alternatives, clients' right to refuse or withdraw consent, and the time frame covered by the consent. Social workers should provide clients with an opportunity to ask questions (1.03a).

If a client is not capable of providing informed consent, then permission should be sought from an appropriate third party (1.03c). If a social worker is serving involuntary clients, then she "should provide information about the nature and extent of services and about the extent of clients' right to refuse service" (1.03d). Further, in cases where a social worker may be required to report findings of an investigation or assessment, such as in a child custody hearing or in probation and parole settings, the client should be warned about the limits of confidentiality as part of the informed consent process (Luftman, Veltkamp, Clark, Lannacone, & Snooks, 2005). Palmer and Kaufman (2003) emphasize the importance of obtaining informed consent in a culturally sensitive manner. The social worker must not assume that such basic values as individualism, self-determination, obedience, and democracy will have the same meaning for her client as they do for her. By keeping this in mind, she can give her clients a meaningful experience in self-determination.

While everyone agrees that clients should provide informed consent before starting treatment or before having confidential information shared, there is little agreement on what information needs to be included in informed consent and whether written consent is needed. In a qualitative review of 37 written family therapy informed consent documents, Haslam and Harris (2004) found a general consistency in the main categories of information included (e.g., process or nature of therapy, confidentiality, insurance issues, etc.), but there was great variability in some of the details, such as indicating the risks of the treatment provided. Pollack (2004) warns of the risk of providing too much information:

> There is no single way to ensure that every potential question a client might have can be adequately addressed. What we can do is be vigilant of paternalism that leaves clients dependent, and be mindful of giving clients so much autonomy that, in the name of good professional practice, they are left unanchored and helpless.... Self-respect, self-direction, and a sense of fair play are at stake (p. 28).

Disclosure of Information, Voluntariness, and Competence

Three issues integral to informed consent are disclosure of information, voluntariness, and competency (Grisso & Appelbaum, 1998; Moreno, Caplan, & Wolpe, 1998; Palmer & Kaufman, 2003). Problems involving any one or all of these issues make for difficult ethical dilemmas in social work practice. We will discuss briefly the ethical aspects of each of these issues.

DISCLOSURE OF INFORMATION A person can be considered sufficiently informed to give consent only if he knows what will occur during the intervention or treatment, what the results of the intervention will be, and what will happen if he does not consent. He should know how much better (or worse) he will be if he agrees to the intervention than he will be if he does not agree. This is not only a problem for the client; the problem also exists for the social worker, who does not know in any definitive way what will actually transpire. The client should also have full knowledge about alternate options and their associated risks and benefits. In situations in which the client is being asked to consent to the disclosure of confidential information to a third party, he should know what information will be released, to whom, for what purposes, and with what consequences. He should also know the consequences of not agreeing. Finally, the disclosure of information must be done in a clear and understandable manner (Grisso & Appelbaum, 1998).

In some cases, fundamental problems of communication may exist when attempting to communicate technical and value-laden information, particularly to those who are in stressful situations. For example, some persons may have difficulty understanding the idea of probability, whereas different styles of communication may be intimidating to some clients (Moreno et al., 1998). Much of the required information can be provided by the social worker, but even she may not be cognizant of some of the possible outcomes because there are always secondary and unanticipated consequences. In fact, the nature and consequences of any option are never entirely clear and may be interpreted differently by different experts.

There is much evidence that many people do not pay attention or fully comprehend information presented to them, no matter how carefully the details and possible risks are explained. It is not always clear whether this is a case of selective listening or of suppressing unpleasant information. In a study of patient/physician communication following general physical exams, the patients could not remember almost 70% of the problems physicians diagnosed (American College of Physicians Observer, 1997). Some have estimated that only 20% of adult Americans have the ability to read, fully understand, and act appropriately on health care information they have received (Dent, 2000). Other patients simply do not want to know the risks involved in the procedure or treatment that has been provided. Still others literally do not hear because they have hearing problems.

Social workers differ in many ways from physicians, but many social workers also report that their clients really do not want to know all the details. They have a problem, and they want help from an expert whom they trust. Yet the social worker is ethically committed to the principle of providing services and treatment only on the basis of informed consent. One of the ethical dilemmas facing the social worker in this area is that she does not want to overwhelm the client with too much information, yet is obligated to provide sufficient information to enable the client to make a meaningful decision. Should the worker be satisfied and proceed when the client has given permission, even though she suspects that this client does not fully understand the information and its meaning, or should she delay help so that she can give the client additional information that she believes is necessary to obtain informed consent?

Think back to the exemplar presented at the beginning of Chapter 1, where the social worker, Ellen Ashton, suspects that Basanti Madurai is in a violent relationship. How did you think the social worker should respond to the situation? If Mrs. Madurai was at risk of harm, should the social worker encourage her to leave her husband? As discussed earlier, women who leave violent relationships tend to return to the relationship several times before leaving permanently. Does full disclosure of information require that Ms. Ashton tell Mrs. Madurai that even if she leaves, it is likely that she will return to her husband? How might such information impact Mrs. Madurai's decision to leave?

VOLUNTARINESS Consent is meaningful only when it is not coerced, but rather given freely. Though there is wide agreement with this ethical rule, some social workers practice in settings where the client has little or no freedom. Prisoners, parolees, and patients hospitalized with mental illnesses are classic examples of involuntary clients. When working with court-mandated clients, there are three barriers to informed consent. First, the risks and benefit of the court-ordered assessment cannot be fully anticipated. Second, the power imbalance results in client vulnerability that undermines voluntariness of consent. Third, while the "ability to form a therapeutic alliance and obtain relevant information is valued by the court, the therapeutic alliance may not always serve the best interest of the client, who may not be aware of the complexity of the relationship" (Regehr & Antle, 1997, p. 301).

Consent may also be less than voluntary in some other settings. Voluntariness is often presented as a dichotomous value—a decision either is or is not voluntary. However, closer inspection will suggest that there is a wide range between the two extremes. For example, how voluntary is the consent of a client who believes that it is important to gain the worker's goodwill in order to obtain the services or goods desired? A destitute single mother may agree with almost everything her social worker suggests because she desperately wants to qualify for assistance. The man who is eager for reconciliation with his estranged wife may agree with everything his social worker mentions because he believes that in this way he may be able to salvage his marriage. The family that desperately needs help and services for their autistic child knows they can obtain these only through the social worker. Even though these people are not forced to come to a social agency or to agree with the social worker's assessment and recommendation, is their informed consent really voluntary?

The importance of developing client trust may lead to another ethical dilemma. Research has demonstrated that trust or faith in the practitioner is a key component in furthering effective change. Yet faith or trust may result in a surrender of decision-making participation. Instead of giving voluntary consent, the client who has blind faith in her social worker will agree to much this worker says. Developing and encouraging trust, while strengthening voluntary consent and decision-making participation, is a challenge for every social worker. Grisso and Appelbaum (1998) comment that "encouraging patients to pursue a particular option is not coercion, unless unfair threats are involved. Clinicians need not simply lay out the alternatives for patients. They can distinguish among the options they consider more or less viable" (p. 9).

Competence Informed consent presupposes that the person who gives consent is competent to do so. However, many social work clients are less than fully competent. Persons with dementia, Alzheimer's disease, or developmental disabilities, and the seriously emotionally disturbed, as well as young children, may not be competent to give informed consent for some or all decisions. However, even clients with serious mental or physical illness may be competent to provide consent. Moser and colleagues (2002) found that 80% of participants with schizophrenia and 96% of persons with HIV had adequate capacity to provide informed consent. Only a court of law can declare a person incompetent, but there are many situations in which a social worker must make a professional assessment of a person's competency to participate in decision making.

The ethical problem is complicated because ostensibly the issue of competency is raised only when a client disagrees with his social worker's recommendation. Rarely does the social worker question his competency when he agrees with her. Ethical problems that arise in this area are especially well known to social workers who are working with adoption, foster placement, custody, abortion, contraception, and end-of-life decisions. The social worker's dilemma may become a difficult one, particularly when young children are involved. Although there is no agreement about how old a child must be before he or she is considered competent, everyone agrees that an infant is not competent to make decisions. Children, like adults, may not always mean what they say or say what they mean, and stated preferences may not reflect actual preferences.

The decision to intervene in a person's life must never be taken lightly. To limit a person's freedom by removing her from her home and placing her in an institution is a very serious decision, which ordinarily should not be made without the person's consent. At the same time, it may be a mistake to always accept that person's consent or refusal at face value. A client may be temporarily depressed, may not understand the reality of the situation or the dangers involved in it, may change her mind upon further reflection, or may be reacting to a situational fear. Consider the ethical issues involved in Exemplar 8.3.

8.3 | Archie Walker's Golden Years

EP 2.1.2

Muriel Palmieri is an outreach worker for the Downtown Elderly Program (DEP). She has organized a group of volunteers who regularly visit with homebound older people. These volunteers have been trained to identify older people who need additional help so that they can report their names to the DEP. One of the volunteers recently told Muriel that she had discovered a bedridden older man in a cold and dirty fourth-floor walk-up apartment.

Archie Walker was probably not as old or as feeble as he appeared, but the volunteer thought that he required more care than the occasional help provided by his 79-year-old neighbor, who brought him food whenever he thought of it. When this neighbor forgot to come, as happened not infrequently, Archie subsisted for days on cold water and bread. It had been years since Archie last saw a doctor. He seemed delighted with the volunteer's visit and begged her to come again soon. Muriel told the volunteer that she would see what could be done to make Archie more comfortable.

When Muriel visited Archie, he welcomed her warmly. She was able to confirm the volunteer's observations. Archie seemed relatively alert. Muriel thought that his dissatisfaction with his present condition was realistic and a hopeful sign, indicative of a capacity to participate in developing plans for the future. Archie explained that his only income came from Social Security. He had never heard of the federal Supplemental Security Income (SSI) program. Muriel suspected that he would qualify for SSI. Archie said that he could not afford to move to another apartment, but he insisted that he did not want to go to an "old folks' home." Muriel explained about many of the programs that were available to help persons in his situation. She listed the advantages and disadvantages of each and indicated the time it might take before each program or service would start for him. She also noted how she could help him qualify. Among the programs they discussed were SSI, Meals-on-Wheels, health visitors, homemakers, Title 8 housing, and the Manor Apartments. Archie seemed bewildered by the many programs from which he could choose and by the many decisions he had to make. He asked Muriel to do whatever was best for him.

If you were in Muriel's place, what would you have done? Here are some of the ethical issues that may arise in trying to help Archie:

- What did Archie mean when he told Muriel to do whatever was best for him? Does this mean that he gave his consent for her to make all kinds of arrangements on his behalf? Is this a satisfactory way of giving informed consent? If not, in what ways does it fall short?
- Instead of overwhelming Archie with so many choices, should Muriel have simplified the decisions he has to make by presenting only a few options or programs at a time? Perhaps it would have been better to have Archie decide first whether he would utilize Meals-on-Wheels, leaving the discussion of whether he really wanted to stay in his present apartment or move elsewhere for a later time. Can he make either decision without having a full knowledge of all options? Do social work ethics require that a client have full knowledge of *all* the relevant options?
- Muriel tried to present all of the advantages and consequences of every option. Did she really know *all* of the consequences? Does Archie really care about *all* of the consequences? Is he not much more interested in what will happen to him in the next few months? How much knowledge must a client have before the social worker can be sure that she has met the demands of the Code of Ethics?
- Would it be ethical for Muriel to design a package of relevant services on the basis of her assessment—and on the basis of Archie's wishes—and then ask Archie whether this package was acceptable?

Additional questions could be asked, but it is already clear that in social work practice informed consent is beset with many difficulties and that these difficulties often lead to ethical dilemmas.

COMMUNITY ORGANIZING AND INFORMED CONSENT

The ethical dimensions of obtaining of informed consent are especially problematic when the client is a community or neighborhood, as may be the case for social workers engaged in community organizing. A social worker involved in a neighborhood renewal program must consider whether the elected representatives really represent all residents. Does their informed consent suffice or must every resident consent? What is the situation when the initiative for intervention comes from the outside? What does it mean to obtain informed consent when the social worker's initial objective is to raise the residents' consciousness to the fact that there is a problem in their community and that they can do something about it? Requiring every person's consent in this latter situation may be tantamount to ruling out any intervention activity, yet intervening without informed consent is a violation of professional ethics. What should a social worker do in these circumstances? Hardina (2004) suggests that the best method for ensuring that most participants agree with an approach is to hold a "meeting in which all members debate risks and benefits of the proposed action and attempt to reach a consensus" (p. 599). This approach can be time consuming, and there is no guarantee that consensus can be reached, however "constituents should be fully informed about the consequences of their actions, especially when personal sacrifices (such as job loss, arrest, or social stigma) are great" (Hardina, 2004, p. 599).

WAYS OF CONSENTING

Oliver Goldsmith (1764) wrote that "silence gives consent," but social workers have learned that silence and other nonverbal signals, such as a nod, or even a verbal yes may be deceptive and may indicate something other than consent. Clients may be ashamed to withhold consent or simply not understand what they have been asked to agree to. A social worker is obligated to offer a full explanation of what the intervention involves, what the projected benefits and risks will be, what other options may be available, and what might happen if the client does not consent. All this must be presented in language that the client can understand. Language per se is important. But even more important may be how the social worker presents the information. Many clients have short attention spans. Exceeding that time span may mean turning the client off, even if the language is simple.

Aside from questions of disclosure of information, voluntariness, and competency, the various forms of consent also make for ethical problems. Consider the following possibilities:

- *Direct or tacit. Direct* refers to the client's verbal response, whereas *tacit* means that the client remained silent. Is it ethical for the social worker to assume that the client agrees when he does not respond to her suggestion?
- *Oral or written.* Written consent is often preferred, but is the use of oral consent necessarily unethical? Does using a written consent form automatically eliminate all ethical dilemmas? Should services that are typically provided via telephone (e.g., suicide hotlines) be withheld until written consent can be obtained? Can other forms of documentation that consent was obtained

(e.g., audio recordings of the verbal consent or copies of e-mail messages) substitute for written consent?

- *Past/present.* Does current dissent invalidate all previous consents? Is this a case of change of mind, diminished competence, situational fear, or something else? To state this dilemma differently, how much credence should a social worker give to a person's change of mind when she knows that in the past the client consistently expressed a contrary view?

- *Present/future.* Can a social worker assume that the client would (or will) agree with her decision if he were (or when he becomes) more aware of what is involved? Can a social worker wait to obtain informed consent until the client and the process is far enough along so the client understands fully the consequences of the decision?

- *Forced consent.* One way to obtain a client's consent is to frame options in such a way that the client will consent, no matter what the response. For example, the social worker may ask, "Do you want to move to the nursing home this week or next?" Is this an ethical way of obtaining consent? Another form of forced consent is by threatening undesirable consequences unless the client consents. What if the agency provides only one kind of service and if the client does not agree, he cannot be served? In this situation, is it ethical to threaten no-service-unless-you-agree?

As we have indicated repeatedly, each of these forms of consent presents ethical problems and dilemmas. One thing is certain: Involving the client in providing informed consent cannot be a one-time activity, but must be an ongoing process. Some have suggested that all of the problems around informed consent can be avoided or resolved by employing good clinical practice. For example, if a client is fully involved in the decision-making process, questions of consent will not arise. It is a fact, however, that even formal contracting does not resolve all the problems involved in obtaining informed consent. The power gap between client and worker inevitably results in contract negotiations between unequals. Some unintended coercion may be brought into play, leading the client to agree to choices that are not entirely of his choosing.

What methods could you use to improve the client's ability to provide informed consent? Is it appropriate to give the client time to consider the options whenever possible? What are the advantages and disadvantages of providing the client with a written summary of his options to take home and think about? Are there times when providing a written document could place a client at risk (e.g., what might happen if Mrs. Madurai's husband found a form listing the women's shelters in her area)? Would it be helpful to encourage the client to discuss options with others before making a decision?

DUTY TO PROTECT

The ground rules that govern how all mental health professionals, including social workers, must deal with violent or potentially violent clients were fundamentally changed by a landmark legal decision (*Tarasoff v. The Regents of the University of California*). This landmark legal case was based on a murder that took place in 1969 in California. A young man—Prosenjit Poddar—who was a voluntary outpatient at the student health service at the University of California, Berkeley, told his therapist that he intended to kill his former girlfriend just as soon as she returned from an out-of-town trip. Shortly thereafter, the young woman—Tatiana Tarasoff—was killed by the young man. The young woman's parents subsequently charged the therapist with neglect. The therapist argued that he was not guilty because his professional relationship with the young client/killer meant that all information he received was confidential. However, the judge held that:

> Public policy favoring protection of the confidential character of patient/psychotherapist relationship must yield in instances in which disclosure is essential to avert danger to others; the protective privilege ends where the public peril begins.
>
> When a therapist determines, or should determine, that his patient presents a serious danger of violence to another, *he incurs an obligation to use reasonable care to protect the intended victim* against such danger. This duty may call for him (1) to warn the intended victim or (2) [to inform] others likely to apprise the victim of the danger, (3) to notify the police, or (4) to take whatever other steps are reasonably necessary under the circumstances (*Tarasoff v. The Regents of the University of California,* 1976, 551 P 2d 334 at 340; emphasis added).

We have cited the *Tarasoff* ruling at length because it has become very important for all mental health professionals, including social workers. Although it was a California court case, this case has had a nationwide impact. The case not only changed the ground rules for mental health professionals when dealing with violent or potentially violent clients but it also stimulated anxiety among many mental health professionals. Major concerns were expressed at the time by many professionals who feared the decision would undermine the practice of therapy by destroying its confidential nature.

Since 1976, mental health practitioners have been required to take reasonable measures to protect potential victims from a client's foreseeable violent acts. Subsequent court decisions further defined the *Tarasoff* doctrine. One decision explained that under the *Tarasoff* doctrine, a social worker or other professional (1) must be able to predict "pursuant to the standards of his profession" that the client is violently dangerous and (2) must be able to specify one or more clearly identifiable victims (*Brady v. Hopper,* 1983, 751 F 2d 329).

In another decision involving the murder of the victim's minor children, the California Supreme Court extended the *Tarasoff* doctrine beyond the identified intended victim to others who also might be in danger. In the same decision, the court ruled that a therapist's failure to use reasonable care to protect a third party from harm constituted "professional negligence," rather than "ordinary negligence." This definition allows suits to be initiated for up to three years after the injury occurred, rather than the usual one-year limitation (Butz, 1985, p. 87, citing *Hedlund v. Superior Court,* 1983, 669, P 2d 41).

In recent years, the duty to protect (sometimes called the duty to warn) has been further extended by various legal decisions, but practice applications are not always entirely clear. Decisions by various courts clarify some questions that professional practitioners face. For example, a 1994 "California appellate court case, *Gross v. Allen,* (22Cal.App.4th.354) expands the *Tarasoff* duty to include suicide threats. It also makes explicit that a psychotherapist's 'duty to warn' includes informing a subsequent therapist about a patient's known dangerousness" Meyers, 1997, p. 365). In *Ewing v. Goldstein* (120 Cal. App. 4th 807 [2004]) and *Ewing v. Northridge Hospital Medical Center* (120 Cal. App. 4th 1289 [2004]), a California Court of Appeal found that family members' reports of threats could also trigger a clinician's duty to warn, suggesting that the clinician does not need to have heard the threats directly in order to have a duty to protect (Ewing, 2005).

The details of the duty to protect vary from state to state (Beck, 1998); it may be ill defined in states where laws regulating professions (or legal decisions interpreting these laws) do not make reference to the *Tarasoff* duty. Some states have enacted *Tarasoff* legislation, and others have not. Some states have adopted and extended the *Tarasoff* principle; others have contained third-party liability within the context of the state's protective disclosure law. Some states acknowledge circumscribed duties to warn or protect (Felthous & Kachigian, 2001). Even the state of California revisited these issues in a criminal case (*People v. Felix,* Court of Appeals, 2001) and tested the limits of the duty to protect. This court held that applying the duty to protect principle without limitations would mean that those who need therapy for homicidal thoughts would not seek it because they would incriminate themselves while in the therapeutic relationship. Mental health professionals praised this ruling, but law enforcement personnel claimed it undermined the rights and safety of potential victims (Ewing, 2002).

Social workers should be alert to the legal dimensions regarding the duty to protect because these differ from state to state and from profession to profession. Some professions may receive the benefit of immunity from liability for breaches of confidentiality, and others may not. Some state laws create legal confidentiality as a right of the client but do not provide liability waivers for mental health practitioners who warn a potential victim. There is no general agreement on what is meant by "serious threat of physical violence," nor on the meaning of "intended" or "capable of being carried out." However, "most state statutes require an actual or serious threat; thus therapists in these jurisdictions no longer have to attempt to predict dangerousness" (Almason, 1997, p. 481).

Different states also vary in their requirements in regard to how the duty to protect should be discharged: warning the potential victim or someone close to the victim, notifying the police, starting commitment proceedings, or informing mental health evaluators of the nature of the threat. Each of the alternatives may present new ethical dilemmas. Reporting to the police, for example, may fulfill the duty to protect, but the police may use this information in ways that social workers would consider unethical (Egley, 1992). Does a social worker who practices in a state without a legal duty to warn have an ethical responsibility to do so when her client presents a danger to another person?

In addition to varying state legislation and court decisions concerning the duty to protect, a fundamental issue of concern is the assessment of the probability of violence. Consider, for example, the situation described in Exemplar 8.4.

8.4	AN IDLE OR SERIOUS THREAT?

EP 2.1.2

Rufus Hall is seeking help with his four-year marriage. According to Rufus, his wife, Sara, refuses to come to counseling with him and has been threatening to get a divorce. Rufus reports that on occasion he gets very angry with his wife and has slapped her once or twice. During one session, he said that he loves his wife and would kill her if she goes through with her threat to get a divorce. His social worker, Jillian Adams, who lives in the same community as Rufus and Sara, knows that Sara recently saw a lawyer about a divorce. To date, Rufus has only spoken of slaps, but Jillian is uncertain how to respond to his comment that he would kill Sara if she divorces him.

Should Jillian report the husband's comment as a threat? If yes, to whom? How can she assess the seriousness of his statement? Would it matter if she knew his "slaps" had been more violent than he reported? What information would be helpful in deciding whether the threat to Sara's safety should be reported?

Admittedly, the prediction of violence is not a hard science. While some personality characteristics have been found to be related to a higher probability of violent behavior, potential violence cannot be predicted with any certainty. Beck (1998) commented on the difficulty of predicting violent behavior, especially for clients who are likely to be impulsive, such as those with certain mental disorders. "When violence appears to be impulsive for whatever reason, courts are reluctant to find the defendants negligent" for not warning a potential victim (Beck, 1998, p. 381).

Some ethical problems that arise in regard to the *Tarasoff* duty are not readily answered in the NASW (2008) Code of Ethics. Social work ethics prohibit revealing confidential information, but this ethical imperative may be overridden "for compelling professional reasons. The general expectation that social workers will keep information confidential does not apply when disclosure is necessary to prevent serious, foreseeable, and imminent harm to a client or other identifiable person" (1.07c). However, there remains much ambiguity about the precise meaning of "foreseeable and imminent harm."

Currently, there is no statute or model law that provides a comprehensive definition of all the components of the duty to protect. The major question is under what conditions do social workers have a duty to protect potential victims. Because the legal situation changes so frequently in this area of the law, even social workers who practice in states where there is no clear precedent would be well advised to use legal and professional consultations where the situation makes it possible to do so.

There are those who hold that the *Tarasoff* doctrine does not present social workers with any new ethical problems because the requirement to break confidentiality and protect the intended victim applies only in specific instances. Beck (1998) suggests that the legal and ethical issues surrounding the duty to warn are "remarkably congruent with good clinical practice" (p. 375). When the duty to protect does apply, the ethical decision screens in Chapter 4 provide guidance because saving human life from direct and immediate danger is a higher-order ethical principle than confidentiality. The ethical issue becomes problematic only because the risk to life is often ambiguous.

Since the initial establishment of a clinician's duty to warn in order to protect third parties from violence, courts have adopted and expanded *Tarasoff*-like duties. At the same time, although more gradually, limits have also been placed on this duty by courts. These limits on the duty to protect have often been codified in state statutes that explicitly make reference to the *Tarasoff* duty and the acceptable ways of discharging this duty. Given the "mixed" and changing legal definition of the duty to protect, social workers should be certain that they know the law in their state and use professional supervision and legal consultation to determine appropriate actions (Walcott, Cerundolo, & Beck, 2001).

CRITICAL THINKING EXERCISES

EP 2.1.3

1. Investigate the laws in your state (or neighboring states or your home state) concerning confidentiality, privileged communication, and the duty to protect, as they apply to social workers.

2. If you are in a field placement, find out what kinds of informed consent documents exist. If the agency permits, share the documents with the class and compare and contrast the different types of forms used. What are the strengths and limitations of each form?

3. Prepare a brief to be presented to your state legislature, urging that the privileged communication rule be extended to the client/social worker relationship and that it include group, couple, and family therapy. What, if any, limits would you suggest placing on privileged communication?

4. Divide the class into groups of two. In each group, have one person assume the role of the social worker and the other the role of an applicant who is seeking help for coping with an alcoholic and physically abusive significant other. The specific task is for the social worker to inform the applicant/client of the limits of confidentiality. Students should try several different approaches and report to the class the one they think is most effective and best meets the demands of the Code of Ethics.

5. Divide the class into groups of two. In each group, have one person assume the role of the social worker and the other the role of an applicant who is seeking help with parenting issues. The specific task is for the social worker to inform the applicant/client of the limits of confidentiality, especially given the possibility of the need to report child maltreatment to the appropriate agency. Students should try several different approaches and report to the class the one they think is most effective and best meets the demands of the Code of Ethics.

6. Earlier in this chapter we discussed a number of situations in Great Britain requiring breaches of confidentiality that were described by Bond and Mitchell (2008). Can you identify the situations in your state that require mandatory breaches of confidentiality?

7. What methods do social workers in your agency or who are known to you use to make certain they comply with providing informed consent to clients or patients? What are some of the practical difficulties they have experienced? How did they solve the problems?

8. Your agency is reviewing its policy on giving clients access to their own case records. Almost all staff members agree to abide by the Code of Ethics, but there is a difference of opinion on how to define "reasonable access" and "exceptional circumstances when there is compelling evidence that such access would cause serious harm to the client"

(1.08a). Try to define these in ways that are congruent with both professional ethics and clients' rights. If there are differences of opinion in your class, organize a discussion to examine the strengths and weaknesses of each position. Can the class reach consensus on how to best define these issues?

SUGGESTIONS FOR ADDITIONAL READINGS

Palmer and Kaufman (2003) explore informed consent and how it applies to the multicultural context of many therapy and other situations. Galambos (2005) examines issues related to confidentiality in rural social work practice and maintaining confidentiality in the face of dual relationships. Reamer (2005) reviews the situation regarding confidentiality issues in practice with children regarding ethics risk management. Slaughter and colleagues (2007) provide guidelines for obtaining consent and assent to participate in research from people with dementia; while these guidelines were developed for research, many of them could be adapted for practice as well. Zayas, Cabassa, and Perez (2005) report on a tool developed for screening capacity to consent.

WEBSITES OF INTEREST

- For extensive information on HIPAA, including the statute and consumer information: www.hhs.gov/ocr/hipaa/
- NASW provides extensive information on HIPAA for social workers at: http://www.socialworkers.org/hipaa/default.asp
- For information on Megan's Law, which requires sex offender registration and community notification, as well as links to state laws: www.klaaskids.org/pg-legmeg.htm
- For information on the Adam Walsh Child Protection and Safety Act of 2006: http://www.fd.org/odstb_AdamWalsh.htm
- For an extensive list of publications on legal issues, including the *Tarasoff* duty and Megan's Law (this site is password protected, so you will only have access to these articles if you are a member of NASW): www.socialworkers.org/ldf/legal_issue/

COMPETENCY NOTES

Identify as a professional social worker and conduct oneself accordingly: This chapter addresses issues of confidentiality, duty to protect, and informed consent, which are EP 2.1.1 important aspects of professional social work practice.

Apply social work ethical principles to guide professional practice: In this chapter, we discussed ethical issues related to confidentiality, duty to protect, and informed EP 2.1.2 consent.

Apply critical thinking to inform and communicate professional judgments: Exemplars and questions throughout the chapter, as well as critical thinking exercise at EP 2.1.3 the end of the chapter, provide opportunities for critical thinking.

SOCIAL JUSTICE, LIMITED RESOURCES, AND ADVOCACY

CHAPTER **9**

This chapter addresses the CSWE 2008 EPAS Educational Policy 2.1.1 on becoming a professional social worker, and we continue content on Educational Policy 2.1.2 about using social work ethical principles to guide professional practice, specifically related to issues of social justice, limited resources, and advocacy. We provide several exemplars, questions, and critical thinking exercises that we hope you will use to apply critical thinking to inform and communicate professional judgments (Educational Policy 2.1.3). This chapter addresses Educational Policy 2.1.4 to engage diversity and difference in practice through discussion of issues related to diversity and social justice. Finally, this chapter addresses Educational Policy 2.1.5 to advance human rights and social and economic justice.

It is a basic law of contemporary democratic societies that every person has an equal right to obtain social benefits and an equal obligation to carry social burdens. This principle is based on the first-order societal value of equity and suggests that goods should be distributed as widely and as equally as possible. Persons in similar situations should be treated in the same way, unless this equality of treatment is outweighed by other considerations such as fairness and beneficence. A corollary of this first-order value is that those in the most needy and most vulnerable groups need to receive greater resources and more services in order to obtain their "fair share" and "fair opportunities" (Rawls, 2001). From this societal value, social workers have derived the professional rule that obligates them to work for social justice and to distribute available resources on an equal basis to all clients, unless unequal distribution is indicated for the reasons suggested by beneficence and fairness.

COMMITMENT TO SOCIAL JUSTICE

Many social workers agree that everyone is entitled to an equal share of available resources, yet an ethical problem occurs when the available resources are so limited that an equal distribution is not possible and choices must be made about to whom to allocate these. In other words, some will receive these resources and others will not, thus resulting in unequal treatment. For example, when a county has only 20 beds for chronically ill older people, these cannot be distributed on an equal basis to 30 clients who qualify and who desperately need this service. The equity value may create ethical problems even with respect to goods and services that lend themselves to an equal division (e.g., the social worker's time or the department's budget), because another professional value may obligate the practitioner to allocate more of her time or resources to meet the specific needs of a certain client. In the sections that follow, we will discuss how time, inequality, societal factors, diversity, and discrimination are related to a commitment to equality and social justice.

TIME

Time is a very limited and precious resource in the social work process. For example, if a social worker in a family agency is available 30 hours each week for direct service to clients, is each of her 30 clients entitled to a one-hour session every week? For some clients, an hour a week may be more than what they need, while for others it may not be sufficient. Is it ethical for a social worker to devote several hours to one client this week to help him cope with an unexpected and sudden family crisis, even if this results in less time being available for other clients? Many social workers recall situations when a client could have received more effective service if only there had been more time available. Ethical dilemmas can occur both in regard to fairness (equity) and equality (equally situated persons receiving equal treatment). For example, the attempt to observe equity in the allocation of time to clients results in several ethical dilemmas, one of which is illustrated in Exemplar 9.1.

What would you do? What other ethical issues, in addition to the equity issue, does this worker face? What are the social worker's obligations to Doreen, her parents, other clients with whom she has appointments scheduled, and the community? How should a social worker be prepared to deal with such unexpected situations?

 EP 2.1.2

INEQUALITY AND THE DISTRIBUTION OF SCARCE RESOURCES

Americans have accepted as a self-evident truth that all persons are created equal. From this first-order value, social workers have derived the ethical rules of "equal distribution of resources" and "equal access to opportunities." Equality is often equated with democracy and social justice. Those raised in this tradition often find it difficult to understand how anyone can raise questions about it. They are upset when it is suggested that an equal distribution of resources is not always ethical and may result in serious injustices.

It is self-evident that all people are entitled to the best medical services, but some have asked whether it is right that medical resources, especially scarce and expensive life-extending technologies and instruments, are distributed equally to all, regardless of a patient's age. Daniel Callahan (1987), a philosopher and medical ethicist, does not seem to think that such an equalitarian approach is ethical. He writes that medicine should "resist the tendency to provide to the aged life-extending capabilities developed primarily to help younger people avoid premature and untimely death" (p. 24). He suggests that age be used as a decision criterion for allocating life-extending therapies. Does this mean that open-heart surgery should not be available to people over a given age, such as 80? Is not the life of an 84-year-old person as important and valuable as that of a 74-year-old person? Some would argue that the chances of a successful operation decrease rapidly as people grow older. Others avoid this statistical argument by noting that it is preferable to use limited resources to add 20 years of life rather than one or two years, particularly when the younger person can still make a valuable contribution to society, while the aging person may be totally dependent on others for the rest of his life. In recent years, a version of this problem has been noted in Oregon, which uses a prioritized list of health services for its Medicaid program. Services are listed from most important to least important for their comparative benefit to the population served (Oregon Health Services Commission, 2006).

9.1 | **INCEST IN THE SCHILD FAMILY**

Doreen Schild is a 13-year-old with a history of school truancy, alcohol and drug experimentation, and several attempts at running away from home. Her parents appear warm and accepting, but the family agency worker who has been meeting with Doreen for the past four weeks suspects that the real problem is Doreen's home life. Today was the fifth session with Doreen. The conversation was routine, and little of significance was said until three minutes before the next client's scheduled appointment. Suddenly, Doreen said that both her father and older brother have tried repeatedly to have sex with her, but thus far she has not let them go all the way. When she told her mother about this, she was told to forget it had ever happened. As Doreen related this information, she became noticeably more upset.

The social worker realized that this interview could not be terminated just because time was up. Doreen was agitated, and the session could not be ended at that point. Later, the worker would need to make a report of suspected child abuse to child protective services. She was not sure how long the discussion with Doreen would take and was worried about how long she could keep the next client waiting. Doreen could easily use all of the next client's hour, but that would not be fair to the other clients scheduled for that day, who may also be experiencing serious difficulties.

Oregon was the first state in the United States to draw up a formal procedure for prioritizing health care. The Oregon Health Plan (OHP) is administered mainly by private health plans. The principle behind the OHP was that, when funds are limited, the state should deliver fewer services to more people. When costs rise or revenues are diminished, cuts should be made to lower-priority services, not to the number of people covered (Saha, Coffman, & Smits, 2010). However, the federal Health Care Financing Administration began denying Oregon's requests to move the priority line upward, and the number of people who were covered steadily declined. The priority list remains in force, and a million and a half people are covered whom otherwise would not be covered. At the time this is being written, it is unclear how Medicaid and the Oregon Health Plan will be affected by the Patient Protection and Affordable Care Act (2010), generally known as "ObamaCare." There are suggestions that many persons lacking insurance will be enrolled in state Medicaid programs.

Under the OHP, health care dollars available determine which priorities are met. As the program costs have grown, the list of covered procedures has become shorter. In 2009, the state would only pay for the first 503 procedures. Between 2002 and 2009, priorities were reordered. Life-saving procedures ranked high in 2002, but they were moved to lower positions in 2009, whereas procedures less related to life and death have climbed to the top. For example, Type 1 diabetes was ranked second in 2002 but dropped to 10th place in 2009, thus being placed behind spending on smoking cessation, sterilization, and drug abuse treatment. Bariatric surgery for people with Type II diabetes and a 35 or greater Body Mass Index (BMI) is ranked 33rd. Stomach surgery to control obesity is prioritized as more important than surgery to repair internal organs, a hip fracture, or a hernia showing symptoms of obstruction or strangulation. In 2006, a Citizens Council recommended that the program consider the rule of rescue; death is final, and the processes of prevention, prolonging life, and promoting health all start with the saving of life. According to Gorman (2009), this did not mean that lives must be saved at any cost, but it did mean that individuals in desperate circumstances should sometimes receive more help than can be justified, as a general rule, because of special circumstances. Nevertheless, the 2009, list emphasized preventive care and chronic disease management because these services are less expensive and more effective than treatment later in the course of a disease. According to Gorman (2009) this policy change was a result of the efforts of active political constituencies in regard to preventive care for the healthy and management of chronic illnesses.

There are, of course, defenders and detractors of the program. The case for prioritizing health care is straightforward. Life and health are basic goods and people have a strong claim on the means necessary to sustain them. But the claims must compete with other claims that might be more important for the good of the society. Hackler (2009) suggests the following considerations regarding the ethic of prioritizing:

1. There are other equally important needs competing for scarce resources.
2. There are no alternative ways to produce equivalent savings.
3. Savings from denied services will benefit other patients or be invested in equally important social needs.
4. Policies and procedures for limiting access to treatment are applied equitably to all.
5. Limits are self-imposed through democratic processes.

Based on the description of Oregon's priority system, is the program ethical? What roles should social workers have in the debate about this issue? How might a health care priority system such as the one in Oregon impact social workers' work with clients in need of health care services?

Hackler (2009) argues that prioritizing is ethical if funding is truly needed for other essential social goods and services; if alternative ways of limiting medical spending have been attempted; if the money saved will be directed to more compelling needs; and if limits are applied equitably to everyone. Limits should be self-imposed in the sense that they are openly developed and generally accepted as fair. Accepting prioritizing is painful for most Americans because of our conviction that human life is priceless. There is a proposed universal coverage plan for all Oregonians. If approved, this package will serve as a minimum set of covered benefits, beginning with public programs and health plans participating in a state insurance exchange.

Deciding the allocation of societal resources on the basis of potential returns to society gives rise to other serious ethical problems. The social contribution of highly intelligent people may be more valuable than that of people with a lower intelligence and perhaps more significant than that of persons with developmental disabilities. But does this give society the ethical right to provide open-heart surgery only to those whose IQ is above 140 or some other arbitrary line or only to people with a college degree? Is it ethical for society to limit such open-heart surgery to those with sufficient income to be able to pay for this life-saving operation? This diabolic argument can be pushed even further by arguing for the elimination of all undesirables, a policy implemented by Nazi Germany in the 1940s. Although few will maintain that the "final solution" was ethical or moral, the implication of this approach for the unequal distribution of resources demands further careful thought. These examples come from the health field, but parallel problems occur in social work situations. Can you think of any?

Even if you have not yet encountered such situations, many social work resources in health, mental health, and child welfare are not distributed equally. In 2003, infants born to Black mothers in the United States died before their first birthdays at the rate of 14 per 1,000 live births (Barr, 2008). For the same year, the infant mortality rate for babies born to White mothers was 5.7 per 1,000 live births. One main contributing factor to this difference in infant mortality is the much higher frequency with which babies born to Black mothers are of low or very low birth weight. Babies at these weights are much more likely to die before their first birthday than babies with normal birth weight. Health disparities also exist for adult men and women. For example, in 2002, the highest rate of high blood pressure was among Black women (more than 50% higher than for White women), and the rate of high blood pressure among black men is nearly 50% greater than that of white men (Barr, 2008).

Members of minority groups also suffer disproportionately from mental illness because they often lack access to services, receive lower quality care, and are less likely to seek help when in distress (Goode, 2001). These inequalities appear to be inequitable and most probably are the result of the distribution of health and other resources. Some of the health and mental health disparities are also likely due to exposure to unhealthy stressful living and work conditions and to inadequate access to essential health and other public services (King, 2009.)

Similarly, in a review of child welfare research, it was found that "children of color and their families experience poorer outcomes and receive fewer services than their Caucasian counterparts" (Courtney et al., 1996, p. 99). A similar conclusion was reached by Rodenborg (2004), who found that when African American children were child welfare clients, they received fewer and lower quality services, fewer parental supports were made available, and these children were more likely to be placed in institutional placements. It is urgent that, wherever such unequal distribution of resources exists, this issue be reexamined and, if necessary, corrected by providing unequal (i.e., more and better) services to those who are in critical need.

The provision of unequal treatment can be overt but more often occurs in social agencies in more subtle and less formal ways. Exemplar 9.2 illustrates how unequal treatment can take place unofficially.

9.2	A FRIEND IN NEED IS A FRIEND INDEED

EP 2.1.2

Latoya Jefferson is a volunteer social worker in an emergency food pantry where persons come to obtain needed food for themselves and their families. The only requirement is that people answer several questions: name, household size, and source of income, not subject to verification. No one asks about living situations (a place to cook, ages of children, or special dietary needs). There are not enough paid staff and volunteers to run the pantry as it should be operated. Because of the shortage of supplies, families can only receive food once a month, but over time the staff and volunteers still get to know individuals and their situations.

Latoya, the paid director of the pantry, recently discovered that Keisha Attlee, a volunteer social worker, favors some clients over others. She chooses favorites who are especially friendly or who have well-disciplined and cute children. She also identifies those she thinks abuse the system; when food is in short supply, she refers the "abusers" to another pantry while assisting her favorites. When Latoya questioned Keisha about her discriminating so that some get needed supplies while others are referred elsewhere, Keisha replied, "In my view I am giving food to those who are most needy and cooperative. Aren't they entitled to the help? I know they will make good use of the food. Those I refer elsewhere may be selling the food and buying beer and whiskey. Furthermore, as a volunteer I don't want to be supervised. If you keep bothering me, I will just leave and you can do the distribution yourself."

What should Latoya do? If she bothers Keisha, the pantry loses an experienced volunteer worker whom they need because they are short of staff. Do the so-called abusers actually misuse the food? Does it make a difference if they do so? If Latoya keeps quiet, some families receive supplies while others do not. As it is now, who gets food often depends on who the volunteer is and only the luck of the draw determines who gets what.

As noted in Chapter 4, there is another side to inequality. Those who are not equal should receive special help (both services and resources) in order to gain equal access to life opportunities. It is this consideration that often justifies the unequal allocation of resources. Children with disabilities, for example, may receive more attention and greater resources than other children in order to compensate for their disabilities. A blind child will not have the same access to education as a sighted child unless society provides the blind child with extra resources, such as talking books and/or a reader. In other words, unequal allocation of resources to those who are not equal or who do not have equal access to life opportunities is more ethical than sticking to equality at all costs.

SOCIETAL RESPONSES TO DISTRIBUTION OF SCARCE RESOURCES

On a societal level, the United States and other countries are faced with many issues, including national security, health care, education, nutrition, and housing, and there is never enough money to fulfill all the needs completely. Between 1946 and 1964, the United States experienced a surge in births, totaling 78 million, known as the baby boomer generation. This group, now approaching (or already in) retirement, continues to grow as a percentage of the population. Consequently, the United States is now facing the cost of the baby boomers in regard to financial support in retirement (e.g., Social Security and other retirement funds) and health care, among other factors.

Simultaneously, as of 2009, there were approximately 14 million children in the United States (one fifth of all children) living in families with incomes below the federal poverty level (National Center for Child Poverty, 2010). When the true costs of raising a family are considered, there are estimates that up to 41% of children live in low-income families. Most of these children have parents who work but earn low wages, have unstable employment, or are unemployed, leaving families struggling to make ends meet. As a result, the children's ability to learn is impeded, and this problem can cascade into social, emotional, and behavioral problems. Poor health and mental health are associated with living in poverty (National Center for Child Poverty, 2010).

Whose needs should take priority? Or if priority cannot be assigned, then what should be the balance (trade-off) between caring for the older baby boomers and caring for the children in poverty? How would you answer this question, given limited societal resources?

Let us suggest several principles:

1. According to John Rawls (1971) in *A Theory of Justice*, the principle of justice should be considered: decisions should be to the greatest benefit of the least advantaged members of society. This latter point suggests the decision should be absolutist (deontological) and follow a fixed moral rule. Are the baby boomers or poor children "the least advantaged members of society"? Some argue that absolute justice demands that all needy people receive help. If there are insufficient resources, then the resources available should be evenly divided among those who need help. Do you agree with that perspective? What if there are measurable differences in degrees of need or other special circumstances?

2. On the other hand, ethical relativists (utilitarians) could argue that on the basis of the potential consequences of the decision, the lives of the young should take precedence. They are the future of the nation. The consequences of not providing them with adequate health, education, housing, and other resources are too costly in many ways. In addition, because they have not lived their lives, providing them support will enable them to have longer, healthier, more productive, and more constructive lives as citizens and workers.

3. We introduce a third choice. Neither argument is correct. The decision must be a tradeoff in which pragmatic ethics decides. The nation should do as much as possible for both aging and young people.

Which decision do you believe to be the most ethical? Would your decision differ if you had the following information available? The United States spends almost two and a half times as much on older adults as on children, measured on a per capita basis. When considering only the federal budget, the ratio rises to 7 to 1 (Isaacs, 2009). Furthermore, for the first time in history, in 2009 every single revenue dollar was committed before Congress voted on any spending program. This means that most of the government's basic functions are paid for out of growing (and believed by many to be unsustainable) deficits (Steuerle, 2010). The vast and growing size of unfunded health and retirement benefits will require that today's children will have to bear very heavy tax burdens when they become working age adults. Given this information, would you change your decision?

DISCRIMINATION AND DIVERSITY

Despite the continuing efforts of many social workers and other citizens, discrimination persists in the United States. In what has become increasingly a multiracial, multiethnic, and highly diverse society, competition for various resources undoubtedly exacerbates conflicts between groups; this conflict is especially evident during times of recession, economic changes, and increased international economic competition. But discrimination is not only the result of competition for scarce resources; discrimination can also be the result of prejudices and stereotypes, such as prejudging others on the basis of unproven assumptions about individuals and groups, and preexisting feelings and attitudes that are not relevant to the actual persons. For social workers, discrimination is a societal and professional problem that directly affects their practice, the availability of resources, and the delivery of social services. The NASW Code of Ethics (2008) states that:

> Social workers should not practice, condone, facilitate, or collaborate with any form of discrimination on the basis of race, ethnicity, national origin, color, sex, sexual orientation, *gender identity or expression*, age, marital status, political belief, religion, *immigration status*, or mental or physical disability. (4.02, the emphasis indicates the two new elements that were added in the 2008 revision to the NASW Code of Ethics)

Discrimination is contrary to the ethical standards of the profession. Whenever and wherever discrimination occurs, social workers cannot achieve their professional aims.

The ethical principles enunciated in the NASW Code (2008) call on social workers "to help people in need and to address social problems," to "pursue social change, particularly with and on behalf of vulnerable and oppressed individuals and groups of people," to be "mindful of individual differences and cultural and ethnic diversity," and to "promote, restore, maintain, and enhance the well-being of individuals, families, social groups, organizations, and communities" (Ethical Principles). There is a whole range of activities that are needed to fight discrimination, ranging from individual interactions to confrontation of institutional and societal racism. Some have suggested that there is a difference between the individual social worker's obligation to fight discrimination and the profession's obligation to root out discrimination. However, both individual social workers and the profession as an organization have a responsibility to address discrimination.

The NASW (2001) Standards for Cultural Competence in Social Work Practice call on social workers to become proficient "to respond respectfully and effectively to people of all cultures, languages, classes, races, ethnic backgrounds, religions, and other diversity factors in a manner that recognizes, affirms, and values the worth of individuals, families, and communities and protects and preserves the dignity of each" (p. 11).

EP 2.1.4

The Council on Social Work Education (CSWE) (2010) addressed these issues by including educational policies 2.1.4 and 2.1.5. Specifically, social workers understand how diversity characterizes and shapes the human experience and is critical to the formation of identity. The dimensions of diversity are understood as the intersectionality of multiple factors including age, class, color, culture, disability, ethnicity, gender, gender identity and expression, immigration status, political ideology, race, religion, sex, and sexual orientation. Social workers appreciate that, as a consequence of difference, a person's life experiences may include oppression, poverty, marginalization, and alienation as well as privilege, power, and acclaim. Social workers:

- recognize the extent to which a culture's structures and values may oppress, marginalize, alienate, or create or enhance privilege and power;
- gain sufficient self-awareness to eliminate the influence of personal biases and values in working with diverse groups;
- recognize and communicate their understanding of the importance of difference in shaping life experience; and
- view themselves as learners and engage those with whom they work as informants. (pp. 4–5 of 16)

EP 2.1.5

Each person, regardless of position in society, has basic human rights, such as freedom, safety, privacy, an adequate standard of living, health care, and education. Social workers recognize the global interconnections of oppression and are knowledgeable about theories of justice and strategies to promote human and civil rights. Social work incorporates social justice practices in organizations, institutions, and society to ensure that these basic human rights are distributed equitably and without prejudice. Social workers

- understand the forms and mechanisms of oppression and discrimination;
- advocate for human rights and social and economic justice; and
- engage in practices that advance social and economic justice. (p. 5 of 16)

NASW and other social work professional associations have responsibilities to eliminate discrimination through advocacy, social action, legal, and other efforts within their organizations and in society. Discrimination in society and the profession makes it difficult to achieve social work's goals and ethical aims of equal access—equitable services and resources—for the fulfillment of individuals and society. Discrimination is unethical, and its existence tends to create additional social problems. Individual social workers also have an ethical responsibility to work toward the elimination of discrimination in their practice, employment, and in society, first because it is unethical and second because it contributes to the creation of additional social problems.

Earlier in this chapter, we reviewed reports that suggest that discrimination exists in provision of health, mental health, and child welfare services. It has been suggested that in these services some social workers may have been responsible for serious ethical breaches. Even though they did not necessarily engage in deliberate unethical activities, their behavior was unethical if they remained silent in the face of systematic institutional discrimination. The single child welfare worker may not be able to change the entire system, but this is hardly a justification to avoid attempts to change as much of one's local system as possible. What are the ethical obligations of social workers who encounter such ethics violations by systems or institutions? What advice does the NASW (2008) Code of Ethics provide social workers who find themselves in these situations?

What should you do if you are on the staff of a training program for young adults whose funding will be cut unless the program serves both White and African American young adults? At present, few Whites are enrolled. In order to meet the demands of the funding agency, staff are now making strenuous efforts to recruit qualified White applicants, even though there is a waiting list of eligible African American candidates. In these circumstances, is it ethical to give preference to Whites? Should you report the situation publicly, even though as a result the program may lose its major funding base? If you do not serve more White young adults, funding will stop, and no one—neither White nor African American young adults—will receive the service they now receive. If you do comply and recruit more White participants, the result will be that the program will serve fewer African American young adults. Weigh the alternatives: What is the ethical thing to do?

DISCRIMINATION AND ADOPTIONS

Many more children are available for adoption than there are families to adopt them. Child welfare agencies usually seek adoptive families from heterosexual two-parent or single-parent families. Gay men and lesbians often encounter legal and other barriers when they attempt to adopt children. This discriminatory pattern prevails even though the traditional heterosexual two-parent nuclear family has decreased and now is a diminishing percentage of the various types of U.S. families. As of 2006, while the total number of married couples was higher than ever before, less than half of the nation's households were made up of married couples (with and without children) (Roberts, 2006). The effect of excluding nontraditional families from adopting means that some children will remain in foster care longer before they are placed in permanent adoptive homes. Yet social workers who advocate placement of a child with a homosexual person or couple may be subjected to ridicule, ostracism, and other career-damaging reactions (Ryan, Perlmutter, & Groza, 2004). Pressures to deselect gay men or lesbians as adoptive parents can come from peer and/or supervisor influences. Similarly, a social worker who believes that it is in the best interest of the child to be adopted by a traditional family could be pressured by a supervisor and peers to facilitate adoption into a gay or lesbian family. In such cases, a social worker may have to choose among loyalty to herself and her career, loyalty to her supervisor, and loyalty to her professional values.

Child custody disputes may be complicated by parents' sexual orientations—for example, between a formerly married parent who now identifies as homosexual and the former spouse, or two gay people who agreed to co-parent but are now separated. When two gay individuals co-parent, they may both be adoptive parents or one may have conceived the child through artificial insemination while the other has shared in the care giving without adopting the child. If the couple separates, who receives custody of the child may depend on the prevailing community attitudes toward homosexuality and toward gay or lesbian parents, as discussed in Exemplar 9.3.

EP 2.1.2

| 9.3 | FAILURE TO ADOPT |

Janice McNally, a highly successful attorney with a very busy professional life, including frequent work-related travel, and Virginia Barker, a sales clerk in a mall who frequently changes jobs, have been in a long-term relationship. They agreed to have a child to be conceived by Janice as the biological mother. When Susan was born, Virginia began, but failed to complete, the adoption process. Both Janice and Virginia love the child and at first shared equally in the parenting. Janice's high income made possible many extras for Susan such as play groups, day camps, arts and crafts classes, and music lessons. For a number of years, the couple remained compatible and cared for Susan together, and the child bonded with both of them. When Susan was 8 years old, Virginia and Janice separated; Virginia asked for joint custody of Susan, which Janice refused to provide.

Judge Watson assigned Roberta Stevenson, a social worker employed by the court, to study the situation and to make recommendations to him as to what he should decide. Roberta, who had special training regarding lesbian adoptions, recommended to Judge Watson that Virginia should have major visitation rights because she has been a significant parental figure and that the best interest of the child is best served by a two-parent relationship.

However, the judge has views not supported by the history and behaviors of all involved. The prevailing community belief is that children raised by lesbians suffer harm, and Judge Watson believes that having a lesbian parent—whatever the legalities—will by itself affect a child's sexual identity, lead to peer rejection, or expose the child to unusual images of family life. He thinks that to allow Virginia visitation rights would only make a bad situation worse, and there is room in the law for leeway for his decision.

What should Roberta do? She is an employee of the court but has dual responsibilities—to the child Susan and to the court. As long as she is employed by the court, her duties are clear. She can try to persuade the judge, but in the final analysis, the judge makes decisions to be implemented by social workers and others. If Roberta believes the judge's decision is contrary to her professional and ethical judgments, how should she respond? What is in the best interest of Susan? How should Roberta respond to Judge Watson's request, and what should she recommend about Susan's future? What ethical dilemmas can you identify? Where can guidance be found for dealing with this situation? Are there other ethical dilemmas in different situations where a social worker is asked to make recommendations to a judge, for example, if the social worker recommended probation but the judge ruled imprisonment? Does the social worker have the right (legal, professional, and/or ethical) to accept some of the judge's rulings and not others?

LIMITED RESOURCES

The ethical problems resulting from the equality-and-inequality principle are often aggravated by limited resources. If resources were unlimited, in theory there would be no problem in providing all persons with the help they need. However, in the real world, there are never enough resources to do everything that should be done. Life is a zero-sum game—allocating a scarce resource to one person means that another will not receive it. The concept of limited resources, however, may be a manipulation of language, used to conceal certain deliberate decisions. Often it means that the available resources have already been allocated elsewhere or that commitments or priorities have been shifted. During George W. Bush's presidency, tax cuts, Iraq and Afghanistan, and the war on terrorism became top priorities. It has been argued that waging the war on terrorism makes it necessary to assign a lower priority and make fewer resources available to other important programs, including social programs designed to eradicate poverty, eliminate discrimination, and improve human services. Even though overall societal resources are limited, it is possible to assign vast resources to particular programs when this has been decided on the highest level. If there is a wide consensus that a certain program deserves the highest priority, or powerful decision-making forces conclude it is necessary, this program will receive funding even at the expense of limiting allocations for other important projects.

If this is the meaning of limited resources, the focus of ethical decision making shifts from the micro to the macro, from the specific case to societal allocations. This process occurs on the organizational and agency level when one program has been prioritized. As a result, other programs may not receive the support necessary. Even on the individual level, this process operates when a worker makes a decision that a certain project or population group or intervention method should receive priority—this decision is always made at the expense of all other projects, populations, or methods.

On one level, the ethical problem facing the social work practitioner will be how to allocate the resources that she controls. On another level, the profession as an organized group and individual social workers as citizens have an ethical responsibility to become involved in the societal allocation process—that is, the political process. For example, home health care, a major segment of community-based long-term care, is especially important for frail older adults. When budgets for this program are cut back because of soaring costs, many of these older adults are pushed into nursing homes and hospitals, even though this creates unnecessary dependency and is more costly. Social workers have a responsibility on ethical and other grounds to advocate for continued and adequate home health care services (Beder, 1998).

Much of what social workers can and cannot do is determined by political decision makers. When the legislature passes budgets, it determines to a large extent priorities and resources available both for public and voluntary agencies and institutions. Other political decisions have a major impact on the nation's economic health, rate of economic growth, availability of jobs, and other indicators that have a direct or indirect impact on what social workers are or should be doing. Are social workers merely passive observers of these political processes? Or is there an ethic of responsibility that obligates social workers to take an active part in these societal processes? We agree with Siporin (1985b) and Goldstein (1998) that social workers are moral agents who have a responsibility to influence organizations and communities. Priorities and commitments determine resource allocations. Significant resources have been allocated to drug wars and rehabilitation programs, whereas considerably less money has been allocated to solve the problems of the homeless. What are the ethical implications of such decisions? What can social workers do about this? Should social workers become active in political campaigns? Run for political office?

Ethical Problems in Allocating Limited Resources

Many allocation decisions are made at the highest political level in Washington or at a state capitol, settings in which most social workers do not feel at home, but which nevertheless require the ethical attention and skills of social workers. At other times, such decisions are made much closer to home. Consider the decision facing the social workers in Exemplar 9.4.

EP 2.1.2

| 9.4 | Refugees in Westport |

Centro Latino is an agency in Westport, a community that has always had a large concentration of Spanish-speaking immigrants. Centro Latino was started as an indigenous self-help group in the 1960s by immigrants from Latin America. Today, its budget is met largely by the United Way and supplemented at times by specific state and federal grants. Though volunteers are still used, most assignments are now handled by professional staff members. The decision-making powers are vested in the agency's board of directors, made up largely of Spanish-speaking residents of the community.

Early last year, more than 400 new Central American refugee families arrived in Westport. Centro Latino was able to generate a special onetime $100,000 grant to help in the adjustment of these refugees. The board of directors decided after lengthy discussion to allocate 20% of this grant to employ two more part-time social workers and to distribute the remaining funds directly to families to help them in their adjustment.

The detailed rules for distributing these funds were to be developed by the agency's staff. The current staff meeting was devoted to developing criteria for distributing the funds. The agency's director, Sandra Lopez, argued that equity demanded that each of the families receive an equal cash grant of approximately $200, which each family could use as it wished. Several staff members agreed with Sandra. But others urged that the limited funds be used where they could do the most good. Because the basic needs were already met, the new monies should be earmarked for special needs where an intensive use of resources could best achieve the desired objective. Each staff group believed that its proposal was professionally sound and supported by the professional ethics code.

If you had been participating in this staff meeting, which position would you have supported? Look at the NASW or other Code of Ethics. Do you find guidance there for your proposal? Consider the ethical principles screen in Chapter 4. What ethical considerations, including those of social justice and equity and equality, should be weighed before making a decision? What would you say is the ethically correct decision? Why?

Although social workers have an ideal of equality of treatment for those similarly placed, the distribution of scarce resources often reflects discrimination against various groups. The NASW (2008) Code of Ethics takes a strong stand for social workers to be proactive against discriminatory behaviors, both formal and informal, as individual professionals and for the profession itself. But there also can be ethical dilemmas connected to the distribution of scarce resources. In some instances, it is more ethical to make distinctions that favor those who are most needy rather than simply defending the idea of equality of treatment.

SOCIAL JUSTICE AND CLINICAL SOCIAL WORK

Wakefield (1988a, 1988b) suggests that social work clinical therapy is a factor in distributive justice. Therapy strives, according to this perspective, to ensure that no person is deprived of a fair minimum level of those basic social goods relevant to justice. Asking what psychological goods are essential to effective goal-oriented action, he answered that they include self-respect, self-esteem, social skills, assertiveness, self-confidence, self-knowledge, problem-solving skills, and self-organization. Increasing these mental and physical capacities provides for a fairer range of opportunities. Possession of these psychological goods makes it possible for people to pursue their own distinctive visions of life.

Swenson (2001) also argued—as Wakefield had done—that alleviating various deprivations (not just economic) can contribute to social justice. She notes that "populations at risk are people from whom social resources have been unjustly withheld; diversity entails respecting the cultures of everyone, not just the privileged few; and social work ethics and values emphasize the dignity and worth of each person, respect for difference, promoting social change, and multicultural competence" (p. 218). Swenson (2001) suggests some clinical theories are incongruent with social work ethics, while others are congruent. From her perspective, she suggests the strengths perspective in practice is congruent, but theories that pathologize, emphasize deficits, and blame the victim are incongruent. The latter theories cut people off from potential internal and external resources, thus increasing their relative deprivation.

Ethnic-sensitive social work practice emphasizes the significance of race, class, and ethnicity as mediators of people's daily objective experience and of their subjective sense of self (Swenson, 2001). Ethnic-sensitive practice can restore to people an appreciation for their particular cultural experience and identity. According to Swenson (2001), more universalistic approaches to people can deprive people of the social dimensions of their existence by not acknowledging the negative effects of racism, classism, and so on, and not emphasizing their strengths as positive resources. Feminist practice includes an analysis of power and offers a critique of power relations based on domination and subordination. Such practice suggests an alternative way of understanding and using power based on collaboration and cooperation instead of competition. Do you agree that those concepts she designates as incongruent with the ethics and values of the profession are unethical? Where in the Code do you see support for your decision? Similarly, do you agree with her view of the theories she views as congruent that they do indeed agree with the ethics and values of the profession? Where in the Code do you find support for your decision?

ETHICAL DILEMMAS IN ADVOCACY

The NASW (2008) Code of Ethics requires social workers to "advocate for living conditions conducive to the fulfillment of basic human needs and ... promote social, economic, political, and cultural values and institutions that are compatible with the realization of social justice" (6.01). Other circumstances that call for a social worker to serve as an advocate include situations where clients are served by an impaired, incompetent, or unethical social worker (Code, 2.09a, b; 2.10a, 2.11a, d) or when the practices of the employing organization are inconsistent with the NASW Code of Ethics (3.09c, d). The purpose of advocacy should always be "to ensure that all people have equal access to the resources, employment, services, and opportunities they require to meet their basic human needs and to develop fully" (6.04a). To be an advocate and to engage in advocacy is to adopt a particular stance about an issue of concern, advance a cause, and attempt to produce a result on behalf of an interest of a person, group, or cause (Cohen, 2004). Hoefer (2006) defines social work advocacy as taking "action in a systematic and purposeful way to defend, represent, or otherwise advance the cause of one or more clients at the individual, group, organizational, or community level, in order to promote social justice" (p. 8). Admittedly, there is no end to the issues that confront social workers and that suggest their serving as advocates, either individually or in groups. Any person who lives in our society can easily recognize that there are ever-present human needs that require advocacy for clients, patients, and others. Because the social worker's time and resources are limited, she must give serious thought to determining priorities in this area.

CASE ADVOCACY

On the individual case level, the objective of advocacy intervention is to obtain a needed resource or service for an individual client or group of clients. On the class level, the goal is to alter the environment through social policy changes or concessions from resistant or unresponsive systems (Mickelson, 1995). The ethical principle of equality and inequality provides the ethical justification for engaging in the advocacy role. Empowerment techniques are necessary in order to give disadvantaged groups and individuals a chance for equal access to life opportunities. However, this ethical justification does not mean that social worker advocates automatically avoid all ethical dilemmas.

Suppose there is only one bed available in the only home for senior citizens in your community. Your client needs to enter this institution because he can no longer cope at home. You also know that there are other older adults (not your clients) whose situations are even more critical. Should you become an aggressive advocate on behalf of your client, knowing that his admission will be at the expense of other older people who have a greater need for this service? Should you advocate his admission even if you are fairly certain that your success will result in irreversible harm to others? How do the "who is your client" considerations discussed in earlier chapters affect your decision? Are there other ways in which you can meet your ethical obligation to everyone who needs this service?

Exemplar 9.5 is an example of a different kind of case advocacy, even though it also involves a request for advocacy by an older client who is a resident of a nursing home.

9.5	A "SQUEAKY WHEEL" GOES UNHEARD

EP 2.1.2

Thomas Wayland is a resident of Room 209 in the Serenity Nursing Home. His roommate has a serious cognitive impairment, is generally incompetent, is incontinent, and makes continual repetitive noises that Thomas finds deeply disturbing. He spoke to a nurse's aide a week ago requesting that his room be changed. He repeated his request to that aide and several others, but so far there have been no changes. This morning he asked that his social worker, Kelli Forsbeck, come visit him. When Kelli arrived, Thomas was quite disturbed and angry; he explained to her that he had asked several times over a full week for a change of room, but nothing had been done to correct his situation. All of his requests had been ignored. He is still in the same room with the same roommate and the same noises. Kelli said she would speak to the head nurse to ask if his room can be changed. When she did so, she was told that the home has no beds available to meet Thomas's request. There are a number of people waiting to be admitted to the home. Other residents also have made requests that cannot be met at this time. Furthermore, she noted, the problem is not unique to Thomas and his current roommate. Other residents also have disconcerting and annoying characteristics, so there is no assurance that if Thomas is moved he will go to a room without some disturbance. She suggested impatiently that Kelli calm Thomas as best as she can, and when Kelli persisted in advocating with the head nurse, the nurse became visibly upset.

What are the ethical dilemmas present in this situation? How much autonomy does Thomas or Kelli really have? What does Kelli's professional role demand she do? Should she try to reassure and calm Thomas in the hope that a bed will open up in a few days, strongly advocate for him, or explain to him that there is little to no chance he will be placed in a different setting but that she will continue to work on his situation? To whom does Kelli owe loyalty? Thomas, the nursing home, or the head nurse? What is the correct ethical decision? Are there other possible options?

CAUSE/CLASS ADVOCACY

Another ethical dilemma a social worker advocate may encounter is illustrated by Exemplar 9.6, which is an example of cause or class advocacy, in which a social worker confronts an issue of importance to a group of persons.

What should you do in this situation? Should you become an advocate to press for institutional changes, such as more adequate public welfare allowances or special clothing allowances? Should you mobilize your volunteer network to locate suitable clothing donations so that the children can return to school as quickly as possible? Or should you do both? The former option will likely take time and will not get the children dressed appropriately so that they can return to school before the end of winter, while the latter option will get the children appropriately dressed and back in school quickly, but will not address the underlying problems. What are the ethical implications of causing short-run harm to your client (i.e., not getting the children back to school quickly) in order to gain an uncertain ultimate benefit (i.e., getting policies changed)? This situation is complicated by the fact that in one strategy (i.e., advocacy to change the policy) the cost is certain (the children will not attend school for a number of weeks or even months) while the benefit is uncertain because there is no guarantee of success, but if successful, such advocacy will help many people. The other strategy (i.e., depending on volunteers to contribute winter clothing to these specific children) may result in early benefits for your clients, but will not solve this problem, which many other children also have.

EP 2.1.2

| 9.6 | NO WINTER CLOTHING |

Three children in a family receiving public aid are sent home from school because despite the cold winter weather they are still dressed in summer clothing. There is no money available at home because their mother has used every last cent she has to pay off more pressing bills. You, the family's social worker, have no emergency funds available to help these three children obtain winter clothing.

Social worker advocates will encounter many ethical problems when their practice role is not fully supported by the employing agency, as is demonstrated in Exemplar 9.7.

EP 2.1.2

| 9.7 | TRAFFIC IN SHADY HILL |

Shady Hill was a quiet residential neighborhood until last year, when a new expressway exit brought a great amount of traffic onto its streets. As a result, there are now several very dangerous intersections. Last month, three children on their way to school were seriously injured when crossing one of these intersections. Parents and neighborhood residents are enraged and demand that the city close the exit or put up traffic lights. A meeting with the mayor has not produced any results. Lou Seward is the neighborhood worker who for the past two years has been staffing the Shady Hill Neighborhood Council, an arm of the Bay City Community Development Department. Under Lou's guidance, the council has undertaken several projects that have improved the quality of life in the neighborhood; everyone has been happy with the results achieved by these projects. Since the current problem has become acute, Lou has helped council officers organize a coalition of all neighborhood groups that are interested in this problem, including the PTA, churches, and fraternal organizations.

At last night's meeting of the coalition, it was agreed that ways must be found to put additional pressure on city hall. It was decided to call a news conference tomorrow morning to announce that a protest rally would be held across the street from city hall next Monday afternoon. If no positive response is received, the residents plan to block the exit the following week. Lou participated in last night's meeting by raising a number of questions, by encouraging the group, and by providing technical information and advice. In this morning's conference with his supervisor, Lou reviewed the Shady Hill situation to see if there were additional ways he could be helpful. His supervisor, the assistant director of the Community Development Department, thought that Lou had not done enough to calm the neighborhood. Though agreeing that the problem demanded attention, his supervisor did not think that an aggressive conflict strategy was helpful. He and the agency expected Lou to use his influence to keep the neighborhood quiet. That, after all, was the major reason why the city allocated monies to this department. The message was clear and so was the problem.

To whom does Lou Seward owe loyalty—to the Neighborhood Council that has successfully improved life in the neighborhood, to his supervisor and the agency, to his profession, or to himself as a professional who wants to place service to clients as his highest priority but who also wants to retain his job?

ADVOCACY AS WHISTLE BLOWING

In addition to case and class advocacy, there are situations in which social workers engage in whistle blowing (reporting or informing on a superior's or organization's ethical, professional, or legal misconduct) as a special type of advocacy. However, this is not a common phenomenon in social work (Green & Kantambu, 2004). Examples of such actions might include protecting clients or patients from abuse by staff members, relatives, custodians, or others; or attempting to protect social workers or other staff members from unwarranted vindictive retribution by other employees or administrators. Another example could be protecting an organization against the misuse of funds by administrators or others with access to funds that could result in depleting the availability of funds for human services as well as exposure to legal actions and depressed fund-raising ability.

Whistle blowing to protect clients against those who are abusing them requires great care and skill. It can expose the agency to potential public criticism or expose misuse of funds, both of which may harm services. By exposure, better services may be provided, but this action also raises issues of loyalty to the agency. Although there are laws at both the federal and state levels to protect whistle blowers from retaliation, social workers anticipating such advocacy need to take special care to consult with an experienced employment/labor lawyer (Whistleblower.org, 2007). According to a survey by the National Whistle Blower Center, most employees who expose wrongdoing in the workplace face some form of retaliation, despite existing laws (*New York Times*, 2002, September 3, Whistle-Blowers Being Punished a Survey Shows, p. A14).

Greene and Latting (2004) reviewed social work's stance on advocacy to protect clients' rights, explained whistle blowing as a type of advocacy, and offered guidance to social workers on handling whistle blowing when it is a relevant option for action. Exemplar 9.8 focuses on an organizational problem in a community fund-raising agency with implications for the organization, the human service agencies it serves, the staff, and the social worker.

EP 2.1.2

| 9.8 | WHO WILL BLOW THE WHISTLE? |

> Julie Greenacre is employed as a fundraiser by the Alliance for Human Services Fund-raising, a community-wide effort to raise money to fund human services. Recently, in discussion with the executive director's secretary, Lillian Radkin, a long-time friend who also attends her church regularly, Julie learned that the executive director has been skimming funds by manipulating his expenses. He also established a business with his son as a subdivision of the organization with a separate legal status and IRS designation. The executive director and his son are receiving excessive salaries and using the resources of the Alliance to operate this business. Lillian explained that she needed to tell someone she trusted because it has been bothering her since she found out about these illegal activities, but there is nothing that she can do about it because she desperately needs her job. She asked Julie if she would do something about the situation.

Should Julie believe these charges, even though Lillian did not provide any cor-roborating evidence? How should Julie respond? Should she find a way to commu-nicate with the executive director to let him know that some staff members are aware of what is happening, even if this means risking her own job or putting Lillian's job at risk (since the executive director can easily figure out who provided information on his activities)? Would it be more effective and safer to inform people outside the organization, such as the district attorney? Or should she just wait, hop-ing the information will come out eventually? To whom does Julie owe primary loyalty: the agency, the community, herself, her friend Lillian, or her profession and its ethical stances?

ADVOCACY AND PRIVATIZATION OF SERVICES

As a result of increased third-party contracting in recent years, the fundamental rela-tionship between clients, social agencies, and governmental agencies has been altered. As illustrated in Exemplar 9.9, the employment of third-parties to be responsible for the delivery of services can raise dilemmas about where advocacy can be directed and also about the relationships of the parties: clients, social workers, agencies, govern-ment, and third-party service providers.

How should Thelma respond and what should she do? If she and the group move ahead, they will almost certainly upset the agency's relationship with Emporium. On the other hand, from the committee's point of view, their efforts will build other sup-port in the community. No matter what happens, there is a danger referrals to South-west may slow down and other assistance will be withheld, depriving some persons of the help they need. To whom does the social worker owe loyalty: her committee, her agency, the clients served by Emporium and potentially by Southwest, her boss, or herself? Because Emporium is a private for profit company, does advocacy di-rected at such a third-party corporation require different ethical stances than those directed at a governmental agency or another non-profit agency?

EP 2.1.3

9.9 | REFERRALS AND COMPLAINTS

Thelma Hicks is a social worker employed by Southwest Rehabilitation and Nursing Home, a nonprofit agency that receives most of its referrals from Emporium Health Services. In addition, physicians and other employees of Emporium provide both paid and volunteer services for Southwest, including membership on Southwest's Board. Mac Grooms, the agency executive director of Southwest, has been concerned that the reputation of the nursing home has been falling in the community. At Mac's suggestion, Thelma created a community advisory committee to provide input for the agency from a consumer's perspective and to improve the nursing home's reputation and relationships in the community. However, over time, as the group learned more about the agency's and the community's needs, the focus has shifted to identifying criticisms of Emporium Health Services.

This morning Mac approached Thelma and said he received a phone call from a committee member last night at home. The committee member told Mac that the group was planning to advocate for change by publicly criticizing Emporium through several community meetings, newspapers, and local community blogs. He expressed concern that any criticism of Emporium would not be good for Southwest because it might reduce the number of referrals, antagonize board members and volunteers, potentially alienate several big donors associated with Emporium and, in general, create problems for Southwest. He asked Thelma to find a way to halt and/or slow the advocacy effort.

CYBERACTIVISM (ELECTRONIC ADVOCACY)

The Internet provides new technologies for advocacy (McNutt & Menon, 2008). These tools have been of growing use in the social welfare arena to protect and advocate for social change and human services. In fact, a major element in the 2008 successful presidential campaign by President Obama was the use of electronic means as an organizing and advocacy tool through websites, news groups, and e-mail, as well as information selection and community organizing activities.

Here we want to identify several electronic techniques for your consideration from an ethical point of view. There are techniques that are unlawful or unethical or both. Ethical decisions may be relatively clear concerning virtual sit-ins when a group ties up the server of a target by overloading its website or when a group attempts hacking into an organization's computer system. However, the answers to the following questions may be less clear. Suppose a social worker or social agency wishes to join a coalition to advocate for improved human services? Is it ethical to cooperate with organizations that have previously used unethical techniques or been found guilty of illegal activities? What if a social worker has to choose among several groups all of whom need greater resources; to which group should the available technological knowledge, skills, and time be devoted? Or, what is the ethical stance for a social worker when the community she serves as an advocate begins to clash with the policies and administration of her employing agency? What if the social worker advocate receives a request from a group member who wants to continue as an active member of the group, but wants to delete his name from petitions or group membership lists that are being sent out electronically? Should the social worker respect this request or try to convince the member to continue his public support by being named on petitions and membership lists?

CONCLUSION

In this chapter, the fact that social workers are constantly forced to make ethical decisions about the use of scarce resources to help individuals and communities was explored. Resources such as available time, health and mental health care, child welfare services, and food are not in limitless supply. In fact, they are usually in short supply. As we have seen, social workers frequently have to make ethical choices about how the resources available will be distributed. Discrimination and social justice also enter the picture. To serve one group may mean other groups receive less than they legitimately also need. Advocacy necessary to attain equitable distribution of resources was introduced through case advocacy, cause and class advocacy, and whistle blowing, as well as cyberactivism.

CRITICAL THINKING EXERCISES

EP 2.1.3

1. We have used the term *social justice* throughout this chapter. What does this term mean to you, and how does it relate to ethical social work practice? What have you personally done to promote social justice? What actions can social work agencies and community organizations do to promote social justice?

2. What would you do if you were the neighborhood worker in Shady Hill (Exemplar 9.7)? What are the ethical problems this neighborhood worker faces? How would you resolve them? Do you think that the supervisor's comments are in accord with the Code of Ethics? What are the supervisor's ethical dilemmas, and what would you do if you were the agency director?

3. The East Side Neighborhood Council has received a small grant to mount an educational program for Central American refugees now settling in large numbers on the East Side. The board is considering two projects: One would fund supplementary classes in local schools; the other would establish English classes for adult refugees. There is a need for both projects, but there is barely enough money to mount one. What are the ethical problems facing the social worker who staffs the board? What ethical considerations should the social worker keep in mind? How can the social worker find guidance that helps to make an ethical decision? If the social worker makes an ethical choice about the programs, does she have a responsibility to tell the board what the relevant professional ethics are, her stance, and how the decision was reached? Suggest ways this social worker can reach an ethically correct decision and what ethical actions should be implemented.

4. In addition to the NASW advocacy efforts (see Websites of Interest), many of the state chapters of NASW have local or state level advocacy efforts. Go to the website for your local NASW chapter, and examine the advocacy activities they are engaged in. Do you agree with the issues identified as the most important and with the actions being taken?

SUGGESTIONS FOR ADDITIONAL READINGS

Schools of social work and the Council on Social Work Education have made strenuous efforts to eradicate racism in individual schools and in social work education (Trolander, 1997). See Basham, Donner, Killough, and Rozas (1997), who describe the efforts and process by which the Smith College School of Social Work moved to become an antiracist institution. Dodd and Jansson (2004) argue that contextual barriers often prevent social workers from ensuring that clients' and patients' perspectives are sufficiently represented in ethical deliberations in multidiscipline settings. They propose that social workers, in addition to rational ethical reasoning, should be prepared with strategies and skills to engage in effective ethical advocacy. Faust (2008) discusses the role of clinical social workers as patient advocates in a community mental health center.

WEBSITES OF INTEREST

- Check out the National Association of Social Workers' advocacy efforts, including grassroots, national, and legislative efforts: www.socialworkers.org/advocacy/
- The Action Network for Social Work Education and Research (ANSWER) "coalition's mission is to increase legislative and executive branch advocacy on behalf of social work education, training, and research. This goal is accomplished through collaboration among social work education, research, and practice organizations, social work education programs, and other interested groups": www.socialworkers.org/advocacy/answer/
- For extensive information on whistle-blowing laws, visit: www.whistleblowerlaws.com

COMPETENCY NOTES

 Identify as a professional social worker and conduct oneself accordingly: In this chapter, we focused on issues of social justice and how they related to ethical issues and
EP 2.1.1   decision making.

 Apply social work ethical principles to guide professional practice: In this chapter, we provided multiple opportunities to apply ethical principles to social work practice.
EP 2.1.2

 Apply critical thinking to inform and communicate professional judgments: Several exemplars asked you to consider and decide how you would respond to ethical dilemmas. In addition, critical thinking exercises presented above also address this educational policy.
EP 2.1.3

 Engage diversity and difference in practice: Cultural diversity is addressed throughout this chapter.
EP 2.1.4

Advance human rights and social and economic justice: This chapter addresses issues of social justice throughout.
EP 2.1.5

ORGANIZATIONAL AND WORK RELATIONSHIPS

This chapter addresses the CSWE 2008 EPAS Educational Policy 2.1.1 on becoming a professional social worker, specifically focusing on organizational and work relationships. We also continue content on Educational Policy 2.1.2 about using social work ethical principles to guide professional practice. We will provide opportunities through numerous exemplars and questions for you to examine your personal and professional values and to work with the ethical decision-making model, which we hope you will use to apply critical thinking to inform and communicate professional judgments (Educational Policy 2.1.3).

So far, our discussion has focused primarily on ethical problems and ethical dilemmas occurring in the professional relationship between social workers and clients and/or other people in the client's system. In this chapter, our attention will be directed to ethical issues arising out of the relationships among social work colleagues and between social workers and their employers, agencies, supervisors, and administrators. Special attention will be paid to social work in the military.

We noted in Chapter 2 that one of the functions of professional codes of ethics is to permit colleagues to work together in harmony. The NASW Code of Ethics "informs other professionals with whom the professional must work about the kind of cooperation they have a right to expect from the professional and the limits to the cooperation that a professional ought to give" (Beyerstein, 1993, p. 420). This information reduces bickering and infighting that might lead to professional self-destruction. One section of the NASW Code deals with the social worker's ethical responsibilities toward colleagues, and another section with her ethical responsibilities to employers and practice settings. Several additional ethical rules dealing with relationships with colleagues are found in the section devoted to ethical responsibilities toward the profession.

Strom-Gottfried (2003) examined 894 ethics complaints filed with NASW for the years 1986 to 1997. Of the 894 complaints, 93 (10.4%) were filed against persons identified in the study as colleagues, an additional 40 (4.4%) complaints were filed against an employer or supervisor, and 174 (19.4%) complaints were filed against employees or supervisees. Thus, one third of the complaints were filed against colleagues, employers, or supervisors, all of whom are work associates. In an earlier published report based on the same 1986 to 1997 data cited above, Strom-Gottfried (1999) found that the most commonly occurring violation concerned poor supervision—involving failure to maintain or share performance standards with workers, using insufficient investigation and documentation in performance review processes, not holding regular supervisory sessions, or holding sessions that were unclear and ineffective. The second most common violation involved employee dismissals that were judged to have been based on insufficient or absent personnel policies, or that diverged from accepted processes of progressive discipline, such as counseling or disciplinary actions. The data from 1997 were the most recent available, and it is unclear whether there have been changes since that time. It is likely that these complaints represent only the tip of the proverbial iceberg because many complaints about unethical behaviors of this type are not filed with NASW but are handled in other ways, as will be discussed later in this chapter and in Chapter 13.

RELATIONS WITH PROFESSIONAL COLLEAGUES

What is a social worker to do when she discovers that a colleague engages in unethical or unprofessional conduct? How should she respond when she realizes that a fellow worker provides poor quality client services? What are her obligations when she believes that another social worker harms a client? What is her responsibility when she discovers that another worker engages in activities prohibited by their agency? What are her responsibilities when she learns that a colleague has violated the Code of Ethics?

The ethical rule obligating social workers to treat colleagues with respect (NASW Code, 2008, 2.01a) is one of those rules that ordinarily do not create an ethical quandary. Social workers face relatively few ethical problems as long as the rules governing relations with professional colleagues are unambiguous and not challenged by other ethical rules. However, as accountability to clients and others becomes more important, the unspoken rule to "protect your own" becomes increasingly problematic. Some examples of unethical behavior that might arise include knowing a colleague is: (a) sharing confidential information about a client inappropriately with colleagues; (b) having sexual relations with a client or a supervisee; (c) an alcoholic and is berating some clients; (d) sharing confidential information about a colleague with clients or other colleagues; or (e) bad mouthing a team leader after failing to convince an interdisciplinary team to proceed with a particular treatment plan.

Today, most social workers are no longer willing to overlook their colleagues' unethical behavior, but it is not always clear what should be done. On learning that a colleague has engaged in unethical behavior, a social worker may choose one or more of the following options:

- *Option A.* One can decide not to report the violating behavior because reporting it may be too troublesome, past experience suggests that nothing will be done about it even if it is reported, or the conduct may be so widespread that it is unlikely that anyone will take the complaint seriously.

- *Option B.* An informal approach to the colleague may resolve the problematic behavior, especially if the violation is of a minor or technical nature or appears to be the result of lack of experience or knowledge. The situation may differ depending on whether your colleague is a peer, a supervisee, or a supervisor.
- *Option C.* If the alleged unethical conduct also violates agency rules, it may be brought to the attention of one's supervisor or it may be raised formally by using agency procedures established for this purpose.
- *Option D.* The alleged unethical behavior may be brought to the attention of the NASW Committee on Inquiry. In order to use this procedure, the colleague who allegedly engaged in the unethical behavior must have been an NASW member at the time of the alleged violation, the complaint must charge a specific violation of the Code of Ethics, the complainant must have personal knowledge about the alleged behavior, and the complainant must be able and willing to provide the Committee on Inquiry with relevant and reliable testimony (NASW, 2005). The National Committee on Inquiry has primary administrative responsibility in all professional review matters. (The NASW professional review procedures will be discussed in more detail in Chapter 13.)
- *Option E.* Where a state licensing board regulates social work practice, unethical conduct harmful to clients can be reported to the board.
- *Option F.* The unethical conduct may be brought to the attention of the general public (whistle blowing), with the expectation that an aroused public will demand appropriate action to bring an end to the violation. (See Chapter 9 for more on whistle blowing.)

There are a number of possible alternatives within each option. Option A is unethical. Options B, C, D, and E are sanctioned by the Code of Ethics. Are there times and occasions when going public is the only way to proceed (Option F)? The decision to go public should never be a routine one and should be taken only after careful consideration of all possibilities. Before choosing which option to follow, the social worker should attempt to clarify what she hopes to achieve by the action she intends to initiate. Loewenberg (1987) suggests the following as possible objectives:

1. Ensure discontinuance of the unethical behavior.
2. Punish the offending social worker.
3. Identify the unethical practitioner so that potential clients and/or employers will avoid this person and turn to another, more ethical practitioner.
4. Prevent others from engaging in this behavior by warning them that it is unethical and will result in sanctions against the practitioner.
5. Protect the good name of the profession by declaring publicly that the unethical behavior is not approved by the profession.

Exemplars 10.1 and 10.2 highlight some of the problems involved in this ethical dilemma.

EP 2.1.2

In Exemplar 10.1, the violation of the Code of Ethics as reported is obvious, but what you should do is not clear because there are many conflicting demands on you. Your most serious consideration is: How trustworthy is this client's report? Can you/should you act if you have questions about what happened? However, assuming you believe the client's report, let us examine some things to consider, one by one, but not in any order of priority.

<table>
<tr><td>10.1</td><td>THREATENING A CLIENT WITH A CHILD PROTECTIVE SERVICES REPORT</td></tr>
</table>

Your colleague Mitchell Moore has been hospitalized quite suddenly. While he is on sick leave, you have been assigned to cover some of his cases. You learn from one of his clients that Mitch has threatened to report one of his clients to Child Protective Services if she does not help him obtain illegal drugs. She says that she was uncomfortable complying with his request but was afraid she would lose her children if she didn't do as Mitch asked. She also asks you to protect her confidentiality and that she will handle the situation when he returns. This behavior is clearly illegal and in violation of the Code.

- Your obligation to promote the well-being of clients (NASW Code, 2008, 1.01).
- Your obligation to respect confidential material received in the course of the professional relationship, except for compelling professional reasons (NASW Code, 2008, 1.07c).
- Your obligation to "take adequate measures to discourage, prevent, expose, and correct the unethical conduct of colleagues" (NASW Code, 2008, 2.11a).
- Your obligation to uphold the values, ethics, knowledge, and mission of the profession (NASW Code, 2008, 5.01b).
- Making a fuss about it might result in making you look ridiculous.

The last consideration argues against your taking any action (Option A—Not report), whereas the earlier considerations suggest a more active response (perhaps Option B—Informal approach, Option C—Use agency procedures, Option D—NASW and professional review, or even Option E—Report to the state licensing board). (The descriptions of these options were provided earlier in this section.) How can a social worker prioritize these considerations by importance? Does the ethical principles screen (EPS) help you in unraveling this conundrum? Which is the priority ethical obligation?

Let's consider another situation that presents the social worker with ethical quandaries in her relation to colleagues in Exemplar 10.2.

<table>
<tr><td>10.2</td><td>FAILURE TO REPORT A CASE OF CHILD ABUSE</td></tr>
</table>

Jake Dember, a frail 5 year old, was brought to the emergency room of Mt. Ebal Hospital unconscious, covered with blood from head to toe, with severe internal injuries. His father, Hiram, said that Jake fell from their second-floor apartment and landed headfirst on the cement sidewalk. The medical team was able to save Jake's life, though serious brain damage could not be reversed. Now, two weeks later, Jake is still in the hospital's critical care unit. The attending physicians are going to report this as a case of child abuse. Before doing so, they have asked the hospital social worker, Josie Perry, to pull together all the relevant information they possess so that it can be provided to child protective services (CPS) at the time of the report.

Erica Dember, Jake's mother, did not want to talk to Josie. She said that she and her husband were already in family therapy at the family service agency, and if Josie wanted to know anything about them, she should talk to their therapist, Ed Custer. Josie arranged to meet with Ed on the following afternoon. He was willing to share his assessment of the Dember family because both parents had signed the appropriate consent forms when Jake was admitted to the hospital. In the course of their conversation, Ed acknowledged that he had been aware of ongoing child abuse in this family, but because he thought that it was not too serious, he did not file a report. He feared that such a report would have interfered with the therapeutic relationship that he was trying to develop with this family.

EP 2.1.2

There are similarities and differences between this exemplar and the previous one. In both cases, one social worker became aware that another social worker may have violated ethical standards. In the first case, continuation of the unethical behavior might result in further harm to the client. In the present case, the harm to Jake had already been done and perhaps will not be repeated with Jake, but Ed Custer's possibly criminal conduct and his failure to report other cases of child abuse may cause harm to other clients. Are the conflicting claims on Josie Perry similar to those that faced Mitch Moore's colleague? How valid is Ed's fear that reporting a client's child abuse may interfere with the therapeutic relationship?

Research findings do *not* support the claim that reporting child abuse interferes with maintaining a therapeutic relationship. A national survey of psychologists who are psychotherapists and who had filed at least one mandated child abuse report found that clients remained in treatment when such reports were made, especially when certain factors were present. Important for maintaining this relationship was the explicit involvement of the client in the informed consent procedures. It was also important that the limits of confidentiality were fully discussed with the client. Moreover, clients were more likely to continue when there were positive therapeutic relationships prior to the report and when the perpetrator was a third party (someone not engaged directly in the treatment). Most surprising, clients reacted more positively when sexual abuse—rather than other forms of abuse—was reported (Steinberg, Levine, & Doueck, 1997). How should Josie Perry resolve the ethical dilemma facing her? Should she report Ed's negligence to the NASW chapter or the legal authorities? Ignore it? Choose another action?

So far, our consideration of the ethical quandaries arising out of this issue has focused on social work colleagues. Social workers also interact with practitioners from other professions and with nonprofessional human service workers. Although the nature of these relations may be different, the NASW (2008) Code of Ethics states that social workers should treat colleagues with respect (2.01a), and presumably this includes those colleagues in other professions. In one sense, the ethical problems arising out of these relationships will be the same as those that occur in relationships with social work colleagues. In other ways, the ethical dilemma may be more complicated because these non–social work colleagues are not subject to the provisions of the NASW Code of Ethics. They may follow other norms of confidentiality or may routinely engage in behaviors that professional social workers define as unethical. What should social workers do if their values and ethics are in conflict with the values and ethics of team members from other professions when the respective ethical obligations have not been clearly established as suggested by the NASW (2008) Code (2.03a) or the disagreement cannot be resolved through appropriate channels (2.03b)? Which other avenues should be pursued to address their concerns consistent with client well-being?

If a social worker learns of the incompetence of a team member from another discipline, what is one's ethical responsibility? What if social workers are working in cooperation with educators, psychologists, lawyers, physicians, or other disciplines? Is the ethical responsibility of the social worker always the same in whatever setting concerning abuse, confidentiality, sexual impropriety, inadequate professional performance, conflicts of interest, and the like? Suppose as a social worker you are employed in a agency led by lawyers. In some states, they may have no legal responsibility to report child abuse that is discovered in the course of their professional activity with clients; a social worker finding out about similar situations has a legal and ethical responsibility to report the situation. In the face of these conflicts and obligations, to whom does the social worker owe responsibility—the client or patient, the team, herself, the social work profession, the other involved professions, or society?

PRACTITIONER IMPAIRMENT

There are social workers who suffer from some type of impairment, including burnout or compassion fatigue (discussed in Chapter 7), substance abuse, psychological stresses due to aging, physical illness, financial hardship, extreme working conditions, marital and family difficulties, or acute or chronic psychological disorders. These problems can affect a social worker and her family, friends, and colleagues. Furthermore, these problems may result in a social worker's inability to provide professionally competent services. Social workers are thought to have about the same rates of alcohol and substance abuse problems as members of other stressful health professions. A survey of all Indiana NASW chapter members reported that 53% knew a social worker whose performance was affected by emotional or mental health problems, substance abuse, burnout, or sexual misconduct (Hiratsuka, 1994).

Siebert (2003) reported on an anonymous survey of a representative sample of North Carolina NASW members (N = 751). She found that 12% (one in eight) of the respondents were at serious risk of alcohol or other drug (AOD) abuse. Twenty-eight percent reported binge drinking during the preceding year; and 21% had used drugs illegally since becoming a social worker. In addition, 34% of the respondents at serious risk of AOD abuse reported at least one impairment incident, and 39% agreed that they had worked when too distressed to be effective. Nine percent of those at serious risk reported current problems. Siebert (2003) points out that denial is a characteristic defense among people with AOD issues and believes the respondents were no exception. Further, she concluded the study's findings are likely under-reports of the prevalence. Also, she stated that based on the sample studied, social workers seem to be drinking at higher rates than other helping professionals and the general public. Siebert (2004) also found that 19% of the respondents reported having depressive symptoms, 14% were currently depressed, and almost half the respondents reported past depression. Some social workers were currently taking medications for depression, and a number reported they had considered suicide at some point in their lives (Siebert, 2004). In a third article based on the same North Carolina data 12% of the study group scored above a threshold on more than one measure of alcohol or drug use and were at high risk for alcohol and drug abuse (Siebert, 2005).

It is an ethical imperative for the profession to ensure that every professional practitioner is able to provide quality professional services and respect all ethical norms, including confidentiality. However, impaired social workers may act in undisciplined, insensitive, erratic, unprofessional, and unethical ways. Sometimes they use inappropriate language or behavior with clients and colleagues, pay haphazard attention to their clients, fail to follow through on assignments, or engage in excessive absenteeism. Impairments can lead to inadequate and even unethical behaviors, which result in actions detrimental to clients and others, can lower the public's estimate of and trust of the profession, and present ethical problems for other social workers.

The NASW (2008) Code of Ethics includes four standards directly related to the impairment or incompetence of professional social workers. Social workers who have direct knowledge of such impairment or incompetence should consult with the impaired colleague where feasible and assist the colleague in taking remedial action. When the colleague has not taken adequate steps to address the impairment, social workers who are aware of such situations are expected to take action through appropriate channels established by NASW, licensing and regulatory bodies, employers, agencies, and other professional organizations (NASW Code, 2008, 2.09a, b; 2.10a, b). However, these standards do not provide answers for all the ethical dilemmas that occur in this area. Consider the situation presented in Exemplar 10.3.

EP 2.1.2

| 10.3 | My Friend, Mentor, Supervisor, and Alcohol |

You are a social worker assigned to a satellite unit of a family service agency. You and Davis Jones, your supervisor, are the only two social workers who work in the unit. Your relationship with Davis goes back at least 15 years; he has been very important in your life at several junctions. He helped you get into social work school; he recommended you for an advanced treatment institute; and once, when your child was ill, he helped you obtain medical care from the best specialist in town. Recently, however, Davis, who is also responsible for evaluating you for pay and possible promotions, has been arriving late for work and has missed some meetings. You have had to cover for him more than a few times with his clients. You are still somewhat in awe of Davis and owe him a lot, but you suspect that his current erratic behavior may be related to alcohol and family difficulties.

So far Davis has done little, if any, harm. At what point must you act? What about loyalty to a mentor, friend, and colleague from whom you have learned much? What about loyalty to yourself, your career, and your family? What about the risks to which you may expose yourself by acting? What should you do? What would be the ethical option? Consider the ethical implications for each of the following options you may select.

- Gather more information if possible to confirm or not confirm your suspicions.
- Encourage one of the clients for whom you have had to replace Davis for several sessions to register a complaint with the agency.
- Call in sick one day, and ask for a substitute to cover cases so that another social worker also becomes aware of the problem.
- Ignore the situation. Wait for someone else to blow the whistle. Meanwhile, cover his cases.
- Ask a mutual friend to call Davis and say that he has heard about his behavior on the job and suggest that it is important that he do something about his problems.
- Report the situation to a high-level agency administrator.
- Speak to Davis directly. State that you want to keep quiet about the situation, but that he must go for help before things become worse.

What are some other options that you could consider?

ADHERENCE TO AGENCY POLICIES AND REGULATIONS

The fact that most social workers are employed by bureaucratic organizations makes for another set of ethical dilemmas. Every organization has rules and policies. Those individuals who accept employment voluntarily agree to abide by these regulations. The NASW (2008) Code of Ethics considers this commitment to the employing organization a basic ethical obligation: "Social workers generally should adhere to commitments made to employers and employing organizations" (3.09a). The goals and objectives of some organizations, even of some social service agencies, however, are not always congruent with the values of the social work profession. Organization maintenance and survival demands may result in rules that contradict the primary obligation of social workers to give priority to their clients' interests. Efficiency measures may limit intervention options so that the most effective option for a given client may not be available. Budgetary considerations may result in service cutbacks that will not be in the client's best interest. This is the type of ethical dilemma that is especially demanding for social work administrators. They must resolve a critical ethical dilemma—whether to give priority to adherence to agency rules or to service to clients.

One response to these situations is collusion with clients to violate agency policies. This approach is often rationalized by the social worker by defining her activities as promoting the client's welfare or contributing fairness and social justice. Is it ever ethical to violate agency policies? For example, what should a social worker do upon learning that a client has occasional additional income, which she is supposed to report to her public assistance worker so that part of this income can be deducted from the following month's welfare check? Or a Supplemental Security Income (SSI) beneficiary is working off the books and not reporting the extra income that would cause her to lose support? If the social worker does not report this income, all of the extra money will be available to the clients. In the first case, the additional cash may help her to return to employment and independence and, in the second case, enable the beneficiary to live at a relatively minimal subsistence level. Keeping quiet may be in the best interest of both clients. Do the amount and the regularity of the extra income make a difference? In each case, what about the worker's obligations to the law, her employer, and society?

A particularly difficult ethical dilemma is faced by social workers when they discover that their agency's policies or regulations are unethical. For example, a hospital social worker discovers soon after employment that it is hospital policy to pressure social workers to encourage mentally competent patients to move into nursing homes. Intended to counter excessive concern by the hospital staff about patient safety following discharge, these actions override patients' rights to autonomy and self-determination (Clemens, 1995). As another example, the administrator of a child protective agency finds that his budget forces him to hire inadequately trained paraprofessional workers to investigate complaints of child abuse, even though this assignment requires a particularly high skill level.

The examples in the previous paragraph present a question as to what are ethical responses to budget cuts for the administrator and direct practitioner. Exemplar 10.4 provides another example where the purposes of the staff are served without due consideration of the needs of the client.

EP 2.1.2

10.4	PREGNANT WOMEN NEED SUPPORT

Terry Newton is a social worker in a private organization, Upward Strivers, that performs contract work for a local Department of Social Services (DSS). The clients receive public assistance under the Temporary Assistance to Needy Families (TANF) program as long as they are enrolled and active in a program that is designed to prepare them for regular employment through job readiness training. After completing the three weeks of job readiness training, those clients not enrolled in other training programs must begin job searches with the help of a placement specialist and may be enrolled part-time in GED preparation or literacy training, if needed. The Department of Social Services frequently refers pregnant women to the job readiness program. None of these women are able to find employment following the training because most employers won't hire pregnant women. The pregnant women are then enrolled in GED preparation in order to avoid the loss of their financial support. Both Upward Strivers and the DSS created this informal policy, which enables both DSS and Upward Strivers to receive payments from the state even though this informal policy is not consistent with the official state policy. The purpose of these informal policies is to maintain payments for the client, the Upward Strivers, and the DSS. The client needs financial support as do the two agencies, both of which are engaged in many important and constructive activities.

If you were a social worker who discovered this pattern, where would you look in the Code of Ethics for guidance on how to choose in an ethical manner among the clients and their needs, Upward Strivers, and the DSS? To which persons, organizations, or institutions do you have an ethical commitment? How would you implement your ethical decision?

EP 2.1.2

A different aspect of the conflict between agency interests and client interests that results in ethical quandaries is illustrated by Exemplar 10.5.

The agency executive requires an institution that runs smoothly. He also needs a physician who is willing to cooperate with the institution's staff. The social workers in this case argue that David has engaged in some asocial behavior—behavior they believe can be controlled more productively in other ways. Whose welfare takes priority? Is their responsibility to David and their own treatment plans, the executive director, the physician, or the other children in the institution who also have rights the social workers are obligated to support?

| 10.5 | A CASE OF A BOY WITH ADHD |

David lives a in a residential institution. He has been diagnosed with severe attention deficit hyperactivity disorder (ADHD) and in the last few weeks, his acting out behavior has become especially problematic. He frequently tosses food at other children during meals, short sheets other children's beds, pulls fire alarms, arrives late wherever he is expected, throws pencils in class, and other such behaviors. Although he is not physically harmful to himself or others, he has been highly disruptive of the institution's daily routine. The consulting physician has prescribed medication to calm David and make him easier to manage, but the cottage social worker has refused on ethical grounds to administer this medicine to David. She feels strongly that such pharmaceutical control will interfere with the child's welfare and freedom and will be counterproductive in any therapy attempted. Her social work supervisor supports this decision. The physician insists the medication prescribed be given to David. The institution's director, a psychologist, supports the doctor against the decision of the social worker.

NON–SOCIAL WORK EMPLOYERS

When a social worker is employed by an organization that is outside the human services field, she may face even more perplexing ethical problems. Today, social workers are employed by hospitals, industry, police, prisons, the military, colleges, long-term care facilities, and a variety of other organizations that are not social work oriented. To whom do these social workers owe their *primary* loyalty? Who is the client of these social workers? For example, the employees of a large manufacturer may consult about personal problems with the social worker whom their employer has hired. Should the employer be informed when a worker's problems may affect the production schedule of a factory or may have security implications? Should detectives have access to confidential information that a prison social worker has obtained from her contacts with prisoners?

SOCIAL WORK AND THE MILITARY

At a high level of abstraction, the values of the military and the values of social work may appear similar. They both value honesty, integrity, loyalty, accountability, fairness, caring, and respect, among other values. However, Simmons and Rycraft (2010) suggest that in day-to-day activities the values of social work and the military actually can be in conflict. "Among the most conspicuous of these is the social work value of social justice, a concept relatively contrary to the military practice of sacrificing individual freedom for the greater good of society. In addition, ethical principles of autonomy, self-determination, privacy/confidentiality, quality of life, and even the right to life take on different meanings in the military, where the Uniformed Code of Military Justice and the needs of the military prevail" (p. 10).

Confidentiality, for example, in a military clinical setting is guided by federal legislation, Department of Defense regulations, and service specific regulations. Although privacy is to be respected, these regulations mandate access to confidential files by military personnel on a need-to-know basis. The need-to-know basis, admittedly ambiguously defined, does not require the service member's signature for release. While there may be ambiguity in certain situations about what need-to-know means, where safety or security are involved in a military environment, confidentiality does not take priority (Jacques & Folen, 1998).

Simmons and Rycraft (2010) studied the ethically challenging experiences of military social workers deployed in Operation Iraqi Freedom and Operation Enduring Freedom in Afghanistan. Their respondents were 24 MSWs with advanced clinical social work licenses working in the Army, Air Force, and Navy. Among the ethical dilemmas faced by the respondents were: the needs of the client versus the needs of the unit (e.g., a soldier/client with mild trauma symptoms wants to go home but the unit requires his combat skills until a replacement arrives); issues of confidentiality and privacy (e.g., keeping the soldier/client's presenting problem secret); conflicts with commanders (who in certain situations can be other than mental health focused); relationships and boundaries (e.g., maintaining boundaries with clients and having personal relationships with non-clients in austere and challenging or dangerous situations); and diagnosis and treatment (e.g., feigning symptoms or truly suffering). A small number of respondents stated they experienced no ethical dilemmas in their deployment. Balancing the needs of the individual and the needs of the unit and its mission is an important challenge. For these social workers, achieving the unit's mission has become the priority value, so that the traditional social work values such as self-determination and clinical judgment become a lower-rank imperative.

As identified above, privacy and confidentiality issues can confront the military social worker. The problem of identifying who is the client and issues of confidentiality may be especially difficult for social workers in military service. Consider Exemplar 10.6.

EP 2.1.2

| 10.6 | THE MILITARY IS A SPECIAL ENVIRONMENT |

Sergeant Richard Mozart recently discussed some personal difficulties with Captain Emilio Pacifico, a social worker on an army base. Sgt. Mozart is assigned to hazardous duty and told Capt. Pacifico that he is a moderate alcohol user. Capt. Pacifico was recently transferred to a new duty station. As a result, he transferred Sgt. Mozart's case file to the new social worker assigned to the base. When the newly assigned social worker—Lt. Ted Maddox—read the file, he reported Sgt. Mozart and had him taken off hazardous duty; he did not consult with Capt. Pacifico or talk to Sgt. Mozart before making this report. As a result of this, Sgt. Mozart filed an ethics complaint against Capt. Pacifico.

What are the ethical dilemmas in this case situation? Should Capt. Pacifico have made a report earlier and had Sgt. Mozart removed from hazardous duty? Was Lt. Maddox's action appropriate? Would it make a difference if these events were taking place in a war zone? What difference would it make if Sgt. Mozart were not assigned to hazardous duty?

As social workers in the military, Capt. Pacifico and Lt. Maddox have to adhere to the NASW Code of Ethics *and* to the guidelines of the Department of Defense. These two sets of guidelines view confidentiality differently. This conflict can create difficulties for the social worker who may find that the demands of the military contradict the standards of the professional Code of Ethics. Should Capt. Pacifico and/or Lt. Maddox be reprimanded by a social work ethics committee? Should signed verbal consent or signed consent forms have been obtained from Sgt. Mozart by either or both social workers prior to the transfer of the case file?

EP 2.1.2

SOCIAL WORKERS NOT IN THE MILITARY BUT IN WAR-RELATED ACTIVITIES

Ethical dilemmas in relation to war are not limited to social workers who are employed in the military. Exemplar 10.7 describes an ethical dilemma that a social worker involved in international service may encounter, but it has implications for workers in many other settings.

| 10.7 | SERVING ONLY THE GOOD PEOPLE |

EP 2.1.2

Amanda Frankel is a social worker for an international aid organization in a war zone. The forces of one side of the conflict are particularly cruel, attacking civilians, raping young girls and older women, and murdering groups of men and burying their bodies to do away with evidence. Until yesterday, Amanda was happy and proud to serve those in need who were being attacked. Then her supervisor sent a message that she was going to be transferred to the other side to serve the people there. Just as here, she would serve all people, including military and paramilitary personnel. She was awake all night considering what she should do.

What is the ethically correct choice in this situation? In what way is Ethical Principle 2 (social justice) relevant to Amanda's situation and dilemma? In what ways do her personal values conflict with her employing agency's values and requirements? Does the NASW (2008) Code of Ethics suggest there is a correct choice for Amanda? Can you identify in your local community situations in which social workers might have their personal values challenged by similar decisions by the agencies for which they work?

Noteworthy for social workers in military and homeland security settings is the struggle of the American Psychological Association and the American Psychiatric Association in response to reports of harsh interrogations of detainees at Abu Ghraib, Guantanamo Bay, and other locations. According to the American Psychological Association, there is a role for psychologists in the interrogation of detainees by the U.S. military and government, but they also warn of the ethical dangers of such activities (Lewis, 2005). Psychologists are permitted to serve in consultative roles in interrogation and information-gathering processes for national security–related purposes. However, psychologists should not engage in, support, facilitate, or offer training related to torture or other cruel, inhuman, or degrading treatment, and they should not use a detainee's medical information to the detriment and harm of the individual. Psychologists serving as consultants to interrogations involving national security should be aware of factors unique to these roles and contexts that require special ethical consideration. The report avoided explicit answers to the question of whether psychologists may advise interrogators on how to increase stress to make detainees more cooperative if the advice is not based on medical files but only on observation of the detainee (Lewis, 2005).

War and Pacifism

Verschelden (1993) argued, following the Gulf War, that social work values and ethics suggest that social work professionals should be pacifists. Her argument is that the basic values of the social work profession suggest that social workers should work to oppose war. Among the relevant values, according to Verschelden (1993), are: commitment to the primary importance of the individual in society; respect and appreciation for individual and group differences; commitment to social justice and the economic, physical, and mental well-being of all in society; and a willingness to persist in efforts on behalf of clients despite frustration. By pacifism, we mean opposition to war and violence to settle conflicts. Do you agree with Verschelden's (1993) reading of the NASW Code of Ethics? When you review the Code of Ethics, can you find any proof that social workers should or should not be pacifists and opposed to all wars and violence as a means of settling conflicts?

Other Non–Social Work Settings

Dilemmas related to issues concerning confidentiality can also occur in other settings, such as employee assistance programs (EAP). Exemplar 10.8 describes an EAP situation and its ethical dilemmas.

EP 2.1.2

| 10.8 | Confidentiality and Threatening Behavior |

You are a social worker in an employment assistance program (EAP) and friendly with Margaret Di Constanza. Margaret recently told you that a male colleague—Ethan Starkey—has been hanging around her work space and making strange sounds. Ethan is an average employee, and the only reports of inappropriate behavior by him concern his keeping piles of magazines and other printed materials in his work space. These piles of printed materials only intrude in the area around his desk, but they are unsightly and may be a fire hazard. He has been asked several times to remove the materials. He does so, and then, shortly afterward, the piles return. His job performance otherwise has been generally adequate. Margaret told you that she feels threatened by his behavior; she doesn't know what to expect next. She asked you to do something about the situation but not tell anyone else. When you attempted to observe Ethan when he was near Margaret, you were unable to confirm her observations and complaint.

To whom do you owe loyalty in such an ambiguous situation: to the EAP, your friendship with Margaret, Ethan Starkey, or yourself as the EAP social worker? Could Ethan's behavior escalate, and what are the implications for others in the workplace? Should you believe and trust your friend and report the incidents to management by revealing her confidence? Should you avoid reporting the incidents but raise what could be a regular concern about Ethan, a concern that would at least keep attention focused on Ethan for a period of time? What is the ethical thing to do?

Ethical problems arising out of adherence to agency policies occur in all settings. Some of our illustrations are taken from non–social work settings because the ethical dilemmas may be more evident there. Social workers employed by social agencies, however, should not think these problems cannot happen to them, as Exemplar 10.9 illustrates.

EP 2.1.2

| 10.9 | Apple Hill Young Adult Social Club |

The Apple Hill Community Center is a group service and recreation agency in a changing neighborhood. When it was established almost 50 years ago, it served an immigrant population and was instrumental in the Americanization of many thousands of newcomers. It now sees character building and strengthening democratic decision making as its major contribution to the community. As a matter of policy, it avoids all political activities. Neither staff nor groups affiliated with the center are allowed to take a public stand on controversial issues.

Otto Zupan, a social group worker, staffs the Young Adult Social Club. This group is composed of 25 young men, ages 18 to 21, almost all of whom are high school graduates. They spend a great deal of time at the community center because most of them are unemployed. Lately, they have talked a lot about why there are no jobs for them. Some thought that the recession was to blame; others felt it was because they were African Americans. Otto urged them to do some research and see if they could come up with some answers to their question. The results of their field study left little doubt that they were the victims of discriminatory hiring practices. Otto urged them to go public because discrimination in hiring was against the law. Letting the public know about their findings might help them get a better break when applying for the next job. They thought that Otto's idea was great and decided to call a news conference. They asked Otto to arrange for a room at the center for the news conference.

When Otto talked over their plan with the center's director, he was flatly rebuffed. Not only could they not have a room for the news conference, but as a center social club they could not engage at all in this type of action program. Furthermore, Otto must do everything to bring the group back to its original objectives as a social club. The center director added that if Otto could not do this, he should ask for another assignment.

Loyalty to agency rules or meeting client needs—these are two conflicting professional obligations that create a serious ethical problem for social worker Otto Zupan. Is it ethical for him to abide by the agency's directives and abandon the young adults at this critical point in their development? Should he ignore his obligations to his employer and help group members organize outside the center? What is the ethical stance demanded of a social worker who faces this situation?

Another type of ethical dilemma occurs when an agency channels clients into programs that are not beneficial for them. For example, what are the ethical issues faced by social workers when a large number of unskilled men and women are directed into job-training programs that lead only to dead-end or nonexistent jobs? Should social workers act against agency policy and tell their clients all that they know about these programs? Is it more ethical to follow organizational directives and keep quiet? How does a social worker make ethical decisions in these situations?

What are the ethical implications when a social agency engages in discriminatory practices? There was a time when such practices were blatant and open; now they are less obvious but may be equally damaging. One child welfare agency places white children in adoptive homes and minority children in institutions because there are no adoptive homes for them. In another agency, homosexuals living with AIDS receive one type of service, while heterosexuals living with AIDS receive another type of service. Whatever the reason, discriminatory practices never benefit the client who is being discriminated against. The NASW (2008) Code of Ethics clearly states, "Social workers should not practice, condone, facilitate, or collaborate with any form of discrimination on the basis of race, ethnicity, national origin, color, sex, sexual orientation, gender identity or expression, age, marital status, political belief, religion, immigration status, or mental or physical disability" (4.02). What does this mean in practice? Should a social worker refuse to accept employment in an agency that practices discrimination? Must she resign when she discovers such practices? Should she ignore such agency policies and, whenever possible, not follow them? Or should she accept a job with the intention to change the agency? What would you do if you had Dale Jenkins's job in Exemplar 10.10? What are the ethical implications of each of the options that Dale is considering?

| 10.10 | Social Work in a Bank |

Social worker Dale Jenkins is employed by a large bank as a community representative in a minority neighborhood. Dale is African American, and part of his assignment is to be visible and become accepted in the community. He has been very successful in meeting this objective. He is accepted by the neighborhood's residents and is liked by nearly everyone. In the past several years, he has been able to help a number of residents qualify for business loans and mortgages. Nick Stamos, vice president of the bank to whom he reports, recently told Jenkins that the bank has decided to direct less money and services to this neighborhood, but that his job is safe. Nick implied that in a few years the bank might again direct monies to this neighborhood. In the meantime, Dale should be more selective in referring residents to the bank for loans and mortgages.

Because none of the loans he facilitated have gone into foreclosure or short sale, Dale understood this message as meaning that the bank no longer would give mortgages to minority group applicants. He considered the options he had, including making sure that he had understood correctly. If he hadn't, then he could discuss with Nick how the misunderstanding had occurred and how to avoid it in the future. However, if he had understood correctly, then he could consider other options, such as trying to persuade Nick and other bank officials to change the new and discriminating policy; ignoring the new policy and operate as he had in the past; or telling community leaders about the new policy and encouraging them to apply political pressure on the bank to change its policy.

SOCIAL WORK ADMINISTRATION AND SUPERVISION

Social work administrators and supervisors have an ethical responsibility to protect clients' rights and to foster an atmosphere in which workers will do the same. At the same time, they are accountable to the agency's sponsors for productivity and for operating within the authorized budget. With diminishing budgets and rising demands, this can be a difficult task. In addition to ethical obligations toward the agency, an administrator also has responsibilities toward his or her employees, as well as to the agency's clients. Many administrators think that the line between ethical and unethical behavior is crossed only when their activities result in personal gain. They feel that it is ethical to do whatever is necessary as long as their activities benefit clients or the agency. If a government contract provides money for staff training but not for staff supervision, they do not hesitate to redefine supervision as training. Recreation services are renamed respite services if government funding for recreation is dropped. In such cases, an illusion of compliance is achieved by playing semantic games. But do such practices present ethical problems?

Another ethical dilemma that some administrators face occurs when there is a conflict between their responsibility for organizational maintenance on the one hand and professional or communal responsibility on the other. Take the case of the director of a children's home that for decades has provided institutional care for infants aged three days to one year. From a professional point of view, there is no longer any justification for continuing this type service, but what about the director's responsibilities to the sponsors, to staff, and to others for ensuring that the agency continues to function. How would you respond to the ethical dilemma facing this social work administrator?

An ethical dilemma of a different nature is presented in Exemplar 10.11.

| 10.11 | THE GOOD OF THE AGENCY, THE COMMUNITY, OR THE STAFF? |

EP 2.1.2

John Meenaghan is a social planner in a United Way community fund-raising and social planning agency. Over lunch, Melissa Bridgewater, a longtime friend and a member of the executive staff, told him that the executive director—who is not a social worker—and several favored members of his personal staff have been living lavishly on their expense accounts and padding their expenses. All the information she provided in the past has been completely accurate. The executive director is tyrannical and punitive but has been extremely creative and improved productivity many times over. The fund drive has reached new heights. Later, in his office, John spent almost an hour contemplating why Melissa shared this information with him. Why doesn't she go public herself? What should he do, if anything?

John Meenaghan understands that whistle blowing can do good as well as harm. If he goes public with the information about agency corruption, he could do much harm to the agency and undermine its fund-raising capacity for some time into the future. Alternately, if he goes public with the information (for which he has no direct evidence), he could perform a public service, protecting the community's resources while ensuring that funds will be spent on the problems for which they were intended. At the same time, the element of trust that generally exists in the agency will be destroyed. The authority structure of the agency will be damaged, at least for a time, thus potentially creating havoc in the administration. If he reports the problem to his supervisor or to a member of the board of directors, he might further his good relations with some superiors and colleagues, and perhaps with members of the board, but the executive director and others will be angry and will be liable to legal actions.

A number of standards in the Code (2008) are relevant to this situation: "Social workers' primary responsibility is to promote the well-being of clients" (1.01). "Social workers should treat colleagues with respect and should represent accurately and fairly the qualifications, views, and obligations of colleagues" (2.01 a, c). In addition, "social workers should take adequate measures to discourage, prevent, expose, and correct the unethical conduct of colleagues" (2.11 a, b, c, d); and "social work administrators should take reasonable steps to ensure that the working environment for which they are responsible is consistent with and encourages compliance with the NASW Code of Ethics. Social work administrators should take reasonable steps to eliminate any conditions in their organizations that violate, interfere with, or discourage compliance with the Code" (3.07d). Finally, "social workers should be diligent stewards of the resources of their employing organizations, wisely conserving funds where appropriate and never misappropriating funds or using them for unintended purposes" (3.09g).

Who is the client or what are the priorities in this situation—Melissa, who shared the information; the executive director, who has done an outstanding job for the agency, maintaining its viability; the community agencies that benefit from the United Way; or those being served by communal agencies? What does John owe Melissa? Lacking detailed information about the improprieties, would he be treating any of his colleagues with respect if he were to move forward? Does he have the right to correct a non–social worker, someone who is not bound by the Code? What would you advise John to do? More generally, both supervisors and administrators have a responsibility to support workers' ethical behaviors and to stop workers' unethical behaviors.

DUAL-ROLE RELATIONS WITH SUPERVISORS

Supervisors and agency administrators are powerful persons because they have considerable influence over the social workers and students whom they employ or supervise. They make assignments, evaluate work, decide on promotions, and at times terminate employment. They are obligated to use this power in ethical ways. This rule has a number of implications. Any relationship with employees or students in which an administrator/supervisor takes advantage, exploits, or harms persons with less power is unethical, even if the initiative comes from the employee or supervisee. This holds not only for sexual relations but also for other types of relations that create bonds that may negatively affect the professional relationship. Several standards in the Code of Ethics provide clear guidance for social workers in regard to dual/multiple relationships. This area of unethical behavior has received increased attention in recent years. Here we wish to highlight the need for social workers to consider seriously the ethical problems that may arise in work settings among persons with different degrees of power.

Consider how you would assess the following supervisory situations:

- Your supervisee's husband is an insurance broker. She tells you that her husband will give you a large discount on your automobile insurance. Will you avoid any ethical problems if you place your insurance with him but pay the full insurance rate?
- Your agency is employing your wife as a caseworker and assigns you to work on a team with her.
- Your supervisee has a summer home in the mountains. She invites you and your children to use it this summer while she and her husband are vacationing elsewhere.

In each of these situations, there is a potential for an ethical difficulty. Do the standards give clear answers to these problems?

OTHER CONFLICTING OBLIGATIONS

Social work supervisors are often in the position of the person "in between" with multiple pressures and obligations. Supervisors have many roles and obligations in social agencies. In addition to their primary responsibility to ensure the delivery of high-quality services, their responsibilities include committee meetings, assignments representing the agency in the community, phone calls, emergencies, and other demands on their time and energy. Exemplars 10.12, 10.13, and 10.14 illustrate several of the ethical dilemmas that can arise.

EP 2.1.2

| 10.12 | FRIEND, SELF, FAMILY, AGENCY—LOYALTY TO WHOM? |

Thomas Kinane was recently promoted to supervisor, a job that pays much more than his prior position. His teenage daughter has been in therapy, and he feels lucky because the money is arriving just when the family needs it. He is responsible for the supervision of 12 workers who are on a task force to implement a new service in Gordonsville, a satellite location. He has an enormous amount of record keeping and report writing to do. Because of demands of the job on his time, both in Gordonsville and at central headquarters, he frequently has to cancel supervisory sessions with individual workers, not fulfilling his responsibilities to supervisees and clients. Yet he does not feel ready to use group supervision, which would help him to better control his time and do his job.

Thomas's situation is not unusual. He wants to succeed in his job, and has a responsibility to his employer. But he also has a responsibility to his supervisees' clients, to his family, and to his supervisees. How would you choose among these conflicting obligations? What would you choose to do?

EP 2.1.2

10.13 | THE ETHICS OF MOONLIGHTING

The employment contract of the Bay City Human Services Agency states: "Social workers may not work for another employer in their professional social work capacity, even outside of their regular working hours." Every new social work employee in the agency is made aware of this provision and acknowledges her agreement to it in writing. The other evening, Ellen and Bill Stock rushed their infant daughter Sharon to the hospital because she had a very high fever. While Ellen stayed with the baby in the emergency room, Bill handled the admission routines.

Later on, Bill told Ellen that among the people with whom he had to speak in the admissions office was a social worker. He had been very impressed by her warm and sympathetic interest in their sick child. Ellen asked Bill if he recalled the worker's name and was surprised to learn that it was Joan Gilligan, one of the social workers she supervises. On the way out of the hospital, Ellen peeked into the admissions office to make sure that this was the same social worker she supervises. It was. Because Ellen did not use her husband's name at work, she was sure that Joan did not realize that she had been helping her supervisor's husband.

Ellen did not know what she should do about her discovery. On the one hand, Joan's moonlighting was in violation of the commitment she made to the agency. The Code of Ethics states clearly, "Social workers generally should adhere to commitments made to employers and employing organizations" (NASW Code, 2008, 3.09a). On the other hand, Joan's moonlighting did not harm anyone. As a matter of fact, her presence in the hospital admissions office benefits many patients at a time when they are in a state of crisis. What are Ellen's obligations to her employer, to her colleague, and to the profession? Are there other ways to address this dilemma, such as working to change the agency policy?

Exemplar 10.14 deals with yet another work-related issue. It will be difficult to differentiate between Wilma's administrative/supervisory responsibilities and her professional social work responsibilities. Any decision she will reach will necessarily include both aspects. Whatever her decision, it will have ethical implications.

10.14 | A CARIBBEAN CRUISE

Wilma Stevens supervises a unit of six social workers, of whom Carla Bick is the most qualified and most effective. Last week, Carla was not at work. Her boyfriend called in to say that Carla had a bad case of the flu and would probably be out all week. Today, she returned to work, bringing a note from her doctor stating that she had been sick all week. Aside from the note, there was no evidence of her having been sick. She explained that yesterday she went to the beach, and this accounted for her suntan. Wilma's cousin had been on a Caribbean cruise last week. When they had supper together, her cousin told Wilma all about the trip and about the many interesting people she met onboard the cruise ship. One of those people was a young social worker—Carla Bick. The cousin wondered whether Wilma happened to know her.

As Wilma thought about Carla's absence from work last week, she noted the following points:

EP 2.1.3

- Carla's absence was not authorized and was in violation of agency policy.
- Carla's behavior was unethical and unprofessional.
- Carla may have harmed her clients by failing to provide them with regular service.
- Carla had not told the truth when she claimed that she had been sick.
- Carla was her best worker, and Wilma did not want to lose her.
- Other workers probably also misused sick leave but were not caught. Would making an example of Carla persuade others to desist from this unethical behavior? If Wilma does so, what will be the cost? Would making an example of Carla be unethical because her privacy would be violated?

One of the assignments of an agency director is to staff the board of directors, the agency's policy-making group. Establishing a good working relationship with board members is essential for every successful agency director. At times, the agency director will encounter ethical dilemmas because of conflicting ethical principles. Consider Exemplar 10.15. What are the ethical problems that this exemplar raises, and how would you address them?

10.15	THE BOARD OF DIRECTORS OF THE ALZHEIMER'S ASSOCIATION

EP 2.1.2

The Alzheimer's Association is a local, voluntary agency established about 10 years ago to provide a wide range of community services to caregivers of people with Alzheimer's disease. At last night's meeting, the board of directors voted to eliminate all homemaker services because the insurance carrier had again raised the premium for liability insurance that homemakers must carry. You, the agency director, know that the demand for homemaker services has always exceeded the staff available. It is not only a popular service, but a resource that has enabled many families to keep their relative with Alzheimer's disease at home instead of placing him or her in an institutional facility. You know that the agency provides other services for which there are fewer demands; reducing these services could pay for the higher insurance premiums. These other services, however, are of special interest to several board members; they will do anything to protect their favorite services.

SUPERVISOR ETHICS AND LIABILITIES

Ethics complaints and legal actions can be brought by clients and employees against supervisors that allege ethical breaches or negligence by the supervisors and by those whom they supervise. Supervisors are affected by two types of liability. **Direct liability** may be charged when harm is caused by the supervisor's acts of omission or commission, such as when the supervisee is assigned duties for which the supervisee is inadequately trained or experienced, or when supervisors do not follow supervision guidelines promulgated by their state boards and/or professional associations. Supervisors may also be charged when the supervisee makes mistakes. Some claims may implicate supervisors under the legal doctrine of *respondeat superior*—"let the master respond." This doctrine—also known as **vicarious liability**—means a supervisor is responsible for the actions of a supervisee that were conducted during the course of employment, training, or field instruction, including potential ethical lapses. Worthington, Tan, and Poulin (2002) conducted an exploratory study of ethically questionable behaviors among 230 graduate counseling psychology supervisees. Among the ethical lapses they identified as unique to supervisees (which could be true also of professional employees) were the following: intentional nondisclosure of important information, mismanagement of case records, actively operating at an inappropriate level of autonomy, failure to address personal biases that impact counseling, inappropriate methods of managing conflict with supervisors, and failure to engage in necessary professional development activities. Two actions were viewed as the most unethical behaviors by both supervisors and supervisees: intentionally fabricating information about a client in supervision and forging a supervisor's signature. Supervisees covertly seeking approval from another person to justify acting on a plan his or her supervisor had rejected was the action with the widest discrepancy between the views of supervisors and supervisees. A similar discrepancy was found regarding the failure to complete documentation of client records within the required time. Otherwise, supervisor and supervisee rating reflected a considerable amount of agreement.

This chapter makes clear that ethical dilemmas can be encountered in direct practice, as well as in relations with professional colleagues, and in relationship to agency policies and regulations. Ethical dilemmas can also occur in the work of supervisors and administrators, and can occur in human service agencies, the military, and business situations.

CRITICAL THINKING EXERCISES

EP 2.1.3

1. Does your state have a list of unethical professional behaviors that are actionable by your state social work licensing authority? What are the unethical professional behaviors on the authority's promulgated list? Are there actions that you would add to the list? What sanctions or punishments are available to this authority? Are there other sanctions you would like to add?
2. Review the employee handbook for the agency where you are employed or in field instruction. Are any of the agency policies inconsistent with the Code of Ethics? How would you address these inconsistencies?
3. In a community organization, you are a member of the staff at a staff meeting when several employees advocate that only African American professionals should work with African American groups and neighborhoods and that only lesbians and gays can be successful in working with lesbian and gay communities (Shillington, Dotson, & Faulkner, 1994; Tully, Craig, & Nugent, 1994). What should you do?
4. Verschelden (1993) argues that social work values and ethics suggest social workers should be pacifists. Do you agree with Verschelden in the belief that social work ethics require a social worker to be a pacifist?
5. Select one of the exemplars involving a supervisor and supervisee in this chapter and role play a meeting between the two addressing the issues raised in the exemplar.

SUGGESTIONS FOR ADDITIONAL READINGS

Egan and Kadushin (2004) report on a survey of home health social workers and their job satisfaction. Among the issues examined are ethical conflicts between patient access to services and agency financial priorities. Compromising professional ethics contributed to significantly less job satisfaction. See Frost, Robinson, and Anning (2005), which examines how child and family interdisciplinary teams work together. Among the issues explored are models of professional practice, status and power, and confidentiality and information sharing. Desai (2003) in *Ethical Decision Making within the Bureaucratic Context: A Case Study* illustrates how the expectation of transparent decision making in bureaucracies forces practitioners to seek guidance in ethical decision making.

Websites of Interest

- The Association for Community Organization and Social Administration (ACOSA) site includes a number of resources and links for social workers involved in administration and community organizing: www.acosa.org
- The National Network for Social Work Managers site offers information on the organization as well as links to articles and presentations: www.socialworkmanager.org
- For information about social workers in the military, go to www.todaysmilitary.com and search social work.

Competency Notes

Identify as a professional social worker and conduct oneself accordingly: In this chapter, we discuss organizational and work relationships and how they relate to EP 2.1.1 ethical dilemmas for social workers.

Apply social work ethical principles to guide professional practice: In this chapter we discuss ethical social work practice in the work setting. EP 2.1.2

Apply critical thinking to inform and communicate professional judgments: Multiple exemplars asked you to consider and decide how you would respond to ethical EP 2.1.3 dilemmas, and exercises at the end of the chapter address critical thinking.

SOCIAL WORK WITH SELECTED CLIENT GROUPS

This chapter addresses the CSWE 2008 EPAS Educational Policy 2.1.1 on becoming a professional social worker, specifically focusing on social work with selected client groups. We also continue content on Educational Policy 2.1.2 about using social work ethical principles to guide professional practice. We will provide opportunities through exemplars and questions that we hope you will use to apply critical thinking to inform and communicate professional judgments (Educational Policy 2.1.3). This chapter will also consider the Educational Policy 2.1.4 to engage diversity and difference in practice.

In this chapter, we cover a medley of topics related to ethical issues and dilemmas in areas that are frequently encountered in direct practice situations, as well as several newer, rapidly evolving problem areas, such as intimate partner violence, elder abuse, end of life decisions, HIV and AIDS, religion and spirituality, and a plurality of identities and client groups.

INTIMATE PARTNER VIOLENCE

Intimate partner violence (IPV), also known as domestic violence and spouse or partner abuse, refers to violence between adults who are intimates, regardless of their marital status, living arrangements, or sexual orientations. Intimate partner violence comes in several forms: physical, sexual, psychological, economic, social isolation, stalking, and coercive control (Austin & Dankwort, 1999, Murphy & Ouimet, 2008).

Violence against women and men has reached epidemic proportions in the United States. During any given year, women experience approximately 4.8 million physical assaults and rapes, whereas men experience somewhat less than 3 million assaults. In 2004, 1,544 deaths were attributed to IPV. Of these deaths, 75% were women and 25% were men. The economic cost of IPV has been estimated at $8.3 billion per year, including medical care, mental health services, and lost productivity in the workplace.

Victims, their families, and significant others pay the personal, economic, and psychological costs of intimate partner violence, but there are also societal costs for providing medical, judicial, police, shelter, and mental health and counseling services as well as lost productivity in the workplace (Cavaiola & Colford, 2006).

Women are more likely to be murdered by an intimate partner than by any other assailant. Homicide by intimate partners is the seventh leading cause of premature death for American women (Hines & Malley-Morrison, 2005). Licensed therapists often fail to identify—or minimize the significance of—domestic violence in their clients' relationships. Clients may not report violence because:

- They view the violence as trivial or tolerable or normal.
- They see violence as a way to resolve conflict.
- They fear what will happen to their public image if the violence becomes known.
- They feel shame.
- They fear further victimization.

Therapists often fail to ask about violence or may only ask one partner (Hamel, 2005).

Although the occurrence of family violence hinders therapy and harms the quality of family life and welfare of clients, clients may need time to develop a trusting relationship with a social worker before they are ready to reveal incidents of domestic violence. Even if someone denies the occurrence of domestic violence early in the client/social worker relationship, the social worker needs to be aware of possible signs of domestic violence and be willing to bring the issue up again later on. What should a social worker do who is working with a client on a time-limited basis when she suspects, but the client denies, a violent relationship, such as Basanti Madurai did in Exemplar 1.1? After all, clients determine what information they will share. Should the social worker use valuable time to come back to this issue again? When IPV is suspected, how can the social worker balance the need to probe for information (because she knows about reluctance to disclose this early in the helping relationship) with her ethical responsibility to respect the client's right to privacy and self-determination?

Social workers who work in intimate partner violence situations are often asked to make predictions about their clients' (or the client's partner's) violent behavior. They may be asked by law enforcement personnel, child and elder protective service workers, and civil and criminal courts to predict the likelihood of future violence of alleged or convicted perpetrators. Clinicians, in general, have been found to perform poorly when making predictions about the future occurrence of violence among perpetrators of violent behavior. Although an assessment of danger to others and/or to oneself is a basic assessment in any case of involuntary confinement or psychiatric treatment, individual clinicians have not been very successful in accurately predicting this danger for potential victims of violence (Sheridan, Glass, Limandri, & Poulos, 2007). At the same time, it must be remembered that clinical predictions often result in decisions that are inconsistent, inequitable, biased, and inaccurate (Milner & Campbell, 2007, p. 26).

There are, however, indications that when clinicians consult with each other in multidisciplinary groups and with victims of violence, they are able to pool their respective knowledge and expertise to reach a consensus. Because interdisciplinary groups view the assessment of risk for future violence from many different perspectives, they often arrive at a more complete and more accurate evaluation. Predictions also can be made even more accurate when evaluators take into consideration such interactive factors as age, gender, unemployment, perpetrator-victim relationship status, the perpetrator's history of violence, use of alcohol and or illegal substances, history of mental health issues and availability of guns. Some factors such as age, gender, and prior history of violence cannot be changed. However, risk factors such as unemployment, access to guns, use of alcohol and illegal drugs may provide clues for intervention. If some of these factors are altered, the risks may be reduced (Sheridan, Glass, Limandri, & Poulos, 2007, p. 10).

The Tarasoff duty to protect (see Chapter 8) and the legal duty to warn require social workers to take appropriate action to protect potential victims wherever and whenever violence is anticipated. A practitioner has a legal and an ethical duty to protect potential victims. To the extent that biases and ignorance influence one's judgment and contribute to inaccurate predictions, one can subject a person to unfair criminal justice penalties on the basis of the biased and inaccurate predictions. Preparation for these legal and ethical responsibilities includes becoming as knowledgeable as possible about the dynamics of violence, particularly in terms of potential further violence, as well as being careful to account for one's own biases.

Studies on the effectiveness of couple therapy for IPV indicate that therapy results in temporary decreases in violence, but generally, therapy does not result in stopping violence in the long term (Jory, Anderson, & Greer, 1997). Babcock, Green, and Robie (2004) conducted a meta-analysis of 22 treatment evaluations and concluded that "effects due to treatment were in the small range, meaning that the current interventions have a minimal impact on reducing recidivism beyond the effect of being arrested" (p. 1023). Feder and Wilson (2005) examined court-mandated batterer intervention programs and reached a similar conclusion "raising doubts about the effectiveness" (p. 239) of these programs. However, more recent research suggests that some strategies, such as integrating substance abuse treatment and interventions to improve program attendance and motivation to change, may reduce abusive behavior (Murphy & Ting, 2010, p. 26). In addition to the potential lack of demonstrated effective interventions, many agencies are understaffed, others have long waiting lists, and most, if not all, give priority to serving those currently in treatment. Remember this when you consider the ethical implications of not providing frequent follow-up services to present and past clients who have been involved in violence relationships. In Exemplar 11.1, we return to Basanti Madurai and Ellen Ashton, the case we have been following throughout the book.

EP 2.1.2

| 11.1 | LEAVING AND RETURNING |

Basanti Madurai has been attending the South Asia Women's Support Group for several months. After some initial resistance, her husband's family decided that it would be good for her to get out once in a while, and they have supported her attendance at the group meetings. Her mother-in-law has even been watching the children so that Basanti can attend the meetings without looking for child care.

As Basanti has become more comfortable with the group, she has admitted that her husband, Prajeet, often yells at her, sometimes hits her, and has occasionally left bruises. Whenever she suggests that he might need help, Prajeet becomes very angry and says that he wouldn't have to yell and hit her if she would just do what she is supposed to. Last month they had a fight, and Basanti had to go to the emergency room for a broken arm. She was afraid that the children will become aware of the violence or that her husband would strike out at the children next, so she took the children and moved into a shelter. Prajeet was very upset that his wife and children had moved to the shelter, and he agreed to attend a treatment program. After he has completed the treatment program, Basanti is planning to return home.

What is social worker Ellen Ashton's ethical responsibility in this situation? If you were in Ellen's position, how would you balance your desire to protect Basanti with her right to self-determination? Would your choice differ if there were no children involved? Would it make a difference if you don't agree with her view that a woman's place is with her husband? If you know the effectiveness or success rate of the treatment program Prajeet completed, how would that affect your decision?

ELDER ABUSE

In this section, we will briefly discuss some of the ethical issues that can arise in situations where older adults are victims of abuse. According to the National Center for Elder Abuse (2005), there are estimates that for every case of elder abuse, neglect, exploitation, or self-neglect reported to local authorities, about five other cases go unreported. There are also estimates that annually 2 million older Americans are maltreated by family members, an estimate that probably reflects underreporting (Hines & Malley-Morrison, 2005). Elderly persons are often easy targets for financial abuse both in their private homes and in institutional settings, often giving control over their finances to their caregivers. Any illegal or improper use of an elderly person's funds is considered financial abuse, including forging the person's signature, forcing them to sign documents that will benefit the forcing person or others, and stealing and misappropriating funds from the elderly person (Fryling, Summers, & Hoffman, 2006). In addition to abuse by family members or caretakers, abuse, gross neglect, and exploitation can occur in nursing homes. Of the 20,673 complaints filed with state long-term care ombudsmen programs nationally in the United States, physical abuse was the most common type of maltreatment reported (Bonnie & Wallace, 2003; National Center for Elder Abuse, 2005).

Approximately two thirds of all elder abuse perpetrators are family members, most often the victim's child or spouse. Furthermore, in many cases, they are financially dependent on the older person's resources and have alcohol and substance abuse problems (National Center for Elder Abuse, 2005). Caregivers of many kinds are responsible for much of the abuse of elders. Bergeron and Gray (2003) discuss the ethical issues that can arise for social workers who facilitate caregiver support groups, and make the following recommendations:

1. Know the elder abuse reporting laws. All 50 states, the District of Columbia, Guam, Puerto Rico, and the Virgin Islands have enacted legislation authorizing the provision of adult protective services in cases of elder abuse (reporting, investigation, and provision of social services to help the victim and ameliorate the abuse). Definitions of abuse differ, as does classification of the abuse as criminal or civil.

2. Develop rapport with adult protective services workers. Many of the potential ethical dilemmas that arise in caregiver support groups have no definitive answers, and developing rapport with elder abuse professionals in advance can help the facilitator be prepared to address issues as they arise.

3. Develop clear expectations of confidentiality with group members who need to be informed of the limits of confidentiality in relation to elder abuse reporting requirements.

4. Facilitators need to "monitor the group process so that information is not being shared prematurely and to ensure that members have sufficient knowledge about the outcome of their disclosures" (p. 103).

5. Prepare support group members for potential reports; group members should be informed of the policies for working with members who reveal abusive behaviors.

6. Cultivate peer supervision and mentoring among facilitators.

7. Contribute to the research in this area.

These recommendations provide some guidance for social workers who facilitate caregiver support groups. If one of the purposes of the caregiver support group is to allow members to vent frustrations and concerns, it is possible that the "normalization of feelings may send subtle messages to members that certain levels of consistent abusive actions, such as yelling, isolating the elderly person, or not obtaining adequate in-home services, are acceptable" (Bergeron & Gray, 2003, pp. 103–104). In earlier chapters, we raised the "who is the client" issue: Who is the client for these recommendations? Does the elderly abused person who is not physically present ever become the group facilitator's client? Is the facilitator's only responsibility to make the report to an elder abuse protection agency?

Questions have been raised about the importance of self-determination when it comes to elder abuse. Bergeron (2006) argues that social work's unrestrained assertion that self-determination is the premier principle of practice derives from the U.S. notion that individualism is of the highest value. But, Bergeron suggests further that "professionals entrusted with the duty-to-protect victims of elder abuse absolutely cannot use the principle of self-determination as the primary reason to leave elder victims in life-threatening situations, or to unconditionally accept victims' refusal for services" (p. 99). Clients who are depressed may refuse treatment out of a concern that no treatment can help; a person can be so abused and beaten down that she believes her situation is unsolvable; or an elderly parent can refuse help to protect the family's good name. Is the acceptance of an abused victim's refusal of help a rejection of the standard that "social workers act on behalf of clients who lack the capacity to make informed decisions, [and] social workers should take reasonable steps to safeguard the interests and rights of those clients" (NASW Code, 2008, 1.14)?

Social workers should bear in mind that they are responsible ethically *and* legally when confronted by abuse of elderly persons. Aside from ethical issues, social workers should know that legal remedies for difficult situations may have to be employed. Most physical, sexual, and financial abuses are considered crimes in all states because these acts violate laws prohibiting assault, battery, rape, theft, and other criminal acts. Under certain circumstances, emotional abuse and neglect may also be subject to criminal prosecution depending on the perpetrator's intent and the consequences for the victim.

END-OF-LIFE DECISIONS

The NASW (2007) policy statement on "End-of-Life Care" provides policy guidance to social workers and is based on the principle that client self-determination should apply to all aspects of life and death. This policy statement states:

> Decisions regarding end-of-life care should be considered numerous times during a person's life, not just at the diagnosis of a terminal illness or in an acute, life-threatening event. End-of-life decisions encompass a broad range of medical, spiritual, and psychosocial determinations that each individual should make before the end of his or her life.... NASW does not take a position concerning the morality of end-of-life decisions, but affirms the right of any individual to direct his or her care wishes at the end of life (Social Work Speaks Abstracts, 2007, p. 1).

The policy statement contains the following ideas:

- The social work profession strives to enhance the quality of life, to encourage the exploration of life options, and to advocate for access to options, including providing all information to make appropriate choices.
- Social workers have an important role in helping individuals identify the end-of-life options available to them.
- Competent individuals should have the opportunity to make their own choices but only after being informed of all options and consequences. Choices should be made without coercion.
- Social workers should not promote any particular means to end one's life but should be open to full discussion of the issues and care options.
- Social workers should be free to participate or not participate in assisted suicide matters or other discussions concerning end-of-life decisions depending on their own beliefs, attitudes, and value systems. If a social worker is unable to help with decisions about assisted suicide or other end-of-life choices, he or she has a professional obligation to refer patients and their families to competent professionals who are available to address end-of-life issues.
- It is inappropriate for social workers to deliver, supply, or personally participate in the commission of an act of assisted suicide when acting in their professional role.
- If legally permissible, it is not inappropriate for a social worker to be present during an assisted suicide if the client requests the social worker's presence.
- The involvement of social workers in assisted-suicide cases should not depend on race or ethnicity, religion, age, gender, economic factors, sexual orientation, or disability.

There are several ambiguities suggested by the last guideline above. Although social workers should not discriminate, different racial and ethnic groups have nevertheless been found to have different views on end-of-life decision making that imply differential interventions by group.

In addition to the statement on end-of-life and self-determination, the NASW published NASW Standards for Palliative and End of Life Care. This publication includes 11 standards for social workers dealing with palliative and end-of-life care. Among the standards included are ethics and values, knowledge required, assessment, and intervention/treatment planning, as well as other features of social work in such situations (NASW, 2007). Reybould and Adler (2006) examined the Standards for Palliative and End of Life Care in regard to end-of-life care for culturally diverse older adults and their families. They emphasize the fact that people from diverse cultures have different perceptions of medical and health care personnel and can have various traditions, beliefs, values, and desires. They can have different values about autonomy and self-determination, death and dying, uncertainty or certainty about whether one is terminally ill, communication (including languages and language barriers), truth telling or not, level of care desired, and other culture-bound perceptions and values.

Gross and Mukamel (2005) argue that any decision-making model focused on the individual practitioner omits the organizational and other contexts in which the decisions have to be made. They studied the process of advance care planning of 3,548 participants in managed care programs. When all the known participant characteristics were accounted for, program effects were found to account for 36% of the variation in do-not-resuscitate choice, 66% in the choice of artificial feeding, and 50% relating to the presence of health care proxy. These findings suggest that individual professionals as well as program and organizational factors can have a large impact on individuals' decisions about advance care planning.

Essentially, end-of-life decisions focus on three different stages of ethical concern: life-palliative care, death by choice or otherwise, and grief among survivors. Social workers have a long history of care with persons involving life-limiting illness, the process of dying, and dealing with grief and bereavement following deaths. The end-of-life policy promulgated by the NASW is a relatively new development in social work, which is met by social workers and others with differing sets of values. Little is known about these phenomena. Some social workers believe that promulgation by the NASW of guidelines regarding social workers' potential roles in physician-assisted suicide in effect suggests it is ethical to do so. Others oppose providing assistance in ending-of-life situations (Manetta & Wells, 2001). In some states, assisting in a suicide is against the law. A major argument presented in opposition to social workers' participation in physician-assisted suicide is the slippery slope argument. Although assisted suicide begins with those who are terminally ill, some persons have expressed fears that the definition of those eligible will—over time—include other vulnerable groups.

Werth and Rogers (2005) emphasize the duty of social workers to protect clients who are identified as suicidal. They propose that the duty to protect should apply whenever a client is engaging in a behavior that may lead to serious self-harm or death within a reasonably short period of time. To do so requires an assessment of impaired judgment, followed by appropriate interventions after the evaluation. The values of the mental health practitioner and the values of the client are both considerations in the situation. Werth and Rogers set forth a summary of the issues to consider when exploring end-of-life decisions. The scheme includes four major issues with a number of subquestions to be considered: (1) assessment of capacity to give informed consent to participate in the review and the capacity to make informed health care decisions; (2) the decision-making process, including physical pain and

suffering, fear of loss of control, financial concerns, cultural factors, underlying issues, overall quality of life, and so forth; (3) the person's social support system; and
(4) systemic and environmental issues. Even if all the above issues are assessed positively, a social worker must decide what her perspective and values are in relation to
end-of-life decisions.

Although the NASW policy statement is based on the principle of self-determination,
many doubt whether meaningful self-determination and voluntary consent prevail in
situations in which a person wishes to harm himself or commit suicide, because "only
abysmal ignorance or deep emotional trauma can lead persons to extreme measures
like these" (Gewirth, 1978, p. 264). But there are those who criticize this view. They
claim that mental illness per se does not preclude competence (Mishna, Antle, &
Regehr, 2002). Others also take issue with the autonomy (self-determination) argument by suggesting that active physician-assisted suicide is more than a matter of
self-determination. From this point of view, it has been suggested that it is a mutual
decision by two people, one of whom is to be killed and the other who is to do the
killing (Callahan, 1994). In certain situations, medical treatment for palliative care
or harsh treatments such as chemotherapy reach a limit beyond which there is no ultimate benefit to the patients and no enhancement of quality of life. Some persons feel
that quality of life is ethically irrelevant, and the ethical issue is to take or not take a
life. If a social worker is faced with such a situation, does the ethical principles screen
(EPS) introduced in Chapter 4 provide any help in clarifying the ethical choices being
faced and in what priority order?

The policy statement raises many questions, among which are the following:
Whose quality of life is supported by assisted suicide? Whose life is harmed?
What is competence in such a situation? How does one judge competency? Is coercion entirely absent when people are considering suicide? What should one do
if the option chosen creates issues for other family members, significant others,
friends, or other professionals? What should one do if there are conflicts among
those involved—some wanting to maintain life at all costs, others supporting the
person's decision? What does it mean to be present but not participate? Is this just
another form of approval of the act? The definition of terminal illness is not always
clear. Sometimes even the best of medical practitioners makes a mistake, and persons judged to be terminally ill live beyond the projected time. Can palliative care
and the control of pain offset the desire to end one's life?

Assisted Suicide

Physician-assisted suicide has been legal in Oregon since 1997, when Oregon voters
approved the Death with Dignity Act. During 2008, voters in the State of Washington
approved a ballot initiative allowing terminally ill, legally competent adults to obtain
lethal prescriptions without exposing themselves or their doctors to criminal prosecution. Montana became the third state to allow physician-assisted suicide in 2010 when
the State Supreme Court ruled that suicide even when a physician plays a role is not a
crime. The Court found that neither state law nor public policy prevented physicians
from prescribing lethal drugs to terminally ill patients who wanted to end their lives.
Supreme Court rulings on physician-assisted suicide for terminally ill persons left the
door open for individual states to define their own statutes in this area and suggested

the Court could revisit the issue. Thirty-nine states explicitly prohibit physician-assisted suicide; six states prohibit suicide through common law; and three states (North Carolina, Utah, and Wyoming) do not have laws prohibiting physician-assisted suicide (Sherer, 2004). Physician-assisted suicide remains quite controversial.

Two basic ethical issues have to be weighed: one concerns society and the second concerns the social work profession itself. In regard to society, there are those concerned about the slippery slope effect of condoning assisted suicide. In at least one nation where assisted suicide has been permitted, the Netherlands, the definition of who is eligible has grown looser and outside the specific guidelines over time (Citizen Link, 2003). The assisted suicide laws in Oregon and the Netherlands differ in important respects. In Oregon the physician prescribes a lethal dose of a medication; in the Netherlands, a physician may prescribe or directly administer a lethal dose. When is the assistance justified? In Oregon, termination is justified when the person has a terminal illness that will lead to death within six months.

In a study to assess the attitudes of 306 hospice nurses and 85 social workers in Oregon in 2001, it was found that almost two-thirds of the respondents reported that at least one patient had discussed assisted suicide as a potential option during the past year. Social workers were generally more supportive of the Death with Dignity Act and of patients choosing suicide than were nurses. Social workers can encounter patient questions about physician-assisted suicide, whether legalized or not, and must be prepared to have these discussions (Miller et al., 2004).

Callahan (1994) argues that "the ethical position for social workers—most in keeping with the spirit and overall content of the NASW Code of Ethics—[is] to oppose assisted suicide and especially to oppose legislation that would change our social policy to one of condoning suicide instead of preventing it" (p. 243). One of his concerns is that participating in assisted suicide can have the effect of destigmatizing the act, leading to greater acceptability of suicide by those who are vulnerable but not terminally ill. Mackelprang and Mackelprang (2005) further suggest that Standard 1.02 of the NASW (1999) Code asserts that social workers have a responsibility to limit self-determination when people pose a serious risk to themselves or others. These perspectives are at variance with NASW Standards for Palliative and End of Life Care (NASW, 2006). The question then is: How is one to choose and on what basis?

As far as social work is concerned, there are additional questions. Assisted suicide requires assistance being provided only for those who are undeniably competent to make such requests and for whom there are no alternative ways of relieving their suffering through palliative care. One observer suggests that there are two essential ethical requirements of professionals: to seek to deliver the kinds of services they profess to provide and to be trustworthy. To be trusted as a profession, social work must be viewed as honest, fair, and just (Jackson, 2000). It is against these ethical standards that assisted-suicide participation needs to be weighed.

CLIENTS LIVING WITH HIV AND AIDS

The HIV (human immunodeficiency virus) infection has now spread to every nation in the world and has infected millions of people. In the United States in 2007, an estimated 468,578 persons were living with AIDS, while the number of persons living with HIV was estimated at 850,000 to 950,000 (in 2004); an additional 40,000 new infections are estimated to occur annually (Morgan & Levi, 2006).

BIASES ABOUT AIDS

AIDS is not an ordinary disease. People who have AIDS or who test HIV positive cannot be discussed in quite the same way as people who suffer other kinds of diseases. There is a high degree of stigma associated with AIDS, more stigma than is true for almost any other illness. Because of this stigma, many people with AIDS do not want others to know they have the disease. They often go to considerable lengths to conceal the illness, even from those who are closest to them. They need support to ask for the help they desperately need.

The AIDS epidemic has become widespread. Many persons have become infected, including spouses and significant others of infected persons, recipients of infected blood, newborn babies of infected parents, persons who shared needles, and others. Some of these persons may share the general public's biases about HIV and AIDS, and the stigma associated with HIV/AIDS may keep them from asking for the help they need when they know they are HIV positive. Social workers must find ways to open communication channels with all of these people, both those who are diagnosed as HIV positive and those who have developed AIDS.

CONFIDENTIALITY AND HIV/AIDS

Ethical dilemmas often arise for social workers when they learn that a client is HIV positive or has contracted AIDS. There are issues concerning the person's efforts to take care of his health needs. Does he use health care appropriately? And there are issues related to how the person relates to other persons. When sexually active, does the person inform partners or keep his health state private, thus potentially putting partners at risk?

Earlier, issues concerning protecting confidentiality were explored in regard to a number of concerns, including threats made by a client that he would seek to harm someone physically. Although complex, the Tarasoff decision provides legal support for a social worker who learns of the client's intentions. But, how should social workers deal ethically with a situation in which the client is HIV positive and refuses to inform his partners? Is this situation parallel to Tarasoff potential violence? Are there laws in your state that set guidelines for social workers dealing with clients living with HIV or AIDs?

SOCIAL WORK ADVOCACY FOR CLIENTS LIVING WITH HIV

There are many ethical dilemmas and problems that social workers face when working with clients living with HIV. Rationing medical care presents one set of ethical problems that require a social worker's advocacy services. Childless adults living with HIV infection typically only qualify for Medicaid coverage once they become eligible for SSI. Becoming eligible for SSI or Social Security Disability depends on becoming disabled—that is, severely limited in his or her ability to work (Federal Globe, 2007). Those persons with asymptomatic HIV infection are not eligible for Medicaid until the condition has become fully developed AIDS. As a result, childless adults who are HIV positive are ineligible for Medicaid except in several states with Medicaid waivers, which extend benefits to nondisabled persons living with HIV. These states conduct demonstration projects to evaluate the cost effectiveness of expanding services to this group in order to slow the progress of the disease and prevent opportunistic infections (Human Rights Campaign, 2003). Does a social worker have an ethical obligation to advocate for such services? Should social workers advocate for other services or rights for persons living with HIV or AIDS?

TECHNOLOGY IN DIRECT PRACTICE

Experiences with the delivery of counseling services through new technological means, lack of services in rural locations, the search for less expensive means of delivering services, and increasing use of the Internet have fostered new ways of delivering services. Telephone counseling is one alternative to face-to-face delivery of services, and can be used as an adjunct to a primary face-to-face relationship or as a primary method for some clients such as those who are mobility-impaired or rural clients who lack transportation. These contacts may be mental health treatment oriented or for information sharing, problem-solving, and support.

In 2001, Medicare expanded its coverage of tele-health services for Medicare beneficiaries to include certain individual psychotherapy services. Eligible clinical social workers can receive reimbursement for specified services. However, the services are reimbursable only if clients receive the services at "originating sites" that provide videoconferencing capabilities, such as physician and practitioner offices, hospitals, and rural health care clinics. In general, these sites must be in rural areas designated as health professional shortage areas or counties that are not part of a metropolitan statistical area (a city with more than 50,000 people) (Ballie, 2001). In these situations, the client must be at the designated site at a specific time to access the services from a social worker available at another distant site.

The telephone has been used to provide services in these ways for years, but now there are many more options for using technology to deliver services, including Internet and online therapy, as well as online self-help groups. To date, these methods have not been scientifically tested as to their effectiveness (NASW, n.d.). NASW and the Association of Social Work Boards (2005) published Standards for Technology and Social Work Practice to provide guidance for the use of services delivered through technological means when technology is used as an adjunct to practice or exclusively delivered through technological means.

There are controversies about the pros and cons of online practice, and questions have also been raised about ethical and legal issues. One concern is about the protection of confidentiality and the misdirection of electronic transmissions, as well as the possibility that hackers could invade the communication. The NASW Code (2008) recognizes the limitations of services using technology. As a result, social workers who provide services via electronic media (such as computer, telephone, radio, and television) are advised to inform recipients of the limitations and risks associated with such services (Code, 2008, 1.03e) and to take precautions to ensure and maintain the confidentiality of information transmitted to other parties (Code, 2008, 1.07m). Encryption of online communication may offer adequate protections, but many individual service providers and clients may not have access or know how to use the necessary software. Confidential e-mail can be misdirected to a wrong person or even to an entire address book or list of people. Is contracting with the services of a technology consultant sufficient assurance that the practitioner is compliant with ethical standards?

A second issue is the appropriateness of treatment services. Which presenting symptoms are appropriate for online treatment? Is online therapy therapeutic? Can therapeutic alliances be developed online? What are the differences between online and face-to-face therapy? To date, no conclusive research exists as to which topics are inappropriate for online therapy. Some topics that might be included in such a list are sexual abuse as a primary issue, violent relationships, eating disorders, and psychiatric disorders that involve distortions of reality (Helton, 2003). Even if there were agreement and evidence about which difficulties can be assisted by online treatment, how can adequate assessments be made without visual and auditory, as well as other, cues? Even if the therapist and client can see each other via videoconferencing or Skype, it is likely that experience will be different from traditional treatment methods and require different skills.

A third concern is whether social workers are sufficiently trained to provide these services. Are the knowledge and skills of traditionally trained and educated social workers transferable to online interventions? Another issue is whether there are credentialing and cross-state issues. Is a therapist in Maryland licensed for therapy in California? Where is the service taking place, Maryland or California? California law, for instance, states that online mental health practitioners cannot practice outside California. What national organization would best standardize credentials and provide licenses and credentials? Finally, what if any issues are there for providing professional insurance coverage for those practicing online? Social workers have an ethical responsibility to seek training for these services and to ascertain how the laws of their state impact on the delivery of services through technological means.

On the positive side, some of the benefits of online therapy are accessibility for rural and isolated areas and home-bound clients; anonymity for those reluctant to see a therapist; 24/7 availability; low cost; and screening and follow-up care. Scheduling problems can be minimized because of the flexibility of the Internet, which can be used day or night, weekday or weekend. Ease of recording for the practitioner may also be increased. There are those who believe that clients may be even more open about self-disclosure in an online setting (Abney & Maddux, 2004).

Although there are claims that social workers who provide these services do so at low risk, there are ethical issues involved. For example, in some crisis situations (such as suicidal ideation) the social worker and the client can be dependent on distant and perhaps unknown persons for assessment and provision of emergency treatment. Where in the Code would you find support suggesting that providing services in this way is ethical or unethical? As with all therapy situations, there are housekeeping matters, including completing intake forms; obtaining informed consent; explaining the limits of confidentiality and mandated reporting laws; describing how any grievances will be handled and by whom; providing the fee structure; and covering record keeping, security measures, and termination policies. How can these issues be ethically addressed in online sessions?

O'Neill (2002) found that some social workers thought it a mistake and unethical for social workers to offer online therapy prior to the establishment of practice standards and before the liability issues have been clarified. Other social workers were critical of the criticisms and claimed that online therapists are equally as well prepared as those who provide offline therapy, relative anonymity can increase willingness of clients to participate in the therapy, and both client and therapist can be freed from preconceived notions about each other (O'Neill, 2002).

The following issues are addressed in the NASW and Association of Social Work Boards (ASWB) (2005) Standards for Technology and Social Work Practice:

- social work advocacy for technology access by clients with special needs or limited access
- compliance with applicable laws and regulations in all states where the social work services are provided
- appropriate matching of online methods, skills, and techniques to the cultural and ethnic characteristics of the treatment population
- accurate marketing practices and verification of client identity
- privacy protection requirements
- knowledge about appropriateness of certain types of online technologies for specific clients
- development of security policies and procedures, as well as contingency plans for electronic failures or emergencies
- retention of technology consultants (list quoted from http://www.socialwor kers.org/ldf/legal_issue/200704.asp?back=yes)

For the reader's consideration, we also include guidelines prepared for the National Board for Certified Counselors. Among their suggested guidelines are:

- Ensure client confidentiality through encryption methods
- Check on liability issues
- Inform the client how long session data will be saved
- Check on client and counselor identities through codes
- Verify identities of adults when consent is needed for minors
- Establish local on-call counselor or crisis resources
- Screen out problems not appropriate for Internet counseling
- Explain and have contingency plans if technical problems occur
- Explain how to cope with potential misunderstandings that arise due to lack of visual cues
- Discuss what to do if the counselor is offline or when there are delays in sending and receiving messages (Fukuyama, 2001)

The commonplace use of e-mail makes unsought information available that may confront a practitioner with critical ethical dilemmas, such as the case presented in Exemplar 11.2.

EP 2.1.2

11.2	E-MAIL FROM EUROPE AND SUICIDAL THOUGHTS

A university student used an electronic mail discussion group to inquire about a drug that could be used for a painless suicide. A professor in Europe who read this request communicated his concern to the sender's university, which forwarded this message to the university's counseling department. The counselor assigned to this case obtained more information before deciding what to do. She contacted the director of the computer center, who broke into the student's account where additional messages on suicide were discovered. At this point, the counselor decided to contact the student's parents. (This situation was described on a social work electronic discussion list and is used with permission of Steve Marson of Pembroke University. The counselor was not a social worker.)

Exemplar 11.2 has been presented because it reflects the use of e-mail and potentially other common forms of electronic communication such as social networking sites, and because it raises some issues that social workers must consider. One issue facing the counselor is whether to act on the basis of third-party information from someone unknown to her. Because the situation was potentially life threatening, this counselor decided to take the information conveyed by the third party seriously, but she also wanted to obtain verification of the facts, if possible. Here, the worker decided that intervention was justified. More generally, questions can be raised regarding the circumstances under which a social worker should seek access to a confidential electronic file. Is there any issue short of life-threatening situations that might support such an action? Under what circumstances does the computer center or a social agency have a right to examine someone's personal computer account?

What should the counselor have done if the computer center (or agency) stated such an invasion was illegal or against the rules? Although the counselor felt justified in asking the computer center for verification because of the potential life-threatening nature of the situation, was it ethical for her to enter the student's computer account without obtaining his permission? Because the student is at the university and the counselor is a university employee, she has some responsibility for his welfare, especially after she gained information about what was in his file. What should she have done if the student's account did not include life-threatening materials?

We do not know the counselor's reasons for contacting the student's parents rather than the student himself. Is telling the parents about their son's behavior an improper invasion of the student's right to privacy and confidentiality? What should the counselor do if, instead of contacting the student's parents, she spoke to the student, and he simply stated that he has an intellectual interest in painless suicide as a chemical problem? Which standards in the Code of Ethics provide guidance in this type of situation?

The use of technologies by social workers is open—as all practice is—to possible ethical dilemmas and unethical behaviors. NASW identified several questionable practices associated with on-line behavior. Among these are: unfounded claims of successful outcomes, use of unprofessional photographs, failure to identify the professional by name and licensure status, single state therapy practices providing nationwide therapy services without indicating licensure in the states where the clients are located, providing services to anonymous clients, and permitting public internet posting of client's comments where confidentiality is not assured (NASW, n.d.).

The extent of the use of social networking sites, including Facebook, MySpace, and LinkedIn, as well as micro-blogging on tools such as Twitter, is unknown. What are some of the possible ethical dilemmas associated with a social worker's participation in social networking sites or blogs? Does it matter if she is participating socially rather than professionally? It is likely that regardless of the undecided practical and ethical issues, Internet-based and other technology-based services will continue to expand.

RELIGION AND SPIRITUALITY

Historically, religious content was sparsely included in social work education and in social work literature. Little information was conveyed on spirituality and religion as part of the educational preparation of practitioners, and there was—for long periods—an almost complete exclusion of such content from journals, textbooks, and course outlines (Hodge, 2004). Canda, Nakashima, and Furman (2004) surveyed 2,069 NASW members about spirituality and religion in their educations and practices. The majority of the respondents pointed out the inadequacy of their social work educations about the two topics. The need to engage more specifically with notions of spirituality and religion has more recently begun to occupy a growing presence in social work education and practice.

Although agreement about definitions of spirituality and religion remains scarce, nevertheless, their place in social work and social work education has steadily broadened. We will use the definitions of Canda et al. (2004), who define religion as "an organized, structured set of beliefs and practices shared by a community related to spirituality" (p. 28) and spirituality as involving "the search for meaning, purpose, and morally fulfilling relations with self, other people, the encompassing universe and ultimate reality, however a person understands it" (p. 28).

Religion and spirituality inform clients' and social workers' worldviews. As Sherwood (1997) points out, "Everyone operates on the basis of some worldview or faith-based understanding of the universe and persons—examined or unexamined, implicit or explicit, simplistic or sophisticated" (p. 115). Sherwood's point is that these worldviews affect our approach to social work practice and how we understand people.

RELIGION, SOCIAL WORK VALUES, AND SECULARISM

According to Stewart (2009), fundamental differences exist between traditionally understood Christian world views and the social work world view. His view is that the NASW-adopted official positions are based on a secular and humanistic interpretation of social work, influenced by humanism, postmodernism, and liberalism, which signaled a movement away from traditional Judeo-Christian religious values. In this world view the nature of humanity, the role of sin, the importance of revealed truth, free will, and the purpose of suffering, all vary significantly from the traditional philosophical perspective. This value conflict with a traditional Christian perspective does not remain strictly theoretical but has practical consequences. This conflict was exemplified by the experience of one school of social work, located within a theological seminary that was entirely dismantled because of a clash of values. Stewart (2009) concludes that conflicts between stated social work values and traditional religious values will continue to be problematic.

Thyer and Myers (2009) reviewed media reports of discrimination against social work students, both in BSW and MSW programs, due to their religious beliefs and provide additional examples of religious discrimination, including faculty evaluations of students and students being unfairly dismissed from social work programs. These charges suggest that accusations of religious discrimination in social work education remain an ongoing problem—not unlike discrimination on the basis of race, gender, and sexual orientation. These reports also support the comments of Stewart (2009), noted above, regarding continuing conflicts between religious and social work values.

At the same time, Hodge (2007) uses the NASW Code of Ethics to argue there is a need to advocate for social justice through the elimination of religious discrimination. Hodge (2007) also refers to the United Nations' (1948) Universal Declaration of Human Rights Article 2 that prohibits religious discrimination and to Article 18 that presents an even broader statement: "everyone has the right to freedom of … religion; this right includes freedom to change his religion or belief, and freedom, either alone or in community with others and in public or private to manifest his religion or belief in teaching, practice, worship and observance". There is much religious discrimination around the world, and Hodge (2007) advocates that social workers should actively work to ensure that all people are able to freely express the rights identified previously. These rights are consistent with the NASW (2008) Code of Ethics standards on autonomy (1.02) and religious nondiscrimination (6.01, 6.04d). Hodge (2007), finally, suggests that social work has a duty to advocate for religious freedom because many of the victims of religious persecution are members of marginalized and vulnerable populations, often disproportionately poor, women, and marginalized subgroups with few advocates worldwide. He advocates that social work as a profession dedicated to social justice should give voice to those religious groups that experience persecution.

Hodge (2009) describes what he perceives as the pervasiveness, yet invisibility, of secularism and secular privilege in the United States. He suggests it is important for social workers to be aware of this phenomenon. Secularists focus on worldly matters rather than the spiritual world and are—in general—little concerned with spiritual, religious, or sacred things. This group is not limited to atheists and agnostics but includes those unaffiliated with a spiritual tradition who are also unconcerned, uninterested, or lack investment in spirituality or religion. Hodge (2009) suggests that in our society secularists largely determine the norms and values of the society. They dominate the professional landscape and the worlds of entertainment, industry, the news media, education, and government. From his perspective, secularism plays a central role in forming the values of broader society and occupies a privileged position.

Hodge's (2009) argument is that understanding the importance of secularism and secular privilege enables social workers to experience a greater appreciation of diversity and cultural differences. With this knowledge, social workers are better positioned to provide ethical professional services in a society with increasingly diverse spiritual cultures. If you agree with Hodge's (2009) assessment, in what ways—from an ethical point of view—can your acknowledgement of secularist privilege affect your ethical decision making? Is tacit acceptance of secular privilege responsible for practitioners—including those who use religious materials and spiritually based interventions in their social work practice—being unprepared during their social work educations for these interventions? What is social work education's ethical responsibility to recognize and deal constructively with what Hodge identifies as secular privilege?

SPIRITUALITY AND SOCIAL WORK PRACTICE

Several authors have drawn attention to the ways in which spiritual matters can be introduced into social work practice. Among these are uses of ritual; exploration of sacred stories and symbols; incorporation of art, dance, and poetry; meditation and prayer; and a focus on caring for the body (Maidment, 2006). Canda et al. (2004) explored other dimensions concerned with spirituality and religion in social workers' practices. There was very high agreement that making referrals to clergy and collaborating with them was appropriate. Lesser numbers agreed to the appropriateness of using prayer, meditation, visualization, rituals and symbols, inspirational readings, touch for helping purposes, spiritual narrative and dialogue, or religious language. The major disagreements focused on the use of prayer, healing touch, and worker self-disclosure; some thought their use appropriate and others inappropriate.

There is little empirical research about if and when to use spiritual interventions and the ethical decision making involved. Any prior questions, such as the constitutionality of these interventions, apparently are being answered in a pragmatic and incremental fashion without being challenged legally. For example, one can ask: What are the constitutional questions concerning the use of religious interventions in public governmental institutions? Assuming there are federal funds involved, what Constitutional questions might be asked when religious/spiritual interventions are used in a voluntary nonprofit agency sponsored by a religious group that serves the broad community, including persons who are not members of the sponsoring religious group? In the United States, there is a careful balance between not establishing a state religion and the religious liberty provisions of federal and state constitutions. Moberg (2005) suggests that focusing on spirituality and not on religion only partly solves the dilemma. Although spirituality may be viewed by some persons as separate from organized religious groups, the concept of spirituality remains open to argument as to whether it refers to the establishment of religion. However, many clients served by social workers have spiritual or religious orientations that are important to them and can be helpful in treatment. Omitting consideration of these basic beliefs and their effects may limit the effectiveness of the social worker's efforts.

Hodge (2005) reports that the largest health care accrediting body in the United States—the Joint Commission on Accreditation of Health Care Organizations (JCAHO)—now requires in mental health settings the administration of an initial exploratory spiritual assessment. Hodge (2005) also describes the "spiritual life map" and its use for spiritual assessment. He introduces several value conflicts that can emerge with the use of spiritual assessment. First, client self-determination and autonomy must be protected. Second, social workers must be alert to the issue of religious counter transference, both as a result of their own developmental issues and decisions as well as the beliefs and values of their clients and patients. Third, even when the value systems of practitioners and clients are congruent, there exists the possibility of the social worker falling into spiritual guidance instead of focusing on the client's problems.

In a subsequent article, Hodge (2006) provides social workers with guidelines for the implementation of spiritual assessments. He suggests four principles, each of which has ethical implications: (1) respect for client self-determination; (2) the practitioner's ability to provide culturally competent services; (3) the degree to which the norms of the client's faith tradition relate to service provision; and (4) the salience of spirituality to the client's life. As part of his discussion, Hodge introduces research that indicates a link between spirituality and religion and mental and physical health outcomes. Arguably, this knowledge supports the ethical correctness of competently using spiritual assessments and interventions specifically designed for particular groups.

A major ethical dilemma in the sphere of religion and spirituality has arisen in relation to the Code of Ethics. In regard to discrimination, the NASW (2008) Code states: "Social workers should not practice, condone, facilitate, or collaborate with any form of discrimination on the basis of race, ethnicity, national origin, color, sex, sexual orientation, gender identity or expression, age, marital status, political belief, *religion,* immigration status, or mental or physical disability" (4.02, emphasis added). Some religious and minority groups are viewed by other groups as being discriminatory. Both religious and minority group discrimination are unethical. There is an ongoing debate and discussion about this dilemma. How can the conflicting claims of different minority groups be accommodated within the parameters of freedom of speech and freedom of conscience to which both groups are entitled? Can the claims of differing religious values be accommodated between those whose religious values condone abortion and those who oppose abortion; those who allow assisted suicide and those who oppose suicide; those who support gay marriage and those who oppose it? All these groups are entitled to freedom of speech and the expression of their freedom of conscience. What ethical dilemmas arise when groups with opposing values meet in the public square and their speech and actions affect other groups?

For the individual social worker and client, perhaps the most difficult issue regarding spirituality and religion focuses on the authority of the social worker and the vulnerability of the client. There are few ways to avoid exerting the social worker's authority, which has been gained from licensing, education, agency-granted authority, and skills. The client needs help and may be vulnerable and needy. Aside from issues of the psychological transference of the client, the authority of the social worker is at play. Is teaching religious ideas by example or through words appropriate in the service relationship? Is it appropriate to encourage a person raised in one religion to drop out or change to another? What are the effects of suggesting that a client pray with you, the social worker? What are the effects of subtly demeaning religious beliefs and practices that differ from yours?

A PLURALITY OF IDENTITIES AND CLIENT GROUPS

U.S. society is growing more and more diverse, leading to an increasing number of group identities in the United States. Such identities serve as political and social forces, as a means of personal expression, and as a way of achieving meaning in people's lives. One result of this increasing diversity is that social workers deal with a growing number of people who come from a variety of cultures that differ from the traditional view of mainstream U.S. society; these people are often more affected by their own cultures than by what might be considered the U.S. culture.

Among general U.S. society and among social workers, there is an affirmation of diversity. Enunciated in the NASW (2008) Code is the expectation that "social workers treat each person in a caring and respectful fashion, mindful of individual differences and cultural and ethnic diversity." The Code standard on cultural competence and social diversity (2008, 1.05) requires that ethical social workers understand culture and its function in human behavior, and have a knowledge base of and be sensitive to their clients' cultures. Furthermore, social workers are expected "to obtain education about and seek to understand the nature of social diversity and oppression with respect to race, ethnicity, national origin, color, sex, sexual orientation, gender identity or expression, age, marital status, political belief, religion, immigration status, and mental or physical disability" (1.05c).

Most people may belong to several groups and have multiple identities. Even when a person is strongly identified with a single culture, his identity can be based on additional characteristics such as national origin, gender, social class, sexual orientation, disability, and age, among others. In the process of learning much about many different groups, there are dangers of stereotyping persons by a primary group identity. Cultures are varied and complex, and social workers need to create methods to avoid false generalizations or overgeneralization about groups (Walker & Staton, 2000). A White woman, for example, can be poor, Baptist, 80 years old, lesbian, and have been born and raised in Africa.

Illustrative of this point, Fellin (2000) proposed a way of assessing cultures of identification and participation, which emphasizes the multiple groups and degrees of group membership and participation an individual may have. Clients belong to various racial and ethnic groups and subgroups, religions, social classes, and sexual orientations, and may have disabilities of various types. When dealing with these differing persons and families, a social worker has to determine the degree of identification each person has with the groups they belong to, the level of their psychological sense of membership, and their level of participation in the groups.

Thus, a person can hold membership in various groups, identify himself psychologically more or less with various groupings, and participate socially to varying degrees in each of the groups. We have introduced this conceptual scheme because it enables social workers to more correctly/ethically understand and assess the clients and families whom they serve from a multicultural and complex perspective. To think a person possesses only one identity is to engage in stereotyping, as each person belongs to many groups and the strength of his identities may shift over time. To understand each person as an individual requires being sensitive to and informed about a client's set of identities.

Because there are often major cultural differences within cultural groups, it is difficult to offer generalizations that apply to a community as a whole. For example, the Filipino community is a diverse population itself. Individuals and their families differ in respect to when they arrived in the United States, socioeconomic background, educational level, language, factors surrounding their immigration, dialect, geographic orientation, social class, and level of acculturation. There is diversity among groups and within groups.

In addition to the treatment of cultural competence in the Code of Ethics, a milestone in this area of concern was the promulgation of the NASW Standards for Cultural Competence in Social Work Practice (2001). Historically, culture and diversity have been associated in social work with race and ethnicity. However, diversity in today's United States includes "the sociocultural experiences of people of different genders, social classes, religious and spiritual beliefs, sexual orientations, ages, and physical and mental abilities" (NASW, 2001, p. 8). In 2008, the NASW Delegate Assembly voted to add gender identity or expression and immigration status to the Code sections on cultural competence and social diversity (1.05), respect (2.01), discrimination (4.02), and social and political action (6.04).

DISCRIMINATION AND MISDIAGNOSIS

Understanding of a particular person and culture can be informed and accurate, but discrimination exists at many levels, including at the practitioner level. Discrimination may affect diagnosis and treatment; for example, Leach and Sullivan (2002) found:

- People in lower socioeconomic classes consistently receive more frequent and severe diagnoses than individuals in other class levels.
- Blacks and Hispanics are more likely than Whites to be diagnosed with personality disorders or schizophrenia.
- African American children are more likely to receive a diagnosis of hyperactivity than White and Asian American children.
- Racial-ethnic minorities are more likely than Whites to be diagnosed with chronic disorders rather than acute disorders.

Discrimination in mental health services has been linked to racial and cultural factors, socioeconomic class, and the gender of clients (Toporek, 2002). At least two theories are suggested to explain these discrepancies: (1) misdiagnosis is a result of different cultural expressions of symptoms, or (2) clinician bias. Regardless of the cause, these kinds of misdiagnoses based on misunderstanding or on bias are unethical. Is the practitioner's intention to misdiagnose necessary before a person can be held guilty of an ethical violation? (See the section on Diagnosis and Misdiagnosis in Chapter 7 for further discussion of ethical issues related to misdiagnosis.)

CULTURE AND TREATMENT

A social worker can also encounter ethical dilemmas related to confidentiality and respecting a client's culture. For example, a young Asian American woman might be extremely shy about truth telling and disclosure. In her culture, many important decisions may be made by elders and not by young persons. On the other hand, social workers are trained to encourage disclosure and honesty in their clients. For a social worker to report bad news (e.g., that they need to make a report for child abuse or suggest HIV testing) to clients who come from some cultures could be interpreted as contributing to the illness, depriving the client of hope, and even casting a curse on the client and her family, in addition to bringing shame on them. Is it ethical to probe for more information when the client is culturally protective of family and personal secrets? What should one do if the client does not want you to report abuse because that would shame her family and ruin their life in their community? Consider the situation described in Exemplar 11.3.

| 11.3 | How Much to Tell Hyun Cho? |

EP 2.1.2

Hyun Cho, an Asian American and recent immigrant in her early 50s, was referred to the Western Neighborhood Counseling Center by a non-Asian friend whom she admired and who had been helped at the Center. Hyun explained to Haley Traylor, her social worker, that she started having stomachaches, accompanied by becoming quite anxious, following her husband's being laid off. A visit to a physician found no physical problems. As treatment proceeded, things went quite well for a time, and Hyun began to feel better and more in control of her life.

At that point Hyun told Haley that although she is feeling better, a woman at her church told her she should not be using the Western Neighborhood Counseling Center but should use Asian methods and Asian persons to deal with her problems. Hyun announced that she appreciates the help she has been given, but she thinks her friend is correct and intends to go to a healer who emphasizes meditation and green tea. This decision surprised Haley because she had heard that the particular healer Hyun is going to visit is not helpful and that several persons had their physical problems worsen after his treatment.

What is the ethical choice for Haley? Should she tell Hyun what she knows about other persons' experiences with the neighborhood healer? Would that lead to an informed choice? Should she remain silent about her knowledge and accept without question Hyun's decision?

Sensitive and informed social work practice can demand that social workers practice in various and counterintuitive ways, ways that may be considered unethical. For example, people of Chinese backgrounds who are under the influence of Taoistic concepts of mental health can see the world in ways very different from what social workers are accustomed to meeting. Yet as Yip (2005) explains, social work practice stresses cognitive and emotional change of the individual in order to face their problems. Persons of Chinese background and influenced by Taoistic concepts seek change through inaction and regressive self-preservation. According to Tao thought, inaction is not static or passive but suggests insight into the laws of nature, and the client is allowing her mind or behavior to occur naturally. Is it ethically correct to remain silent and accept the person's behavior? Does this mean choosing between ordinary accountability to the agency and loyalty to the client? How might a social worker respond in Exemplar 11.4?

11.4 | CALLING A SHAMAN

EP 2.1.2

Evelyn Waters was on a home visit with Mr. Lee when he asked her to contact a shaman (a member of certain tribal societies who acts as a medium between the visible
and spirit worlds for healing, divination, or control over events) because he has been
feeling quite ill. When the social worker instead suggested he should be taken to a local walk-in clinic, he was very resistant and insisted on seeing a shaman. Because the
client was conscious and seemed to be in control of himself, Ms. Waters decided to
take the phone number and called the shaman, who said he would come immediately.
When the shaman arrived, he spoke to Mr. Lee briefly in private and then started the
healing process by looping a coiled thread around Mr. Lee's wrist. The shaman
explained that he was summoning Mr. Lee's runaway soul. In addition, the shaman
traced with his finger a protective invisible shield around Mr. Lee. Given Mr. Lee's
history of diabetes and hypertension, Ms. Waters was concerned that the shaman's
treatment might not be sufficient or may even be harmful.

Is it helpful to know that Hmong people rely on their spiritual beliefs to get
them through illnesses? Was it ethical to accept Mr. Lee's self-determination and
assessment of his situation? What ethical alternatives existed before calling the shaman, after his arrival, and after his treatment began? Would it make a difference if
the shaman decided to treat Mr. Lee in his own way and insisted Mr. Lee could be
brought to the clinic but not before tomorrow morning?

In their practices, practitioners may encounter culture-bound syndromes. For
example, social workers in certain locations may be confronted with client symptoms, such as *ataque de nervios* (out-of-consciousness state resulting from evil spir-
its); amok (outbursts of violent and aggressive behavior); and *dhat* (extreme anxiety
associated with a sense of weakness and exhaustion) (Castillo, 2007). When the
social worker is confronted by these unfamiliar syndromes, she must consider
several ethical issues: (a) Does she have sufficient training to recognize and deal
with them? (b) What should she do when managed care will not reimburse unless
a practitioner assigns a DSM-IV-TR (Diagnostic and Statistical Manual of Mental
Disorders) diagnosis? (c) What should she do when managed care refuses to reimburse treatment for the symptoms identified? (d) Can a social worker raised in U.S.
culture accept these as valid symptoms even though they are not part of her own
cultural experience? (e) Finally, how much multicultural training is required for a
practitioner to practice ethically with diverse populations?

CRITICAL THINKING EXERCISES

EP 2.1.3

1. If you were confronted as a social worker with the issue of assisted suicide, can you identify your personal values about such actions? What would be your position? What justification would you provide for your decision?
2. The legislature in your state has been alarmed by a sudden sharp increase in the incidence
   of HIV-positive findings among several population groups. A bill has been introduced
   calling for mandatory HIV screening for all persons applying for a marriage license. The

problem is a real one; the solution may or may not be effective, but it does raise a number of ethical issues. Your local NASW chapter has asked you to discuss these questions at the next membership meeting.

3. The agency at which you are employed wants to begin offering services over the Internet. In a group, discuss what you see as the ethical dilemmas for the agency and for social workers. Identify how these dilemmas could be avoided and/or dealt with ethically. How are HIPAA requirements being addressed?

4. If you were the social worker in the situation described in Exemplar 11.3 and Hyun Cho were your client, what would you have done? What is the basis of your decision?

5. You are thinking about starting a blog on your experiences as a social work student. Is this a good idea? What are some of the ethical issues that could come up?

6. Using your favorite search engine, search "social work blog." After reading some of these blogs, what, if any, ethical issues can you identify in them?

Suggestions for Additional Readings

Palmer and Kaufman (2003) highlight the importance of self-determination in social work and the United States. It is viewed as a core value and ethical standard. They explore how practitioner and institutional biases about diverse populations relate to informed consent in a multicultural context. Yip (2005) illustrates how traditional Taoism impacts on the mental health of Chinese people. They may not be in favor of empowerment or environmental change, and may favor inaction instead of cognitive and behavioral change, as well as question values such as self-actualization. Hodge (2004) examines the development of cultural competence (attitudes, knowledge) with evangelical Christians, suggesting that unresolved issues of the practitioner may play out in practice situations. Similar issues exist in regard to many and diverse populations. In 2009, the *Journal of Religion & Spirituality in Social Work: Social Thought* published a special issue (volume 28, issue 1 & 2) on controversial issues in religion, spirituality, and social work, including an article on ethical issues in the use of spiritually based interventions by Sheridan (2009).

Websites of Interest

- Georgetown University's National Center for Cultural Competence: http://www11. georgetown.edu/research/gucchd/nccc/
- Extensive information on cultural competence for health care providers (including assessment tools and training curricula) is available at the USDHHS Health Resources and Services Administration (HRSA): www.hrsa.gov/culturalcompetence/
- The USDHHS Centers for Disease Control and Prevention (CDC) provides information on IPV: http://www.cdc.gov/ViolencePrevention/intimatepartnerviolence/index.html
- The World Health Organization (WHO) provides information on IPV: www.who.int/ violence_injury_prevention/violence/world_report/factsheets/en/ipvfacts.pdf
- Additional information from WHO on the link between IPV and HIV/AIDS is available at: www.who.int/hac/techguidance/pht/InfoBulletinIntimatePartnerViolenceFinal.pdf
- Extensive information about elder abuse is available from the National Center on Elder Abuse: http://www.ncea.aoa.gov/ncearoot/Main_Site/index.aspx
- Information about the Society for Spirituality and Social Work: http://ssw.asu.edu/portal/ research/spirituality

COMPETENCY NOTES

Identify as a professional social worker and conduct oneself accordingly: In this chapter, we discuss work with various client groups and how they relate to ethical dilemmas for social workers.

EP 2.1.1

Apply social work ethical principles to guide professional practice: In this chapter, we discuss ethical social work practice with various client groups.

EP 2.1.2

Apply critical thinking to inform and communicate professional judgments: Exemplars asked you to consider and decide how you would respond to ethical dilemmas, and exercises at the end of the chapter address critical thinking.

EP 2.1.3

Engage diversity and difference in practice: Cultural diversity is addressed throughout this chapter.

EP 2.1.4

Changing World, Changing Dilemmas

This chapter addresses the CSWE 2008 EPAS Educational Policy 2.1.1 on becoming a professional social worker, specifically focusing on ethical issues related to a number of social work practice issues. We also continue content on Educational Policy 2.1.2 about using social work ethical principles to guide professional practice. We will provide opportunities through numerous exemplars and questions that we hope you will use to apply critical thinking to inform and communicate professional judgments (Educational Policy 2.1.3). We also discuss diversity (Educational Policy 2.1.4) and social justice and advocacy (Educational Policy 2.1.5) in this chapter, as each relates to ethical issues.

In this chapter, we discuss ethical dilemmas that result from factors that impact on practitioners and influence the kinds of interventions and decisions that can be made, including managed care and mental health; technology; research and evaluation in practice settings; evidence-based practice; private practice issues; practice in rural or isolated settings; and neighborhoods, society, and community organizing.

MANAGED CARE AND MENTAL HEALTH

The cost of health care has escalated beyond the rate of inflation in the United States for a number of years. This cost spiral has been due to a number of factors, including the growth of an aging population that requires more intensive health care, the availability of new technologies and costly new treatments, an emphasis on acute care rather than preventive services, and varying standards of treatment according to geographic locations. These and other factors have resulted in an increasing demand to control medical expenditures and to make use of managed health and mental health care systems in order to reduce costs wherever possible. Managed care developed as one major strategy devised in an attempt to control health and mental health costs by monitoring access to, and the type of, health care patients receive from health care practitioners or health maintenance organizations (HMOs). Costs are reduced by placing controls on health practitioners and by fostering competition among HMOs. Managed care plans also attempt to reduce costs through controlling the type of health practitioners used, limiting access to service, and prescribing the type and length of service provided.

Managed care was specifically designed to "eliminate unnecessary and inappropriate care and to reduce costs" (Wineburgh, 1998, p. 433). In 2007, 73.9 million people, or about one fourth of the U.S. population, were enrolled in health maintenance organizations or managed care entities (U.S. Census Bureau, 2010). Whatever the successes of managed care towards the reduction of the escalating costs of health care in the United States, the costs continue to increase. In 2010, health care costs were 17% of gross domestic product, meaning health care accounted for 1 in every 6 dollars spent in the United States. There continues to be tremendous concern about the heavy burden of health care expenditures on the national budget; at the same time, there is concern about the large number of children and adults who do not have health insurance and who may not be able to afford health care.

On March 23, 2010, the Patient Protection and Affordable Care Act was signed into law by President Barack Obama. The Act has a large number of health-related provisions, including the provision of health care benefits by businesses, subsidized insurance benefits, establishment of health insurance exchanges, and a host of other factors. This comprehensive and complex legislation was passed because there was wide agreement that health expenditures had to be reined in and the number of uninsured people reduced. Unless health care costs can be controlled, the U.S. budget will not be able to cover other programs necessary for society, and/or the deficit will continue to increase. Further, the needs of a growing population, including services for those without health insurance, as well as an expanding aging population, could not be served or served sufficiently if health care costs are not managed well.

Managed care addresses primarily health care providers, but it also impacts many professional social workers. It challenges the autonomy of both the social worker and the patient, and it requires a high degree of accountability (Hall & Keefe, 2006). Professional service stresses the importance of practitioner assessment and judgment, and the Code of Ethics promotes "clients' socially responsible self-determination" (NASW, 2008, Ethical Principles). But autonomy for both the practitioner and the patient tends to be diminished in managed care settings. The choice of treatment can be determined by the practitioner alone or together with a managed care reviewer. However, the managed care reviewer may reduce the autonomy of both practitioner and patients through quality assurance, utilization review, and selection of appropriate forms of treatment (Wineburgh, 1998).

Practitioners must select their treatment choices from those authorized by the managed care organization. Failing to abide by these rules risks a decrease in referrals, which can mean a potential loss of status and income. Brief therapy appears to be the preferred mode of intervention (Cohen, 2003); as a result, long-term therapy may only be available to those who can pay privately for this treatment modality. McBeath and Meezan (2008) examined in-agency and out-of-agency service provision to a sample of 243 foster children and their families who were served by non-profit agencies. The agency operated under either a performance-based managed care purchase of service contract or a fee-for-service reimbursement mechanism.

Children and families served by agencies with performance-based managed care contracts received fewer services than those served by fee-for-service contracts. The researchers suggest that performance based managed care contracting is related to suppressed service provision and leads to service disparities between foster children and families served under different market environments. Bennett and colleagues (2009) surveyed Illinois social work members of NASW regarding their views of the influence of managed care on their clinical decision making. The study found that social workers are more likely to be influenced by managed care in regard to altering the number of sessions, reducing fees, and advocating for clients and less likely to change a diagnosis or treatment plan because of ethical reasons.

Many social workers may be pressured by managed care organizations to provide group therapy for their clients in place of individual treatment because group service is time and cost efficient. One practitioner can treat many people with similar problems at the same time, thus reducing the number of billable hours. The insurance companies stress that outpatient services in time-limited groups have been found to be very effective. For example, persons with panic disorder who received cognitive-behavioral group therapy in addition to medication "had lower posttest anxiety scores than those who received medication alone" (Mitchell, 1999, p. 188). What is the ethical responsibility of a social worker inexperienced with groups who has a client whom a managed care entity has only approved for group treatment? Should she offer group service (even while learning how to do this) or should she tell the client that he must look for help elsewhere? Does it matter if a client lives in a rural area or has limited transportation available and does not have access to other locations for treatment or services?

Practitioners may be tempted to agree to emphasize group treatment because this can result in greater income—even when professional judgment contraindicates this mode of treatment. Here, the social worker faces another ethical dilemma: how to juggle the demands of her own professional judgments, those of the insurance company, and her desire for economic security. This dilemma can occur in any practice setting, as shown in Exemplar 12.1.

The influence of the managed care organization can affect the practitioner's choice of intervention, the length of service, and the expected outcome of the service. Gibelman and Mason (2002) reported that managed care influenced practice decisions about treatment planning; the amount and types of treatment; limiting who could be seen in treatment; elimination of collateral visits with other family members, lawyers, teachers, and employers; and premature discharge of patients. Uncertainty about the reaction of the managed care representative can lead practitioners to fudge the diagnosis in an effort to get approval for the treatment needed (see Chapter 7 for further discussion of the ethical issues related to misdiagnosis). Many practitioners have reported that patients whose care has been denied often reappear later with the same complaints that led to their seeking treatment. Such experiences can lead to the view that managed care organizations can be capricious in their decisions. A national study of 582 social workers, psychologists, and psychiatrists found that they do not see themselves as having the requisite skills to interact adequately with managed care organizations to ensure that their clients receive appropriate care (Hall & Keefe, 2006).

| 12.1 | WHAT THE PINE TREE INSURANCE COMPANY WANTS |

Dr. Felicia Montevideo, director of social work clinical services for Family and Children's Services of Pleasant City, was surprised when she received a letter from the Pine Tree Insurance Company (Managed Care Division) and later a phone call, both of which subtly suggested that more of the agency's treatment services be offered in time-limited groups. When she raised the issue with the agency's administrative executive committee, some argued in favor of complying because the money received from the insurance company made up a substantial part of the agency's income. Others were concerned that such a change in operating procedures would upset the staff. Still others wanted to know what would be most helpful to clients, and some argued that compliance would mean yielding their professional judgment to the Pine Tree Insurance Company.

Among the options suggested by committee members are the following: (a) ignore the suggestion because it had not been explicitly stated; (b) comply as soon as possible with the suggestion; (c) refuse to comply and begin to advocate with Pine Tree Insurance for the current mix of service modalities; (d) examine and review research on the relative effectiveness of various treatment methods; and (e) meet with Pine Tree representatives to explore ways to slowly phase in more group treatment. What are the ethical implications of each option?

The Code of Ethics has several standards regarding third-party payers, which are of special relevance in managed care situations: (a) "Social workers should use clear and understandable language to inform clients of the purpose of the services, risks related to the services, limits to services because of the requirements of a third-party payer, relevant costs, reasonable alternatives, clients' right to refuse or withdraw consent, and the time frame covered by the consent" (NASW, 2008, 1.03a); (b) "Social workers should not disclose confidential information to third-party payers unless clients have authorized such disclosure" (1.07h); and (c) "Social workers should take reasonable steps to avoid abandoning clients who are still in need of services" (1.16b).

Other standards may also be relevant to managed care settings. Consider, for example, the issue of informed consent (1.03). Clients may have limited financial resources that force them to choose their health plans on the basis of cost. As a result, because of this earlier choice, they may now face limitations of services. Similarly, the client may face a choice between no service and the service authorized by the managed care program, thus minimizing their sense of voluntariness. Managed care programs may place the social worker in situations in which their compliance with standard 4.04 ("Social workers should not participate in, condone, or be associated with dishonesty, fraud, or deception") (NASW Code, 2008) may become questionable. For example, in order to provide a reimbursable service for a client, the practitioner may have to consider fudging the diagnosis in some way. If deception is used, it is not only vis-á-vis the managed care organization but also concerns the client because the more severe diagnosis may jeopardize the client in the future.

There are many other ethical dilemmas practitioners can encounter in regard to managed care situations. Difficult issues arise when the cost containment goals of managed care place limits on the length of treatment, deny care, or insist on certain treatments. When a client's situation is not improved or the problem is unresolved, managed care may deny further reimbursed treatment. Nonetheless, the client may require a continuation of services. This problem becomes accentuated for a practitioner when two similarly situated clients both need professional social work service but have different benefit packages. On what basis does this social worker decide how to distribute services when both have equal needs? Should the client with the more generous benefit package receive more service?

Certain ethical dilemmas arise from the requirement to continue treatment if it is needed (Code, 2008, 1.16b) or terminate treatment once it is no longer needed (Code, 1.16a). What should the practitioner do if the client who needs continued treatment has reached the maximum on his annual or lifetime benefits and is unable to pay? A practitioner can state at the beginning of treatment that the family agency policy limits the number of sessions. What if, during treatment, the client resolved several of the problems that had brought him into treatment but another problem had emerged, and the social worker's supervisor denied permission for additional sessions? What is the ethical thing to do?

Davis (1997) discusses the need to ensure the availability of culturally competent standards of care and diagnostic and treatment services to underserved groups. In addition, managed care organizations need to provide accessible services "located within reasonable geographic distance to Black neighborhoods" (Davis, 1997, p. 636). What should the social worker do in Exemplar 12.2?

EP 2.1.2

| 12.2 | WHERE ARE THE SERVICES? |

Anita Dee is a social worker in a state psychiatric hospital that primarily serves low-income people of color. The Medicaid recipients are served through a managed care system that is privately operated. Generally, administrators and supervisors in this public hospital seek harmonious relationships with the managed care organization, located in another state. Anita recently realized that when chronically ill psychiatric patients are discharged, the managed care company refers them to outpatient sites that are seldom near where they reside, and transportation to the treatment sites is not provided. Consequently, the discharged persons are not receiving the help they need. Anita believes the managed care company is discriminating against poor and minority persons because there are services available closer to clients' homes, but these services are not allowed because they are more expensive. Anita would like to challenge the managed care organization's decisions, but her supervisor says her job is to help prepare persons to leave the hospital and anything after that is not her concern.

It is clear from the NASW (2008) Code of Ethics (6.01) that a practitioner should advocate for her client to receive appropriate services. The issue of advocacy raises several questions. How does one balance advocacy for one client versus the services that other clients need? Advocacy for one client can be time consuming and deprive others of services they need. How far should one appeal? How much unpaid time should be devoted to such efforts? Should one appeal when there is little chance for success? Furthermore, one can advocate once too many times and risk being removed from the managed care panel (Wineburgh, 1998). (See Chapter 13 for more on advocacy.)

TECHNOLOGY

In Chapter 11, we discussed technology in direct practice, specifically the delivery of services online and through other technologies; in this chapter we will discuss other ways in which technology can produce ethical dilemmas. Social work, like many other professions, has been affected by computers and other modern technologies. Many people, including social workers, believe that things, unlike people, are value free. However, because technology exists within a human context, it reflects and shapes human choices, which always involve value choices and ethical priorities.

Initially, social workers were concerned that the introduction of information technologies into social agencies and social work practice would result in more critical ethical dilemmas because these technologies were thought to be insensitive to variations in human needs and individual differential values and cultures. For example, electronic technology used by organizations to provide services for HIV-positive persons may provide support, empowerment, and practical advice about how to cope with the disease. But these patients may be especially vulnerable if the system is unable to protect the confidentiality of communications to and from them (Benotch et al., 2006).

As coordinating agencies, grant-funding agencies, third-party payers, and others create large, interconnected computerized databases, methods are needed to guarantee the confidentiality of records from hackers and other intruders. When multiple agencies become linked in networks in order to promote collaborative case management, new problems arise. Is client permission needed for one agency or worker to share or receive the information held by another agency about a common client? To what extent should agencies limit the client data they have computerized? How can clients be sufficiently informed about data sharing between agencies? How well informed should clients be about the realities of the information networks to which agencies and their personal records are tied? The increased ease and speed of information transfer make these ethical issues ever more critical in social work practice.

Other issues arise from the use of computers. For example, employees in social agencies may work at computer monitors whose screens face common areas and are exposed to view by anyone who passes by, or computers may be left with information visible while the social worker is away from her desk. There are several things that social workers can do to address these issues. Computer monitor screens are available that make it difficult to view anything on the monitor unless one is looking directly at it, which can reduce the ability of other people to read confidential information from a distance. It is good practice to lock a computer account whenever it is not in use so others will not have access to it; alternatively, software is available to automatically lock a computer that has not been used for more than a certain period of time. Sensitivity to these concerns has undoubtedly increased as a result of confidentiality, privacy, and HIPAA issues discussed in Chapter 8.

Furthermore, if an agency's computer system can be accessed externally, it is potentially open to hackers, even when security systems are in place. Just as anyone can observe what remains in view on an employee's monitor, organizations have the ability to monitor employees' phone calls, e-mail messages, Internet connections, and computer files. Video surveillance also exists for security reasons in many agency locations. Electronic communications accessed through employers belong to the employer, not the employee. Social workers employed in governmental agencies may find that their electronic messages are public records that can be monitored without prior notice (Levine, 2000; Lorenz, 2006). How do these practices affect social workers' and clients' privacy rights? Should a social worker inform her clients that her agency may monitor phone calls and e-mail messages?

Concerns about computer security are not limited to inter-organizational electronic communications. Caputo (1991) set forth an ethical framework for information systems that asserts the primacy of clients as citizens. The ethical framework fulfills the following functions:

1. It provides a way to inform clients about the existence of a computerized client-information system.
2. It enables clients to give informed consent in regard to the uses of information about themselves.
3. It offers an opportunity for individuals to inspect, correct, or add information about themselves, allowing them to expunge all or parts of their records, except where such records are legally required.
4. It develops an information-needs matrix to guide unit allocation decisions on the basis of critical success factors.
5. It holds professionals to a professional practice that is mindful of ethical standards, including respect for clients' autonomy, their right to information and privacy, the need to weigh the efficacy of demands for efficiency against the principle of human dignity, and adherence to confidentiality regarding the use of routinely collected information about clients.

Although Caputo (1991) developed this framework a number of years ago, the recommendations are still relevant today and are likely to continue to be so as long as computerized databases are used.

Other ethical issues arise out of still newer developments. Among these are computerized screening and assessment; selection of practice and service recommendations; expert systems for evaluating various risks, such as foster care, parole, and suicide; and interactive treatment games and various forms of therapy. Among the ethical dilemmas that have developed as a result of these technologies are questions of beneficence (autonomy versus paternalism), equity of access to scarce resources (ensuring equality of opportunity), and the promotion of the common good (ensuring that the maximum number of individuals benefit from the introduction of information technology). The assumption of many advanced software and expert systems (computerized decision making) is that there is always one "right" decision that should be followed. As a result, problems concerning client autonomy and worker flexibility have become more critical. How can the worker simultaneously defend the autonomy of the client, meet the expectations of the agency, and avoid paternalism and control of clients when computerized decision-making software is used?

Technology has advanced to a point beyond data collection and interpretation where *interactivity* can support the use of influential communications for behavioral change. *Persuasive technology* is designed to potentially increase the capacity of a person to act or act differently. Persuasive tools can be used for conditioning (e.g., reinforcement), self-monitoring (e.g., tracking performance to help people to achieve outcomes), and offering suggestions at opportune moments, among other uses (LaMendola & Krysik, 2008). A number of ethical principles have been identified related to the use of persuasive technologies by an agency: (1) motivations, methods, and outcomes that are unethical in nontechnical situations are also unethical when used in persuasive technology; (2) privacy must be respected; (3) personal information about the user must not be relayed to others without the user's agreement; and (4) the creators of a persuasive technology must assume responsibility for all reasonably predictable outcomes of its use. Because individuals tend to reveal more criminal and sensitive personal information to a computer than to a human, clarity about accessibility of the information developed through the use of persuasive tools and the uses of that information may be growing issues for social agencies and social workers (LaMendola & Krysik, 2009).

The introduction of information systems into social agencies with very tight budgets may mean that scarce resources must be deployed to pay for the new technology and for staff with specific expertise even while other agency programs and client supports will be reduced or eliminated. Work patterns and organizational structure will change, and some resources will not be available for some kinds of client services. Consider the dilemma that confronts the social worker in Exemplar 12.3.

12.3   COMPUTERIZED INFORMATION SYSTEM OR SERVICES?

EP 2.1.2

Miri Neidig, a social worker, is a member of the board of directors of a neighborhood service center that provides counseling and other services, including services for low-income minority teens at a local shopping mall. This service has recently been instituted and is highly valued by community members and by teenagers because of the privacy afforded by the location and the likable staff. The agency's computers and databases have become very dated, and there have been concerns about security. Now some members of the board are pressuring the executive director to upgrade their computers, information systems, and security systems. They believe it is essential for agencies to be technologically up to date, however funding has been cut back this year and the budget is very tight; increasing technology use may be at the cost of reduced services to clients. The board will meet tonight to set priorities and review the agency budget.

The board and Miri are faced with the question of what services to reduce or cut. Some argue that it is more important to upgrade the technology in the agency, and others argue there are too few services provided now. There are waiting lists for almost all services. The board, including Miri, is faced with difficult choices. For the future, improved use of computers by the agency will be a positive step. If they vote in favor of further computerization, other services will be diminished. A vote for computerization will deny the community services that are desperately needed. What recommendation would you make to Miri about her vote? How would you choose?

RESEARCH AND EVALUATION IN PRACTICE SETTINGS

In addition to keeping up to date with current research findings, social workers are encouraged to "promote and facilitate evaluation and research to contribute to the development of knowledge" (NASW Code, 2008, 5.02b). Many funding sources now require that agencies provide outcome data in order to continue receiving funding. While this requirement is not inconsistent with the Code of Ethics, it may create a number of ethical dilemmas for social workers such as informed consent, the client's right to withdraw from participation, the need for support services, the protection of confidentiality, and others. Consider the situation in Exemplar 12.4.

EP 2.1.2

| 12.4 | Fundalot Foundation Wants Evidence |

The Sidestreet Agency provides services to runaway adolescents; for the past three years, over 80% of their funding has been provided by the Fundalot Foundation. The board of directors of the Fundalot Foundation recently voted to change the criteria for continued funding; specifically, they now want all programs to provide evidence of their efficacy. They have not been specific about what type of evidence will be acceptable, but rather, they have decided to let each agency determine what types of data should be collected and reported. Funding will be discontinued if programs have inadequate data collection and reporting or offer findings that do not support the program's efficacy.

Kathleen Hall is the social worker for the Sidestreet Agency. For the past three years, she has written the funding proposal for the Fundalot Foundation. Given the new requirements, Kathleen has asked to meet with the other members of the staff to discuss how they will address them. During the meeting, a number of issues are raised: (a) Should the agency respond or not respond to these requirements? (b) Is informed consent required to collect and report outcome data? What if clients refuse to give consent? Will they be dropped from the treatment program? (c) If the agency's clients are children and adolescents, at what age can they give informed consent, and how can it be obtained for those clients who are too young or not competent to give consent? Is the consent of their parents required? (d) What if the findings do not provide evidence for the efficacy of the program? (e) Who or what takes ethical priority here: the agency that needs funding, the clients being served, the staff who want to retain their jobs, or honesty that requires accurate recording? How should a social worker respond to these issues?

When an agency decides to evaluate its services, it must make sure that it avoids a number of potential ethical issues. Among these issues may be the use of deception, violation of confidentiality and privacy, conflicts of interest, and disclosing or not disclosing the results to the research participants (Grinnell & Unrau, 2005). The collection of outcome data potentially raises a number of ethical dilemmas. The NASW Code of Ethics (2008) has standards for evaluation and research (see 5.02 a–p), including an injunction against conflicts of interest and dual relationships with participants (5.02o). The result may be a conflict of interest that forces the practitioner to choose: the research or professional service to the client. Despite this injunction, the current priority given to establishing the efficacy of clinical programs through research demands that clinicians include research in the scope of their practice. The dual role of clinician and researcher, although advantageous, poses risks to the self-determination of clients who are also potential study participants (Antle & Regehr, 2003, p. 140). On the other hand, ethical questions can be raised when a clinician practices without including evaluation research as a fundamental part of her practice.

Is the clinician-researcher dual role avoidable for a social worker in an agency that requires the collection of outcome data? If this dual role is unavoidable, how can the social worker protect the client's rights, including self-determination, while meeting the needs of the agency to establish its efficacy? What should a social worker do who works for an agency that will not provide services without the client's agreement to provide outcome data? Finally, let us consider the case of an agency that has collected the outcome data required by its funding agency, but the results are not positive (e.g., there is no evidence that the agency's services are effective). What would you do in this situation?

Although most evaluation and research activities do not call for deception, there can be situations in which deception is used. For instance, the real reason for evaluating client satisfaction might be kept from the clients. Perhaps honest explanations would bias the results in some way. The protection of confidentiality may also be a problem. Who will have access to the responses and data? In addition to personal failures to protect privacy and confidentiality, there can be security problems associated with computers and electronic transmission of data. In Exemplar 12.4, we saw potential issues regarding conflicts of interest and reporting of the results. Involving clients in research efforts may also create potential conflicts of interest of a different type, by creating stress and discomfort for clients because they feel they have no free choice to participate or not. This discussion of research and evaluation in practice leads directly into concerns about accountability, effectiveness, and the emphasis on evidence-based practice.

EVIDENCE-BASED PRACTICE (EBP)

What is evidence-based practice[1]? Gambrill (2006) suggests that evidence-based practice "is a new educational and practice paradigm for closing the gaps between research and practice to maximize opportunities to help clients and avoid harm" (p. 339). Keeping in mind the ethical obligations described in the NASW (2008) Code of Ethics, she suggests evidence-based practice is "a philosophy and process designed to forward effective use of professional judgment in integrating information regarding each client's unique characteristics, circumstances, preferences, and actions and external research findings" (Gambrill, 2006, p. 339). Would any ethical practitioner dismiss the use of empirical, scientific, and relevant information that can be helpful in providing effective and efficient services?

Public and private organizations and third-party payers increasingly are pressuring social workers and human service organizations for evidence that they are accountable and their services are beneficial to those they are serving. This trend is reflected in the NASW (2008) Code of Ethics, where several standards are relevant to discussions of evidence-based practice and the use of research findings:

---

[1] Evidence-based practice (EBP) is a process of using evidence to inform practice, which is different from an evidence-based intervention (EBI), which is a specific intervention that is supported by empirical evidence.

"Social workers should critically examine and keep current with emerging knowledge relevant to social work ... [and] should routinely review the professional literature" (4.01b). In addition, "social workers should base practice on recognized knowledge, including empirically based knowledge" (4.01c). Furthermore, social workers are also encouraged to "fully use evaluation and research evidence in their professional practice" (5.02c). There are social workers, especially students, who are not convinced that research is relevant to what they do. (What was your own response, or that of your classmates, to having to take a research course or two as part of your BSW or MSW program?) But more and more demands are made on social workers that they be accountable for their methods and the outcomes of their services.

There has been a great deal of discussion about evidence-based practice and how it should be used in social work (see Gambrill, 2003; Howard, McMillen, & Pollio, 2003). There have been many earlier developments and changes in social work practice that engendered debates. For example, the introduction of behavioral and cognitive therapies and time-limited and task-structured interventions were the occasion of debates, followed by research and gradual acceptance. Evidence-based practice has been touted as another among the major advances in social work, with the promise of achieving major change in the profession and its services. Whether evidence-based practice will prove revolutionary for social work or will simply be integrated into the profession with a more emphatic stress on empirical and scientific evidence in the choice of interventions remains to be seen.

How might a social worker use evidence-based practice? Research knowledge, clinical expertise, and client values are all integrated in the process of evidence-based practice, which involves five steps:

1. Convert the information needs related to practice decisions into answerable questions.
2. Track down the best evidence with which to answer them.
3. Critically appraise that evidence in terms of its validity, clinical significance, and usefulness.
4. Integrate this critical appraisal of research evidence with one's clinical expertise and the patient's values and circumstances.
5. Evaluate one's effectiveness and efficiency in undertaking the four previous steps, and strive for self-improvement. (Thyer, 2004, p. 168)

Social workers may feel unprepared or unable to perform these five steps, and/or they may feel that they are already overburdened and do not have the time to perform them. A social worker may even wonder if evidence-based practice is really ethically necessary. The Code (2008, 4.01) suggests that clients have a right to expect that social workers will be competent in their area of practice. Can a social worker remain competent if she does not stay up-to-date with current developments in the field? Consider Exemplar 12.5.

What are the ethical dilemmas facing Sheryl? Who is her client—the infant, Claire, the physician? How can she decide who takes priority? What additional information is needed so that Claire can give informed consent for the treatment? Are there non-medication treatments for depression? Is this situation a repeat of Claire's earlier depressive episode or postpartum depression? How much time will it take to find and review the relevant research literature? What harm can be done in the interim? Should Claire be told about the available treatment options, the risks and benefits of each, and the likely efficacy of each, including the fact that Sheryl is not experienced in delivering some of these treatment options? What should Sheryl do if she cannot learn the most effective new treatments easily or if Claire refuses to participate when informed of the situation? Review the Code of Ethics (2008) for relevant standards.

12.5	Claire Johnson Is Depressed but Doesn't Want to Take Antidepressants

EP 2.1.2

One of Sheryl Hall's clients, Claire Johnson, was referred to her after Claire's physician made a diagnosis of depression. Claire's physician wanted to prescribe an antidepressant, but Claire refused to take the medication prescribed. She is afraid that the medicine will harm her 3-month-old baby because she is breastfeeding, and she previously had been prescribed medications for depression that made her life miserable with headaches, dry mouth, and sweating. Because of Claire's refusal to take the antidepressants, her physician referred her to Sheryl for counseling. He expected Sheryl to convince Claire to take her medication. The physician expressed great concern about the infant's health. Sheryl has little experience treating depression, but there are no other licensed social workers in the area. At the first session, Claire stated that she is very concerned that, due to her depression, she is not adequately caring for her baby and that she needs immediate relief so she can be a better mother, but she cannot cope with the side effects of the medication.

Let us consider how Sheryl could apply the five steps of evidence-based practice (Thyer, 2004) described above to this situation. First, she could develop "answerable questions," such as what non–medication-based treatments are available for depression. Also, given that Claire has a 3-month-old son, what distinguishes major depression from postpartum depression, which is the most appropriate diagnosis for her, and are the treatment options different?

Once Sheryl has developed answerable questions, she can move to the second step, "track down the best evidence." How should Sheryl proceed? Assuming that she is a busy professional, does she have time to find and review all the relevant research literature? There are a growing number of Internet-based resources available that provide summaries and critiques of the research literature in a number of areas. What if Claire has heard about a treatment for depression and has asked Sheryl to convince the insurance company to pay for this treatment? Should Sheryl do so even if she does not have any experience providing that form of treatment? How could she decide if this is an appropriate form of treatment? Sheryl could check with a library or look for Internet-based resources, such as the Cochrane collaboration, which provides systematic reviews on a number of health-related topics, including depression. As of August 2010, the Cochrane Library at http://www.thecochranelibrary. com/details/browseReviews/576825/Depressive-disorders–major-depression.html has published reviews on the treatment of depression, including one on psychosocial and psychological interventions for treating postpartum depression.

Once Sheryl has found the relevant research evidence, she needs to move to step 3 and "critically appraise that evidence." Some social workers find research intimidating and/or have difficulty evaluating research methodology—how should they proceed with this step? Is it ethical to uncritically accept the conclusions of study authors without examining the adequacy of the research methodology used? Is this step easier if one has reliable and trustworthy sources of information such as the Cochrane Library?

In step 4, the results of steps 1 through 3 are applied, including considerations of whether what has been found is relevant to the client's issue and how these findings relate to the client's values. What should Sheryl do if after all of this she finds that the most effective treatment is one she does not know how to provide or is unacceptable to Claire? Finally, in step 5, the effectiveness and efficacy of steps 1 through 4 are evaluated. For most social workers, this evidence-based practice process may be quite time consuming, especially the first few times it is used. Does this cause any ethical dilemmas?

Philosophical criticisms have also been expressed about EBP. Those who make these arguments suggest that "an evidence based, rational model of decision making does not fit the realities of individualized, contextualized practice, especially where problems are less well defined" (Mullen & Streiner, 2004, p. 114). The NASW (2008) Code requirements include that "social workers should strive to become and remain proficient in professional practice" (4.01b) and they should "base practice on recognized knowledge, including empirically based knowledge, relevant to social work and social work ethics" (4.01c). Reflecting this point of view, Howard and Jenson (1999) advocate for guidelines to direct practice in the most effective and proven ways, faulting the professional association for failing to implement practice guidelines. Others argue that solving human problems through the use of an approved list of techniques would violate the richness and dignity of human struggles and triumphs. Social workers "deal with enormously complex and difficult issues. To do this well, they must be analytical, reflective, and compassionate in their approach to human suffering. They must recognize that they often know very little about the lives of those they serve and that, therefore, they must listen and learn from them" (Witkin, 1998, pp. 79–80).

PRIVATE PRACTICE

In this section, we will address several issues that may be particularly relevant to social work in private practice or in agencies that have very tight budgets, where social workers are forced to make difficult decisions based on finances. Later in this chapter, we will also address issues that are more common in macro practice settings.

CLIENT DUMPING

What is the ethical thing to do when, during the course of treatment, a client's financial situation changes, and he can no longer pay for services? Consider the situation of Larry Firth in Exemplar 12.6.

"Dumping the client" is one way that some practitioners have responded to clients who can no longer pay for services. There are various ways to dump a client. A worker may tell a client that his problem has been solved successfully (when it has not yet been solved) or that no more can be done for him (when, in fact, the worker could still be helpful). The worker may cancel appointments so frequently that the client loses interest, or the worker may refer a client who no longer can afford her services to another agency that does provide free services. No matter what technique is used, the worker's objective is to stop serving the client who can no longer pay. What can an ethical practitioner do when this situation arises? Similarly, when insurance companies place limits on the number of sessions that they will cover, how should a social worker address problems that she feels will require more sessions than the insurance company will reimburse?

EP 2.1.2

12.6	A DIFFICULT FAMILY SITUATION

Larry Firth came to consult with you about a difficult family situation. His wife has left him and their two sons in order to live with her boyfriend. He himself has formed a relationship with a married neighbor. However, he is concerned what his teenage sons will say and do when they find out the truth about their parents. You are making good progress in helping Larry come to grips with his problem. Today, however, Larry tells you that he has lost his job and can no longer afford to pay for counseling. What should you do?

MISREPRESENTATION

The NASW (2008) Code of Ethics specifically states: "Social workers should ensure that their representations to clients, agencies, and the public of professional qualification, credentials, education, competence, affiliations, services provided, or results to be achieved are accurate" (4.06c). What seems like a simple ethical rule gives rise to a number of questions, including the following:

- Is it ethical for a social worker to identify herself as something other than a social worker (such as a marriage counselor or psychotherapist)?
- Is it ethical for a social worker to call herself "Doctor" when she has not earned a Ph.D., D.S.W., or other doctoral degree?
- Must a student social worker always identify herself as a student in field instruction placements, or can she present herself as "your social worker"?

Those who engage in these practices claim that they do so to give clients greater confidence in their worker and thus increase the chances for a successful outcome. Is this ethical? Similarly, a social worker may claim or promise that she can help a client who comes to her seeking treatment. Can she ethically make such a promise?

PRACTICE IN RURAL OR ISOLATED SETTINGS

Rural and isolated settings are different from suburban and urban settings in several ways that can create ethical challenges for social workers. By rural or isolated settings, we mean those communities that have small populations, limited services available, and large distances between communities. Small populations increase the likelihood that community members will know each other and have opportunities to interact with each other in many different ways. Limited services availability may mean that some needed resources cannot be easily accessed. Finally, large distances between communities may mean that even when services are available in a neighboring community, residents may not be able to use them due to lack of transportation. Even within suburban and urban areas, members of some religious, ethnic, or cultural groups may be isolated from the broader society and seek services and relationships only within their own community. Other communities within suburban and urban areas may be isolated because public transportation is not available or is not affordable. Whatever the reason for the isolation, there are possibilities for ethical dilemmas within these settings.

According to Green (2003), "while all social work practice must be contextualised, a review of the literature regarding the nature of rural social work practice indicates the context impacts on the nature of professional practice in significant ways. These include the styles of practice, the impact on the professional of managing dual and multiple relationships, confidentiality, privacy and personal safety and the challenges of providing accessible, ethical and competent practice in a climate of poor funding, geographical distance, and complex and multi-layered networks" (p. 210). Because of their visibility in the community, personal social acceptability and safety issues may arise for social workers who advocate for change, remove children from abusive homes, or try to assist those, for example, who are trying to leave a violent relationship (Green, 2003).

Many of the ethical dilemmas in rural settings are related to dual or multiple roles with clients. Whereas it may be possible to avoid social relationships with clients, ex-clients, and their families in urban areas, it may be impossible to do so in rural areas (Green, 2003; Scopelliti, Judd, Grigg, Hodgins, Fraser, Hulbert, Endacott, & Wood, 2004; Sidell, 2007) unless the social worker does not participate in community activities or shop locally. It can become harder to separate personal and professional roles the longer a social worker lives in the community (Scopelliti et al., 2004). Is it reasonable, or appropriate, to expect that a social worker should avoid participating in community activities because of potential dual roles with clients or ex-clients? Should the social worker have to travel to another community to shop or bank? Should the social worker avoid attending her children's school events or serving on school committees because she may have to interact with a client or his family in that setting? How much interaction would be appropriate in these situations?

Halverson and Brownlee (2010) conducted a qualitative study of 10 social workers' and social service workers' dual relationships in rural and remote communities in Canada (p. 248). Three themes were identified:

1. The ubiquitous nature of dual relationships in small communities.
2. Factors for consideration when entering into and/or maintaining dual relationships.
3. Perceived benefits of additional education and training around dual relationships. (Halverson & Brownlee, 2010, p. 252)

Participants described dual relationships as "inevitable" (p. 252). A common way to handle dual relationships in urban settings is to refer the client to another social worker. However, in rural and isolated settings, even when there was more than one social worker in a community, it was common for both of them to have a relationship with someone in need of services (Halverson & Brownlee, 2010).

Interestingly, those who had always worked in rural settings were more accepting of dual relationships than those who had previously worked in urban settings, and even indicated that at times it is helpful for the social worker to have a very close (nonsexual) relationship with the client. These rural social workers felt that they could do their most effective work when they had developed a "circle of trust" or "mutual trust" (Halverson & Brownlee, 2010, p. 255). According to Scopelliti and colleagues (2004), it is argued that "dual relationships and familiarity with patients ... tend to decrease the probability of exploitation—not increase it—as the power differential in a more egalitarian relationship is reduced" (p. 955). However, research on this topic is limited (Scopelliti et al., 2004), and it is unclear if this argument is accurate.

Sidell (2007) examined perceptions of dual relationships among 43 county child welfare workers in rural Pennsylvania. Although all respondents were employed in social work positions, only 40% held social work degrees. Participants were asked to indicate how ethical (on a scale from 1 = *never ethical* to 5 = *always ethical*) six behaviors were. Eighty-four percent thought it was never ethical to invite clients to a personal party or social event, and 79% thought it was never ethical to sell a product to a client (p. 100). However, only 33% thought it was never ethical to buy goods or services from a client; 40% thought it was never ethical to employ a client; 53% thought it was never ethical to "provide individual therapy to a relative, friend or lover of an ongoing client;" and 56% thought it was never ethical to provide therapy to an employee (pp. 100–101). Very few (only one or two for each item) respondents thought it was "mostly ethical" to engage in any of these situations; however, the remainder thought each was rarely or sometimes ethical. No significant differences were found between social work and non—social work educated respondents, but the lack of differences could be due to the small sample size in this study.

It is necessary to conduct "ongoing assessment of the effectiveness of a dual relationship made 'inevitable' by the absence of other alternatives" (Halverson & Brownlee, 2010, p. 253). Social workers should ask themselves if the dual relationship is necessary, exploitive, beneficial, damaging to the client, or disruptive to the therapeutic relationship. In addition, social workers should examine whether they are being objective about the relationship, document the decision-making process, and address the potential risks of the dual relationship as part of the informed consent process (Scopelliti et al., 2004, p. 957). Consider the situation in Exemplar 12.7.

What should Valerie do? Is it appropriate for her to provide assessment and treatment services to one of her students? If so, why or, if not, why not? Are there other potential ethical dilemmas in this situation?

Social workers in rural settings may also experience boundary issues in their work settings. Rural agencies may have a very small number (perhaps only one) of social workers who are expected to function in a variety of flexible roles (Green, 2003). Within this context, it is possible that a social worker may be asked to work with a client who has very different values. In an urban area, the social worker could refer the client to another social worker who has similar values, however that option may not be available in a rural area. Hancock (2008) raises the question of "how conservatively religious students who plan to practice in rural areas or small towns may view their professional responsibilities in practice situations in which, for example, women are seeking assistance with abortion or emergency conception or a gay couple is applying to provide foster care" (p. 349). We discussed value neutrality and imposing values in Chapter 6. Do the issues raised in that chapter help you address this issue?

EP 2.1.2

12.7	75 MILES FROM AN ALTERNATIVE

Valerie Crowe, the lone social worker and counselor at Littleton Community College, teaches Human Behavior 101 and works in the Student Counseling Center. Littleton Community College is in a remote mountainous section of a western state approximately 75 miles from Bigton, the nearest town with mental health services other than those offered at the community college. Today, when Valerie went to the counseling center, she found that she was scheduled to meet with Raymond Silver, a student in her Human Behavior 101 class. He told her that he has been having very disturbing thoughts about his inadequacies and feelings of guilt that are making it difficult for him to study and to sleep. Valerie made a judgment that additional assessment and possible treatment was needed. Valerie was conflicted about whether it would be appropriate for her to provide assessment and counseling services to one of her students, but she is the only counselor at the center and based on her prior experiences, getting an appointment to see a psychiatrist in Bigton would take at least two months. Even then, seeing the psychiatrist would require Raymond driving through snow on icy roads to reach the appointment.

MACRO PRACTICE

The NASW (2008) Code of Ethics includes a number of standards that expect social workers to accept a responsibility to engage in efforts to improve their communities and society (6.01, 6.02, 6.03, and 6.04). Among these are to promote the general welfare of society, participate in the community to shape policies and institutions, provide services during emergencies, and engage in social and political action. Nevertheless, the Code makes no specific provisions for ethical dilemmas encountered in social work with groups and communities.

COMMUNITY GROUPS

Although the NASW (2008) Code refers to "clients" as individuals, families, groups, organizations, and communities and refers to social groups in passing, the only direct attention to groups and families is in the context of confidentiality. Perhaps reflecting the Code's sparse attention, social work has paid rather scarce attention to ethical dilemmas in work with groups. Dolgoff and Skolnik (1992, 1996) studied the bases upon which social workers with groups make ethical decisions when faced with ethical dilemmas and on what basis they made these decisions. The results overwhelmingly indicated that practice wisdom was the primary basis for ethical decision making by these social workers. Congress and Lynn (1997) examined a number of ethical dilemmas encountered in task groups in the community, including confidentiality, self-determination of the group and individual members, inclusion or exclusion of members, and conflicts of interest. Consider the following situations where social work in the community may raise ethical dilemmas:

- You are a social worker employed by a city housing authority, and you are working with a group of mothers to improve a playground for their children. One resident brings a friend to the meeting. During the meeting, you discover that the friend is living in the group member's apartment. This is against the law and is not known to the housing authority (your employer). What should you do?
- You are a social worker assigned to work with a community group concerned about trash pickup, speeding traffic that endangers neighborhood children, and public transportation accessibility. Your values and those of the group have been congruent regarding every concern so far. At this evening's meeting, a highly influential group member reported that the state mental health department intends to establish a community residence in the neighborhood. Under her leadership, everyone present agreed to make their opposition to the proposed residence the group's highest priority. You know there is a great need for such residences, but you are concerned that your opposition to this action may undermine your effectiveness on all the other issues. How will you balance your values with those of the group? To whom do you owe loyalty: the group, yourself, the neighborhood, your profession, those who need such residences, or society in general?

Social workers with community groups may have somewhat different views about the implications of developing a friendship with a client or member, about serving on community boards or committees together with clients or members, or about having another type of relationship with a client or member. For example, social workers who are community organizers or social planners may go to a local diner or coffeehouse with a group of clients/members after a session, whereas social workers who work with individuals may or may not draw a line on such behavior. Social work administrators often make their most important contacts with board members in social settings. Obviously, the definition of who is a client/member, the purpose of the professional relationship, and the context are factors that affect the ethical assessment of such dual-role relationships. The dual relationships formed by community organizers may be reflective of what have become changing views in the social work profession. Earlier, in Chapter 7, the views of Maidment (2006) were introduced that the profession should be more open to client-worker relationship boundaries that fall both within and outside conventional ethical parameters in professional practice. Do you agree with this position? Why or why not?

Community and Societal Issues

Standard 6.01 of the NASW (2008) Code states "social workers should promote the general welfare of society ... their communities, and their environments." Before leaving this section, we want to point out an example of ethical responsibility of social workers at a societal level. Blacks in the United States do not live as long as Whites. A Black male born in 1999 had a life expectancy of slightly more than 67 years. A White male born in that same year could expect to live until 74, an additional seven years of life. American Indians and Alaskan Native people born today will live five years fewer than people of any other U.S. racial or ethnic group. When compared to Whites, Asian Americans, Blacks, and Hispanics are less likely to have a regular doctor. Poor people are more likely to go without needed medical care. Clearly, some groups in the United States are healthier in general than others and receive better health care (Center for Health Equity Research and Promotion, 2005).

For all social workers, the Code of Ethics sets forth several standards concerned with social workers' ethical responsibilities to the broader society. Among these responsibilities are the identification of disparities such as those cited above and working to address them. Doing so requires macro-level organizing and advocacy either in professional roles or as concerned citizens. For example, standard 6.04 (NASW Code, 2008) states: "Social workers should engage in social and political action that seeks to ensure that all people have equal access to the resources, employment, services, and opportunities they require to meet their basic human needs and to develop fully."

Community organizers, policy and social planning practitioners, advocates, and others involved with societal issues take as their focus issues at the community and societal levels. Are such matters the ethical concern only of social workers who are practicing macro methods? If not, what does this suggest are the ethical roles of direct service and clinical social workers in regard to these situations? Whatever the difficulties and dilemmas for social workers in macro practice, the Code of Ethics— for all social workers—explicitly requires engagement by social workers in social and political action.

Some professional social workers hold stereotyped views of their colleagues who engage in macro practice. They believe that practitioners who engage in agency-wide change efforts, social planning, neighborhood and community organization and development, social action, and social policy efforts are operating in a highly politicized arena. They think that this practice area is grounded on techniques and methods based on pragmatism rather than on ethical considerations. This perception is fostered not only by the nature of the settings in which macro practitioners practice but also by the language they use, especially such terms as tactics, strategies, conflict, and advocacy. Indeed, with a few exceptions, references to ethics are only rarely found in macro practice textbooks.

Nevertheless, macro social workers may encounter many more difficult ethical dilemmas in their daily practice than do their colleagues in direct practice. The 2008 Code of Ethics applies to all NASW members, including those in macro practice. The Code states that "Social workers' primary responsibility is to promote the well-being of clients" (1.01) and "Social workers should promote the general welfare of society, from local to global levels" (6.01). Further, "the social worker should engage in social and political action that seeks to ensure that all people have access to the resources, employment, services, and opportunities they require to meet their basic human needs and to develop fully" (6.04a).

When the social worker is attempting to comply with all of these standards, many dilemmas are encountered. These include determining who is the client to whom primary responsibility is owed and selecting the persons who have access to resources when not every needy person can be supplied because these resources are in short supply. Another type of dilemma occurs when there are several similarly disadvantaged groups. How does the worker choose the one group that will receive her priority attention? In the social planning situation in Exemplar 12.8, the social worker has to choose between many different groups. The choices to be made clearly deal with promoting the "general welfare of society." In this instance, who is society? Which group deserves priority consideration?

12.8 | ESTABLISHING A CANCER TREATMENT UNIT

EP 2.1.2

You are the director of social work in a large urban community hospital located in a low-income area serving people from various economic levels. You have been assigned to staff the planning committee charged with creating a plan for the future of the hospital. You grew up in the community and have family and long-standing friends who reside there. You also have relationships with many community human service administrators and staff members.

As the planning process proceeds, it becomes clear that most committee members favor the creation of a specialized cancer treatment unit, which will gain status and recognition for the hospital and also attract patients from throughout the state. Such a recommendation, however, will make it impossible to recommend improvements for emergency and ambulatory care that are desperately needed by the neighborhood. A recommendation for a cancer treatment unit will change the nature of the available health care, who will get the jobs, use of community space, kinds of housing that will be available, and so forth.

It becomes clear to you that the local community will gain very little and may lose much if a cancer treatment unit is installed. You are torn between loyalties to the hospital, to the community in general, to the social and human service agencies in the community, and to the community's population, including your friends and relatives who need a different type of service.

As a member of the planning group, you are faced with the dilemma of choosing between groups to determine who will benefit from the distribution of resources. What criteria will help you choose between the cancer patients who need this service but who do not necessarily come from the immediate community and the health needs of the local community, including your family, friends, and neighbors? Choosing between two groups, both of which have real needs, is a typical ethical dilemma faced by social workers who are social planners. Whose good is primary? As a social worker, you owe first priority to the potential recipients of health services, but which of the groups has a higher priority? In addition, is the hospital's long-term viability a consideration that should affect the ethical decision-making process?

A review of the ethical principles screen (EPS) in Chapter 4 can be helpful as you think about this dilemma. We would suggest that a consideration of Ethical Principles 1 and 2 is most compelling in the present case.

Principle 1—Protection of life. All medical services ultimately deal with the protection of life. Cancer patients are at a great risk and inevitably face life-threatening situations that require early treatment—the earlier the better. On the other hand, the emergencies typically treated in a hospital ER range from routine treatments to life-threatening situations that require immediate treatment; for the latter, any delay may be a death sentence. Principle 1 does not provide unambiguous guidance, but it can be used to buttress either choice.

Principle 2—Social Justice. Cancer is a very high-profile disease. A cancer treatment unit will be established in at least one hospital in the state, no matter what the board of Neighborhood Hospital decides. For the neighborhood residents, however, Neighborhood Hospital is the only chance for receiving timely emergency services; transportation to the next nearest hospital would add 10 to 15 minutes' travel time—too much when every minute counts. Under this principle, neighborhood persons have the ethical right to expect preferred consideration. The social worker, therefore, can support a recommendation in favor of improving emergency services.

Social workers are expected to be open and honest. Among the standards in the NASW (2008) Code of Ethics is the expectation that "social workers should not participate in, condone, or be associated with dishonesty, fraud, or deception" (4.04). At every step in their education and later in practice, social workers are encouraged not to engage in secretive, hidden, or disguised actions or to be manipulative. Much attention has been paid in the literature to efforts to change social agencies, always with the justification that one's efforts are designed to improve services for clients or to attain some general good. In some cases, concealed and unacknowledged action may be thought necessary to gain a greater good for a community or for clients. In these cases, social workers have to weigh the ethical balance between a greater good and hidden actions. What is the best way for the worker to respond in the situation presented in Exemplar 12.9?

EP 2.1.2

| 12.9 | Fighting the Half-Truths of the Real Estate Lobby |

Ed Corey is a community organizer employed by a social agency to develop new housing in a neighborhood. Ed staffs a community coalition that is vigorously working on the new housing. The early activities of the coalition were very successful, but powerful real estate interests who wanted to block the development of the new housing began to spread rumors about Ed's personal history and life. They also used deceptive and distorted facts in advertisements to destroy the coalition's efforts and to undercut Ed's potential influence. Ed, for his part, knows about the shady dealings of some members of the real estate group. He senses there will be no new housing unless aggressive action is taken, but he is unsure what he should do to combat the half-truths and lies of the opponents of the new housing.

How should Ed use the information he has? Should he be open and rebut the charges of the opponents? Should he retaliate and fight fire with fire behind the scenes? Should he use the facts he possesses with strategically located opinion molders to undermine the influence of the real estate group?

Community Organizing

Hardina (2004) explored the ways in which community organizers encounter ethical dilemmas in practice. Concepts such as self-determination, informed consent, and protection of confidentiality are relevant to both micro and macro practice, but their application in community organization is different than in direct or clinical practice. She identifies the values inherent in community practice, describes ethical issues encountered, and examines available tools for resolving common ethical dilemmas. Consider Exemplar 12.10.

EP 2.1.2

12.10	THE SOCIAL WORKER SEES AN INJUSTICE

Paulina Dill is a community organizer working in Milltown. She is helping the mill workers organize for better benefits, including sick leave and health insurance. Milltown is in a very rural region, and the community is almost entirely dependent on the mill for its economic survival. The families of the current mill workers have lived in town and been employed by the mill for generations. Most of the residents have very traditional gender roles and values.

Over the past several months, Paulina has been to several community meetings and met with individual workers. As she spoke with the workers, she noted that none of the women were supervisors or managers, even though the women had as much education and experience as the men did. Paulina was upset by the gender discrimination and wanted to organize the women to address the issue. When she suggested this to the women at one of the community meetings, she was told that the women did not want to be supervisors or managers so they never applied for those positions.

How should Paulina respond? Should she encourage women to apply for these positions? Should she try to organize the workers to advocate for women in supervisory or administrative positions even though they are resistant to the idea? If she does try to organize them, is she imposing her feminist values on the people of Milltown? If she does not do anything, is she helping perpetuate discrimination? How would you respond?

Among the ethical dilemmas Hardina (2004) identifies for community organizers are conflicts of interest and choice of tactics. Many community organizers are members of the neighborhood or community they are trying to organize. The interventions involved in the organizing effort may force the organizer to choose between loyalty to the organizing effort and participants and friends, relatives, and other neighborhood residents. Patronizing some businesses so as to obtain information may create a conflict with other businesses in the area, influencing who can be involved in the organizing effort and how. Financial conflicts can also occur when an organizing group invests in some businesses in the community, only to find that their organizing efforts will help or hinder their organization's own investments, creating conflicts of interest. Conflicts may also occur when organizers develop friendships or inappropriate personal boundaries with persons involved in the organizing efforts. Furthermore, the choice of tactics, including confrontational tactics, may present ethical dilemmas for organizers. Do the ends to be attained justify the tactics chosen to pursue the outcome?

The literature regarding ethics and community organizing is in its early developmental stages. In fact, sparse attention has been paid to the many ethical issues that confront community organizers and the ways in which they can be dealt with. Hardina (2004) introduces several tools for use by community organizers to deal with the ethical dilemmas they encounter, including the NASW Code of Ethics, the ethical principles screen presented earlier in this book, and an ethical decision-making framework for organizers (Reisch & Lowe, 2000). Reisch and Lowe (2000) propose a series of steps for community organizers to use to resolve ethical dilemmas. The following are their recommended steps and ethical decision-making framework for organizers:

- Identify the ethical principles that apply to the situation at hand.
- Collect additional information necessary to examine the ethical dilemma in question.
- Identify the relevant ethical values and/or rules that apply to the ethical problem.
- Identify any potential conflicts of interest and the people who are likely to benefit from such a conflict.
- Identify appropriate ethical rules and rank order them in terms of importance.
- Determine the consequences of applying different ethical rules or ranking these rules differently.

If you were serving as a community organizer, to what extent do the NASW (2008) Code of Ethics and the decision-making framework for community organizers described immediately above provide guidance for your ethical decision making? To what extent do you think this proposed framework for community organizers would assist you in making ethical decisions?

Hardina (2004) suggests the practitioner construct her own ethics model using the above mentioned tools, to which can be added other principles such as mutual learning and empowerment to develop a personal framework to be used in community practice. Efforts to develop ethical decision-making literature and exploration of issues in social work with community groups and in macro practice are in their initial stages, although both areas of practice deal continuously with ethical dilemmas.

Earlier, Hardina (2000) reported on a study of 44 members of the Association for Community Organization and Social Administration (ACOSA) who teach community organization in schools of social work. The study identified models of community organization, as well as tactics taught in those classes. One additional question was explored: Are there tactics that the respondents feel are incompatible with social work ethics? In regard to this last question, 37 respondents indicated that they found at least one tactical method to be unethical. The tactics that were viewed as unethical in descending frequency were: violence (37%); personal degradation/harm (17%); deceit/ lie (15%); terrorism/insurrection (8%); manipulation of constituents (5%); and tactics that serve the power elite (3%). Interestingly, respondents saw social action to be the least effective method of promoting social change because of its potential for conflict and the alienation of key decision makers. Hardina (2000) suggests that some respondents associate confrontation with violence, personal verbal and physical attacks, and the manipulation of constituency groups. She also concluded that social workers reject tactics associated with social action such as demonstrations, picketing, and boycotts.

The finding that social workers are uncomfortable with social action tactics is significant. Reisch and Lowe (2000) identified the principle of justice in the distribution of social benefits, rights, power, status, and opportunities as of special importance to community organizers. Interventions in regard to social justice necessarily involve actions aimed at altering the pattern of resources and power distribution in the community. Discussion of social action as an important strategy for community organizers is widespread (Mondros, 2009; Weil & Gamble, 2009). Nevertheless, it is difficult to reconcile the discomfort with social action expressed by the teachers and the prevalence of social action in the literature.

Social justice is a core value in the NASW (2008) Code of Ethics (Preamble) and is second among the ethical principles espoused by the Code: Social workers challenge social injustice. Social workers pursue social change, particularly with and on behalf of vulnerable and oppressed individuals and groups of people. "Social workers' social change efforts are focused primarily on issues of poverty, unemployment, discrimination, and other forms of social injustice" (NASW, 2008, Ethical principles). On the face of it, redistribution of resources and power are seldom, if ever, accomplished without social action. To what extent is social action being practiced, and can individual community organizers and social workers in general and the profession itself claim their efforts are congruent with the demands of the Code?

McNutt and Menon (2008) discuss cyberactivism that can be used for organizing and for advocacy. They identify several barriers to the use of technology by community organizers, including "the digital divide," potential efforts by corporations to control the Internet, and growing concerns about privacy on the Internet. Access to the Internet is becoming more universal but many groups, especially traditional groups at risk, lack the technology to engage in online advocacy. Thus, persons and groups from the middle and upper socio-economic levels have greater access to these organizing tools while lower-income persons and groups may be without access and therefore less able to take part in the political process. For example, several types of technology were used in the successful effort to elect President Barack Obama, including e-mail, the Internet, conferencing, teleconferencing, faxes, videoconferences, and videotapes.

From an ethical decision-making point of view, these facts raise issues of equality and inequality, limited resources, and advocacy, which were discussed in Chapter 9. When resources are limited, who gets priority? What if in a community a wealthier group is working to achieve an important goal, let us say a community youth center (a goal clearly to the benefit of many people), and a poorer group is attempting to advocate for a nursery school that will affect many fewer but more needy people? If you as a community organizer got to choose which group gets the technological tools needed, how and what would you choose?

CRITICAL THINKING EXERCISES

EP 2.1.3

1. In a group, discuss how technologies present ethical dilemmas for your agencies and for social workers. Identify how these ethical dilemmas could be avoided and/or dealt with ethically.
2. You are serving on the committee in Exemplar 12.1, "What the Pine Tree Insurance Company Wants." Which of the options suggested by committee members would you choose? What standards in the Code of Ethics support your choice?
3. Have a class discussion or debate about whether evidence-based practice is ethically necessary.

4. If you are confronted by the ethical dilemma that faces the director of social work in Exemplar 12.8, "Establishing a Cancer Treatment Unit," what do you think your decision would be? What arguments support your decision? What arguments exist contrary to your point of view?

SUGGESTIONS FOR ADDITIONAL READINGS

Keefe, Hall, and Corvo (2002) examined a sample of clinical social workers, psychologists, and psychiatrists to determine what percentage of their caseloads consisted of persons who had been denied reimbursement by managed care organizations for ongoing therapy. Their findings have potential ethical and legal complications for private practitioners. Santhiveeran (2004) presents an historical overview of e-therapy and the state of the art as it related to social work at that time. Available research is evaluated, and ethical concerns based on the NASW Code of Ethics are considered. Marziali, Donahue, and Cross in (2005) report on Internet video conferencing supports for family caregivers of persons with neurodegenerative disease (dementia, stroke, and Parkinson's disease) and discuss the professional and ethical implications of providing clinical interventions using the Internet. Jewell, Collins, Gargotto, and Dishon (2009) discuss community organizing for human rights. Silvestre, Quinn, and Rinaldo (2010) report on a community advisory board for health research that provided opportunities for social change and community organizing; they also discuss relevant ethical issues. Scopelliti et al. (2004) present several models for assessing dual relationships in rural communities.

WEBSITES OF INTEREST

- The University of Maryland, Baltimore Health and Human Services Library provides links to a number of evidence-based practice resources: http://guides.hshsl.umaryland.edu/content.php?pid=61701&sid=453802
- Haworth Press publishes the *Journal of Evidence-Based Social Work:* http://www.informaworld.com/smpp/title~content=t792303996~db=all
- The NASW and ASWB Standards for Technology and Social Work Practice are available at: www.socialworkers.org/practice/standards/NASWTechnologyStandards.pdf
- NASW resources on evidence-based practice are available at: http://www.naswdc.org/research/naswResearch/0108EvidenceBased/default.asp
- The Social Work Policy Institute resources on evidence-based practice are available at: http://www.socialworkpolicy.org/research/evidence-based-practice-2.html
- The Association for Community Organization and Social Administration (ACOSA): http://www.acosa.org/ and their professional journal, *Journal of Community Practice: Organizing, Planning, Development & Change* at http://www.acosa.org/jcpwhat.html

COMPETENCY NOTES

Identify as a professional social worker and conduct oneself accordingly: In this chapter, we discuss a number of practice settings and issues and how they relate to ethical dilemmas for social workers.

EP 2.1.1

Apply social work ethical principles to guide professional practice: In this chapter, we discuss managed care, technology, evidence based practice, and direct and macro practice related ethical issues.

EP 2.1.2

Apply critical thinking to inform and communicate professional judgments: Exemplars asked you to consider and decide how you would respond to ethical dilemmas, and exercises at the end of the chapter address critical thinking.

EP 2.1.3

Engage diversity and difference in practice: We discuss issues related to rural and isolated communities and the ethical issues that may be encountered in these settings.

EP 2.1.4

Advance human rights and social and economic justice: We discuss social justice and advocacy.

EP 2.1.5

WHOSE RESPONSIBILITY ARE PROFESSIONAL ETHICS?

CHAPTER **13**

In this chapter, we continue to address the CSWE 2008 EPAS Educational Policy 2.1.1 on becoming a professional social worker and Educational Policy 2.1.2 on using social work ethical principles to guide professional practice, specifically related to individual and organizational responsibility. We provide questions and critical thinking exercises that we hope you will use to apply critical thinking to inform and communicate professional judgments (Educational Policy 2.1.3). These educational policies have been addressed throughout this book. We hope that you now have a better sense of the ethical dilemmas that occur in social work practice and that you have developed a set of tools with which to address the dilemmas you will encounter in your own practice. In this final chapter, we address additional resources that may be helpful to you in this effort.

Ethical decision making is often presented in a way that suggests that the social worker who must make a decision is completely alone and cut off from every support system that might give her guidance. Many have questioned this view. Thus, philosopher W. D. Walsh (1969) wrote, "Morality is first and foremost a social institution, performing a social role, and only secondarily, if at all, a field for individual self-expression" (cited in Frankena, 1980, p. 33).

While every social worker is, of course, responsible for her ethical decisions, it must be recognized that she is a participant in a number of networks and social systems that support—or should support—her ethical decision making. One of the purposes of codes of ethics is to help social workers "identify relevant considerations when professional obligations conflict or ethical uncertainties arise" (NASW Code, 2008, Purpose of the NASW Code of Ethics). Decision making, however, always occurs within a social setting that influences, rewards, or guides certain behaviors and limits, while it sanctions or disapproves others. The social agency employing the social worker is one such setting; the service delivery team, unit, or office is another; and the professional association is a third. Any discussion of steps designed to facilitate and strengthen ethical decision making in professional practice is incomplete if it fails to take these systems into consideration. In other words, professional ethical actions involve much more than merely individual choices.

Organizations also must play a part in supporting ethical decision making by social workers. Essential to all techniques that agencies employ to establish ethical norms and enhance ethical conduct (e.g., staff education and training, accountability systems, etc.) is the establishment of an ethical climate in the agency that is visible, deemed important, and understood by all participants. The establishment of such a climate involves the use of the executive leadership influence and the participation of staff members and other parties at every level of the system to ensure high ethical standards throughout the work and life of the agency (Grundstein-Amado, 1999).

RESOURCES THAT SUPPORT ETHICAL DECISION MAKING

There will never be a time when clear guidelines will be available for every ethical decision that a social worker must make, but various societal and institutional mechanisms have been developed to provide guidance and support. In this chapter we will discuss a number of mechanisms that may be particularly helpful for social workers.

CLIENTS' BILL OF RIGHTS

Many hospitals and other service organizations distribute a bill of rights to new clients and patients. These brief statements inform people of the type of information they are entitled to know about their situation. They are also told they can expect to be treated with dignity and respect, they will participate in decision making about their situation, they will be informed about available options, and they have a right to speak to an ombudsman or other person if they are dissatisfied with their treatment.

Social workers should consider the use of a clear and informative statement to advise new clients about what they can expect from the professional personnel they will encounter, the mechanisms for raising questions or seeking clarification where needed, and the procedures for registering grievances. While social workers can and should inform their clients about these things, transmitting such information verbally is not the same as a bill of rights. Such a statement must be in writing and can be issued only by the agency, not by the individual social worker. The situation is different for those in private practice, who can and should issue such a written document to every new client. The document should include statements about what the client can and cannot expect to happen in the professional service. The rules promulgated by the Health Insurance Portability and Accountability Act (HIPAA) safeguard personal information of clients from being released without prior written consent by the client, with the exception of child abuse and neglect, thoughts about harming someone, or thoughts about harming themselves. Part of the compliance procedure for social workers and agencies is provision to each client of a copy of the policy that explains clients' rights.

AGENCY RISK AUDITS

Many types of audits are conducted in human service agencies—financial, safety, quality control, and utilization review. Agencies can also conduct an audit of professional knowledge of social work ethics that can include two major foci: (1) social workers' knowledge of identified ethics-related risks (such as complaints and lawsuits filed against social workers, ethics committees' past experience, and court cases not specific to social work but with implications for social workers and social agencies) in their field of service and practice settings; and (2) current agency procedures for handling ethical issues, dilemmas, and decisions. Among the ethical risks are client rights, confidentiality and privacy, informed consent, service delivery, boundary issues, conflicts of interest, documentation, defamation of character, client records, supervision, staff development and training, consultation, client referrals, fraud, termination of services and client abandonment, practitioner impairment, and evaluation and research. Agencies that periodically engage in social work ethics audits have the opportunity to strengthen their own ethical performance, but they also provide support and preparation for practitioners and supervisors, thus sharing as an organization the burden of ethical decision making by staff members (Reamer, 2001).

The importance of ethics risk management has begun to be recognized in social work and other human service professions. The social work ethics audit provides for systematic attention to steps that can minimize the likelihood of harm to clients and staff, prevent ethics complaints, and prevent lawsuits alleging some kind of ethics-related negligence. Kirkpatrick, Reamer, and Skyulski (2006) conducted and reported on an ethics audit in three health care settings that were part of a large hospital corporation affiliated with a medical school. The results for each of the sites differed, but the most significant risks were related to policies and procedures concerning informed consent (e.g., interpreter and translation for non–English speaking persons; and handling of confidential information, such as disclosure of a patient's substance abuse history or sensitive information to managed care organizations); maintenance of proper boundaries with patients (e.g., developing friendships with patients); supervision of staff (e.g., frequency, quality, and documentation of supervision); staff consultation (e.g., when and how to obtain consultation); and documenting ethical decisions The audit provided administrators and staff with opportunities to examine their policies and practices, identify risk areas, and develop strategies for improving their handling of ethical issues (Kirkpatrick, Reamer, & Skyulski, 2006).

In addition, a series of guidelines regarding documentation have been developed that can help ensure risk-management standards to enhance the delivery of services to clients and to protect practitioners who may be required to defend themselves against ethics complaints brought either to state licensing boards or professional associations. Reamer (2005) places these guidelines into four categories: (1) content of documentation, (2) language and terminology, (3) credibility, and (4) access to records and documents. Essentially, these guidelines suggest balancing detail against overly sparse record keeping, as well as careful uses of language. "Too much content, too little content, or the wrong content can harm clients and expose practitioners to considerable risk of liability" (Reamer, 2005, p. 328). Too little detail in some circumstances can compromise the quality of service so that an on-call backup person only has vague or incomplete information for dealing with the situation, or the record of steps taken has insufficient detail in the event of a complaint or lawsuit. Be cautious with personal notes when documenting services to families and couples in a unified record, and be careful not to expose confidential information, as records and personal notes may be subpoenaed. Social workers should also avoid defamatory language, acknowledge errors, be familiar with relevant laws, and make certain records are secure.

McAuliffe (2005), an Australian social worker, focused not on avoidance of risk but, instead, studied agencies that agreed to participate in a funded research project on the institution of social work ethics audits. Participants included three hospitals, three counseling and support agencies, two community-based services for women, one community health service, one community-based disability support service, and one volunteer-based unfunded service. The research on the implementation of the audits highlighted a number of benefits and challenges for the staffs and agencies: (1) providing a legitimate space for discussion of ethical issues; (2) identifying the gaps in knowledge and skills of the staff; and (3) identifying implications for quality assurance and accreditation. McAuliffe (2005) concluded that the most important beneficial outcomes of implementing social work ethics audits are the explicit focusing of attention on ethical practice and the legitimacy that an ethics audit gives to addressing issues of ethical sensitivity.

Chase (2008) suggests increasing liability and risk are the result of ethics and other practice violations. She therefore proposes six strategies to reduce risk:

1. Assume a proactive stance by considering the preventive aspects of risk management.
2. Minimize risk through familiarity with policies and procedures so as to minimize risks that occur because of lack of knowledge.
3. Take a comprehensive look at the context and eliminate or reduce risk wherever possible.
4. Stress education in the area of ethics, good practices, transference, and counter-transference.
5. Supervision and consultation should be available.
6. Share the burden of risk by being aware of agency policies and procedures, and take additional precautions such as carrying malpractice insurance and arranging to have on-going consultation and/or supervision. (p. 428)

Peer Review and Committees on the Ethics of Social Work Practice

Peer review permits a social worker to test her ethical decision making against that of her colleagues, either informally in groups that practitioners create for mutual aid or formally in agencies. In the past, social workers have used informal groupings to review their professional practice decisions. Such groupings can also be useful for reviewing ethical decisions. Peer review groups are particularly important for social workers in private practice because they are more isolated than workers in agency-based practice and because they have less opportunity for interaction with peers. Controls and accountability of private practice social workers depend almost entirely upon the sensitivity and knowledge of the individual practitioner. Peer pressures, which are so immediate in agency practice, are much less evident in private practice. Because of these considerations, social workers in private practice may want to organize peer review systems that are specifically geared to provide review and advice regarding their ethical decision making. In this way, they can be more certain that their decisions will be of the highest quality.

Each agency should establish a *Committee on the Ethics of Social Work Practice*, analogous to Human Research Protections Offices (HRPO) or Institutional Review Boards (IRB) that exist in academic research organizations. Practitioners who have an ethical question may consult with the committee about a problem. Such a committee is a forum where social workers can think through difficult ethical questions occurring in everyday practice. Most important, this committee can be the locus for the routine monitoring of ethical practice within the agency.

As a service to current members, the NASW Office of Ethics and Professional Review provides ethics consultations to those members who are experiencing an ethical dilemma. These consultations guide people through the Code and point them toward the relevant standards related to their concerns. Dialogues may help members to make ethical decisions. Members may be referred to particular resources if the questions are not related to ethics but to legal issues or standards of social work practice.

ACCOUNTABILITY SYSTEMS

Professional social workers working in agencies or in private practice will be held accountable for their professional activities. Courts, third-party payers, governmental regulators, and empowered clients and patients as citizens play roles in regard to accountability in our increasingly litigious society. Social agencies are accountable for what their employees do. Social agencies that want to implement this responsibility in a positive way must develop and operate internal accountability systems. These systems are characterized by the following features: information systems and monitoring; methods for sampling activities and decisions; clear indicators of the desired quality of performance; clear indicators or criteria of the desired quality of ethical decision making; and feedback systems that permit an early alert to problem situations.

Accountability systems relate primarily to practice performance, but there is no reason why such systems could not incorporate additional indicators that focus on the ethical aspects of practice. Just as agencies evaluate the effectiveness and efficiency of the services they deliver and the social work practices of their social work employees, agencies can also track and systematically evaluate the ethical decision making of social work practitioners.

TRAINING AND CONSULTATION

Most agencies make a heavy investment in providing in-service training, continuing education opportunities, and consultation for their staff. Though the focus is often on more effective practice and more efficient administration, these sessions should also include a focus on the ethical implications of practice in order to strengthen the ethical level of practice. Social workers in private practice are expected to continue learning about ethical decision making and the further development of their ethical decision-making abilities. Many states now require ethics content as part of the continuing education requirements for relicensure, a factor that may help encourage social workers to remain current in their knowledge of ethics.

Agency Appeals Procedures and Ombudsmen

Many agencies have appeals procedures, yet clients are often not aware of these. Forgetting to inform clients about them may simplify the life of the practitioners and administrators but does not make for a high level of ethical practice. The use of appeals procedures does more than correct mistakes made by social workers. One of their most valuable functions is to sensitize social workers to the ethical aspects of practice. An ombudsman or another type of appeals procedure should be readily available to all clients, who should be able to use these procedures without any risk of stigma or retaliation of any kind. Ethical social workers will welcome such strategies. Administrative review procedures also have a place in the support system, but they do not take the place of appeals procedures that are freely available to clients.

Professional Associations

Professional associations, such as NASW, can play a key role in strengthening ethical practice. The promulgation and periodic revision or updating of the Code of Ethics (last completed in 2008) needs to be strengthened through the inclusion of case references and interpretive guidelines because the standards of practice and the limits of ethical behavior are often difficult to define. Jayaratne et al. (1997) found, in a study of Michigan NASW members, that there is much confusion and disagreement as to what constitutes appropriate ethical practice.

Maidment (2006) argues that in the current context there is a need to explore client/worker relationship boundaries that fall both within and outside conventional ethical professional practice (as discussed in Chapter 7). She argues there are alternative interpretations that can be useful regarding relationship, reciprocity, love, touch, and spirituality, thus suggesting that the NASW and other professional associations of social workers must develop additional strategies if they want to encourage clarification and strengthening of ethical decision making within the profession. The following are some of the ways to do so:

- Continue to revise and refine the Code of Ethics. It may be helpful to add case precedents.
- Encourage the formation of formal and informal groups to study and review critical ethical decisions arising from actual practice experiences.
- Develop a data bank of precedents with ethical implications. Knowledge about ethical decisions is valuable, but identifying and learning about those actions found to be unethical can also have positive consequences, including being instructive and warning members of the profession.
- Continue to schedule activities that focus on the ethical aspects of practice, both at professional conferences and as part of continuing education programs.
- In addition to discussion of monthly dilemmas on NASW's website, publish an "Ethics Reporter" or a regular ethics column in *Social Work* or in the *NASW News* in order to make social workers more familiar with their Code of Ethics.
- Further develop NASW's ethics hotline so that practitioners, supervisors, and administrators can obtain advice on ethical issues that arise in their practice.

Modern communication technologies, such as instant messaging and electronic mail, can provide instant communication over long distances. At the same time, these technologies give the consultant sufficient time to reflect on the question or to consult with others.

- The NASW should publish an annual report, as does the American Psychological Association, regarding the number and types of ethical complaints investigated and the disposition of those cases.

Fine and Teram (2009) studied the daily life experience of social workers who are members of the Canadian Association of Social Workers in regard to their ethical decision making and the professional code. The researchers used individual interviews and focus group methods to collect data from the social workers, all of whom lived and worked in five cities in the Province of Ontario. The total participant sample consisted of 51 women and 20 men. The researchers identified two major groups: The believers abided by the Code; the skeptics were leery about the benefits of the Code. The believers regard the Code as the best representative of what the social work profession embodies. The skeptics, though appreciative of the social work endeavor, question whether the principles of social work as represented in the Code are always in the best interest of the clients. "The Code does not address the particular, the local, and the contextual and ... strict adherence leads to a disconnection with the client (i.e., lack of physical and emotional connection) as well as an obfuscation of power and justice issues that underlie client 'problems' (e.g., further oppression through unfair social assistance policies) which are among the concerns expressed in the literature" (Fine & Teram, 2009, p. 73). If a similar survey were conducted in the United States, what do you think the findings would be?

The Fine and Teram (2009) study underscores the need for the professional organization and its local chapters, as well as individual social agencies, to collect data on ethical decision making. Such a data bank should not be limited to success stories but should also include errors, unanswerable questions, and embarrassing situations. Collection of this type of data will be helpful to practitioners as well as to students. This information will explicate the ethical quandaries experienced by social workers, the preferred solutions, and the results achieved. Such a data bank will also be helpful in the creation of case materials, which are necessary for the systematic development of new social work knowledge. Just as lawyers can draw on case law for guidance in making the difficult decisions, so social workers should be able to receive guidance from the suggested data bank.

NASW Professional Complaint Procedures

Requests for professional review (RPRs) may be submitted in the event of an alleged violation of the NASW Code of Ethics by the following:

- An individual who has engaged in a professional social work relationship with an NASW member
- A group of individuals in an agency or organization who have direct knowledge of an NASW member's professional conduct within a professional social work relationship or setting

- An individual on behalf of another person as long as that person is either mentally or physically incapacitated, or is a minor child, and the person has proper standing to bring such an action on behalf of the incapacitated adult or minor
- An NASW member who has concerns that his or her actions in a situation may have violated the NASW Code of Ethics

The individual against whom the RPR is filed must have been a member of the NASW at the time of the alleged violation.

In addition to particular forms being completed and filed, as well as other procedural matters, a complainant must describe how the alleged misconduct violated the NASW Code of Ethics by citing specific standards from the Code. Whenever possible, hearings and mediation sessions will be conducted by members of the NASW chapter where the violations under review were alleged to have occurred. If a chapter fails to take timely action, the National Ethics Committee may assume jurisdiction. Certain alleged actions will be referred for adjudication, whereas others will be referred for mediation (NASW, 2005).

In October 2009, the NASW Board of Directors approved and immediately implemented two changes to the professional review procedures: (1) if a social work licensing board action requires revocation of the member's license, NASW membership will also be revoked; and (2) if a member is convicted of a felony, NASW membership will also be revoked (NASW, 2010). The two changes were recommended in order to address concerns about protection of the public. When a chapter becomes aware of a substantiated criminal or social work licensure violation by a member based on information available in the public domain that has resulted in an action less than a felony or revocation of a social work license, the chapter will forward serving as a surrogate actor the information to the national office for review. A special review process will then be set in motion. This procedure can also be started by a self-report by the social worker. Members will be provided an opportunity for review before automatic sanctions are implemented by NASW.

ETHICS ADVOCACY, HUMAN SERVICES AGENCIES, AND INTERDISCIPLINARY TEAMS

Social workers are employed at a great variety of human service and other sites where members of the staffs include social workers and other professionals, all of whom may have varying professional powers, statuses, and professional ethical obligations, and exert varying degrees of control. Participation in interdisciplinary situations means working with other social workers, psychologists, nurses, physicians, and correctional personnel, as well as representatives of other disciplines. Both in settings where the predominant profession is social work and in other settings where other professions play host roles, social workers loyal to the NASW Code of Ethics may have to engage in effective ethical advocacy. Dodd and Jansson (2004) recommend that social workers attain knowledge and skills that will allow them to contribute effectively in ethical discussions involving social workers and clients or patients, as well as other professionals.

Csikai (2004) surveyed a sample of 110 hospice social workers to identify ethical issues in hospice care, how the issues were managed, and the extent to which the social workers participated in the resolution of the ethical dilemmas. Social workers on the ethics committees served as advocates for social justice through new policies and assisted in reviewing existing policies concerning ethical issues. Csikai (2004) concluded that interdisciplinary participation that is not limited to the above two activities requires much more preparation than social workers currently receive.

Faust (2008) drew attention to the fact that clinical social work settings often ignore advocacy for patients. Systems, including mental health agencies, are not always responsive to individual patients. But, in addition to the need to advocate for individuals, there arise many patient complaints that require institutional change, complaints related to both treatment and concrete services such as financial aid, transportation, and housing issues. The presence of a skillful ethical advocate prepared for advocacy in regard to the agency itself reminds the staff of the mental health agency of the rights of patients. Faust (2008) identifies other issues for ethical advocacy such as adding information about medical and other students being involved in treatment (and the right to refuse such participation) to the Patient's Bill of Rights; correcting unintentional violations of confidentiality due to architectural characteristics of a lobby; and devising strategies to confirm appointments with patients without violating their confidentiality.

Among the strategies Dodd and Jansson (2004) propose to promote an organization's ability to deal with power and politics in relation to ethical decision making are: seeking written protocols that identify the need for and nature of social work participation in ethical decision making by the team; seeking multidisciplinary ethical training sessions; and educating the members of other professions about the potential role of social workers in ethical decision making. Prior to involvement with the ethical decision making of interdisciplinary groups, social workers must develop their own knowledge of the ethics of the social work profession and the group. They must also develop advocacy skills as well as feelings of self-efficacy that can make them effective advocates for clients and patients. Finally, they must find constructive ways of interacting with other professionals in the ethical decision-making processes.

McBeath and Webb (2002) emphasize the advocacy function in the British social work context with clear implications for U.S. social workers. They describe social work and agencies as "increasingly routinized by accountability, quality control and risk management... [with] an emphasis on regulation and duties. This has produced a culture of following approved or typical processes resulting in defensive forms of social work wholly uncongenial to the development of human qualities likely to promote social workers' engagement in critique and revision of what counts as best practice" (p. 1016). They suggest that "the integrity of the social worker is not found in consistent action or maximizing pay-offs across cases, or in carrying out department policy or the law accurately, rather it is found in the fundamental orientation or good will towards those who one works for and works with, and towards the activities in which one engages" (p. 1028). McBeath and Webb (2002) write of the "iron cage of administrative rationality" and advocate that social workers not let the rightness of action (the ethical action) be determined in relation to a body of law or other rules. In other words, ethical accountability cannot be ruled by administrative rationality, rules, and laws. This conclusion suggests that mechanical applications of the support systems that have evolved may not lead to desired achievement of more ethical practice but rather to the strengthening of bureaucratic procedures that are unresponsive to individual needs.

CONCLUSION

In this final chapter, we have presented ideas that may help social workers in their search for more effective ethical practice. The values of the social work profession form the background for ethical decision making. In turn, ethical decision making is the cornerstone for ethical practice. Ethical decision making begins with familiarity with codes of ethics and the clarification of one's own values. Knowledge of what one really believes is an inescapable basic step for social workers seeking to strengthen their ethical practice. Beyond this, it becomes important for social workers to clarify the values of society and of the various groups with which they work. Clarification of these values permits social workers to become more sensitive to and more aware of the values of others and of possible conflicts between different value systems.

American society has grown more litigious. One result has been that greater expectations are being placed on social workers, those who are new to the profession as well as those who are more experienced. Optimal preparation of social workers to practice ethically requires the efforts of individual practitioners, social work education, employing social agencies, individual and group private practitioners, and the profession (Chase, 2008). Individual practitioners sometimes feel they are alone when facing ethical dilemmas, but there are others who can share these ethical problems. Formal peer review, agency consultations, and the professional association must share the burden of thinking through these dilemmas. Some persons have suggested that ethics do not exist outside of community. To base ethical decisions strictly on one's individual conscience can lead a person into very difficult situations and into playing God. All ethics are integral to community. There are many reasons for a professional social worker to connect with the professional community. Fellow professionals can provide opportunities to think through ethical questions and dilemmas, to discuss one's ethical concerns with other social work professionals, and to gain colleague support in seeking the most ethical of ethical decisions.

RETURNING TO THE BEGINNING

Early in the first chapter of this book, we began our case exemplar of Basanti Madurai, whom our social worker Ellen Ashton had just met. We have returned to Basanti and Ellen several times in this book, adding information each time, much like an actual case might slowly be unveiled. As we end this book, let us assume that it is now two years later, and we find:

> About a year ago, Basanti stopped attending the South Asian women's support group that Ellen ran. During the past year, Ellen has occasionally seen Basanti in the community; when they meet they always say hello and chat for a few minutes in a friendly manner. On their most recent meeting, Basanti mentioned that things are going very well for her, and that she would like to give something back to the group that helped her so much. She asked Ellen if they could schedule a time to meet as friends and to discuss ways that Basanti could help with the South Asian women's support group.

How should Ellen respond to this request? What are the possible ethical dilemmas involved, and where could Ellen turn for help with reaching an ethical decision?

CRITICAL THINKING EXERCISES

EP 2.1.3

1. Identify your strengths and limitations in regard to ethical decision making when you are engaged in social work practice. How can you better prepare yourself for being an ethical social worker?
2. Identify in your field instruction placement, your agency of employment, or other social agency what you consider to be the limitations of the ethical decision-making patterns used. If you could improve one thing about ethical decision making in this organization, what would you choose to alter and how could you go about trying to improve the situation?
3. Review the NASW Procedures for Professional Review (2005) to become familiar with the filing of a complaint with the professional association.

SUGGESTIONS FOR ADDITIONAL READINGS

Strom-Gottfried (2003) helps practitioners and others to increase their understanding of adjudication as she reviews the origins, targets, and outcomes of ethics complaints. Kelly (2005) in "Beyond Problem-Solving: The Social Worker as Risk Manager and Educator in Educational Host Settings" describes how social workers in educational host settings engage in risk management and ethics education to address ethical dilemmas encountered in school settings. Advocacy has been inherent in social work, and a number of the standards in the Code suggest the importance of serving as advocates. Whistle-blowing is explored by Greene and Latting (2004) as a means to protect clients' rights and as an ethical means.

WEBSITES OF INTEREST

- You can find a copy of the NASW (2005) Procedures for Professional Review, Revised at: www.socialworkers.org/nasw/ethics/procedures.pdf
- The Ohio University Institute for Applied and Professional Ethics (see http://www.faculty-commons.org/ethics/) has an "Ask the E-Team!" resource that allows you to e-mail them a question about applied or professional ethics: http://www.faculty-commons.org/ethics/391/

COMPETENCY NOTES

EP 2.1.1

Identify as a professional social worker and conduct oneself accordingly: In this chapter, we focused on professional development in ethical decision making.

EP 2.1.2

Apply social work ethical principles to guide professional practice: In this chapter, we provided multiple resources that can help you apply ethical principles to social work practice.

EP 2.1.3

Apply critical thinking to inform and communicate professional judgments: Questions throughout the chapter and exercises at the end of the chapter address critical thinking.

| # ADDITIONAL EXEMPLARS

1. When Does Confidentiality End?

Clinical social worker Montana Jeffries is employed by Jefferson County Mental Health Center to work with men who have been court ordered to participate in treatment for domestic violence. Taylor Jones was a patient of hers for just over two years. His treatment ended successfully, and there have been no reports of him continuing any abuse of his partner. The Court agreed that he fulfilled the court's order. Ms. Jeffries has had no contact with him for over three years. Yesterday, when Ms. Jeffries was out of the office, a county sheriff left a message asking her to provide information about Mr. Jones's whereabouts in order to serve him with an arrest warrant. The sheriff also wanted as much information from her work with Mr. Jones as possible that would help locate him and understand how he operates. He asked that Ms. Jeffries call him back as soon as possible. When she received the message, Ms. Jeffries was uncertain how to respond. If she is legally required to respond, how much and what kinds of information can she report? Assume the law does not compel the release of information. Should Ms. Jeffries still comply with the request, and, if yes, what information should she report?

2. Protect a Fragile Client or Obey the Law?

Ms. Aspira Montgomery is a female in her late 20s who has been diagnosed as depressed and has a history of suicidal ideation. She has been in individual therapy with Violet Bruder, a social worker, for the last two years. During a recent session, Ms. Montgomery disclosed that she was a victim of sexual abuse during her teenage years and that she had not told anyone about it before. By law, Ms. Bruder is required to report the alleged abuse to the local Child Protective Services agency, but Ms. Montgomery is very resistant to her doing so and fears retaliation because the perpetrator is a relative and still alive. Ms. Bruder is also afraid that if she reports the abuse, Ms. Montgomery will become even more depressed and may harm herself. What should Ms. Bruder's next steps be? What is the ethical thing to do?

3. **What are Ms. Holliday's Ethical Choices?**
Sam Pilsudski is a 67-year-old widower lying unconscious in an intensive care unit. He has a previously undiagnosed cancer of the larynx obstructing his airway, and the physician wants the family to agree to surgery that would remove the patient's cancer and the larynx, depriving him of speech following the operation. When the physician spoke to one daughter of Mr. Pilsudski, she was very resistant about the surgery. The physician asked the social worker, Ms. Holliday, to speak to the family because without surgery Mr. Pilsudski will die.

Ms. Holliday met with the three adult children, none of whom had a health care power of attorney. The daughter who was resistant regarding the surgery persuaded her brother and sister that their father could not tolerate being disabled and unable to speak. She was certain their father would rather die if he was left without the ability to speak. Ms. Holliday has seen many successful voice rehabilitations following laryngectomies, and she described to the family members the rehabilitation methods and the adjustments patients made after the loss of their voices. But their decision remained firm. The physician also was unable to change their minds and was upset with the family and insisted Ms. Holliday try again to persuade the family members. What should Ms. Holliday do?

4. **Potential Harm Versus Confidentiality**
A clinical social worker, Cornelia Gallardo, meets weekly with a 15-year-old female client, Natalie Mays. During their first meeting, Ms. Gallardo explained that she would keep everything she was told confidential unless Natalie told her that she intended to harm herself or someone else. During the last session, Natalie told Ms. Gallardo that she is dealing drugs with a boyfriend who just completed a one-year jail sentence for selling drugs. Natalie's parents have forbidden her to contact her boyfriend and have asked Ms. Gallardo to inform them if their daughter tells her that she is seeing the young man again. Ms. Gallardo is concerned about Natalie's safety, as well as her illegal involvement in the sale of drugs and the dangers she may face from the drug trade. Does this present enough of a potential harm to Natalie to justify telling her parents? Is there an obligation to report Natalie's or her boyfriend's illegal behavior?

5. **Who Owes Loyalty to Whom?**
Jane Smith and John Adams are both in their second year field placement at the Good Will Rehabilitation Program. Jane discovered that John was telling fellow workers that she is a lesbian. Although Jane is open about her sexual orientation, she thinks it is inappropriate for John to share personal information about her with co-workers. When Jane approached John and asked him to stop telling people that she is a lesbian because it is professionally inappropriate, he replied "Why shouldn't I tell people? Everyone knows, and you're out anyway." Feeling disappointed and angry, Jane made an appointment to speak to her field supervisor and described what happened and complained about John's

behavior. Jane's field supervisor responded that she was sorry this had happened, but there was nothing she could do about it because John is the relative of a very powerful board member and she is afraid that reprimanding John will cause problems for her. Given the current economic situation, the field supervisor is afraid that she could lose her job and not be able to find another one. Is the field supervisor's response ethical? To whom does the supervisor owe loyalty? How would you respond in Jane's position? How would you respond in the field supervisor's position?

6. **Protect My Wife or Not?**
   Joseph Young found notes accidentally left on the copy machine by another social worker. Joseph was quickly skimming the notes to see whom he should return them to when he noticed the name of the agency where his wife Alaina was currently working as a contractual employee. Alaina was recently offered a full-time position, so Joseph was very interested in the information about the agency. Without thinking, Joseph read the notes, which described allegations of sexual harassment by the agency executive director—the same man Alaina would be working with if she accepted the full-time position. After reading the materials, Joseph became quite concerned about his wife's situation. What are the ethical issues in this situation? What should Joseph do? Can he tell Alaina about the allegations of sexual harassment? If he can't tell her the specific issues, can he take other action to warn her about the executive director? How would you respond in a similar situation?

7. **Protect Sam Down on His Luck?**
   Samuel Wander is a resident of a homeless shelter, where he stays at night. When the morning comes, he goes to a food bank, walks the streets, visits the library and bus station, and generally roams the city. He is a very likable person who fell on very hard times. Samuel confided in his social worker that he sold his Independence Card (food stamps) to get money for beer that he shares with friends who have even less money than he. To do so is illegal, and Samuel could lose his benefits, but he is a peaceful man, and he is using the money to have a few beers with his friends. Should the social worker report Samuel's behavior? What are the ethical reasons for and against reporting Samuel's behavior?

8. **Dual Roles Can Sometimes Appear Unexpectedly**
   Social worker Delores Lanier and her husband have been searching for a condo apartment for months. Yesterday, they were shown a beautiful condo that was just right for them, and they immediately made an offer to buy the apartment. The realtor made a private phone call and announced that the owner agreed to the offer. Only when they received the signed contract did the Laniers find out that the owner of the apartment is one of Delores's current clients. What is (are) the ethical dilemma(s) in this situation? What should Delores Lanier do?

9. **Silence Can Be a Helping Hand**
   Genevieve Hassan's job is to help low-income students and their families apply for college and financial aid. As she worked with the Bregmans, she discovered

they had included fraudulent information in their tax returns, including claiming children who were self-supporting and lived outside the home and claiming business losses for a non-existent home business. Based on the figures reported, the Bregmans's adjusted gross income decreased by more than $20,000, making them eligible for several financial aid programs that they would be ineligible for based on their actual adjusted gross income. When Genevieve raised a question about the data provided, the Bergmans were adamant that the forms be submitted as they had arranged the figures. Genevieve was uncomfortable with their dishonesty but also fairly sure that her client would only be able to attend college with the financial aid that would be available using the fraudulent tax information. What are the ethical issues for the social worker, Genevieve, in this situation? What is the ethical thing to do?

10. Equal or Unequal Access to Resources?

The Board of the Primary Good Counseling agency established a sliding scale fee policy with a minimum $10 charge per session to insure that services are available to all members of the community. In the past, the Primary Good Counseling agency offices have been located in predominantly White neighborhoods, but they have recently opened the Plains office, which is located in a predominantly African American neighborhood. The Plains neighborhood is lower income than the other neighborhoods where Primary Good Counseling has offices, so, in order to recruit clients, the Board will waive the minimum $10 charge per session for those with incomes below $30,000 per year. The Board hopes that this decision will lead to services being provided to a growing number of African American clients, which would in turn be a positive factor when applying for governmental and foundation grants. But to do so means those who pay fees in other offices will be subsidizing the nonpaying clients who use the Plains office. Is the Board's payment policy ethical? Why or why not?

11. Both Sides Have to Live up to the Contract

Sofia Stowe has been working with the Downs family in brief family therapy. They contracted for 12 sessions, and it was agreed that all interventions will be discussed prior to implementation. In the sixth session, Ms. Stowe decided that a paradoxical intervention would be appropriate; however, this requires that the family not know the nature of the intervention, and she implements it without informing them. No one in the family objected or reminded Ms. Stowe of her early promise. The intervention achieves the goals, and the family successfully completes the 12 weeks of treatment. What ethical problems do you identify for Ms. Stowe in this situation?

12. Doing a Good Deed or Paternalism?

Mr. Ebenezer Fleece, age 78, is ready to be discharged from the hospital after being treated for a cut on his scalp, the result of a fall from a ladder. While discussing discharge, Mr. Fleece tells Hermine Lastig, the social worker, that since his wife died he frequently skips meals, sometimes for a couple of days at a time. He says he does not like to shop and does not like to cook. Ms. Lustig offers to make arrangements with Meals on Wheels, but he tells her not to do so. Ms. Lustig thinks that Mr. Fleece is not in as good a shape as he believes himself to be and that he will only be able to continue in his own home with the support of Meals on Wheels. Therefore she arranges to have meals on wheels delivered to Mr. Fleece five days a week. Ms. Lustig is sure that Mr. Fleece will like having the meals available when they arrive, but if he does not, then he can discontinue the service. Is Ms. Lustig's behavior ethical? Why or why not?

13. Loyalty to Agency, Client, or Self?

Mr. and Mrs. Altona Sofarra requested couples counseling from an agency in their neighborhood because of the increasing miscommunication and arguments in their marriage. They saw an initial intake person who determined that their income requires a $90 fee per session, and they agreed to the fee arrangement. Afterward, they were assigned to a social worker, Hyacinth Deforma, who is trained to do couples counseling. After they began working with Ms. Deforma, they told her the fee is proving to be more stressful for their family than they anticipated. Ms. Deforma says (despite the agency's policies and fee schedule) that there may be a way to solve the financial problem. Because the agency has no written policy about seeing agency clients privately, she could see them privately in her part-time practice for a lower fee. Should she? Why or why not?

14. How to Answer the Question?

Danielle Doyle is a social worker at Farragut Planned Parenthood. Marilyn Hall is a 16-year-old pregnant teenager who visited Farragut Planned Parenthood this morning. Danielle overhears a volunteer call Marilyn's home and ask for her. But when she found out that Marilyn was not home she left her number (without identifying where she was calling from) and asked that Marilyn call her back. Moments later, Danielle answered another phone at Farragut Planned Parenthood. It was a woman who identified herself as Marilyn's mother, wanting to know who had called her daughter and what they were calling for. What is the ethical thing for Danielle to do?

15. Safety, the Law, and Confidentiality

Clarissa Lannan is a social worker at Homestead Youth Services where she serves as a group therapist to eight teenagers, ages 14 to 17. During this week's session, one of the teenagers revealed that this group has been holding Friday night parties. They get together at a home where the parents are away, and alcohol and drugs are involved. Some of the youth have had unprotected sex during the parties, and they have been texting nude photos of themselves to each other, some of which have been posted on the Web. When Clarissa started with the group, she made an agreement with them about what confidentiality they could expect from her and what was expected from the teens. What are the ethical dilemmas for Clarissa? How should she respond to the disclosure about the parties, use of alcohol and drugs, and other behavior? What is her ethical responsibility?

16. Revealing Secrets

Richard Sabino, a social worker, is employed by the San Jacinto Counseling Service where Victoria Finlandia is also employed. Victoria has a long and close friendship with Richard, a relationship both personal and professional: He refers cases to her private practice, and their families are friendly and have vacationed together. Richard often addresses community groups on family, child, and adolescent topics such as family communication, teenagers and sex, and dealing with family stresses when a parent loses a job. Several of Victoria's clients have mentioned hearing Richard speak; they all praised him for his speaking style and his knowledge of family life and of children and adolescents. Each of Victoria's clients says that Richard reports on cases anonymously from his practice and often refers to his private practice and where it is located. Using current cases, even anonymously, and references to his private practice are both forbidden by agency policy.

Several of Victoria's clients who have heard him speak tell her that they are sure they recognize some of the people and families referred to and that they were frustrated by his frequent references to clients and their situations and to his private practice. Furthermore, they worry that if Victoria was to do such talks, she will describe them so that those who know Victoria in the community will be able to recognize and learn of private situations just as they believe they recognize some of his cases. In addition, Stanley Lipp, another one of Victoria's clients, today told her that he believes that Richard's references to his private practice are inappropriate and that he believes Victoria as a social worker, should do something about Richard's behavior. In fact, he discussed this with several friends who also have heard Richard's talks. What should Victoria do?

17. What's a Little Furniture?

Dominico Alfasi is a client with whom you have been working for six months. Your relationship with Dominico is a good one, and he has been making steady progress on his issues, which mainly focus on his relationship to his wife and children. He has a pattern of picking verbal fights and retreating from his family, watching television, and hiding in his garage workshop where he builds furniture. Today, Mr. Alfasi announced at the end of the session that he was unexpectedly let go from his job because the firm is cutting back on staff and consequently he can no longer afford to pay for therapy. He would like to continue in treatment. Both of you think that his situation with his family and at home has been steadily improving, but more progress is needed. During the discussion of the payment question, he asked whether he could pay you by building furniture for your office or home. How should you respond to this offer?

18. Is It OK to Renew a Relationship?

Caldwell Gordon is a social worker employed in a public physical rehabilitation unit. When he was informed that a 27-year-old woman, Amy Dill, was being assigned to him, he realized that she was a former girlfriend. They were together for two years, and the affair ended about four years ago. Because he was once involved with the young woman and still has unresolved feelings for her, he arranged for her to be transferred to another worker. He never informed his supervisor of this prior relationship. Shortly thereafter, Caldwell ran into Amy at the local grocery store; both were single and decided to get together later that week. Caldwell and Amy began dating regularly. On one of their dates, they met

Mike Alonzo, Caldwell's supervisor. The next morning Mike called Caldwell into his office and asked about the situation between Caldwell and Amy. Caldwell told him about his past relationship with Amy and that was why he had asked that her case be transferred to someone else. Is it ethical for Caldwell to date Amy? Why or why not? How should his supervisor, Mike, respond to this situation?

19. My Patient or My Child?

Anna Kazin is a social worker who recently gave birth to a premature infant. After several weeks in the intensive care unit, the infant is now at home with a caretaker with child care experience. Ms. Kazin is the social worker for a middle-aged man at a local counseling center who is extremely upset because he has just learned that he has a terminal cancer. While talking to him bedside about the situation, she was told she has an emergency phone call at the desk. Excusing herself, Ms. Kazin takes the phone call and learns that the woman who is providing care for her infant is calling to tell her the infant doesn't look quite right. She couldn't give a very clear description, but she asked if Ms. Kazin could come home right away. She is very worried. When she returned to her patient, he was crying and extremely upset. Although she is the only social worker on staff today, she decided she must tell him that she will have to leave to look after her infant. When she did so, he said he has no friends or family, and he needs her to stay with him for a little while until he pulls himself together. What are the ethical issues here and what should Ms. Kazin do?

20. Can We Predict the Future?

Robert Jay is a foster care worker who has been working with Mrs. DiBenedetto for the past six months since her two young children were removed from her home because of child neglect. Mrs. DiBenedetto has cooperated with all of the agency's requests, and they are now approaching a six-month court review to determine if the children should be returned home. Mr. Jay and his supervisor know that there is an ongoing criminal investigation of the client. Although the alleged criminal activity would not directly place the children at risk of harm, they are uncertain about whether they should recommend reunification or not. What are the ethical issues involved in this exemplar? What is the ethical response in this situation? Would you recommend that the children be returned home? Why or why not?

21. A Student Thinks Ethically

Martina Burke, a second-year MSW student, has her field placement in a school where many of the children she works with are in out-of-home placements due to child abuse or neglect. One of the children, 8-year-old Ana Bright, is not doing well. Martina suspects that her foster parents are not properly monitoring her medications. She has contacted June Albertson, Ana's foster care worker, twice about this issue, but nothing has been done. Without checking with her field instructor, Martina filed a complaint against June Albertson. When Martina's field instructor received a call asking about the complaint, she did not know anything about it and went to discuss it with Martina. The field instructor was very concerned that Martina filed a complaint without discussing it with her. After they discussed the issues, the field instructor was not convinced that a complaint was appropriate and suggested that Martina should withdraw the complaint. Martina, however, still felt that the complaint was appropriate and that someone needed to investigate the way June Albertson monitors the children assigned to her caseload. Martina's field instructor told her that she did not yet have enough experience to make that judgment, and an unfounded complaint would cause problems between the school and the Department of Social Services. What are the ethical issues for Martina? How should she respond to her field instructor's suggestion? What are the ethical issues for the field instructor? How should she respond if Martina refuses to withdraw the complaint?

22. **Friend or Interpreter?**
You are a social worker, and Tatiana Kaminski, your friend, is a recent Polish immigrant who speaks very little English. Ms. Kaminski has been having difficulty with her 14-year-old daughter, who is not coping well with life in the United States. At your suggestion, Ms. Kaminski phones Family Service of the Seashore for an appointment while you are with her. When the intake worker has difficulty understanding Ms. Kaminski, she asks that you get on the phone, explain the situation, and schedule an appointment. You agree to help in this manner, but when you do, you discover no one in the agency speaks Polish, and the agency does not have the funds to hire an interpreter. The intake worker suggests that you serve as the interpreter, which would allow the agency to help Ms. Kaminski and her daughter. Would it be appropriate for you to serve as the interpreter? Why or why not? What are the ethical dilemmas in this situation?

23. **Informed Consent Requires Professional Knowledge**
Moses Jenkins is 73-years-old and has been diagnosed with Alzheimer's disease. He has periods of lucidity, which are longer than the brief periods when he is not completely aware of his surroundings. A psychologist noted that when Mr. Jenkins is lucid, he can think clearly and provide informed consent about services and treatment options. The psychologist says he is able to discuss important matters during his lucid periods, but Mr. Jenkins's social worker, Marty Cameron, has noticed that Mr. Jenkins sometimes agrees to things when he appears to be lucid, but later Mr. Jenkins says he never agreed and doesn't know what Marty is talking about. Mr. Jenkins lives alone, and he has no living relatives or close friends. How can Marty ensure that Mr. Jenkins provides informed consent? What should he do if he doesn't think Mr. Jenkins is capable of providing informed consent? What is the ethical thing to do?

24. **Individual or Family Therapy?**
The parents and adolescents in the Martin family have been having problems. There has been a series of incidents in which everyone involved has been shouting at each other, calling each other names, or not talking to each other for days. Christine Martin feels that she has failed as a mother. She asked Molly Aberdeen, a private practice social worker, to help her cope with her feelings. After talking with Christine, Molly felt that the problem went beyond Christine's feelings and that family therapy was indicated. Even though Molly is a competent social worker, she has had no training or experience in providing family therapy. However, there

are no family therapists in this rural county. At first, Molly assessed the problem in such a way that individual intervention was appropriate. At least, this assessment makes it possible for her to help Christine. Hopefully, this will lead to changes in the family situation. Or, failing that, Christine will be able to cope more successfully. Is it ethical for Molly to prepare on her own to do family therapy and treat the family? Or to only offer individual therapy to Christine? What should she do?

25. Report Drug Paraphernalia or Not?

Zachariah Jones is a social worker in a child development program run by a Beach County voluntary social agency for children. The program has a liaison relationship with the local child protective services but is not part of the Department of Social Services. This morning, Zachariah was assigned to visit the home of Virginia Dabney to make an assessment of the situation: Virginia's daughter, Beatrice, has not attended the early childhood program for three days, and phone calls made to the home were unanswered. This morning when he visited the home for discussions with Virginia, Zachariah observed what appeared to be illegal drug paraphernalia. Virginia showed no signs of being on drugs and it was unclear whether she uses drugs or not. It turned out that her daughter was sick with a virus, and the doctor she consulted told her to keep her daughter home until the illness cleared up. Obviously, she was not neglecting her child. During his training period, Zachariah was told that if he is on a home visit and observes illegal drugs in the home, he is not to report the presence of the drugs to either legal authorities or child protective services because to do so would destroy any possible constructive relationship with the client and cost the agency reimbursement for its service. Furthermore, the word would go out in the neighborhood and interfere with serving other families. The training personnel and his supervisor suggest that the relationship with the client takes priority over all else because the relationship is necessary for the good of the child. The problem Zachariah perceives, however, is that he knows the law demands that he report the paraphernalia. What should he do? Follow the training guidelines he received that have been reinforced by his supervisor? Suggest to Virginia that if she is using the illegal drugs she could use the local substance abuse counseling services? Tell Virginia that he will report his observations to law enforcement? Forget what he saw? Who is he responsible to? The child? Virginia? The state and the law? His supervisor? The agency?

26. Continuing Treatment

Teenagers sent to the Lasswell Residential treatment facility are hostile, sullen, and angry young people. Many of them have family health insurance, and the staff has to check with the insurance company to determine the length of acceptable treatment. Ordinarily, the insurance company believes that intensive therapy can be accomplished in 30 days. The young residents and the social workers have to form a trusting relationship for the work together to be done at all. Most of the residents take from 30 to 60 days before they are willing to let down their guard and reveal the issues, personal and otherwise, that are bothering them, including issues related to their families' functioning. What should the social worker do when the insurance company informs the treatment center it will not pay for treatment beyond next week and the agency administrators say clearly that the treatment center cannot keep residents without payment? Discharge the resident? File a claim and appeal to the state insurance commission? Try to involve agencies in the local community where the resident lives that will also be interested in some kind of payment, if the agency is equipped to help the youth? If local services can be found, based on past experiences there are few chances the resident and family will follow through. It seems that either way, the young person and the family are set up for failure. What is the ethical thing to do?

27. A Shortage of Beds

While working on an inpatient oncology unit in an acute care hospital, Viveca Chin, a social worker, was told by the physician to discuss follow-up care with the family of a terminally ill patient, Sam Marino. The order also indicated the patient could be discharged today. Sam was not doing well enough to participate in any discussion and his wife and family members were distraught. They didn't understand that Sam couldn't remain in the hospital today but had to choose either home or inpatient hospice care. At the same time, social workers were told to get as many patients out of the hospital today as possible because the hospital is short of beds. The patient's physician was unavailable, and the resident physician was reluctant to meet with the family. Viveca thought about delaying discharge and a referral until the end of the day because doing so might keep Sam in the hospital for a day or two longer. What should she do? To whom does Viveca owe loyalty: Sam, his family, his physician, the hospital?

28. A Little Extra Will Make Her Life More "Worth Living"

Marie Cummings is in her early 70s, lives by herself, and ekes by financially. In previous years, she received Low Income Home Energy Assistance Program (LIHEAP). She just told you that she purposely stopped paying her heating bills—even though she can afford to do so—with the expectation that she will also receive help this year. This strategy has proven successful for several years and leaves her a little money to play bingo once in a while. She feels doing so makes her life worth living. It is your understanding that the funds available for this program are more limited this year. Marie's strategy is helpful for her, but you also know there are more applicants this year than last whose needs are as great as or even greater than Marie's. What ethical issues are involved here? What should you do?

29. Who Decides?

Rochelle Diego is 82-years-old and has been disabled and living at home. Gradually her physical abilities have been eroding. In fact, her physical abilities have deteriorated much more and faster than her cognitive abilities. She has become more dependent physically but remains intellectually alert and active. It appears that her caretaker during the day has been neglecting her. Although there is no hard evidence, there is a suspicion that her caretaker may also be abusing her. Rochelle, however, has been very protective of the caretaker and makes no suggestions of dissatisfaction. Sophia Breckenridge, her social worker, feels Rochelle needs to become a resident of a nursing home. Although no proof of neglect or abuse exists, she obviously needs more care than can be provided by a visiting home health care aide and a day worker. Whenever the topic is raised, Rochelle refuses to be moved. A close younger friend once offered to care for her if she were moved to the friend's spacious home. After Rochelle agreed to do so, several of Rochelle's adult children were furious with her and forced her to back out. But none of them offered to care for her in their homes. There was also an attempt to transfer her to a nursing home, but other adult children objected. What should Sophia do? After all, Rochelle's thoughts are generally clear, but she does not recognize or accept her physical disabilities. Who should decide what to do, especially since Rochelle is growing more and more feeble?

30. Family Tradition or Education?
You have been seeing a quiet but very bright young high school student, an immigrant woman from Ethiopia. She has been offered a full scholarship and room and board at the prestigious Parkside Preparatory School. She says the offer creates a conflict with her traditional family. Her parents want her to marry and have children. Education is for men. She wants to go to school, but her family feels that if she does so, she will be betraying her family and culture. She is sad, torn, and confused. She asks you what she should do. Does it make a difference if you are an ardent feminist? What if you are also an Ethiopian immigrant?

31. Mrs. Walker or Her Husband?
You are seeing Susan Walker for a first session at the base. You learn that her husband is a helicopter pilot, and she tells you that she cannot stand his continual drinking. She has come to see you to get help living with the situation. Captain Walker regularly goes on beer-drinking binges, and although he has never been abusive to her or their children, he often passes out and collapses into bed. Susan asks for treatment for herself but strongly resists your reporting her husband's behavior. Furthermore, she says that if you report her husband, she won't continue in treatment and will move out of the house. She says if you tell, you will be responsible for anything that occurs in her family—because they are getting along just fine now. What should you do? Does his behavior make it difficult for him to perform his duties safely? Is this a life-threatening situation? To whom do you owe loyalty? Susan? The military? Society? Should you reveal Susan's confidences or keep quiet and begin work with her, hoping you can do something later about her husband's flying and drinking? Can you find guidance in the Code as to what your correct actions should be?

32. Should I Tell?
Amanda Winterspoon is a licensed social worker employed by a general hospital in a small town. She has been active in general discharge planning and providing therapy for psychiatric patients after they are discharged from the psychiatry unit. Also, she has developed a small private practice outside the hospital. Over the years, Amanda has developed excellent work relationships with nurses and physicians. She is highly respected. Last week, she was in an automobile accident and was seriously injured so that she could not reach her patients, who did not know what happened to her or where she was. A long-standing social work colleague and friend—Sarita Bonhomme—called the social work department to

inquire about Amanda's situation. The social worker who answered the call told her that because Amanda was an employee, no information about her could be given out, including whether she was a patient or not. Sarita explained that, as a social worker and old friend, she wanted to know how things were going for Amanda, but she also wanted to respond to several patients who anxiously inquired as to Amanda's whereabouts. Again, she was told that no information could be given to her. What is the ethical thing for the hospital social worker to do in this situation?

33. Is an Indeterminate Agreement Binding?

Ruth Martini, a single mother of two young children, had accomplished so much working at the Libertyville Mental Health Center. She was well respected by her colleagues and was promoted to supervisor at the mental health clinic, which was owned by two psychiatrists who—in addition to being owners—saw patients and consulted with the staff. The time was rapidly approaching when Ruth should move on. Not only was she sure she was ready to establish a private practice, but her family needed additional income, and this was the only way she could earn more. As a result, she decided to keep her job but also see patients privately on a part-time basis. She decided that she could approach Julie Goodheart, a middle-aged and middle-class patient with whom she had been working successfully and helpfully for over a year. She would let her know she would be leaving the agency sometime in the near future. If Julie were interested, perhaps Ruth could see her privately. There was only one problem. When Ruth was hired by the center, she agreed verbally to a contract not to see agency clients privately, either while she was employed by the center or for an undefined period following her termination of employment. Does Julie's right to self-determination overrule any commitment to the agency? Would Ruth's patients have a right to follow her if she left the agency, if she did not tell them she was doing so but they found that she was in private practice? Would agreeing to an indeterminate period forbidding a private practice impose an undue hardship on Ruth? She owes loyalty to the agency but also to herself and her family. What are her choices, and what should she do?

34. To Report or Not?

A number of undocumented immigrants recently showed up at the Evergreen Family Social Service Resource Center. The majority of the agency's funds come from state revenues and taxpayers. The immigrants have serious financial, food, and housing needs and are typically under great stress. There are laws that demand that workers report undocumented immigrants to immigration authorities. The agency supervisors inform the workers that if one is working with an immigrant family and some members of the family do not have Social Security numbers, they should not be reported to the U.S. Bureau of Citizenship and Immigration Services as it would be detrimental to the helping relationship. Rosa Martinez is a legal resident, but her husband is an undocumented immigrant. Their three children are U.S. citizens because they were born in the United States. Several workers in the agency disagree with the agency's policy to ignore the law. What should a social worker do? On the one hand, social workers are to obey the law. On the other hand, they want to be helpful to the immigrant families who have serious individual and family needs. To whom should the social workers be loyal? The law and citizen taxpayers? The entire family? The state and society?

35. Your Supervisor, Your Colleague, or the Children?

The Riverside Therapeutic Foster Care Agency requires social workers to see foster parents twice every month in their homes. As a social worker, you are fulfilling this responsibility, but you have discovered accidentally that your colleague, Rene Flambeau has not done so for several families. When he told you about this situation, he explained to you that these parents have jobs where they work odd and changing evening hours. He has found it almost impossible to visit them regularly. As a result, he lies to his supervisor, who is also your supervisor. You are now meeting with your supervisor, Clem LaPoint, with whom you have a long, friendly, and trusting relationship. Clem unexpectedly asks you about Rene's frequency of visits to foster homes. What should you do? Be loyal to the hardworking families? The children in foster care? Your colleague? Your friend and supervisor? The agency?

36. Fran's Son Is Dating Her Client

Fran Reilly is a social worker who has a well-deserved reputation in Pittsfield because of her outstanding work with adolescents. She has been working for approximately a year with Millicent Jasowitz, a shy, lonely young woman, who goes to school but has little other social life. This morning, quite by accident, Fran learned that her son, Wally, who is a loner and has been unpopular for some time both in middle school and in his new high school, has had a couple of dates with Millicent, her patient. What should Fran do? She has a very good relationship with Millicent, who is making good progress in treatment, and she also is hopeful that Wally has begun to make a relationship with another teenager. Is this a dual relationship by proxy? Should she discontinue treatment with Millicent? She cannot imagine asking her son to discontinue his relationship with Millicent. What should she do?

37. A Fellow Student May Be Impaired

Cynthia Messing is a graduate student in social work. She is a highly motivated student who enrolled in the school after several years practice in a drug and alcohol abuse program. She is friendly and forms good relationships with faculty members, field instructors, and her fellow students. Yesterday, one of her fellow students, Claudia Arroz, told her confidentially that she thinks Erika Luft—another classmate—has a substance abuse problem. She said she was speaking to Cynthia because she knows she has work experience in substance abuse and because she didn't trust the faculty member who teaches this class. Cynthia asked her how she knew. Claudia said that she noticed Erika has missed several sessions, and she knows that the faculty member has not discussed absences with Erika. Erika is forgetful, told Claudia she often doesn't feel well, did not pull her weight on a group assignment, misses meetings at their field placement, and is very touchy. Despite the fact that Cynthia is a student and not yet a professional social worker, she understands that student social workers have a responsibility to live up to the standards of the NASW Code of Ethics. What is her responsibility in this situation to Claudia, Erika, the faculty member teaching the course, the school, profession, and herself? What should Cynthia Messing do?

38. Stabilized and Ready to Go?

Three weeks ago, Joseph Clark was admitted involuntarily to Los Gatos Mental Hospital following a psychotic episode. He was involved in a fracas at a local library and caused a disturbance on the street, which resulted in the police taking him to a hospital emergency room, which in turn led to his being admitted to Los Gatos. Jeremy Blake is a social worker who is assigned to the unit in which Joseph is housed and to Joseph's case. The unit has a long waiting list. Joseph is stabilized but resists taking his medications. Today Jeremy was asked by the unit's psychiatrist to somehow persuade Joseph to take his meds so he can be discharged, thus opening a bed for the unit. What ethical issues does this raise, and what should Jeremy do?

39. St. Louis or Singapore?

Several relatives of Derrick Lin, a native of Singapore, crowded into a St. Louis hospital room to meet with a social worker, Linda Flowers, to hear the news that Derrick's kidney cancer is incurable. Derrick was in another room. As soon as his relatives heard the prognosis, they were immediately unanimous in their opinion and made it clear to Linda that they did not want him to know his prognosis. They told Linda that in Singapore the practice of informing a patient of his diagnosis is left to the family's discretion, and it was extremely important to the family that their culture be respected. Linda wondered what she should do. Should she simply tell the oncologist the family demands Derrick not be told his prognosis and tell the physician of their reasons? However, U.S. doctors take action only with the approval of their patients and only after fully informing them of their prognoses. Should she advocate for the relatives' point of view? What role, if any, should Derrick play in any discussions? Who should decide?

40. Testing and Treatment for All?

A state department of social services (DSS) developed a new program to evaluate potential recipients for depression or substance abuse before they enter the public assistance system. The program has been a success: Clients interviewed who are in the program felt it helped them to get back to work because they were treated for depression. You are employed by another state's DSS that has created a similar but different program. Only clients who are receiving cash assistance qualify for the testing. Those clients who already have a job do not get tested. Most of these persons had just taken the job to qualify for the program to begin with. Those clients who are depressed or have other psychological problems who are forced to work without proper treatment usually get fired or quit one job after another. They end up experiencing even more failure, which deepens their depression. A suggestion has been made that a psychiatric assessment should be required for every DSS client, and those who are found to have emotional problems should be forced into treatment in order to receive payments or to have a job. What stance should you take?

41. What If Either Silence or Speaking Does Potential Harm?

Brian Philbrick was called by Irene Courtney asking for an appointment with her husband, Dennis, for marital counseling. They had attended four sessions when Dennis requested an individual session. Irene acknowledged the individual session was a good idea and agreed to it. During the individual session, Dennis indicated he was having an affair with a woman with whom he worked. But when it was suggested that he tell this information to Irene, he refused to do so. Brian maintained the confidentiality of this private information, but he was certain that the possibility of successful marital therapy was compromised and now not possible. Not sharing the information threatens the help he can provide and can undermine the communication of the couple and his reputation for competence. Sharing the information breaks the confidentiality of the individual session. Should Brian suggest the couple discontinue treatment with him? What should he do?

42. To Lie or Just Not Tell Everything?

A licensed clinical social worker employed in an agency and who has a small private practice receives treatment from a psychiatrist and takes medications prescribed for her depression. She is paying by cash and not through health insurance. She functions adequately at her job, and her evaluations have been at a sufficiently high level. She and her therapist agree that she is capable of serving her private clients effectively. She wants to apply to be included in a panel of practitioners who will be referred cases and receive third-party payments. The application asks if she has ever had a diagnosis for mental illness. The extra money is important. She has family expenses, and she has to pay for her treatment and medication. What should she do?

43. Who Has Veto Power?

Joseph Gerden is a member of a therapy group for recently divorced persons. At the suggestion of his probation officer, he requests that group records be submitted to the court. He may be permitted to visit his 7-year-old son if the records show he has made progress in the group. Another member of the group will not agree under any circumstance to the release of the records. As the facilitator of this group, what should you do?

44. A Late Night Phone Call

Your supervisor—Stephanie Hamlet—just called you at 11:30 p.m. at home. She said the state legislature will vote this week to require parental notification of pregnant teenagers seeking abortions. She said, "I know you will want to sign our petition in the morning. Although we have never discussed this issue, I just feel you will agree and want to sign the petition since you have so much empathy for teenagers and their problems." You have no idea how to respond to the comments Stephanie made. Actually, you believe parents should be notified, but your relationship with Stephanie has been less than stellar, and your six-month probation evaluation is due soon. Should you tell Stephanie that you don't want to sign the petition? Should you just agree and somehow fail to sign the petition? Should you tell her that you agree with the petition's ideas and will be glad to sign in the morning? What should you do?

GLOSSARY

autonomy self-determination, self-rule, being able to make free choices.

autonomous ethics ethical systems in which humans determine the moral rules.

beneficence to promote the client's good and take care to prevent, remove, or minimize harm.

client bill of rights a statement distributed to all clients/patients informing them of the information they are entitled to know about their situation, treatment expectations, and participation in decision making; that they will be informed about available options; and that they have a right to speak to an ombudsman or other person if dissatisfied with treatment.

code of ethics a collection of aspirations, regulations, and guidelines that represent the values of a group or profession to which it applies; a compilation of ethical standards.

competence the ability to give informed consent to some or all decisions; clients/patients are located along a range of capabilities, extending from completely competent, to those who are somewhat competent, to those who are not at all competent.

competing loyalties two or more loyalties that cannot be honored at the same time.

competing values two or more values that cannot be honored at the same time.

confidentiality a rule of duty requiring one entrusted with private or secret matters to refrain from divulging them; a contract not to reveal information about an individual except with his or her consent.

conflict of interest a situation in which a social worker in a position of trust that requires exercising judgment on behalf of clients, agencies, or others has competing professional or personal interests, which can make it difficult to fulfill impartially and objectively her professional duties and/or give the appearance of being unable to do so.

conflicting obligations two or more obligations that cannot be fulfilled at the same time.

deontology a philosophy of ethics holding that ethical rules for the right course of action are self-evident, can be formulated, and should hold under all circumstances.

direct liability supervisors may be charged with ethical breaches or negligence when harm is caused by the supervisor's acts of omission or commission.

dual-role relationship situation in which professionals fill more than one role at a time and should avoid conflicts of interest that interfere with the exercise of professional discretion and impartial judgment, especially to protect clients' interests and not to take unfair advantage of them.

duty to warn an obligation to use reasonable care to protect intended victims; also referred to as the *Tarasoff principle*.

effectiveness criterion the degree to which a desired outcome is achieved.

efficiency criterion relative cost of achieving a stated objective.

ethical absolutism any ethical theory that claims there are ethical rules that hold regardless of society, culture, or religion; correct standards applicable to everyone everywhere.

ethical decision making the process of analyzing and assessing the ethical dimensions of practice in order to develop ethically appropriate professional behavior.

ethical dilemmas choice by the social worker between two or more relevant but contradictory ethical directives; when every alternative results in an undesirable outcome for one or more persons.

ethical problem identifying the right thing to do in a given practice situation.

ethical priorities screen (EPS) a guide for rank-ordering ethical principles and priorities.

ethical relativism the belief that there is no absolute or universal moral standard and what is right or wrong is relative to an individual, group, or culture.

ethical rules screen (ERS) used as a step in ethical decision making by consulting the Code of Ethics for guidance.

ethics branch of philosophy that deals with the rightness or wrongness of human actions.

general ethics the obligations that are owed by one person to another.

group values values held by subgroups within a society.

heteronomous ethics ethical systems that derive moral rules from nonhuman sources.

informed consent the knowledgeable and voluntary agreement by a client to undergo an intervention that is in accord with the client's values and preferences.

least harm principle when harm will come to someone in the situation, it is the choice of the option that results in the least harm, the least permanent harm, or the most easily reversible harm.

malpractice professional negligence or misconduct; failure to exercise a degree of care that a similar professional of ordinary prudence would demonstrate under the same circumstances.

morality a concern with personally held ethical beliefs, theories of obligation, and the social elements that reinforce ethical decisions.

paternalism the act of overriding the autonomous decisions of a person or making decisions for the person with the intention of benefiting that person.

personal (individual) values the values held by one person but not necessarily by others.

prima facie **correct** apparently correct upon first viewing.

privacy a zone of individual autonomy in which people ought to be free to behave as they wish; the constitutional right protecting individuals from unwarranted governmental interference in intimate personal relations or activities.

privileged communication a legal concept protecting against forced disclosure in legal proceedings that would break a promise of privacy—based on ethical principles of confidentiality and privacy.

professional code of ethics a compilation of values, ethical principles, and ethical standards of a particular profession.

professional ethics codification of the special obligations that arise out of a person's voluntary choice to become a professional, such as a social worker.

professional social work ethics those ethical standards promulgated by the social work profession through its Codes of Ethics and other publications.

professional values those values proclaimed by a professional group.

religious ethics ethics based upon a religion and its beliefs.

self-determination a person's right to make his or her own decisions.

situational ethics the position that all ethical decisions must be made in the light of individual circumstances and not according to moral rules or universal laws.

societal values values recognized by major portions of the entire social system or, at least, by the leading members or spokespersons of that system.

teleology philosophy of ethics that justifies ethical decisions on the basis of the context in which they are made or on the basis of the consequences they create.

unethical behavior violations of the profession's principles established by the profession's Code of Ethics.

utilitarianism a philosophy of ethics that defines right action as that which results in the greatest happiness for the greatest number of people.

value dilemmas two or more values that cannot be reconciled and simultaneously enacted.

values preferences that serve as guides or criteria for selecting good or desirable behaviors.

vicarious liability a supervisor is responsible for a supervisee's conduct during the course of employment or field instruction, including ethical lapses.

voluntariness acting on the basis of meaningful and free consent obtained without coercion.

BIBLIOGRAPHY

This bibliography lists the books and articles cited in this book, as well as additional literature on ethical problems in professional practice that may be of interest to the reader.

Abbott, A. A. (1999). Measuring social work values: A cross-cultural challenge for global practice. *International Social Work*, 42(4), 455–470.

Abbott, A. A. (2003). A confirmatory factor analysis of the Professional Opinion Scale: A values assessment instrument. *Research on Social Work Practice*, 13(5), 641–666.

Abney, P. C., & Maddux, C. D. (2004). Counseling and technology: Some thoughts about the controversy. *Journal of Technology in Human Services*, 22(3), 1–24.

Abramson, J. S. (1993). Orienting social work employees in interdisciplinary settings: Shaping professional and organizational perspectives. *Social Work*, 38(2), 152–157.

Abramson, M. (1984). Collective responsibility in interdisciplinary collaboration: An ethical perspective for social workers. *Social Work in Health Care*, 10(1), 35–43.

Abramson, M. (1985). The autonomy-paternalism dilemma in social work practice. *Social Casework*, 66, 387–393.

Abramson, M. (1989). Autonomy vs. paternalistic beneficence: Practice strategies. *Social Casework*, 70, 101–105.

Abramson, M. (1996). Toward a more holistic understanding of ethics in social work. *Social Work in Health Care*, 23(2), 1–14.

Acker, G. M. (1999). The impact of clients' illness on social workers' job satisfaction and burnout. *Health and Social Work*, 24(2), 112–119.

Adams, R. E., Boscarino, J. A., & Figley, C. R. (2006). Compassion fatigue and psychological distress among social workers: A validation study. *American Journal of Orthopsychiatry*, 76(1), 103–108.

Addams, J. (1902). *Democracy and social ethics*. New York, NY: The Macmillan Co. Electronic version, no pagination. Chap. 7, Political reform. Retrieved October 4, 2006, from www.gutenberg.org/files/15487/15487-h/15487-h.htm.

Adler, S. S. (1989). Truth telling to the terminally ill. *Social Work*, 34, 158–160.

Advocate Web (2002). Helping overcome professional exploitation. Sexual exploitation litigation issues. Retrieved July 18, 2002, from www.advocateweb.org/hope/litigation.asp.

Agbayani-Siewert, P. (1994). Filipino American culture and family: Guidelines for practitioners. *Families in Society*, 75, 429–438.

Aguilar, G. D. (2004). A comparative study of practitioners' and students' understanding of sexual ethics. *Journal of Social Work Values and Ethics*, 1(1). Retrieved December 27, 2006, from www.socialworker.com/jswve/content/view/7/30

Aguilera, E. (2003, February 10). Cuba's low HIV rate belies the stigma, ignorance many face.

Denver Post. Retrieved March 11, 2003, from www.denverpost.com/stories/O

Ajzen, I. (2005). *Attitudes, personality, and behavior* (2nd ed.). Maidenhead, U.K.: Open University Press.

Ajzen, I., & Madden, T. J. (1997). Prediction of goal-directed behavior: Attitudes, intentions, and perceived behavioral control. In M. Hew-stone, & S. R. Manstead et al., *The Blackwell reader in social psychology* (pp. 245–267). Malden, MA: Blackwell Publishers.

Albert, R. (1986). *Law and social work practice*. New York, NY: Springer Publishing.

Aldarondo, E., & Straus, M. A. (1994). Screening for physical violence in couple therapy: Methodological, practical, and ethical considerations. *Family Process*, 33, 425–439.

Algana, F. J., et al. (1979). Evaluating reaction to interpersonal touch in a counseling interview. *Journal of Counseling Psychology*, 26, 465–472.

Alle-Corliss, L., & Alle-Corliss, R. (1999). *Advanced practice in human services agencies: Issues, trends, and treatment perspectives*. Belmont, CA: Wadsworth Publishing Co.

Almason, A. L. (1997). Personal liability implications of the duty to warn are hard pills to swallow: From *Tarasoff* to *Hutchinson v. Patel* and beyond. *Journal of Contemporary Health, Law and Policy*, 13, 471–496.

Altman, L. K. (1999, August 31). Focusing on prevention in fight against AIDS. *New York Times*, p. F5.

Altman, L. K. (2002, July 3). U.N. forecasts big increase in AIDS death toll. *New York Times*, pp. A1, A6.

American Association of Social Work Boards. (2005). ACE, Approved Continuing Education, Provider News. Retrieved March 13, 2007, from www.aswb.org.

American College of Physicians ACP Observer. (1997). Patients often forget physician's diagnosis. *News Briefs*. www.acponline.org/journals/news/feb97/brief297.htm.

American Medical Association. (1997). Code of Ethics. www.ama-assn.org.

American Medical Association. (2007). Health law. Retrieved January 30, 2007, from www.ama-assn.org/ama/pub/category/15549.html.

American Psychiatric Association. (2000). *Diagnostic and statistical manual of mental disorders* (4th ed.). Washington, DC: American Psychiatric Association.

Anderson, D. K., & Saunders, D. G. (2003). Leaving an abusive partner. *Trauma, Violence, & Abuse*, 4, 163–191.

Andrews, A. B., & Patterson, E. G. (1995). Searching for solutions to alcohol and other drug abuse during pregnancy: Ethics, values, and constitutional principles. *Social Work*, 40, 55–64.

Antle, B. J., & Regehr, C. (2003). Beyond individual rights and freedoms: Meta ethics in social work research. *Social Work*, 40, 135–144.

Arendt, H. (1977). *Eichmann in Jerusalem: A report on the banality of evil*. New York, NY: Penguin Books.

Aristotle (2004). *The Nicomachean Ethics*. New York, NY: Penguin Books.

Ashton, V. (1999). Worker judgments of seriousness about and reporting of suspected child maltreatment. *Child Abuse and Neglect*, 23(6), 539–548.

Ashton, V. (2001). The relationship between attitudes toward corporal punishment and the perception and reporting of child abuse. *Child Abuse and Neglect*, 25(3), 389–400.

Athanassoulis, N. (2006). Virtue ethics. *The Internet encyclopedia of philosophy*. Retrieved September 9, 2006, from www.iep.utm.edu/v/virtue.htm.

Austin, J. B., & Dankwort, J. (1999). Standards for batterer programs. *Journal of Interpersonal Violence*, 14, 152–168.

Babcock, J. C., Green, C. E., & Robie, C. (2004). Does batterers' treatment work? A meta-analytic review of domestic violence treatment. *Clinical Psychology Review*, 23, 1023–1053.

Baier, K. (1958). *The moral point of view: A rational basis of ethics*. New York, NY: Random House.

Ballie, R. (2001). Medicare will now cover some telehealth psychotherapy services. *Monitor on Psychology*, 32(10). www.apa.org/monitor/nov01/telehealth.html

Banks, S. (2004). *Ethics, accountability and the social professions*. New York, NY: Palgrave Macmillan Publishing.

Barker, R. L. (1988a). "Client dumping": Some ethical considerations. *Journal of Independent Social Work*, 2, 1–5.

Barker, R. L. (1988b). Just whose code of ethics should the independent practitioner follow? *Journal of Independent Social Work*, 2(4), 1–5.

Barker, R. L. (1992). *Social work in private practice* (2nd ed.). Washington, DC: NASW Press.

Barksdale, C. (1989). Child abuse reporting: A clinical dilemma. *Smith College Studies in Social Work*, 59, 170–182.

Barnett-Queens, T. (1999). Sexual relationships with educators: A national survey of masters-level practitioners. *The Clinical Supervisor*, 18(1), 151–172.

Baretti, M. (2004). What do we know about the professional socialization of our students? *Journal of Social Work Education*, 40(2), 255–283.

Barr, D. A. (2008). *Health disparities in the United States: Social class, race, ethnicity, and health*. Baltimore, MD: Johns Hopkins Press.

Basham, K. K., Donner, S., Killough, R. M., & Rozas, L. W. (1997). Becoming an anti-racist institution. *Smith College Studies in Social Work*, 67, 564–585.

Bates, C. M., & Brodsky, A. M. (1989). *Sex in the therapy hour: A case of professional incest*. New York, NY: Guilford.

Bauman, Z. (1996). Morality in the age of contingency. In P. Heclas, S. Lash, & P. Morris (Eds.), *Detraditionalization: Critical reflections on authority and identity* (pp. 49–58). Cambridge, MA: Blackwell Publishers.

Bayer, R. (1998). AIDS and the ethics of prevention, research, and care. In G. Wormser (Ed.), *AIDS and other manifestations of HIV infection* (3rd ed., pp. 799–807). Philadelphia: Lippincott-Raven Publishers.

Bayles, M. D. (1981). *Professional Ethics*. Belmont, CA: Wadsworth Publishing.

Beck, J. C. (1998). Legal and ethical duties of the clinician treating a patient who is liable to be impulsively violent. *Behavioral Sciences and the Law*, 16, 375–389.

Beder, J. (1998). The home visit, revisited. *Families in Society*, 79, 514–522.

Behnke, S. (2006). Ethics and interrogations: Comparing and contrasting the American Psychological, American Medical and American Psychiatric Association positions. *Monitor on Psychology*, 37(7).

Bennett, C. C., Naylor, R. B., Perri, C. S., Shirilla, R. G., & Kilbane, T. (2008). Managed care's influence on clinical decision making. *Praxis*, 8, 57–68.

Benotsch, E. G., Wright, V. J., Cassini, T. A. D., Pinkerton, S. D., Weinhardt, L., & Kelly, J. A. (2006). Use of the Internet for HIV prevention by AIDS service organizations in the United States. *Journal of Technology in Human Services*, 24(1), 19–35.

Bergeron, L. R., & Gray. B. (2003). Ethical dilemmas of reporting suspected elder abuse. *Social Work*, 48, 96–105.

Bergin, A. E. (1980). Psychotherapy and religious values. *Journal of Consulting and Clinical Psychology*, 48(1), 95–105.

Bergin, A. E. (1991). Values and religious issues in psychotherapy and mental health, *American Psychologist*, 46(4), 394–403.

Bergeron, M., & Hebert, M. (2006). Evaluation of a group interview using a feminist approach for victims of sexual abuse. *Child Abuse & Neglect*, 30(10), 1143–1159.

Berkman, C. G., Turner, S. G., Cooper, M., Polnerow, D., & Swartz, M. (2000). Sexual contact with clients: Assessment of social workers' attitudes and educational preparation. *Social Work*, 45(3), 223–234.

Berlin, S. (2005). The value of acceptance in social work direct practice: A historical and contemporary view. *Social Service Review*, 79(3), 482–510.

Berliner, A. K. (1989). Misconduct in social work practice. *Social Work*, 34, 69–72.

Bern, D. J. (1970). *Beliefs, attitudes and human affairs*. Pacific Grove, CA: Brooks/Cole Publishing.

Bernsen, A., Tabachnick, B. G., & Pope, K. S. (1994). National survey of social workers' sexual attraction to their clients: Results, implications, and comparison to psychologists. *Ethics & Behavior*, 4(4), 369–388.

Bernstein, S. (1960). Self-determination: "King or citizen in the realm of values." *Social Work*, 5, 3–8.

Bernstein, S. R. (1990). Contracted services: Issues for the nonprofit agency manager. In *Towards the 21st century: Challenges for the voluntary sector*. Proceedings of the 1990 Conference of the Association of Voluntary Action Scholars. London.

Besharov, D. J., & Besharov, S. H. (1987). Teaching about liability. *Social Work*, 32, 517–522.

Besharov, D. J., & Laumann, L. A. (1996). Child abuse reporting. *Society*, 33(4), 40–46.

Beyerstein, D. (1993). The functions and limitations of professional codes of ethics. In E. R. Winkler & J. R. Coombs (Eds.), *Applied ethics* (pp. 416–425). Cambridge, MA: Blackwell Publishers.

Bilson, A. (2007). Promoting compassionate concern in social work: Reflections on ethics, biology, and love. *British Journal of Social Work*, 37(8), 1371–1386.

Bisman, C. (2004). Social work values: The moral core of the profession. *British Journal of Social Work*, 34, 109–123.

Black, D. (1972). The boundaries of legal sociology. *Yale Law Journal*, 81, 1086–1101.

Bloom, M. (1975). The paradox of helping: Introduction to the philosophy of scientific helping. New York, NY: John Wiley & Sons.

Blum, L. (2001). Care. In: L. C. Becker & C. B. Becker (Eds.), *Encyclopedia of Ethics*, Vol. 1 (2nd ed.) (pp. 185–187). New York, NY: Routledge.

Bogodanoff, M., & Elbaum, P. L. (1978). Touching: A legacy from the encounter movement to social work practice. *Social Work in Health Care*, 4, 209–219.

Boland-Prom, K. W. (2009). Results from a national study of social workers sanctioned by state licensing boards. *Social Work*, 54(4), 351–360.

Boland-Prom, K., & Anderson, S. C. (2005). Teaching ethical decision making using dual relationship principles as a case example. *Journal of Social Work Education*, 41(3), 495–510.

Bond, T., & Mitchels, B. (2008). *Confidentiality and record keeping in counseling and psychotherapy*. Los Angeles, CA: Sage Publications.

Bonnie, R. J., & Wallace, R. B. (2003). *Elder mistreatment: Abuse, neglect, and exploitation in aging America*. Washington, DC: The National Academies Press.

Bonosky, N. (1995). Boundary violations in social work supervision: Clinical, educational, and legal implications. *The Clinical Supervisor*, 13(2), 79–95.

Borenzweig, H. (1983). Touching in clinical social work. *Social Casework*, 64, 238–242.

Borys, D. S., & Pope, K. S. (1989). Dual relationships between therapist and client: A national study of psychologists, psychiatrists, and social workers. *Professional Psychology: Research and Practice*, 20, 283–293.

Bowden, P. (1997). *Caring: Gender-sensitive ethics*. New York, NY: Routledge.

Bowers v. Hardwick, 106 S. Ct. 2841 (1986).

Bowles, W., Collinridge, M., Curry, S., & Valentine, B. (2006). *Ethical practice in social work: An applied approach*. New York, NY: McGraw Hill.

Brabeck, M. M., & Ting, K. (2000). Feminist ethics: Lenses for examining ethical psychological practice. In M. M. Grabeck (Ed.), *Practicing feminist ethics in psychology*. Washington, DC: American Psychological Association.

Brager, G. A. (1968). Advocacy and political behavior. *Social Work*, 13(2), 5–15.

Brandeis, L. D., & Warren, S. D. (1890). The right to privacy. *Harvard Law Review*, IV(5), December 15.

Braye, S., & Preston-Shoot, M. (1990). On teaching and applying the law in social work: It is not that simple. *British Journal of Social Work*, 20, 333–353.

Bride, B. E. (2007). Prevalence of secondary traumatic stress among social workers. *Social Work*, 52(1), 63–70.

Bride, B. E., & Figley, C. R. (2007). The fatigue of compassionate social workers: An introduction to the special issue on compassion fatigue. *Clinical Social Work Journal*, 35, 151–153.

Brill, C. K. (2001). Looking at the social work profession through the eye of the NASW Code of Ethics. *Research on Social Work Practice*, 11(2), 223–234.

British Association of Social Workers (nd). Code of ethics for social work. Retrieved from http://www.basw.co.uk/about/codeofethics/

Broadie, S. (1991). *Ethics with Aristotle*. New York, NY: Oxford University Press.

Brown, H. J. (1970). Social work values in a developing country. *Social Work*, 15(1), 107–112.

Bryan, V. (2006). Moving from professionally specific ideals to the common morality: Essential content in social work ethics education. *Journal of Teaching in Social Work*, 26 (3/4), 1–17.

Bufka, L. F., Crawford, J. I., & Levitt, J. T. (2002). Brief screening assessments for managed care and primary care. In M. M. Anthony & D. H. Barlow (Eds.), *Handbook of assessment and treatment planning for psychological disorders* (pp. 38–63). New York, NY: The Guilford Press.

Bush, N. J. (2009). Compassion fatigue: Are you at risk? *Oncology Nursing Forum*, 36(1), 24–28.

Butz, R. A. (1985). Reporting child abuse and confidentiality in counseling. *Social Casework*, 66, 83–90.

Callahan, D. (1987, October/November). Terminating treatment: Age as a standard. *Hastings Center Reporter*, 21–25.

Callahan, J. (1988). *Ethical issues in professional life*. New York, NY: Oxford University Press.

Callahan, J. (1994). The ethics of assisted suicide. *Health and Social Work*, 19, 237–244.

Canda, E. R. (1988). Spirituality, religious diversity, and social work practice. *Social Casework*, 69, 238–247.

Canda, E. R., Nakashima, M., & Furman, L. D. (2004). Ethical considerations about spirituality in social work: Insights from a national qualitative survey. *Families in Society*, 85(1), 27–35.

Caputo, R. K. (1991). Managing information systems: An ethical framework and information needs matrix. *Administration in Social Work*, 15(4), 53–64.

Carey, B. (2006, October 10). An analyst questions the self-perpetuating side of therapy. *New York Times*, p. D2.

Carlson, S. (2002, November 15). Virtual counseling. *The Chronicle of Higher Education*, pp. A35–36.

Carpenter, M. C., & Platt, S. (1997). Professional identity for clinical social workers: Impact of changes in health care delivery systems. *Clinical Social Work Journal*, 25, 337–351.

Carter-Pokras, O., & Zambrana, R. E. (2001). Latin Health Status. In M. Aguirre-Molina, C. W. Molina, & R. E. Zambrana (Eds.), *Health Issues in the Latino Community* (pp. 23–54). San Francisco, CA: Jossey-Bass.

Castillo, R. (2007). Glossary of key terms in culture and mental illness. Retrieved March 27, 2007, from www2.hawaii.edu/~rcastill/Culture_and_Mental_Illness/Glossary.html.

Cavaiola, A. A., & Colford, J. E. (2006). *A practical guide to crisis intervention*. Boston, MA: Houghton Mifflin.

Cervera, N. J. (1993). Decision making for pregnant adolescents: Applying reasoned action theory to research and treatment.

Families in Society: The Journal of Contemporary Human Services, 74, 355–365.

Chan, S. (2007, January 23). New York City puts millions into high-tech worker tracking. *New York Times*, p. C11.

Chase, Y. (2008). Professional liability and malpractice. In T. Mizrahi & L. Davis (Eds.), *Encyclopedia of social work*, volume 3 (20th ed.) (pp. 425–429). New York, NY: Oxford University Press.

Chow, J. (1999). Multi service centers in Chinese American immigrant communities: Practice principles and challenges. *Social Work*, 44, 70–80.

Christensen, K. E. (1986). Ethics of information technology. In G. R. Geiss & N. Viswanathan (Eds.), *The human edge* (pp. 72–91). Binghamton, NY: Haworth Press.

Citizen Link (2003). Dutch (Holland/Netherlands) euthanasia: The Dutch disaster. Retrieved January 8, 2003, from www.family.org/cforum/research/papers/a0001021.html.

Claiborne, N. (2006). Effectiveness of a care coordination model for stroke survivors: A randomized study. *Health and Social Work*, 31(2), 87–96.

Clark, C. (1998). Self-determination and paternalism in community care: Practice and prospects. *British Journal of Social Work*, 28, 387–402.

Clark, C. (1999). Observing the lighthouse: From theory to institutions in social work ethics. *European Journal of Social Work*, 2(3), 259–270.

Clark, C. (2006). Moral character in social work. *British Journal of Social Work*, 36, 75–89.

Clifford, D., & Burke, B. (2005). Developing anti-oppressive ethics in the new curriculum. *Social Work Education*, 24(6), 677–692.

Cohen, E. (2004). Advocacy and advocates: Definitions and ethical dimensions. *Generations*, 28(1), 9–16.

Cohen, J. (2003). Managed care and the evolving role of the clinical social worker in mental health. *Social Work*, 48(1), 34–43.

Cohen, R. (1980). The (revised) NASW Code of Ethics. *NASW News*, 26 (April), 19.

Coleman, E., & Schaefer, S. (1986). Boundaries of sex and intimacy between client and counselor. *Journal of Counseling and Development*, 64, 341–344.

Congress, E., & McAuliffe, D. (2006) Social work ethics: Professional codes in Australia and the United States. *International Social Work*, 49, 151–164.

Congress, E. P., & Lynn, M. (1997). Group work practice in the community: Navigating the slippery slope of ethical dilemmas. *Social Work with Groups*, 20(3), 61–74.

Conte, H. R., Plutchik, R., Picard, S., & Karasu, T. B. (1989). Ethics in the practice of

psychotherapy. *American Journal of Psychotherapy*, 43, 32–42.

Corey, G., Corey, M. S., & Callanan, P. (2003). *Issues and ethics in the helping professions* (6th ed.). Pacific Grove, CA: Brooks/Cole Thomson Learning Publishing Co.

Cottone, R. R., & Tarvydas, V. M. (2007). *Counseling ethics and decision making* (3rd ed.) Upper Saddle River, NJ: Pearson/Merrill Prentice Hall.

Council on Social Work Education. (2004). *Educational policy and accreditation standards*. Alexandria, VA: Council on Social Work Education.

Council on Social Work Education. (2010). *Educational Policy and Accreditation Standards* (Revised March 27, 2010). Retrieved from http://www.cswe.org/File.aspx?id=40200 on 6/2/10.

Courtney, M. E., Barth, R. P., Berrick, J. D., Brooks, E., Needell, B., & Park, L. (1996). Race and child welfare services: Past research and future directions. *Child Welfare*, LXXV, 99–137.

Csikai, E. L. (1999a). Euthanasia and assisted suicide: Issues for social work practice. *Journal of Gerontological Social Work*, 31(3/4), 49–63.

Csikai, E. L. (1999b). The role of values and experience in determining social workers' attitudes toward euthanasia and assisted suicide. *Social Work in Health Care*, 30(1), 75–95.

Csikai, E. L. (1999c). Hospital social workers' attitudes toward euthanasia and assisted suicide. *Social Work in Health Care*, 30(1), 51–73.

Csikai, E. L. (2004). Social workers' participation in the resolution of ethical dilemmas in hospice care. *Health & Social Work*, 29(1), 67–76.

Csikai, E. L., & Sales, E. (1998). The emerging social work role on hospital ethics committees: A comparison of social worker and chair perspectives. *Social Work*, 43(3), 233–242.

Cua, A. S. (2001). Confucian ethics. In: L. C. Becker & C. B. Becker (Eds.), *Encyclopedia of Ethics*, Vol. 1 (2nd ed.) (pp. 287–295). New York, NY: Routledge.

Cummings, S. M., Cooper, R. L., & Cassie, K. M. (2009). Motivational interviewing to affect behavioral change in older adults. *Research in Social Work Practice*, 19(2), 195–204.

Currie v. Doran, U.S. Court of Appeals, 10th Circuit. 2001.

Curtis, P. A., & Lutkus, A. M. (1985). Client confidentiality in police social work settings. *Social Work*, 30, 355–360.

Cwikel, J. G., & Cnaan, R. A. (1991). Ethical dilemmas in applying second wave information technology to social work practice. *Social Work*, 36(2), 114–120.

Cyrns, A. G. (1977). Social work education and student ideology: A multivariate study of professional socialization. *Journal of Education for Social Work*, 13(1), 44–51.

Daley, M. R., & Doughty, M. O. (2006). Ethics complaints in social work practice: A rural-urban comparison. *Journal of Social Work Values and Ethics*, 3(1).

Darlington, Y., Feeney, J. A., & Rixon, K. (2005). Interagency collaboration between child protection and health services: Practice, attitudes, and barriers. *Child Abuse& Neglect*, 29, 1085–1098.

Daro, D. (1988). *Confronting child abuse: Research/or effective program design.* New York, NY: Free Press.

Davis, K. (1997). Managed care, mental illness and African Americans: A prospective analysis of managed care policy in the United States. *Smith College Studies in Social Work*, 67, 623–641.

Dean, H. (1998). The primacy of the ethical aim in clinical social work: Its relationship to social justice and mental health. *Smith College Studies in Social Work*, 69, 9–24.

Dean, R. G., & Rhodes, M. L. (1992). Ethical-clinical tensions in clinical practice. *Social Work*, 37, 128–132.

Delaronde, S., King, G., Bendel, R., & Reece, R. (2000). Opinions among mandated reporters toward child maltreatment reporting policies. *Child Abuse and Neglect*, 24(7), 901–910.

Dent, S. (2000). Illiteracy: "Hidden disability" creates health care confusion. *FP Report*, 6(1). Retrieved October 16, 2002, from www.aafp.org/fpr/20000100/illiteracy.html

Department of Health & Human Services, Centers for Disease Control and Prevention. (2001). *HIV prevalence trends in selected populations in the United States: Results from national serosurveillance, 1993–1997.*

Department of Health and Human Services (2002). Modifications to the standards for privacy of individually identifiable health information—final rule. Retrieved November 25, 2002, from www.hhs.gov/news/press/2002pres/20020809.html.

Desai, K. (2003). Ethical decision making within the bureaucratic context: A case study. *Child Management Journal*, 4(3), 122–128.

Deutscher, I., Pestello, F. P., & Pestello, H. F. G. (1993). *Sentiments and acts.* New York, NY: Aldine de Gruyter.

Devilly, G. J., Wright, R., & Varker, T. (2009). Vicarious trauma, secondary traumatic stress or simply burnout? Effect of trauma therapy on mental health professionals. *Australian and New Zealand Journal of Psychiatry*, 43, 373–385.

DiMarco, M., & Zoline, S. S. (2004). Duty to warn in the context of HIV/AIDS-related psychotherapy: Decision making among psychologists. *Counseling and Clinical Psychology*, 1(2), 68–85.

Dobrin, A. (1989). Ethical judgments of male and female social workers. *Social Work*, 34, 451–455.

Dodd, S., & Jansson, B. (2004). Expanding the boundaries of ethics education: Preparing social workers for ethical advocacy in an organizational setting. *Journal of Social Work Education*, 40(3), 455–465.

Dolgoff, R. (2002). An exploration in social policy and ethics: Ethical judgment before or after the fact? *Social Work Forum, Wurzweiler School of Social Work*, 35(Winter/Spring, 2001–2002), 67–86.

Dolgoff, R., & Skolnik, L. (1992). Ethical decision making: The NASW code of ethics and group work practice: Beginning explorations. *Social Work with Groups*, 15(4), 99–112.

Dolgoff, R., & Skolnik, L. (1996). Ethical decision making in social work with groups: An empirical study. *Social Work with Groups*, 19(2), 49–65.

Dryden, W., & Ellis, A. (1988). Rational-emotive therapy. In *Handbook of Cognitive-Behavioral Therapies* (pp. 214–272). New York, NY: The Guilford Press.

Dumont, M. P. (1996). Privatization and mental health in Massachusetts. *Smith College Studies in Social Work*, 66, 293–303.

Durana, C. (1998). The use of touch in psychotherapy: Ethical and clinical guidelines. *Psychotherapy: Theory, Research, Practice, Training*, 35(2), 269–280.

Dworkin, G. (1985). Behavioral control and design. *Social Research*, 52, 543–554.

Dwyer, S. (2005). Older people and permanent care: Whose decision? *British Journal of Social Work*, 35(7), 1081–1092.

Edward, J. (1999). Is managed mental health treatment psychotherapy? *Clinical Social Work Journal*, 27, 87–102.

Egan, M., & Kadushin, G. (2004). Job satisfaction of home health social workers in the environment of containment. *Health & Social Work*, 29(4), 287–296.

Egley, L. C. (1992). Defining the *Tarasoff* duty. *Journal of Psychiatry and Law*, 19, 93–133.

Ellis, A. (1973). *Humanistic psychotherapy: The rational-emotive approach.* New York, NY: McGraw-Hill.

Eriksen, K., & Kress, V. E. (2005). *Beyond the DSM story: Ethical quandaries, challenges, and best practices.* Thousand Oaks, CA: Sage Publications.

Ewalt, P. L., & Mokuau, N. (1995). Self-determination from a Pacific perspective. *Social Work*, 40, 168–175.

Ewing, C. P. (2002). *Tarasoff* update: Psychotherapy threats alone provide no basis for criminal prosecution. *Monitor on Psychology, 33*(2), 1–3. Retrieved July 17, 2002, from www.apa.org/monitor/feb02/jn.html.

Ewing, C. P. (2005). *Tarasoff* reconsidered: The *Tarasoff* rule has been extended to include threats disclosed by family members. *Monitor on Psychology, 36*(7), 112.

Faust, J. R. (2008). Clinical social workers as patient advocate in a community mental health center. *Clinical Social Work Journal, 36,* 293–300.

Fawcett, B. (2009). Questioning the certainties in social work. *International Social Work, 52*(4), 473–484.

Feder, L., & Wilson, D. B. (2005). A meta-analytic review of court-mandated batterer intervention programs: Can courts affect abusers' behavior? *Journal of Experimental Criminology, 1,* 239–262.

Federal Globe–Federal Employee Benefits FAQ. (2007). What the gay, lesbian, or bisexual employee needs to know. Retrieved January 30, 2007, from www.fedglobe.org/issues/benefitsfaq5.htm.

Federal Psychotherapist-Patient Privilege (*Jaffee v. Redmond,* 518 U.S. 1): History, documents, and opinions. Retrieved September 5, 2002, from http://psa-uny.org/jr/.

Feldman, K. A., & Newcomb, T. M. (1994). *The impact of college on students.* New Brunswick, NJ: Transaction Publishers.

Fellin, P. (2000). Revisiting multiculturalism in social work. *Journal of Social Work Education, 36*(2), 261–278.

Felthous, A. R., & Kachigian, C. (2001). The fin de millénaire duty to warn or protect. *Journal of Forensic Science, 46*(5), 1103–1112.

Festinger, L. (1957). *A theory of cognitive dissonance.* New York, NY: Harper & Row.

Fetter, B., Morgan, D., & Levi, J. (2006). The United States of America. In E. J. Beck, N. Mays, A. W. Whiteside, & J. Zuniga (Eds.), *The HIV epidemic: Local and global implications* (pp. 581–587). New York, NY: Oxford University Press.

Figley, C. R. (1995). *Compassion fatigue: Coping with secondary traumatic stress disorder in those who treat the traumatized.* New York, NY: Brunner/Mazel Publishers.

Figley, C. R. (1999). Compassion fatigue: Toward a new understanding of the costs of caring. In B. Hudnall Stamm (Ed.), *Secondary traumatic stress: Self-care issues for clinicians, researchers, and educators* (2nd ed., pp. 1–28). Baltimore: Sidran Press.

Fine, M., & Teram, E. (2009). Believers and skeptics: Where social workers situate themselves regarding the Code of Ethics. *Ethics & Behavior, 19*(1), 60–78.

Finkelhor, D. (1990). Is child abuse over-reported? *Public Welfare, 48,* 22–29.

Finkelhor, D. (1998). Improving research, policy, and practice to understand child sexual abuse. *Journal of the American Medical Association, 280,* 1864–1865.

Finn, J. (1990). Security, privacy, and confidentiality in agency microcomputer use. *Families in Society: The Journal of Contemporary Human Services* (May), 283–290.

Finn, J., & Banach, M. (2002). Risk management in online human services practice. *Journal of Technology in Human Services, 20*(1/2), 133–153.

Fishkin, J. S. (1982). *The limits of obligation.* New Haven, CT: Yale University Press.

Flaherty, J. (2002, August 14). Girls link their use of family planning clinics to keeping parents in the dark. *New York Times,* p. A14.

Flanagan, E. H., & Blashfield, R. K. (2005). Gender acts as a context for interpreting diagnostic criteria. *Journal of Clinical Psychology, 61*(12), 1485–1498.

Fleck-Henderson, A. (1991). Moral reasoning in social work practice. *Social Service Review* (June), 185–202.

Flexner, A. (1915). Is social work a profession? *Proceedings of National Conference of Charities and Corrections* (pp. 576–590). Chicago, IL: Hindman.

Fodor, J. L. (1999, February). Computer ethics in higher education. *Syllabus,* 12–15.

Francis, C. (1995). Hindu ethics. In: J. Roth (Ed.), *Encyclopedia of Ethics* (pp. 376–377). Chicago, IL: Fitzroy Dearborn Publishers.

Frank, J. (1991). *Persuasion and healing* (Rev. ed.). New York, NY: Schocken Books.

Frankel, A. J., & Gelman, S. R. (2004). *Case Management* (2nd ed.). Chicago, IL: Lyceum Books.

Frankena, W. K. (1973). *Ethics* (2nd ed.). Englewood Cliffs, NJ: Prentice Hall.

Frankena, W. K. (1980). *Thinking about morality.* Ann Arbor, MI: University of Michigan Press.

Frankl, V. (1968). *The doctor and the soul.* New York, NY: Alfred A. Knopf.

Frans, D. J., & Moran, J. R. (1993). Social work education's impact on students' humanistic values and personal empowerment. *Arete, 18*(1), 1–11.

Freedman, T. G. (1998). Genetic susceptibility testing: Ethical and social quandaries. *Health & Social Work, 23,* 214–222.

Freeman, J. M., & McDonnell, K. (2001). *Tough decisions: Cases in medical ethics* (2nd ed.). New York, NY: Oxford University Press.

Freud, S. (1999). The social construction of normality. *Families in Society, 80*(4), 333–339.

Freud, S., & Krug, S. (2002). Beyond the code of ethics, Part 1: Complexities of ethical decision making in social work practice. *Families in Society: The Journal of Contemporary Human Services*, 83(5/6), 474–482.

Frost, N., Robinson, M., & Anning, A. (2005). Social workers in multidisciplinary teams: Issues and dilemmas for professional practice. *Child and Family Social Work*, 10(187–196).

Fryling, T., Summers, R. W., & Hoffman, A. H. (2006). Elder abuse: Definition and scope of the problem. In: R. W. Summers & A. H. Hoffman (Eds.), *Elder abuse: A public health perspective* (pp. 5–18). Washington, DC: American Public Health Association.

Fukuyama, M. A. (2001). Counseling in colleges and universities. In D. C. Locke, E. L. Herr, & J. E. Myers (Eds.), *The handbook of counseling* (pp. 319–341). Thousand Oaks, CA: Sage Publications.

Furlong, M. A. (2003). Self-determination and a critical perspective in casework: Promoting a balance between interdependence and autonomy. *Qualitative Social Work*, 2(2), 177–196.

Furman, R., Downey, E. P., & Jackson, R. L. (2004). Exploring the ethics of treatments for depression: The ethics of care perspective. *Smith College Studies in Social Work*, 74(3), 525–538.

Galambos, C. M. (1999). Resolving ethical conflicts in a managed health care environment. *Health & Social Work*, 24(3), 191–197.

Galambos, C. (2005). Rural social work practice: Maintaining confidentiality in the face of dual relationships, 2 (2). Retrieved July 19, 2006, from www.socialworker.com/jswve/content/view/23/37

Galinsky, M. J., Schopler, J. H., & Abell, M. D. (1997). Connecting group members through telephone and computer groups. *Health & Social Work*, 22, 181–188.

Gambrill, E., & Pruger, R. (Eds.) (1997). *Controversial issues in social work ethics, values, and obligations*. Boston, MA: Allyn & Bacon.

Gambrill, E. D. (2003). From the editor: "Evidence-based practice": Sea change or the emperor's new clothes? *Journal of Social Work Education*, 39, 3–23.

Gambrill, E. (2006). Evidence-based practice and policy: Choices ahead. *Research on Social Work Practice*, 16(3), 338–357.

Ganzani, L., Horvath, T., Jackson, A., Goy, E. R., Miller, L. J., & Delora, M. A. (2002). Experiences of Oregon nurses and social workers with hospice patients who requested assistance with suicide. *New England Journal of Medicine*, 347(8), 582–588.

Garb, H. N. (1994). Cognitive heuristics and biases in personality assessment. In L. Heath (Ed.), *Applications of heuristics and biases to social issues* (pp. 73–90). New York, NY: Plenum Press.

Gerhart, U. C., & Brooks, A. D. (1985). Social workers and malpractice: Law, attitudes, and knowledge. *Social Casework*, 66, 411–416.

Gewirth, A. (1978). *Reason and morality*. Chicago: University of Chicago Press.

Gibelman, M., & Schervish, P. H. (1997). *Who we are: A second look*. Washington, DC: NASW.

Gibelman, M. (2005). Social workers for rent: The contingency human services labor force. *Families in Society: The Journal of Contemporary Social Services*, 86(4), 457–469.

Gibelman, M., & Mason, S. E. (2002). Treatment choices in a managed care environment: A multi-disciplinary exploration. *Clinical Social Work*, 30(2), 199–214.

Givelber, D., Bowers, W., & Blitch, C. (1984). *Tarasoff:* Myth and reliability. *Wisconsin Law Review*, 2, 443–497.

Glaser, R. D., & Thorpe, J. S. (1986). Unethical intimacy: A survey of sexual contact and advances between psychology educators and female graduate students. *American Psychologist*, 41(1), 43–51.

Glassman, C. (1992). Feminist dilemmas in practice. *Affilia*, 7, 160–166.

Goffman, E. (1959). *The presentation of self in everyday life*. Garden City, NY: Doubleday.

Goldenberg, I., & Goldenberg, H. (2000). *Family therapy: An overview* (5th ed.). Belmont, CA: Brooks/Cole.

Goldstein, E. G. (1997). To tell or not to tell: The disclosure of events in the therapist's life to the patient. *Clinical Social Work Journal*, 25, 41–58.

Goldstein, H. (1973). *Social work: A unitary approach*. Columbia, SC: University of South Carolina Press.

Goldstein, H. (1987). The neglected moral link in social work practice. *Social Work*, 32, 181–186.

Goldstein, H. (1998). Education for ethical dilemmas in social work practice. *Families in Society: The Journal of Contemporary Human Services*, 79, 241–253.

Goodban, N. (1985). The psychological impact of being on welfare. *Social Service Review*, 59, 403–422.

Goode, E. (2001, August 27). Disparities seen in mental care for minorities. *New York Times*, pp. 1, 12.

Gorman, L. (2009). Rationing care: Oregon changes its priorities. National Center for Policy Analysis, Brief Analysis #645, February 19, 2009. Retrieved March 11, 2010, http://web.ebscohost.com/ehost/detail

Gorman, S. W. (2009). Sex outside of the therapy hour: Practical and constitutional limits on therapist sexual misconduct regulations. 56

U.C.L.A. Law Review 983, 2009. Retrieved http://uclalawreview.org/pdf/56-4-4.pdf. February 23, 2010.

Gottleib, M. C., & Cooper, C. C. (1993). Some ethical issues for systems-oriented therapists in hospital settings. *Family Relations*, 42(2), 140–144.

Green, R. (2003). Social work in rural areas: A personal and professional challenge. *Australian Social Work*, 56, 209–219.

Greene, A. D., & Latting, J. K. (2004). Whistle-blowing as a form of advocacy: Guidelines for the practitioner and organization. *Social Work*, 49(2), 219–230.

Greenhouse, L. (1998, December 2). High court curbs claim on privacy in a house. *New York Times*, p. A11.

Greenhouse, L. (1999a, April 11). Check out your driver. *New York Times, Week in Review*, p. 2.

Greenhouse, L. (1999b, April 6). Supreme court roundup; police searching car may include passenger's things. *New York Times*, p. A19.

Greenwood, E. (1957). Attributes of a profession. *Social Work*, 2(3), 45–55.

Grinnell, R. M. Jr., & Unrau, Y. A. (2005). *Social work research and evaluation*. New York, NY: Oxford University Press.

Grisso, T., & Appelbaum, P. S. (1998). *Assessing competence to consent to treatment: A guide for physicians and other health professionals*. New York, NY: Oxford University Press.

Group for the Advancement of Psychiatry (1994). *Forced into treatment: The role of coercion in clinical practice*. Report No. 137. Washington, DC: American Psychiatric Press.

Grundstein-Amado, R. (1999). Bilateral transformational leadership: An approach for fostering ethical conduct in public service organizations, *Administration & Society*, 31(2), 247–260.

Gursansky, D., Harvey, J., & Kennedy R. (2003). *Case management: Policy, practice, and professional business*. New York, NY: Columbia University Press.

Guttmann, D. (1996). *Logotherapy for the helping professional: Meaningful social work*. New York, NY: Springer Publishing Co.

Hackler, C. (2009). Is rationing health care ethically defensible? In: E. E. Morrison (Ed.), *Health care ethics: Critical issues for the 21st century* (2nd ed.) (pp. 355–364). Sudbury, MA: Jones and Bartlett Publishers.

Hadjistavropoulos, T., & Malloy, D. C. (1999). Ethical principles of the American Psychological Association: An argument for philosophical and practical ranking. *Ethics & Behavior*, 9, 127–140.

Haley, J. (1976). *Problem-solving therapy*. New York, NY: Harper & Row.

Hall, M. L., & Keefe, R. H. (2006). Interfacing with managed care organizations: A measure of self-perceived competence. *Best Practices in Mental Health*, 2(1), 31–41.

Halmos, P. (1965). *Faith of the counselor*. London, UK: Constable.

Halverson, G., & Brownlee, K. (2010). Managing ethical considerations around dual relationships in small rural and remote Canadian communities. *International Social Work*, 53(2), 247–260.

Hamel, J. (2005). *Gender-inclusive treatment of intimate partner abuse*. New York, NY: Springer Publishing.

Hancock, T. U. (2008). Doing justice: A typology of helping attitudes toward sexual groups. *Affilia: Journal of Women and Social Work*, 23(4), 349–362.

Handler, J. E., & Hollingsworth, E. J. (1971). *The deserving poor*. Chicago, IL: Markham.

Hankins, C. A., Stanecki, K. A., Ghys, P. D., & Marais, H. (2006). The evolving HIV epidemic. In E. J. Beck, N. Mays, A. W. Whiteside, & J. M. Zuniga (Eds.), *The HIV pandemic: Local and global implications* (pp. 21–35). New York, NY: Oxford University Press.

Hardina, D. (2004). Guidelines for ethical practice in community organization. *Social Work*, 49(4), 595–604.

Hardina, D. (2000). Models and tactics taught in community organization courses: Findings from a survey of practice instructors. *Journal of Community Practice*, 7(1), 5–18.

Harrington, D., & Dolgoff, R. (2008). Hierarchies of ethical principles for ethical decision making in social work. *Ethics and Social Welfare*, 2, 183–196.

Harris, G. C. (1999). The dangerous patient exception to the psychotherapist-patient privilege: The *Tarasoff* duty and the *Jaffee* footnote. *Washington Law Review*, 74, 33–68.

Harris, M.B., & Franklin, C. (2009). Helping adolescent mothers to achieve in school: An evaluation of the taking charge group intervention. *Children & Schools*, 31(1), 27–34.

Hartman, A. (1995). Family therapy. In R. L. Edward (Ed.), *Encyclopedia of social work* (19th ed., Vol. 2, pp. 983–991). Washington, DC: National Association of Social Workers.

Hartman, A. (1997). Power issues in social work practice. In A. J. Katz, A. Lurie, & C. M. Vidal (Eds.), *Critical social welfare issues* (pp. 215–226). New York, NY: The Haworth Press.

Haslam, D. R., & Harris, S. M. (2004). Informed consent documents of marriage and family therapists in private practice: A qualitative analysis. *American Journal of Family Therapy*, 32, 359–374.

Hayes, D. D., & Varley, B. K. (1965). The impact of social work education on students' values. *Social Work*, 10(4), 40–46.

Healy, T. C. (1998). The complexity of everyday ethics in home health care: An analysis of social workers' decisions regarding frail elders' autonomy. *Social Work in Health Care*, 27(4), 19–37.

Healy, T. C. (2004). Levels of directiveness: A contextual analysis of social work in health care. *Social Work in Health Care*, 40(1), 71–91.

Held, V. (2006). *The ethics of care: Personal, political, and global*. New York, NY: Oxford University Press.

Helton, D. (2003). Online therapeutic social service provision (Therap-pc): A state of the art review. *Journal of Technology in Human Services*, 21(4), 17–36.

Hetzel, L., & Smith, A. (2001). The 65 years and over population: 2000. *Census 2000 Brief*. Washington, D.C.: U.S. Census Bureau. Retrieved October 9, 2003, from www.census.gov/prod/2001pubs/C2kbr01-10.pdf

Hines, D. A., & Malley-Morrison, K. (2005). *Family violence in the United States: Defining, understanding, and combating abuse*. Thousand Oaks, CA: Sage Publications.

Hiratsuka, J. (1994). When it's a helper who needs help. *NASW News* (June), 3.

Hodge, D. R. (2002). Does social work oppress evangelical Christians? A "new class" analysis of society and social work. *Social Work*, 47(4), 401–414.

Hodge, D. R. (2004). Developing cultural competency with evangelical Christians. *Families in Society*, 85(2), 251–260.

Hodge, D. R. (2004). Who we are, where we come from, and some of our perceptions: Comparison of social workers and general population. *Social Work*, 49 (2), 261–268.

Hodge, D. R. (2005a). Spiritual life maps: A client-centered pictorial instrument for spiritual assessment, planning, and intervention. *Social Work*, 50(1), 77–87.

Hodge, D. R. (2005b). Epistemological frameworks, homosexuality, and religion: How people of faith understand the intersection between homosexuality and religion. *Social Work*, 50(3), 207–218.

Hodge, D. R. (2006). A template for spiritual assessment: A review of the JCAHO requirements and guidelines for implementation. *Social Work*, 51(4), 317–326.

Hodge, D. R. (2007). Social justice and people of faith: A transnational perspective. *Social Work*, 52(2), 139–148.

Hodge, D. R. (2007). Secular privilege: Deconstructing the invisible rose-tinted sunglasses. *Journal of Religion and Spirituality and Social Work Values: Social Thought*, 28 (1/2), 8–34.

Hoefer, R. (2006). *Advocacy practice for social justice*. Chicago, IL: Lyceum Books, Inc.

Hogue, C. J. R., & Hargraves, M. A. (2000). The commonwealth fund minority health survey of 1994: An overview. In C. J. R. Hogue, M. A. Hargraves, & K. S. Collins (Eds.), *Minority Health in America* (pp. 1–18). Baltimore, MD: Johns Hopkins University Press.

Hokenstad, M. C. (1987). Preparation for practice: The ethical dimension. *Social Work Education Reporter*, 25, 1–4.

Hollingsworth, L. D. (2005). Ethical considerations in prenatal sex selection. *Health & Social Work*, 30(2), 126–134.

Holloway, S., Black, P., Hoffman, K., & Pierce, D. (ND). Some considerations of the import of the 2008 EPAS for curriculum design. Retrieved from http://www.cswe.org/File.aspx?id=31578 on 6/2/10.

Holmes, S. A. (1998, December 6). Right to abortion quietly advances in state courts. *New York Times*, Section 1, p. 1.

Holroyd, J., & Brodsky, A. (1977). Psychologists' attitudes and practices regarding erotic and nonerotic physical contact with patients. *American Psychologist*, 32, 843–849.

Home Care & Hospice, National Association for Home Care & Hospice (2006). The Medicare home health benefit: Utilization and outlays have dropped dramatically. Retrieved July 11, 2006, from www.congressweb.com/nahc/positionpapers.htm

Horner, W. C., & Whitbeck, L. B. (1991). Personal versus professional values in social work: A methodological note. *Journal of Social Service Research*, 14(1/2), 21–43.

Houston-Vega, M. K., Nuehring, E. M., & Daguio, E. R. (1997). *Prudent practice*. Washington, DC: NASW Press.

Howard, M. O., & Jenson, J. M. (1999). Clinical practice guidelines: Should social work develop them? *Research on Social Work Practice*, 9, 283–301.

Howard, M. O., McMillen, C. J., & Pollio, D. E. (2003). Teaching evidence-based practice: Toward a new paradigm for social work education. *Research on Social Work Practice*, 13, 234–259.

Howe, E. (1980). Public professions and the private model of professionalism. *Social Work*, 25, 179–191.

Hughes, R. C. (1993a). Child welfare services for the catastrophically ill newborn: Part I—A confusion of responsibility. *Child Welfare*, 72, 32–40.

Hughes, R. C. (1993b). Child welfare services for the catastrophically ill newborn: Part II—A guiding ethical paradigm. *Child Welfare*, 72, 423–437.

Hugman, R. (2003). Professional values and ethics in social work: Reconsidering postmodernism. *British Journal of Social Work*, 33(8), 1025–1041.

Human Rights Campaign (2003). Medicaid expansion. Retrieved January 27, 2003, from www.hrc.org/issues/hiv_aids/background/medicaid.asp.

Illich, I. (2006). Deschooling society. Retrieved October 30, 2006, from http://reactor-core.org/deschooling.html.

Imbert, R. C. (2006). Personal letter (November 20). NASW Insurance Trust and the American Professional Agency.

Imre, R. E. (1989). Moral theory for social work. Social Thought, 15(1), 18–27.

Isaacs, J. B. (November, 2009). Spending on children and the elderly. Brookings Institute. Retrieved March 11, 2010, http://www.brookings.edu/reports/2009/1105_spending_children-isaacs.aspx.

Iserson, K. V. (1986). An approach to ethical problems in emergency medicine. In K. V. Iserson et al. (Eds.), Ethics in emergency medicine (pp. 35–41). Baltimore, MD: Williams & Wilkins.

Iversen, R., Gergen, K. J., & Fairbanks, R. P. II, (2005). Assessment and social construction: Conflict or co-creation? British Journal of Social Work, 35(5), 689–708.

Jackson, J. (2000). Duties and conscience in professional practices. In Q. de Stexhe & J. Verstraeten (Eds.), Matter of breath: Foundations for professional ethics (pp. 239–258). Leuven, Belgium: Peeters.

Jackson, J. S., & Sellers, S.L. (2001). Health and the elderly. In R. L. Braithwaite & S. E. Taylor (Eds.), Health issues in the black community (pp. 81–96). San Francisco, CA: Jossey-Bass Publishers.

Jaques, L. H., & Folen, R. A. (1998). Confidentiality and the military. In R. M. Anderson Jr., T. L. Nardello, & H. V. Hall (Eds.), Avoiding ethical misconduct in psychology specialty areas. Springfield, IL: Charles C. Thomas Publishers.

Jayaratne, S., Croxton, T., & Mattison, D. (1997). Social work professional standards: An exploratory study. Social Work, 42, 187–199.

Jewell, J. R., Collins, K. V., Gargotto, L., & Dishon, A. J. (2009). Building the unsettling force: Social workers and the struggle for human rights. Journal of Community Practice, 17, 309–322.

Jiminez, J. (2006). Epistemological frameworks, homosexuality, and religion: A response to Hodge. Social Work, 51(2), 185–187.

Joint United Nations Programme on HIV/AIDS (UNAIDS) and World Health Organization (WHO). (2009). AIDS epidemic update: November 2009. Geneva, Switzerland: UNAIDS. Retrieved from http://data.unaids.org/pub/Report/2009/JC1700_Epi_Update_2009_en.pdf.

Johner, R. (2006). Dual relationship legitimization and client-self-determination. Journal of Social Work Values and Ethics, 3(1). Retrieved July 19, 2006, from www.socialworker.com/jswve/content/view/30/44.

Johnson, R. (2008). Kant's moral philosophy. In: E. N. Zalta (Ed.), The Stanford Encyclopedia of Philosophy (Summer 2010 edition). Retrieved from http://plato.stanford.edu/entries/kant-moral/.

Jones, W. T., Sontag, F., Beckner, M.O., & Fogelin, R. J. (1977). Approaches to ethics. New York, NY: McGraw-Hill.

Jory, B., Anderson, D., & Greer, C. (1997). Intimate justice: Confronting issues of accountability, respect, and freedom in treatment for abuse and violence. Journal of Marital and Family Therapy, 399–419.

Joseph, M. V. (1983). The ethics of organization. Administration in Social Work, 7, 47–57.

Joseph, M. V. (1985). A model for ethical decision-making in clinical practice. In C. B. Germain (Ed.), Advances in clinical social work practice (pp. 207–217). Silver Spring, MD: NASW.

Judah, E. H. (1979). Values: The uncertain component of social work. Journal of Education for Social Work, 15(2), 79–86.

Kalichman, S. C. (1999). Mandated reporting of suspected child abuse: Ethics, law, and policy. Washington, DC: American Psychological Association.

Kaslow, F. (1998). Ethical problems in mental health practice. Journal of Family Psychotherapy, 9(2), 41–54.

Keefe, R. H., Hall, M. L., & Corvo, K. N. (2002). Providing therapy when managed care organizations deny reimbursement: Are private practitioners and their clients taking the fall? Social Work in Health Care, 36(2), 49–64.

Keith-Lucas, A. (1977). Ethics in social work. Encyclopedia of social work (pp. 350–355). Washington, DC: National Association of Social Workers.

Kelly, D. C. (2005). Beyond problem solving: The social worker as risk manager and educator in educational host settings. School Social Work Journal, 29(2), 40–52.

Kelly, T. B. (1994). Paternalism and the marginally competent: An ethical dilemma, no easy answers. Journal of Gerontological Social Work, 23(1/2), 67–84.

Kim, M. M., Scheyett, A. M., Elbogen, E. B., Van Dorn, R. A., McDaniel, L. A., Swartz, M. S., Swanson, J. W., & Ferron, J. (2008). Front line workers' attitudes towards psychiatric advance directives. Community Mental Health Journal, 44(1), 28–46.

King, N. (2009). Health inequalities and health inequities. In: E. E. Morrison (Ed.), Health care ethics: Critical issues for the 21st century

(2nd ed.) (pp. 339–354). Sudbury, MA: Jones and Bartlett Publishers.

Kirk, S. A., & Kutchins, H. (1988). Deliberate misdiagnosis in mental health practice. *Social Service Review*, 62, 225–237.

Kirk, S., & Kutchins, H. (1992). Diagnosis and uncertainty in mental health organizations. In Y. Hasenfeld (Ed.), *Human services as complex organizations* (pp. 163–183). London: Sage.

Kirkpatrick, W. J., Reamer, F. G., & Sykulski, M. (2006). Social work ethics audits in health care setting: A case study. *Health & Social Work*, 31(3), 225–228.

Kiselica, M. S., & Ramsey, M. L. (2001). Multicultural counselor education. In D. C. Locke, J. E. Myers, & E. L. Herr (Eds.), *The handbook of counseling* (pp. 433–451). Thousand Oaks, CA: Sage Publications.

Kitchner, K. S. (1984). Intuition, critical evaluation and ethical principles: The foundation of ethical decisions in counseling psychology. *Counseling Psychology*, 12, 43–55.

Klosterman, E. M., & Stratton, D. C. (2006). Speaking truth to power: Jane Addams's values base for peacemaking. *Affilia*, 21(2), 158–168.

Kluckhohn, C. (1951). Values and value-orientations in the theory of action: An exploration in definition and clarification. In T. Parsons & E. A. Shils (Eds.), *Toward a general theory of action* (pp. 388–433). Cambridge, MA: Harvard University Press.

Koenig, T. L., & Spano, R. N. (2003). Sex, supervision, and boundary violations: Pressing challenges and possible solutions. *The Clinical Supervisor*, 22(1), 3–19.

Kohlberg, L. (1984). *The psychology of moral development*. New York, NY: Harper & Row.

Kopels, S., & Kagle, J. D. (1993). Do social workers have a duty to warn? *Social Service Review*, 67, 101–126.

Kroll, B. (2004). Living with an elephant: Growing up with parental substance misuse. *Child and Family Social Work*, 9, 129–140.

Kuczynski, K., & Gibbs-Wahlberg, P. (2005). HIPAA the health care hippo: Despite the rhetoric, is privacy still an issue? *Social Work*, 50(3), 283–287.

Kuhse, H., & Singer, P. (1985). Ethics and the handicapped newborn infant. *Social Research*, 52, 505–542.

Kupperman, J. J. (1999). *Value ... and what follows*. New York, NY: Oxford University Press.

Kurri, K. (2005). Placement of responsibility and moral reasoning in couple therapy. *Journal of Family Therapy*, 27(4), 352–369.

Kurzman, P. A. (1995). Professional liability and malpractice (pp. 1921–1927). *Encyclopedia of social work* (19th ed.). Washington, DC: NASW Press.

Kutchins, H. (1991). The fiduciary relationship: The legal basis for social workers' responsibilities to clients. *Social Work*, 36, 106–113.

Kutchins, H., & Kirk, S. A. (1987). DSM-III and social work malpractice. *Social Work*, 32, 205–211.

Kutchins, H., & Kirk, S. A. (1988). The business of diagnosis: DSM-III and clinical social work. *Social Work*, 33, 215–220.

Kutchins, H., & Kirk, S. A. (1995). Review of diagnostic and statistical manual of mental disorders (4th ed.). *Social Work*, 40, 286–287.

Kutchins, H., & Kirk, S.A. (1997). *Making us crazy*. New York, NY: The Free Press.

Kwak, J., & Haley, W. E. (2005). Current research findings on end-of-life decision making among racially or ethnically diverse groups. *The Gerontologist*, 45(5), 634–641.

LaMendola, W., & Krysik, J. (2008). Design imperatives to enhance evidence-based interventions with persuasive technology: A case scenario in preventing child maltreatment. *Journal of Technology in Human Services*, 26(2–4), 397–422.

LaMendola, W., & Krysik, J. (2009). Design imperatives to enhance evidence-based interventions with persuasive technology: A case scenario in preventing child maltreatment. In: J. Finn & D. Schoech (Eds.), *Internet-delivered therapeutic interventions in human services: Methods, interventions, and evaluation*. New York, NY: Routledge.

Landau, R. (1996). Preparing for sudden death or organ donation: An ethical dilemma in social work. *International Social Work*, 39, 431–441.

Landau, R. (1998a). Secrecy, anonymity, and deception in donor insemination: A genetic, psychosocial, and ethical critique. *Social Work in Health Care*, 28(1), 75–89.

Landau, R. (1998b). The management of genetic origins: Secrecy and openness in donor assisted conception in Israel and elsewhere. *Human Reproduction*, 13(11), 3268–3273.

Landau, R. (1999). Professional socialization, ethical judgment and decision making orientation in social work. *Journal of Social Service Research*, 25(4), 57–75.

Landau, R., & Osmo, R. (2003). Professional and personal hierarchies of ethical principles. *International Journal of Social Welfare*, 12, 42–49.

Lange, J. M. (2006). Antiretroviral treatment and care of HIV. In E. J. Beck, N. Mays, et al. (Eds.), *The HIV pandemic: Local and global implications* (pp. 86–104). New York, NY: Oxford University Press.

Leach, M. M. & Sullivan, A. (2001) The intersection of race, class, and gender on diagnosis. In D. B. Pope-Davis, & H. L. K. Coleman, (Eds.), *The Intersection of Race, Class, and Gender in Multicultural Counseling* (pp. 353–383). Thousand Oaks, CA: Sage Publications, Inc.

Lens, V. (2000). Protecting the confidentiality of the therapeutic relationship: *Jaffee v. Redmond. Social Work*, 45(3), 273–276.

Lens, V. (2006). Work sanctions under welfare reform: Are they helping women achieve self-sufficiency? *Duke Journal of Gender Law and Social Policy*, 13(1), 255–280.

Levy, C. (1976a). Personal versus professional values: The practitioner's dilemma. *Clinical Social Work Journal*, 4, 110–120.

Levy, C. (1976b). The value base of social work. *Journal of Education in Social Work*, 9, 34–42.

Lewis, H. (1984). Ethical assessment. *Social Casework*, 65, 203–211.

Lewis, H. (1989). Ethics and the private non-profit human service organization. *Administration in Social Work*, 13(2), 1–14.

Lewis, N. A. (2005, July 6). Psychologists warned on role in detentions. *New York Times*, A14.

Lilienfeld, S. O., Fowler, K. A., Lohr, J. M., & Lynn, S. J. (2005). Pseudoscience, nonscience, and nonsense in clinical psychology: Dangers and remedies. In R. H. Wright & N. A. Cummings (Eds.), *Destructive trends in mental health: The well-intentioned path to harm* (pp. 187–218). New York, NY: Routledge.

Lipsyte, R. (2002, November 17). Johnson and Augusta mask bigger issues. *New York Times, Sports Sunday*, p. 5.

Lloyd, C., King, R., & Chenoweth, L. (2002). Social work, stress, and burnout: A review. *Journal of Mental Health*, II(3), 255–265.

Lo, B., Dornbrand, L., Wolf, L. E., & Groman, M. (2002). The Wendland case—Withdrawing life support from incompetent patients who are not terminally ill. *The New England Journal of Medicine*, 346, 1489–1493.

Loewenberg, F., & Dolgoff, R. (1988). *Ethical decisions for social work practice* (3rd ed.). Itasca, IL: F. E. Peacock Publishers, Inc.

Loewenberg, F. M., & Dolgoff, R. (1992). *Ethical decisions for social work practice* (4th ed.). Itasca, IL: F. E. Peacock Publishers, Inc.

Lorenz, K. (2006). Is your boss spying on you? Retrieved February 8, 2007, from http://edition.cnn.com/2006/US/Careers/03/24/cb.boss.spying/

Lott, B., & Bullock, H. E. (2001). Who are the poor? *Journal of Social Issues*, 57(2), 189–206.

Lovat, T., & Gray, M. (2008). Towards a proportionist social work ethics: A Habermasian perspective. *British Journal of Social Work*, 38 (6), 11–14.

Luftman, V. H., Veltkamp, L. J., Clark, J. J., Lannacone, S., & Snooks, H. (2005). Practice guidelines in child custody evaluations for licensed clinical social workers. *Clinical Social Work Journal*, 33, 327–357.

Lum, D. (2000). *Social work practice and people of color* (4th ed.). Belmont, CA: Brooks/Cole.

Lundahl, B. W., Nimer, J., & Parsons, B. (2006). Preventing child abuse. A meta-analysis of parent training programs. *Research on Social Work Practice*, 16(3), 251–262.

Lystad, M., Rice, M., & Kaplan, S. J. (1996). Family violence. In S. J. Kaplan (Ed.), *Domestic violence* (pp. 139–180). Washington, DC: American Psychiatric Press.

MacIntyre, A. (2001). Virtue ethics. In: L.C. Becker & C. B. Becker (Eds.), *Encyclopedia of Ethics*, Volume III (2nd ed.) (pp. 1757–1763). New York, NY: Routledge.

MacIver, R. (1922). The social significance of professional ethics. *Annals*, 101, 5–11.

Mackelprang, R. W., & Mackelprang, R. D. (2005). Historical and contemporary issues in end-of-life decisions: Implications for social work. *Social Work*, 50(4), 315–324.

MacMurray, J. (1961). *Persons in relation.* Atlantic Highlands, NJ: Humanities Press.

Maesen, W. A. (1991). Fraud in mental health practice: A risk management perspective. *Administration and Policy in Mental Health*, 18, 431–432.

Maher, V. F., & Ford, J. (2002). The heartbreak of parens patriae. *Jona's Healthcare, Law, Ethics, and Regulation*, 4, 18–22.

Mahony, R. (2006, March 22). Called by God to help. *New York Times*, Op. Ed., Section A, p. 25.

Maidment, J. (2006). The quiet remedy: A dialogue on reshaping professional relationships. *Families in Society: The Journal of Contemporary Social Services*, 87(1), 115–121.

Manetta, A. A., & Wells, J. G. (2001). Ethical issues in the social worker's role in physician-assisted suicide. *Health and Social Work*, 26(3), 160–166.

Manning, R. C. (1992). *Speaking from the heart: A feminist perspective on ethics.* Lanham, MD: Rowman & Littlefield Publishers.

Manning, S. S. (1997). The social worker as moral citizen: Ethics in action. *Social Work*, 42, 223–230.

Manning, S. S., & Gaul, C. E. (1997). The ethics of informed consent: A critical variable in the self-determination of health and mental health clients. *Social Work in Health Care*, 25(3), 103–117.

Manstead, A. S. R. (1996). Attitudes and behavior. In G. R. Semin & K. Fiedler (Eds.), *Applied social psychology*. Thousand Oaks, CA: Sage Publications.

Marcuse, P. (1976). Professional ethics and beyond: Values in planning. *Journal of the American Institute of Planners*, 42, 264–274.

Maritain, J. (1934). *Introduction to philosophy*. London, UK: Sheed & Ward.

Marson, S. (1993). Social work discussion list. Retrieved October 18, 1993. socwork@umab.bit-net

Marshall, T., & Solomon, P. (2004). Confidentiality intervention: Effects on provider-consumer-family collaboration. *Research on Social Work Practice*, 14(1), 3–13.

Martin, J. L. R., Barbanoj, M. J., Schlaepfer, T. E., Perez, V., Kulisevsky, J., & Gironell, A. (2002). Transcranial magnetic stimulation for treating depression (Cohrane review). In *The Cochrane Library*, 2, Oxford, U.K.: Update Software.

Marziali, E., Donahue, P., & Crossin, G. (2005). Caring for others: Internet health care support interventions for family caregivers of persons with dementia, stroke, or Parkinson's disease. *Families in Society*, 86(3), 375–383.

Maslow, A. H. (1962). *The farther reaches of human nature*. New York, NY: Penguin Books.

Maslow, A. H. (1969). Toward a humanistic biology. *American Psychologist*, 24, 724–735.

Mason, R. O. (1994). Morality and models. In W. A. Wallace (Ed.), *Ethics in modeling* (pp. 183–194). Tarrytown, NY: Pergamon.

Matorin, S., Rosenberg, B., Levitt, M., & Rosenbaum, S. (1987). Private practice in social work: Readiness and opportunity. *Social Casework*, 68(1), 31–37.

Mattison, D., Jayaratne, S., & Croxton (2002). Client or former client? Implications of ex-client definition on social work practice. *Social Work*, 47(1), 55–64.

Mayer, L. M. (2005). Professional boundaries in dual relationships: A social work dilemma. *Journal of Social Work Values and Ethics*, 2(2). Retrieved July 19, 2006, from www.socialworker.com/jswve/content/view/25/37/

Mayo Clinic. Transcranial magnetic stimulation: An experimental depression treatment. Retrieved April 24, 2007, from www.mayoclinic.com/health/transcranial-magneticstimulation/MH00115

McAuliffe, D. (2005). Putting ethics on the organizational agenda: The social work ethics audit on trial. *Australian Social Work*, 58(4), 357–369.

McBeath, B., & Meezan, W. (2008). Market-based disparities in foster care service provision. *Research on Social Work Practice*, 18(1), 27–41.

McBeath, G., & Webb, S. A. (2002). Virtue ethics and social work: Being lucky, realistic, and

not doing one's duty. *British Journal of Social Work*, 32(8), 1015–1036.

McCann, C. W. (1977). The codes of ethics of the NASW: An inquiry into its problems and perspectives. In B. E. Olvett (Ed.), *Values in Social Work Education* (pp. 10–19). Salt Lake City, UT: University of Utah Graduate School of Social Work.

McCarty, D., & Clancy, C. (2002). Telehealth: Implications for social work practice. *Social Work*, 47(2), 153–161.

McGowen, B. G. (1995). Values and ethics. In C. H. Meyer & M. A. Mattaini (Eds.), *The foundations of social work practice* (pp. 28–41). Washington, DC: NASW Press.

McMahon, A., & Allen-Meares, P. (1992). Is social work racist? A content analysis of recent literature. *Social Work*, 37, 533–539.

McNutt, J. G., & Menon, G. M. (2008). The rise of cyberactivism: Implications for the future of advocacy in the human services. *The Journal of Contemporary Social Services*, 89(1), 33–38.

Melton, G. B. (1988). Ethical and legal issues in ATOS-related practice. *American Psychologist*, 43, 941–947.

Meyer, C. H. (1985). Different voices: Comparable worth. *Social Work*, 30, 99.

Meyers, C. J. (1997). Expanding *Tarasoff*: Protecting patients and the public by keeping subsequent caregivers informed. *The Journal of Psychiatry & Law*, Fall, 365–375.

Mickelson, J. S. (1995). Advocacy. In R. L. Edwards (Ed.), *Encyclopedia of social work*. (Vol. 1, 19th ed., pp. 95–100). Washington, DC: National Association of Social Workers.

Miller, D. J., & Thelen, M. H. (1986). Knowledge and beliefs about confidentiality in psychotherapy. *Professional Psychology: Research and Practice*, 17, 15–19.

Miller, H. (1968). Value dilemmas in social casework. *Social Casework*, 13, 27–33.

Miller, L. L., Harvath, T. A., Ganzini, L., Goy, E. R., Delorit, M. A., & Jackson, A. (2004). Attitudes and experiences of Oregon hospice nurses and social workers regarding assisted suicide. *Palliative Medicine*, 18(8), 685–691.

Millstein, K. (2000). Confidentiality in direct social work practice: Inevitable challenges and ethical dilemmas. *Families in Society*, 81(3), 270–282.

Milner, J. L., & Campbell, J. C. (2007). Prediction issues for practitioners. In: J. C. Campbell (Ed.), *Assessing dangerousness: Violence by batterers and child abusers* (2nd ed.) (pp. 25–43). New York, NY: Springer Publishing Company.

Mishna, F., Antle, B. J., & Regehr, C. (2002). Social work with clients contemplating suicide: Complexity and ambiguity in the clinical, ethical, and legal considerations. *Clinical Social Work Journal*, 30(3), 265–280.

Mitchell, C. G. (1999). Treating anxiety in a managed care setting: A controlled comparison of medication alone versus medication plus cognitive-behavioral group therapy. *Research on Social Work Practice*, 9, 188–200.

Mittendorf, S. H., & Schroeder, J. (2004). Boundaries in social work: The ethical dilemma of worker-client sexual relationships. *Journal of Social Work Values and Ethics*, 1(1). Retrieved July 19, 2006, from socialworker.com/jswve/content/view/11/30.

Moberg, D. O. (2005). Research in spirituality, religion, and aging. *Journal of Gerontological Social Work*, 45(1/2), 11–40.

Mondros, J. B. (2009). Principle and practice: Guidelines for social action. In: A. R. Roberts (Ed.), *Social workers' desk reference* (2nd ed.) (pp. 901–906). New York, NY: Oxford University Press.

Moody, H. R. (2004). Hospital discharge planning: Carrying out orders? *Journal of Gerontological Social Work*, 43(1), 107–118.

Moran, J. R. (1989). Social work education and students' humanistic attitudes. *Journal of Education for Social Work*, 25(1), 13–19.

Moreno, J. D., Caplan, A. L., & Wolpe, P. R. (1998). Informed consent. *Encyclopedia of Applied Ethics* (Vol. 2). New York, NY: Academic Press, 687–697.

Morin, D., Tourigny, A., Pelletier, D., Robichaud, L., Mathieu, L., Vezina, A., Bonin, L., & Buteau, M. (2005). Seniors' views on the use of electronic health records. *Informatics in Primary Care*, 13, 125–134.

Morris, E. K., Laney, C., Bernstein, D. M., & Loftus, E. F. (2006). Susceptibility to memory distortion: How do we decide it has occurred? *American Journal of Psychology*, 119(2), 255–274.

Moser, C. (1980). Letter. *NASW News*, 25(9), 6.

Moser, D. J., Schultz, S. K., Arndt, S., Benjamin, M. L., Fleming, F. W., Brems, C. S., Paulsen, J. S., Appelbaum, P. S., & Andreasen, N. C. (2002). Capacity to provide informed consent for participation in schizophrenia and HIV research. *American Journal of Psychiatry*, 159, 1201–1207.

Mullen, E. J., & Streiner, D. L. (2004). The evidence for and against evidence based practice. *Brief Treatment and Crisis Intervention*, 4(2), 111–121.

Munson, C. E. (2005). Personal communication, October 14, 2005.

Murdock, V. (2005). Guided by ethics: Religion and spirituality. *Journal of Gerontological Social Work*, 45(1/2), 131–154.

Murphy, C. M., & Ting, L. A. (2010). Interventions for perpetrators of intimate partner violence: A review of efficacy research and recent trends. *Partner Abuse*, 1(1), 26–44.

Murphy, M. J., DeBernardo, C., & Shoemaker, E. (1998). Impact of managed care on independent practice and professional ethics: A survey of independent practitioners. *Professional Psychology: Research and Practice*, 29, 43–51.

Murphy, S. B., & Ouimet, L. V. (2008). Intimate partner violence: A call for social work action. *Health & Social Work*, 33(4), 309–314.

Myers, L. L., & Thyer, B. A. (1997). Should social work clients have the right to effective treatment? *Social Work*, 42, 288–298.

National Association of Scholars (2006). National association of scholars urges U.S. Dept. of Health and Human Services to drop CSWE requirement for social workers. Retrieved January 30, 2007, from www.nas.org/print/pressreleases/hqnas/releas_25oct06.htm.

National Association of Social Workers Ad Hoc Committee on Advocacy. (1969). The social worker advocate: Champion of social victims. *Social Work*, 14(2), 16–23.

National Association of Social Workers (n.d.). Social workers and e-therapy. Retrieved from http://www.socialworkers.org/ldf/legal_issue/200704.asp?back=yes.

National Association of Social Workers. (1987). *AIDS: A social work response*. Washington, DC: National Association of Social Workers.

National Association of Social Workers. (1990a). People in the news. *NASW News*, 35(5), 17.

National Association of Social Workers. (1990b). *Standards for social work personnel practices*. Washington, DC: National Association of Social Workers.

National Association of Social Workers. (1992). *NASW standards for social work case management*. Retrieved January 22, 2007, from www.socialworkers.org/practice/standards/sw_case_mgmt.asp.

National Association of Social Workers. (1993). A study of trends in adjudication of complaints concerning violations of NASW's Code of ethics—Overview of results. Washington, DC: National Association of Social Workers.

National Association of Social Workers. (1994). Client self-determination in end-of-life decisions. In *Social work speaks* (pp. 58–61). Washington, DC: National Association of Social Workers.

National Association of Social Workers. (1995a). Lawsuits: No more immunity. *NASW News*, 40(1), 7.

National Association of Social Workers. (1995b). A study cites most reported ethics breaches. *NASW News*, 40(4), 4.

National Association of Social Workers. (1999a, October). Assembly lowers BSW's dues, alters ethics code, eyes itself. *NASW News*, 44(9), 1, 10.

National Association of Social Workers. (1999b). *Code of Ethics*. Washington, DC: National Association of Social Workers.

National Association of Social Workers. (2000). Agency restricts Internet counseling. *NASW News*, 45(8), 12.

National Association of Social Workers. (2001). *NASW standards for cultural competence in social work practice*. Washington, DC: National Association of Social Workers.

National Association of Social Workers. (2001a). Caution urged before web counseling. *NASW News*, 46(January), 5.

National Association of Social Workers. (2002). HIPAA alert! Retrieved October 1, 2002, from www.socialworkers.org/practice/hipaa/default.asp.

National Association of Social Workers. (2003). Practice Research Network. Survey 2002. Private practice. Retrieved February 2007.

National Association of Social Workers. (2003). NASW Standards for Social Work Practice in Palliative and End of Life Care. Retrieved from http://www.socialworkers.org/practice/bereavement/standards/default.asp.

National Association of Social Workers. (2005). *NASW procedures for professional review*. Rev. (4th ed.). Washington, DC: National Association of Social Workers.

National Association of Social Workers (2006a). Executive Director's Office and NASW Insurance Trust. Personal communication. Types of claims.

National Association of Social Workers (2006b). Social work speaks abstracts, professional impairment. Retrieved August 7, 2006, from www.socialworkers.org/resources/abstracts/abstracts/profimpairment.asp.

National Association of Social Workers (2009). Personal communication by e-mail from NASW staff member Lucinda Branaman, December 21, 2009 confirming current malpractice statistics are representative of the 40 year time period for which data have been collected.

National Association of Social Workers (2010). NASW Procedures for Professional Review Revisions (4th edition, 2005, amended December 2009). http://www.naswdc.org/nasw/ethics/procedures.asp Retrieved October 4, 2010.

National Association of Social Workers & Association of Social Work Boards. (2005). Standards for technology and social work practice. Retrieved August 9, 2006, from www.aswb.org/Technology SWPractice.pdf.

National Research Council. (1993). *Child abuse and neglect*. Washington, DC: National Academy Press.

Negretti, M. A., & Weiling, E. (2001). The use of communication technology in private practice: Ethical implications and boundary dilemmas in therapy. *Contemporary Family Therapy*, 23(3), 275–293.

Netting, F. E. (1987). Ethical issues in volunteer management and accountability. *Social Work*, 32, 250–252.

Netting, F. E., Kettner, P. M., & McMurtry, S. L. (1998). *Social work macro practice* (2nd ed.). White Plains, NY: Longman Publishing Group.

Nissen, L.S. (2006). Effective adolescent substance abuse treatment in juvenile justice settings: Practice and policy recommendations. *Child & Adolescent Social Work Journal*, 43(1), 298–315.

North, R. L., & Rothenberg, K. (1993). Partner notification and the threat of domestic violence against women with HIV infection. *New England Journal of Medicine*, 329, 1194–1196.

Northen, H. (1998). Ethical dilemmas in social work with groups. *Social Work with Groups*, 21(1/2), 5–17.

Nugent, W. R. (2004). The role of prevalence rates, sensitivity, and specificity in assessment accuracy: Rolling the dice in social work process. *Journal of Social Service Research*, 31(2), 51–75.

Nyberg, D. (1996). Deception and moral decency. In R. A. French, T. E. Vehling Jr., & H. K. Wettstein (Eds.), *Midwest studies in philosophy Vol. XX, Moral concepts*. Notre Dame, IN: University of Notre Dame Press.

Odell, M., & Stewart, S. P. (1993). Ethical issues associated with client values conversion and therapist value agendas in family therapy. *Family Relations*, 42(2), 128–133.

O'Neill, J. V. (2001). Webcams may transform online therapy. *NASW News*, 46(7), 4.

O'Neill, J. V. (2002). Internet-based therapy draws criticism. *NASW News*, 47(4), 12.

Oppenheim, S., Hay, J. B., Frederich, M. E., & von Gunten, C. F. (2002). Palliative care in human immunodeficiency virus: Acquired immunodeficiency syndrome. In A. M. Berger, R. K. Portenoy, & D. E. Weissman (Eds.), *Principles and practice of palliative care and supportive oncology* (pp. 1071–1085). New York, NY: Lippincott Williams and Wilkins.

Oregon Department of Human Services (2010). Death with Dignity Act annual reports. Year 12 – 2009 Summary (pdf) – Released March 2010. Retrieved from http://www.oregon.gov/DHS/ph/pas/ar-index.shtml

Oregon Health Services Commission (2006). Oregon health plan. Retrieved November 8, 2006, from http://egov.oregon.gov/DAS/OHPPR/HSC/

Orovwuje, P. R. (2001). The business model and social work: A conundrum for social work practice. *Social Work in Health Care*, 34(1/2), 59–70.

Pace, P. R. (2009). Latest HIPAA standards include new breach notification rule. NASW News, November, 8.

Padilla, Y. C. (1997). Immigrant policy: Issues for social work practice. *Social Work*, 42, 595–606.

Palmer, N., & Kaufman, M. (2003). The ethics of informed consent: Implications for multicultural practice. *Journal of Ethnic & Cultural Diversity in Social Work*, 12(1), 1–26.

Panchanadeswaran, S., & Koverola, C. (2003). The voices of battered women in India. *Violence against Women*, 11, 736–758.

Parker, L. (2003). A social justice model for clinical social work. *Affilia*, 18(3), 272–288.

Parker-Oliver, D., & Demiris, G. (2006). Social work informatics: A new specialty. *Social Work*, 51, 127–134.

Parton, N. (2003). Rethinking professional practice: The contributions of social constructionism and the feminist "ethics of care". *British Journal of Social Work*, 33, 1–16.

Pear, R. (2006, June 28). New rules force states to limit welfare rolls. *New York Times*, pp. 1, 17.

Peckover, S. (2002). Supporting and policing mothers: An analysis of the disciplinary practices of health visiting. *Journal of Advanced Nursing*, 38, 369–377.

Pellegrino, E. D. (1991). Trust and distrust in professional ethics. In E. D. Pellegrino, R. M. Veatch, & J. P. Langan (Eds.), *Ethics, trust, and the professions* (pp. 69–85). Washington, DC: Georgetown University Press.

Pemberton, J. D. (1965). Is there a moral right to violate the law? *Social Welfare Forum*, 1965 (pp. 183–196). New York, NY: Columbia University Press.

Perlman, H. H. (1965). Self-determination: Reality or illusion? *Social Service Review*, 39, 410–422.

Perry, C., & Kuruk, J. W. (1993). Psychotherapists' sexual relationships with their patients. *Annals of Health Law*, 2, 35–54.

Pike, C. K. (1996). Development and initial validation of the social work values inventory. *Research in Social Work Practice*, 6, 337–352.

Planned Parenthood of Southeastern Pa. v. Casey, 505 U.S. 833 (1992).

Pollack, D. (2004). Getting informed consent: More than just a signature. *Policy & Practice of Public Services*, 62(2), 28.

Pollack, D., & Marsh, J. (2004). Social work misconduct may lead to liability. *Social Work*, 49(4), 609–612.

Pope, K. S. (2000). Therapists' sexual feelings and behaviors: Research, trends, and quandaries. In L. T. Szuchman & F. Muscarella (Eds.), *Psychological perspectives on human sexuality* (pp. 603–658). New York, NY: John Wiley & Sons.

Pope, K. S., & Bouthoutsos, J. C. (1986). *Sexual intimacy between therapist and patient*. New York, NY: Praeger Publishers.

Pope, K. S., & Feldman-Summers, S. (1992). National survey of psychologists' sexual and physical abuse history and their evaluation of training and competence in these areas. *Professional Psychology: Research and Practice*, 23(1), 353–361.

Pope, K. S., Levenson, H., & Schover, L. R. (1979). Sexual intimacy in psychology training: Results and implications from a national survey. *American Psychologist*, 34(8), 682–689.

Pope, K. S., Tabachnick, B. G., & Keith-Spiegel, P. (1987). Ethics of practice: The beliefs and behaviors of psychologists and therapists. *American Psychologist*, 42, 993–1006.

Pope, K. S., & Vasquez, M. J. T. (1998). *Ethics in psychotherapy and counseling* (2nd ed.). San Francisco, CA: Jossey-Bass.

Powderly, K. (2001). Ethical and legal issues in perinatal HIV. *Clinical Obstetrics and Gynecology*, 44, 300–311.

Powell, W. E. (1994). The relationship between feelings of alienation and burnout in social work. *Families in Society*, 75, 229–235.

Pumphrey, M. W. (1959). *The teaching of values and ethics in social work education*. New York, NY: CSWE.

Rabkin, J. G., & Struening, E. L. (1976). *Ethnicity, social class and mental illness*. New York, NY: Institute on Pluralism & Group Identity.

Rawls, J. (1971). *A theory of justice*. Cambridge, MA: Harvard University Press.

Reamer, F. G. (1983). Ethical dilemmas in social work practice. *Social Work*, 28, 31–35.

Reamer, F. G. (1993). *The philosophical foundations of social work*. New York, NY: Columbia University Press.

Reamer, F. G. (1998). The evolution of social work ethics. *Social Work*, 43, 488–500.

Reamer, F. G. (1999). *Social work values and ethics* (2nd ed.). New York, NY: Columbia University Press.

Reamer, F. G. (2001). *The social work ethics audit: A risk management tool*. Washington, DC: NASW Press.

Reamer, F. G. (2003). Boundary issues in social work: Managing dual relationships. *Social Work*, 48(1), 121–133.

Reamer, F. G. (2004). Ethical decisions and risk management. In M. Austin & K. M. Hopkins (Eds.), *Supervision as collaboration in the human services: Building a learning culture* (pp. 97–109). Thousand Oaks, CA: Sage Publications.

Reamer, F. G. (2005). Documentation in social work: Evolving ethical and risk-management standards. *Social Work*, 50(4), 325–334.

Reamer, F. G. (2005). Update on confidentiality issues in practice with children: Ethics risk management. *Children & Schools*, 27, 117–120.

Reamer, F. G. (2009). Risk management in social work. In: A. R. Roberts (Ed.), *Social worker's desk reference* (2nd ed.) (p. 122). New York, NY: Oxford University Press.

Reamer, F. G., & Shardlow, S. M. (2009). Ethical codes of practice in the US and UK: One profession. Two standards. *Journal of Social Work Values and Ethics*, 26(2), 5–23.

Regehr, C. & Antle, B. (1997). Coercive influences: Informed consent in court-mandated social work. *Social Work*, 42, 300–306.

Reid, W. J. (1997). Research on task-centered practice. *Social Work Research*, 21, 132–137.

Reid, W. J., Kenaley, B. D., & Colvin, J. (2004). Do some interventions work better than others? A review of comparative social work experiments. *Social Work Research*, 20(2), 71–81.

Reisch, M., & Lowe, J. I. (2000). "Of means and ends" revisited: Teaching ethical community organizing in an unethical society. *Journal of Community Practice*, 7(1), 19–38.

Reiser, S. J., Burstajn, H. J., Applebaum, P. S., & Gutheil, T. G. (1987). *Divided staffs, divided selves: A case approach to mental health ethics*. England: Cambridge University Press.

Reybould, C. & Adler, G. (2006). Applying NASW standards to end of life care for a culturally diverse aging population. *Journal of Social Work Values and Ethics*, 3(2). Retrieved October 19, 2006, from http://www.socialworker.com/jswve/content/view/38/46/.

Reynolds (2001). Hindu ethics. In: L. C. Becker & C. B. Becker (Eds.), *Encyclopedia of Ethics*, Volume II (2nd ed.) (pp. 676–683). New York, NY: Routledge.

Riccucci, N., Meyers, M. K., et al. (2004) Implementation of welfare reform policy: The role of public managers in front-line practices. *Public Administration Review*, 64(4), 438–448.

Rice, D. S. (1994). Professional values and moral development: The social work student. Unpublished dissertation. University of South Carolina.

Rizzo, V. M., & Rowe, J. M. (2006). Studies of the cost-effectiveness of social work services in aging: A review of the literature. *Research on Social Work Practice*, 16(1), 67–73.

Roberts, C. S. (1989). Conflicting professional values in social work and medicine. *Health and Social Work*, 14, 211–218.

Roberts, S. (2006, October 15). It's official: To be married means to be outnumbered. *New York Times*, p. 14.

Rock, B. (2001). Social work under managed care: Will we survive, or can we prevail? In R. Perez-Koenig & B. Rock (Eds.), *Social work in the era of devolution: Toward a just practice* (pp. 69–85). New York, NY: Fordham University Press.

Rodenborg, N. A. (2004). Services to African American children in poverty: Institutional discrimination in child welfare. *Journal of Poverty*, 8(3), 109–130.

Rooney, R. H. (1992). *Strategies for work with involuntary clients*. New York, NY: Columbia University Press.

Rosa, L., Rosa, E., Samer, L., & Barrett, S. (1998). A close look at therapeutic touch. *Journal of the American Medical Association*, 279, 1005–1010.

Roseborough, D. J. (2006). Psychodynamic psychotherapy: An effectiveness study. *Research on Social Work Practice*, 16(2), 166–175.

Rosen, A., & Proctor, E. K. (Eds.) (2003). *Developing practice guidelines for social work intervention: Issues, methods, and research agenda*. New York, NY: Columbia University Press.

Rosenthal, R. N. (2004). Overview of evidence-based practice. In A. R. Roberts & K. Yeager (Eds.), *Evidence-based practice manual: Research and outcome measures in health and human services*. New York, NY: Oxford University Press.

Ross, J. W. (1992). Editorial: Are social work ethics compromised? *Health and Social Work*, 17, 163–164.

Rothman, J. (1989). Client self-determination: Untangling the knot. *Social Service Review*, 63, 598–612.

Rothman, J., Smith, W., Nakashima, J., Paterson, M. A., & Mustin, J. (1996). Client self-determination and professional intervention: Striking a balance. *Social Work*, 41, 396–405.

Rothstein, E. (2002, July 13). Moral relativity is a hot topic? True. Absolutely. *New York Times*, pp. A13, A15.

Roy v. Hartogs. 366 N. YS. 2d297 (1975).

Rubin, A., Cardenas, J., Warren, K., Pike, C. K., & Wambach, K. (1998). Outdated practitioner views about family culpability and severe mental disorders. *Social Work*, 43(5), 412–422.

Rubin, A., & Parrish, D. (2007). Views of evidence-based practice among faculty in master of social work programs: A national survey. *Research on Social Work Practice*, 17(1), 110–122.

Rust v. Sullivan, 500 U.S. Supreme Court, 173 (1991).

Ryder, R., & Hepworth, J. (1990). AAMFT ethical code: "Dual relationships." *Journal of Marital and Family Therapy*, 16(2), 127–132.

Ryan, S. D., Pearlmutter, S., & Groza, V. (2004). Coming out of the closet: Opening agencies to gay and lesbian adoptive parents. *Social Work*, 49(1), 85–95.

Sackett, D. L., Straus, S. E., Richardson, W. S., Rosenberg, W., & Haynes, R. B. (2000). *Evidence-based medicine: How to practice and teach EBP* (2nd ed.). New York, NY: Churchill-Livingstone.

Saenz v. Roe, U.S. Supreme Court, 1518, 1999.

Saha, S., Coffman, D. D., Smits, A. K. (2010). Giving teeth to comparative-effectiveness research – The Oregon experience. *New England Journal of Medicine*, e18, 1–3. Retrieved from http://healthcarereform.nejm.org/?p=2936.

Sammons, C. C. (1978). Ethical issues in genetic intervention. *Social Work*, 23, 237–242.

Santhiveeran, J. (2004). E-therapy: Scope, concerns, ethical standards, and feasibility. *Journal of Family Social Work*, 8(3), 37–54.

Santhiveeran, J. (2009). Compliance of social work e-therapy Websites to the NASW Code of Ethics, *Social Work in Health Care*, 48(1), 1–13.

Sasson, S. (2000). Beneficence versus respect for autonomy: An ethical dilemma in social work practice. *Journal of Gerontological Social Work*, 33(1), 5–16.

Schamess, G. (1996). Who profits and who benefits from managed mental health care? *Smith College Studies in Social Work*, 60, 209–220.

Schild, S., & Black, R. B. (1984). *Social work and genetic counseling: A guide to practice*. Binghamton, NY: Haworth Press.

Schlossberger, E., & Hecker, L. (1996). HIV and family therapists' duty to warn: A legal and ethical analysis. *Journal of Marital and Family Therapy*, 22, 27–40.

Schoener, G. R. (1995). Assessment of professionals who have engaged in boundary violations. *Psychiatric Annals*, 25(2), 95–99.

Schopler, J. H., Abell, M. D., & Galinsky, M. J. (1998). Technology-based groups: A review and conceptual framework for practice. *Social Work*, 43, 254–267.

Scopelliti, J., Judd, F., Grigg, M., Hodgins, G., Fraser, C., Hulbert, C., Endacott, R., & Wood, A. (2004). Dual relationships in mental health practice: issues for clinicians in rural settings. *Australian and New Zealand Journal of Psychiatry*, 38, 953–959.

Sedlak, A. J., & Broadhurst, D. D. (1996). *Third national incidence study of child abuse and neglect: Final report*. Washington, DC: U.S. Department of Health and Human Services.

Selznick, P. (1961). Sociology and natural law. *Natural Law Forum*, 6, 84–108.

Sharma, S., & Patenaude, A. (2003). HIV/AIDS. Retrieved January 24, 2003, from www.emedicine.com/aaem/topic252.htm.

Sharwell, G. R. (1974). Can values be taught? *Journal of Education for Social Work*, 10, 99–105.

Shavit, N., & Bucky, S. (2004). Sexual contact between psychologists and their former therapy patients: Psychoanalytic perspectives and professional implications. *American Journal of Psychoanalysis*, 64(3), 229–248.

Shaw, G. B. (1932). *The doctor's dilemma*. London: Constable.

Shea, S. C. (1999). *The practical art of suicide assessment*. New York, NY: John Wiley & Sons.

Sherer, R. A. (2004). The debate over physician-assisted suicide continues. *Psychiatric Times*, 21(1). Retrieved March 21, 2007, from www.psychiatrictimes.com.

Sheridan, D., J., Glass, N., Limandri, B. J., & Poulos, C. A. (2007). Prediction of interpersonal violence: An introduction. In: J. C. Campbell (Ed.), *Assessing dangerousness: Violence by batterers and child abusers* (2nd ed.) (pp. 1–23). New York, NY: Springer Publishing.

Sheridan, M. (2009). Ethical issues in the use of spiritually based interventions in social work practice: What are we doing and why. *Journal of Religion and Spirituality and Social Work Values: Social Thought*, 28 (1/2), 99–126.

Sherwood, D. A. (1997). The relationship between beliefs and values in social work practice: Worldviews make a difference. *Social Work and Christianity*, 24(2), 115–135.

Shillington, A. M., Dotson, W. L., & Faulkner, A. O. (1994). Should only African-American community organizers work in African-American neighborhoods? In M. J. Austin & J. I. Lowe (Eds.), *Controversial issues in communities and organizations* (pp. 128–111). Boston, MA: Allyn & Bacon.

Sidell, N. L. (2007). An exploration of nonsexual dual relationships in rural public child welfare settings. *Journal of Public Child Welfare*, 1(4), 91–104.

Siebert, D. C. (2003). An issue for social workers and the profession. *Health & Social Work*, 28(2), 89–97.

Siebert, D. C. (2004). Depression in North Carolina social workers: Implications for practice and research. *Social Work Research*, 28(1), 30–40.

Siebert, D. C. (2005). Help seeking for AOD misuse among social workers: Patterns, barriers, and implications. *Social Work*, 50(1), 65–75.

Silvestre, A. J., Quinn, S. J., & Rinaldo, C. R. (2010). A 22-year old community advisory board: Health research as an opportunity for social change. *Journal of Community Practice*, 18, 58–75.

Simmons, C. A., & Rycraft, J. R. (2010). Ethical challenges of military social workers serving in a combat zone. *Social Work*, 55(1), 9–18.

Simon, R. I., & Gutheil, T. G. (1997). Ethical and clinical risk management principles in recovered memory cases: Maintaining therapist neutrality. In P. S. Appelbaum,

L. A. Uyehara, & M. R. Elin (Eds.), *Trauma and memory* (pp. 477–495). New York, NY: Oxford University Press.

Siporin, M. (1982). Moral philosophy in social work today. *Social Service Review, 56,* 516–538.

Siporin, M. (1983). Morality and immorality in working with clients. *Social Thought, 9*(Fall), 10–28.

Siporin, M. (1985a). Current social work perspectives for clinical practice. *Clinical Social Work Journal, 13,* 198–217.

Siporin, M. (1985b). Deviance, morality, and social work therapy. *Social Thought, 11*(4), 11–24.

Skolnik, L., & Attinson, L. (1978). Confidentiality in group work practice. *Social Work with Groups, 1*(2), 165–174.

Slaughter, S., Cole, D., Jennings, E., & Reimer, M. A. (2007). Consent and assent to participate in research from people with dementia. *Nursing Ethics, 14*(1), 27–40.

Smith, C. (2004). Trust and confidence: Making the moral case for social work. *Social Work & Social Sciences Review, 11*(3), 5–15.

Smith, C. J., & Devore, W. (2004). African American children in the child welfare and kinship system: From exclusion to over-inclusion. *Children and Youth Services Review, 26*(5), 427–446.

Smith, R. A. (1998). AIDS-related complex (ARC). In: R. A. Smith (Ed.), *Encyclopedia of AIDS: A social, political, cultural, and scientific record of the HIV epidemic.* Chicago, IL: Fitzroy Dearborn Publishers.

Smith, S. (2006). Mandatory reporting of child abuse and neglect. Retrieved September 26, 2006, from www.smith-lawfirm.com/mandatory_reporting.htm.

Social Work (1991) 36(2), 106–144. This issue contains a series of articles on the theme "Ethics and Professional Relationships."

Soderfeldt, M., Soderfeldt, B., & Warg, L. E. (1995). Burnout in social work. *Social Work, 40,* 638–646.

Sokolowski, R. (1991). The fiduciary relationship and the nature of professions. In E. D. Pellegrino, R. M. Veatch, & J. P. Langan (Eds.), *Ethics, trust, and the professions* (pp. 23–39). Washington, DC: Georgetown University Press.

Solomon, A. (1992). Clinical diagnosis among diverse populations: A multicultural perspective. *Families in Society, 73*(6), 371–377.

Soss, J., Schram, S. F., et al. (2004). Welfare policy choices in the states: Does the hard line follow the color line? *Focus, 23*(1), University of Wisconsin–Madison, Institute for Research on Poverty, 9–15.

Soyer, D. (1963). The right to fail. *Social Work, 8*(3) (July), 72–78.

Spelman, E. V. (2004). The household as repair shop. In C. Calhoun (Ed.), *Setting the moral compass: Essays by women philosophers.* New York, NY: Oxford University Press.

Spero, M. H. (1990). Identification between the religious patient and therapist in social work and psychoanalytic psychotherapy. *Journal of Social Work and Policy in Israel, 3,* 83–98.

Sprang, G., Clark, J. J., & Whitt-Woosley, A. (2007). Compassion fatigue, compassion satisfaction, and burnout: Factors impacting a professional's quality of life. *Journal of Loss and Trauma, 12,* 259–280.

State of California, Department of Consumer Affairs (2004). Professional therapy never includes sex. Retrieved June 22, 2006, from www.psych-board.ca.gov/pubs/psychotherapy.pdf.

Steinberg, K. L., Levine, M., & Doueck, H. (1997). Effects of legally mandated child-abuse reports on the therapeutic relationships: A survey of psychotherapists. *American Journal of Orthopsychiatry, 67,* 112–122.

Steuerle, G. (2010). The U.S. is broke: Here's why. *USA Today,* Opinion, January 27, 2010. Retrieved March 16, 2010. http://blogs.usatoday.com/oped/2020/01/column-the-us-is-broke-heres-why-.html.

Stevens, J. W. (1998). A question of values in social work practice: Working with the strengths of black adolescent females. *Families in Society, 79,* 288–296.

Stewart, C. (2009). The inevitable conflict between religious and social work values. *Journal of Religion and Spirituality and Social Work Values: Social Thought, 28*(1/2), 35–47.

Stoesen, L. (2002). Recovering social workers offer support. *NASW News,* www.socialworkers.org/pubs/news/2002/07/recovering.asp?back=yes.

Stout, C. E., & Grand, L. C. (2005). *Getting started in private practice.* Hoboken, NJ: John Wiley & Sons.

Strean, H. S. (1997). Comment on James C. Raines, Self-disclosure in clinical social work, *Clinical Social Work Journal, 25,* 365–366.

Strom, K. (1992). Reimbursement demands and treatment decisions: A growing dilemma for social workers. *Social Work, 37,* 398–403.

Strom, K. (1994). Social workers in private practice: An update. *Clinical Social Work Journal, 22,* 73–89.

Strom-Gottfried, K. (1998a). Informed consent meets managed care. *Health and Social Work, 23,* 25–33.

Strom-Gottfried, K. (1998b). Is "ethical managed care" an oxymoron? *Families in Society: The Journal of Contemporary Human Services, 79,* 297–307.

Strom-Gottfried, K. (1999). When colleague accuses colleague: Adjudicating personnel matters through the filing of ethics complaints. *Administration in Social Work*, 23(2), 1–16.

Strom-Gottfried, K. (2000). Ensuring ethical practice: An examination of NASW code violations, 1986–97. *Social Work*, 45(3), 251–261.

Strom-Gottfried, K. (2003). Understanding adjudication: Origins, targets, and outcomes of ethics complaints. *Social Work*, 48(1), 85–94.

Strom-Gottfried, K., & Mowbray, N. D. (2006). Who heals the healer? Facilitating the social worker's grief. *Families in Society*, 87(1), 9–15.

Strozier, A. L., Kmzek, C., & Sale, K. (2003). Touch: Its use in psychotherapy. *Journal of Social Work Practice*, 17(1), 49–62.

Strozier, M., Brown, R., Fennell, M., Hardee, J., & Vogel, R. et al. (2005). Experiences of mandated reporting among family therapists. *Contemporary Family Therapy*, 27(2), 175–189.

Strug, D. L., Grube, B. A., & Beckerman, N. (2002). Challenges and changing roles in HIV–AIDS social work: Implications for training and education. *Social Work in Health Care*, 35(4), 1–19.

Sunley, R. (1997). Advocacy in the new world of managed care. *Families in Society*, 78, 84–94.

Sutherland, P. K. (2002). Sexual abuse by therapists, physicians, attorneys, and other professionals. *Worldwide Legal Information Association*. Retrieved July 17, 2002, from www.wwlia.org.

Swenson, C. R. (2001). Clinical social work's contribution to a social justice perspective. In J. Rothma, J. L. Ehrlich, & J. E. Tropman (Eds.), *Strategies of Community Intervention* (6th ed.) (pp. 217–229). Itasca, IL: F. E. Peacock Publishers.

Szasz, T. S. (1994). *Cruel compassion: Psychiatric control of society's unwanted.* New York, NY: John Wiley & Sons.

Tarasoff v. Regents of the University of California. S. Ct. of CA (1976).

Taylor, L., & Adelman, H. S. (1989). Reframing the confidentiality dilemma to work in children's best interest. *Professional Psychology: Research and Practice*, 20, 79–83.

Taylor, M. F. (2006). Is self-determination still important? What experienced mental health social workers are saying. *Journal of Social Work Values and Ethics*, 3(1), 1–12. Retrieved October 12, 2006, from www.socialworker.com/jswve/content/view/29/44/.

Taylor-Brown, S., & Garcia, A. (1995). Social workers and HIV-affected families: Is the profession prepared? *Social Work*, 40, 14–15.

Tessitore, A. (1996). *Reading Aristotle's Ethics* (pp. 25–26). Albany, NY: State University of New York.

Thyer, B. A. (2004). What is evidence-based practice? *Brief Treatment and Crisis Intervention*, 4(2), 167–176.

Thyer, B. A., & Myers, L. L. (2009). Religious discrimination in social work academic programs: Whither social justice? *Journal of Religion and Spirituality and Social Work Values: Social Thought*, 28 (1/2), 144–160.

Timms, N. (1983). *Social work values: An enquiry.* London, UK: Routledge & Kegan Paul.

Tong, R. (1998). Feminist ethics. In *Encyclopedia of applied ethics.* (Vol. 2, pp. 261–268). New York, NY: Academic Press.

Tong, R. (2006). Feminist ethics. *Stanford encyclopedia of philosophy.* Retrieved September 5, 2006, from http://plato.stanford.edu/entries/feminism-ethics.

Toporek, R. L., & Liu, W. M. (2002). Advocacy in counseling: Addressing race, class, and gender oppression. In D. B. Pope-Davis & H. L. K. Coleman (Eds.), *The intersection of race, class, and gender in multicultural counseling* (pp. 385–413). Thousand Oaks, CA: Sage Publications.

Torczyner, J. (1991). Discretion, judgment, and informed consent: Ethical and practice issues in social action. *Social Work*, 36, 122–128.

Tower, K. D. (1994). Consumer-centered social work practice: Restoring client self-determination. *Social Work*, 39(2), 191–196.

Towle, C. (1987). *Common human needs.* Silver Spring, MD: National Association of Social Workers.

Trolander, J. A. (1997). Fighting racism and sexism: The CSWE. *Social Service Review*, 71, 110–134.

Tropman, J. E., Erlich, J. L., & Rothman, J. (2001). *Tactics and techniques of community intervention* (4th ed.). Itasca, IL: F. E. Peacock Publishers.

Tully, C. T., Craig, T., & Nugent, G. (1994). Should only gay and lesbian community organizers operate in gay and lesbian communities? In M. J. Austin & J. I. Lowe (Eds.), *Controversial issues in communities and organizations* (pp. 86–96). Boston, MA: Allyn & Bacon.

Turner, F. J. (2002). *Diagnosis in social work: New imperatives.* New York, NY: Haworth Social Work Practice Press.

Ulrich, B., & Beck-Gemsheim, E. (1996). Individualization and "precarious freedoms." In P. Heclas, S. Lash, & P. Morris (Eds.), *Detraditionalization: Critical reflections on authority and identity* (pp. 23–48). Cambridge, MA: Blackwell Publishers.

United Nations (1948). Universal Declaration of Human Rights. Retrieved from http://www.un.org/en/documents/udhr/.

U.S. Census Bureau. (2010). Statistical abstract of the United States: 2010 (129th ed.). Washington, DC: U.S. Census Bureau.

Retrieved from http://www.census.gov/
compendia/statab/.

U.S. Census Bureau; Hobbs, F. B. (2003). The
elderly population. Retrieved January 30,
2003, from www.census.gov/population/
www/pop-profile/elderpop.html.

U.S. Department of Health and Human Services,
Administration on Children, Youth, and
Families (2006). *Child maltreatment 2004.*
Washington, DC: U.S. Government Printing
Office.

Vanderwoerd, J. R. (2005). Ethical conflicts
between religion and sexual orientation in
North American social work education.
Retrieved January 26, 2007, from www.
aspecten.org/teksten/IS2005/
VanderWoerd_Panel.pdf.

Van Hoose, W. H., & Kottler, J. A. (1985). *Ethical
and legal issues in counseling and psychotherapy*
(2nd ed.). San Francisco, CA: Jossey-Bass.

Varley, B. K. (1963). Socialization in social work
education. *Social Work*, 8(4), 102–105.

Varley, B. K. (1968). Social work values: Changes
in value commitment of students from
admission to MSW graduation. *Journal of
Education for Social Work*, 4, 67–76.

VandeCreek, L., Knapp, S., & Herzog, C. (1988).
Privileged communications for social workers.
Social Casework, 69, 28–34.

Vernberg, D., & Schuh, M. J. (2002). Internet
bibliotherapy: A narrative analysis of a
reading simulated support group. *Journal of
Social Work in Disability and Rehabilitation*,
1(1), 81–97.

Verschelden, C. (1993). Social work values and
pacifism: Opposition to war as a professional
responsibility. *Social Work*, 38, 765–769.

Vigilante, J. L. (1974). Between values and science:
Education for the profession during a moral
crisis or is proof truth? *Journal of Education
for Social Work*, 10, 107–115.

Vigilante, J. L. (1983). Professional values. In A.
Rosenblatt & D. Waldfogel (Eds.), *Handbook
of clinical social work* (pp. 58–69). San
Francisco, CA: Jossey-Bass.

Wagner, L., Davis, S., & Handelsman, M. M.
(1998). In search of the abominable consent
form: The impact of readability and
personalization. *Journal of Clinical
Psychology*, 54, 115–120.

Wakefield, J. C. (1988a). Psychotherapy,
distributive justice, and social work: Part 1.
Social Service Review, 62(2), 187–210.

Wakefield, J. C. (1988b). Psychotherapy,
distributive justice, and social work: Part 2.
Social Service Review, 62(3), 353–382.

Walcott, D. M., Cerundolo, P., & Beck, J. C.
(2001). Current analysis of the *Tarasoff* duty:
An evolution towards the limitation of the
duty to protect. *Behavioral Sciences and the
Law*, 19, 325–343.

Walker, R., & Clark, J. J. (1999). Heading off
boundary problems: Clinical supervision as
risk management. *Psychiatric Services*, 50(11),
1435–1439.

Walker, R., & Staton, M. (2000). Multiculturalism
in social work ethics. *Journal of Social Work
Education*, 36(3), 449–462.

Walrond-Skinner, S., & Watson, D. (1987).
Ethical issues in family therapy. London, UK:
Routledge & Kegan Paul.

Walsh, W. D. (1969). *Hegelian ethics.* New York,
NY: St. Martin's Press, pp. 16–17.

Ward, J. W., & Drotman, D. P. (1998).
Epidemiology of HIV and AIDS. In G. P.
Wormser (Ed.), *AIDS and other
manifestations of HIV infection* (3rd ed.,
pp. 1–17). Philadelphia, PA: Lippincott-Raven.

Watanabe, T. (April 20, 2010). Cardinal Mahoney
Criticizes Arizona Immigration Bill, *Los
Angeles Times*, April 20, 2010. Retrieved
from http://articles.latimes.com/2010/apr/20/
local/la-me-0420-mahoney-immigration-
20100420, June 23, 2010.

Webb, S.A. (2009). Against difference and
diversity in social work: The case of human
rights. *International Journal of Social
Welfare*, 18 (3), 307–316.

Weick, A. (1999). Guilty knowledge. *Families in
Society*, 80(4), 327–332.

Weil, M. O., & Gamble, D. N. (2009).
Community practice model for the twenty-
first century. In: A. R. Roberts (Ed.), *Social
workers' desk reference* (2nd ed.)
(pp. 882–892). New York, NY: Oxford
University Press.

Weinberg, J. K. (1998). Balancing autonomy
and resources in health care for elders,
Generations, 22(3), 92–96.

Weinstein, B., Levine, M., Kogan, N., et al. (2000).
Mental health professionals' experiences
reporting suspected child abuse and
maltreatment. *Child Abuse & Neglect*,
24(10), 1317–1328.

Weiss, I., Gal, J., & Cnaan, R. A. (2004). Social
work education as professional socialization:
A study of the impact of social work
education upon students' professional
preferences. *Journal of Social Work Research*,
31(1) 13–31.

Werth, J. L. & Rogers, J. R. (2005). Assessing for
impaired judgment as a means of meeting the
"duty to protect" when a client is a potential
harm-to-self: Implications for clients making
end-of-life decisions. *Mortality*, 10(1), 7–21.

Wheeler, D. L. (1993). Physician-anthropologist
examines what ails America's medical system:
Instead of treating patients, Melvin Konner
probes health care in general. *Chronicle of
Higher Education*, June 2, A6–A7.

WhistleblowerLaws.com (2006). The law: An
overview: False Claims Act whistleblower

employee protections. Retrieved November 7, 2006, from http://whistleblowerlaws.com/protection.htm.

Whistle-blowers being punished, a survey shows. (2002, September 3). *New York Times*, A14.

Williams, R. M., Jr. (1967). Individual and group values. *Annals*, 371, 20–37.

Wilson, C. A., Alexander, J. R., & Turner, C. W. (1996). Family therapy process and outcome research: Relationship to treatment ethics. *Ethics & Behavior*, 6, 345–352.

Wineburgh, M. (1998). Ethics, managed care, and outpatient psychotherapy. *Clinical Social Work Journal*, 26, 433–443.

Witkin, S. L. (1998). The right to effective treatment and the effective treatment of rights: Rhetorical empiricism and the politics of research. *Social Work*, 43, 75–80.

Wodarski, J. S., Pippin, J. A., & Daniels, M. (1988). The effects of graduate social work education on personality, values and interpersonal skills. *Journal of Social Work Education*, 24, 266–277.

Woldeguiorguis, I. S. (2003). Racism and sexism in child welfare: Effects on women of color as mothers and practitioners. *Child Welfare*, 82(2), 273–288.

Wolf, L. E., Lo, B., Beckerman, K. P., Dorenbaum, A., Kilpatrick, S. J., & Weintraub, P. S. (2001). When parents reject interventions to reduce postnatal human immunodeficiency virus transmission. *Archives of Pediatrics & Adolescent Medicine*, 155, 927–933.

Wolfson, E. R. (1999). The fee in social work: Ethical dilemmas for practitioners. *Social Work*, 44(3), 269–273.

Woodside, M. (2003). *Generalist case management*. Pacific Grove, CA: Brooks/Cole, Thomson Publishing.

Worrell, J., & Remer, P. (2003). *Feminist perspectives in therapy: Empowering diverse women* (2nd ed.). New York, NY: John Wiley & Sons.

Worthington, R. L., Tan, J. A., & Poulin, K. (2002). Ethically questionable behaviors among supervisees: An exploratory investigation. *Ethics & Behavior*, 12(4), 1–22.

Wyatt, T., Daniels, M. H., & White, L. J. (2000). Noncompetition agreements and the counseling profession: An unrecognized reality for private practitioners. *Journal of Counseling & Development*, 78(1), 14–20.

Yang, J. A., & Kombarakaran, F. A. (2006). A practitioner's response to the new health privacy regulations. *Health & Social Work*, 31, 129–136.

Yip, K-S. (2005). Taoistic concepts of mental health: Implications for social work practice with Chinese communities. *Families in Society: The Journal of Contemporary Social Service*, 86(1), 35–45.

Yu, M., & O'Neal, B. (1992). Issues of confidentiality when working with persons with AIDS. *Clinical Social Work Journal*, 20, 421–430.

Yurkow, J. (1991). Abuse and neglect of the frail elderly. *Pride Institute Journal of Long Term Home Health Care*, 10(1), 36–39.

Zayas, L. H., Cabassa, L. J., & Perez, M. C. (2005). Capacity-to-consent in psychiatric research: Development and preliminary testing of a screening tool. *Research on Social Work Practice*, 15, 545–556.

Zellman, G. L., & Fair, C. C. (2002). Preventing and reporting abuse. In J. E. B. Myers, L. Berliner et al. (Eds.), *The ASPSAC Handbook on Child Maltreatment* (2nd ed.). Thousand Oaks, CA: Sage Publications.

Zetlin, A. G., Weinberg, L. A., & Shea, N. M. (2006). Seeing the whole picture: Views from diverse participants on barriers to educating foster youths. *Children & Schools*, 28, 165–173.

Zur, O., & Lazarus, A. A. (2002). Six arguments against dual relationships and their rebuttals. In A. A. Lazarus & O. Zur (Eds.), *Dual relationships and psychotherapy* (pp. 3–24). New York, NY: Spring Publishing Co.

Zygmond, M. J., & Boorhem, H. (1989). Ethical decision-making in family therapy. *Family Process*, 28, 269–280.

INDEX

Abortion, 30, 92
Accountability systems, 271
Adam Walsh Child Protection Act of 2006 (H.R. 4472), 150
Administration and supervision, 210–215
  conflicting obligations, 212–214
  dual-role relations, 211–212
  supervisor ethics, 214–215
Administrative records, and privacy, 150–151
Adoptions, and discrimination, 182–183
Advocacy, 187–193
  case advocacy, 187–188
  cause/class advocacy, 188–190
  cyberactivism (electronic advocacy), 192–193
  and HIV, 226–227
  and privatization of services, 191–192
  as whistleblowing, 190–191
Agency
  appeals procedures, 272
  policy, 202–204
  risk audits, 268–270
Alcohol or other drug (AOD) abuse, 200–201
Ambiguity, 101–104
American Association for Organizing Family Social Work, 43
American Association of Social Workers (AASW), 43–44
Appeals procedures, 272
Anorexia, 99
Assessment screen, ethical, 74–76
  protection of clients' rights, 74–75
  protection of society's interests, 75–76
Assisted living residence, 12
Assisted suicide, 224–225

Association for Community Organization and Social Administration (ACOSA), 263
Association of Social Work Boards (ASWB), 7, 229
Attention deficit hyperactivity disorder (ADHD), 204
Autonomy, fostering, 81–82

Bases for malpractice suits, 32
Border Protection, Terrorism, and Illegal Immigration Control Bill (proposed), 32–33

Case advocacy, 132, 187–188
Cause/class advocacy, 133, 188–190
Changing dilemmas in social work, 241–264
  evidence-based practice (EBP), 250–253
  macro practice, 257–264
  managed care and mental health, 241–245
  practice in rural or isolated settings, 254–257
  private practice, 253–254
  research and evaluation, 248–250
  technology, 246–248
Checklist for ethical decisions, 72
  Generalization, 72
  Impartiality, 72
  Justifiability, 86
Child Abuse Prevention and Treatment Act, 27
Child protective services (CPS), 158
Child welfare and confidentiality, 158–159
Clarifying
  group values, 67–68
  personal values, 65–67

professional values, 68–69
  societal values, 68
Client
  bill of rights, 268
  and colleagues from other fields, 149–150
  defined, 91–94, 257
  dumping, 253–254
  examples, See Ethical dilemmas exemplar
  interests versus worker interests, 124–125
  living with HIV and AIDS, 225–227
  rights, 61, 91–104
  sexual relations, 128–132
  social relations, 133–134
Client/worker value gap, 107–109
Client rights, 91–104
  and ambiguity, 101–104
  and privacy, 154–155
  and professional expertise, 94–96
  and self-determination, 96–101
  and welfare, protection of, 61
Clinical pragmatism, 56–57
Clinical social work, 186–187
Code of Ethics of the National Association of Social Workers (NASW, X2008) core values, 24
Codes of ethics, 41–47
  defined, 41–43
  history of, 43–45
  U.S. and international, 44–47, 113
Code of Ethics of the International Federation of Social Workers, 113
Coercion, 40
Colleagues from other fields, and clients, 149–150
Committee on the Ethics of Social Work Practice, 257

Community
groups, 257–258
organizing, 166, 261–264
and privacy, 150
and societal issues, 258–261
Compassion fatigue, 141–143
Competence, 6–7, 24, 39
Competing loyalties, 11
Competing values, 5, 11, 13
Complaints and lawsuits, 30
Conditions to win malpractice suits, 31
Confidentiality, 147–159
and child welfare, 158–159
defined, 147
and HIV and AIDS, 226
limits to, 155–156
and privacy, 147–156
right to, 82
and technology, 157
and threatening behavior, 207
Confucian ethics, 63
Core values of social work, 24–25
Consent, See Informed consent
Council on Social Work Education
(CSWE), 7, 23, 46, 181
CSWE 2008 Educational Policy
and Accreditation Standards
(EPAS), 27–28
Court decisions
Brady v. Hopper (1983), 168
Ewing v. Goldstein (2004), 169
*Ewing v. Northridge Hospital
Medical Center* (2004), 169
Gonzaga v. Doe (2002), 146
Griswold v. Connecticut (1965),
146
Gross v. Allen (1994), 168–169
Hedlund v. Superior Court
(1983), 168
In re Quinlan (1976), 146
Jaffee v. Redmond (1996), 157,
159–160
Minnesota v. Andring (1984), 160
People v. Belous (1969), 30
People v. Felix, Court of Appeals
(2001), 169
Saenz v. Roe (1999), 30
*Tarasoff v. Regents of the
University of California*
(1976), 32, 36, 167–170
United States v. Chase (2002), 160
United States v. Hayes (2001), 160
CSWE, *See* Council on Social Work
Education
Cyberactivism (electronic advocacy),
192–193

Decision-making, ethical
contemporary approaches to,
56–64
defined, 3–17
foundations for, 52–56
guidelines, 50–69
model, 73
process and tools, 72–86
screens, 82–85
Democratization, 121–122
Department of Health and Human
Services (DHHS), 156
Diagnosis and misdiagnosis, 138–141

Diagnostic and Statistical Manual
of Mental Disorders
(DSM-IV-TR), 138–140
Dignity of person, 24
Dilemma, definition p. 10
Direct consent, 166
Disclosure of information, 162–163
Discrimination
and adoptions, 182–183
and diversity, 180–182
Diversity, and discrimination, 180–182
Dual roles, 125–128
with supervisors, 211–212
Duty to protect, 167–171
Duty to warn, 98

E-therapy, 151–152
Educational Policy and Accreditation
Standards (EPAS), 7, 46
Educational Policy and Accreditation
Standards of the Council on
Social Work Education
(2008), 46
Efficiency and effectiveness, 77–78
Elder abuse, 220–222
Electronic advocacy, 192–193
Employment assistance programs
(EAP), 207
End-of-life decisions, 222
Ethical absolutism, 53–54
Ethical assessment screen, 74–76
protection of clients' rights, 74–75
protection of society's interests,
75–76
Ethical decision making
contemporary approaches to, 56–64
and ethics, 8–9

dilemmas, 9
ethical problems in social work
practice, 9–12
ethics, 8
foundations for, 52–56
goal setting, 12
guidelines, 50–69
model, 73
overview, 3–17
process and tools, 72–86
and professional ethics, 14–16
question check, 86
role conflict, 12
screens, 82–85
and social work competencies, 6–7
textbook overview, 16–17
value dilemma, 12–14

Ethical decision making, contemporary
approaches, 56–64
clinical pragmatism, 56–57
Confucian ethics, 63
ethics of caring, 59–61
feminist ethics, 61–62
Hindu ethics, 63–64
humanistic ethics, 57–58
religious ethics, 58–59
virtue ethics, 62–63
Ethical decision making, foundations
for, 52–56
different approaches, 54–56

ethical absolutism, 53–54
ethical relativism, 52–53
Ethical decision-making guidelines,
50–69
Ethical decision-making model, 73
Ethical decision-making process and
tools, 72–86
Ethical assessment screen, 74–76
general model for, 73
least harm principle, 76–78
rank ordering ethical principles,
78–86
Ethical decision-making screens,
application of, 82–85
Ethical dilemmas in advocacy, 187–193
case advocacy, 187–188
cause/class advocacy, 188–190
cyberactivism (electronic
advocacy), 192–193
privatization of services, 191–192
and whistleblowing, 190–191
Ethical offenses, 35
Ethical principles, rank ordering of,
78–86
Ethical principles screen (EPS), 80,
224, 260–261
Ethical problems in social work
practice, 9–12
Ethical relativism, 39, 52–53
Ethical rules screen (ERS), 79–80
Ethics, 8, 25–33
of caring, 59–61
defined, 25–26
general versus professional, 28
and law, 29–33
sources of, 56–64
unethical behavior, 33–38
Ethics advocacy, 274–276
Evidence-based practice (EBP), 39,
250–253
Exemplars, *See* Ethical dilemmas
exemplars

Family secrets, 4
Feminist ethics, 61–62
Forced consent, 167
Freedom, fostering, 81–82
Full disclosure, 82
Future consent, 167

General ethics, 8
General Social Care Council, 45
Generalization, 86
Goal setting, 12
Group values, 67–68

Health Insurance Portability and
Accountability Act (HIPAA),
150–151, 156–157, 246, 268
Health Information Technology and
Clinical Health Act (HITECH),
157–158
Hierarchy of personal principles,
85–86
Hindu ethics, 63–64
HIV and AIDS, 77, 153, 225–227
Human relationships,
importance of, 24
Human Research Protections Offices
(HRPO), 271

Human services agencies, 274–276
Humanistic ethics, 57–58

Impartiality, 86
Inequality, 174
Informed consent, 160–168
    and community organizing, 166
    disclosure of information,
        162–163
    voluntariness, 163–165
    ways of consenting, 166–167
Institutional Review Boards (IRB), 271
Insurance, 139
    Insurance companies and third-
        party payers, 152
Integrity, 24
Interdisciplinary teams, 274–276
International codes of ethics, 44–47
Interpersonal relationships
    ethics of, 27
    importance of, 24
Intimate partner violence (IPV),
    217–220

Joint Commission on Accreditation
    of Health Care Organizations
    (JCAHO), 233
Justifiability, 86

Law, 30–31
    Law and ethics, 29–33
    conflict between, 31–33
    differences between, 31
    unethical but legal, 29–30
Learning disabilities, 140–141
Least harm principle, 76–78, 82
Limitations on professional
    judgments, 121–122
Limited resources, 184–186

Macro practice, 257–264
    community groups, 257–258
    community organizing, 261–264
    community and societal issues,
        258–261
Malpractice, 7, 29, 31, 33–38
Managed care and mental health,
    241–245
Megan's Law, 150
Military, and social work, 204–206
Misdiagnosis, 138–141
Misrepresentation, 134–138, 254
Morality, 26–27
Multiple-client system, 5

National Association of Social
    Workers (NASW), 5, 272–273
NASW Code of Ethics (1960), 41, 44
NASW Code of Ethics (1979), 44
NASW Code of Ethics (1990), 41
NASW Code of Ethics (2008), 5, 6,
    18, 23–27, 32, 36–7, 40–1,
    44–7, 56, 59, 65, 68, 85, 94,
    106–107, 116, 124–128, 132,
    147, 149, 153–154, 161, 180,
    182, 186, 195, 199–202,
    206–209, 211, 234–235, 242,
    250, 257–267, 274
    core values, 24–25
    ethical principles, 107, 125, 242

preamble, 23, 68, 264
    on privacy, 147
    purpose, 106, 267
NASW Insurance Trust, 8, 34, 128
NASW Office of Ethics and
    Professional Review, 271
NASW professional complaint
    procedures, 273–274
NASW Standards for Cultural
    Competence in Social Work
    Practice (2001), 181
NASW Standards for Palliative and
    End of Life Care (2006), 225
National Center for Elder Abuse
    (2005), 220
Non-sexual social relations, 149
Non-social work employers, 204–209

Ombudsmen, 272
Oral or written consent, 166–167
Oregon Health Plan (OHP), 175–177
Organizational and work
    relationships, 195–215
    administration and supervision,
        210–215
    and agency policy, 202–204
    non-social work employers, 204–209
    practitioner impairment, 200–202
    relations with professional
        colleagues, 196–200
Overlap, general and professional
    ethics p.28?

Pacifism, 207
Participants in the social work
    process, 102
Patient Protection and Affordable
    Care Act (2010), 242
Patient Self-Determination Act
    (1990), 97
Peer review and committee on ethics,
    270–271
Personal principles hierarchy, 85–86
Personal Responsibility and Work
    Opportunity Act (1996),
    30, 101
Personal values, 65–67
Plurality of identities, 235–238
Police, 152–153
Posttraumatic stress disorder (PTSD),
    141–142
Practice in rural or isolated settings,
    254–257
Practitioner impairment, 200–202
Present consent, 167
Principle of Generic Consistency,
    124–125
Principle of social justice, 81
Privacy
    administrative and electronic
        records, 150–151
    with clients, 154–155
    with colleagues from other fields,
        149–150
    with the community, 150
    and confidentiality, 82, 147–156
    defined, 147
    disappearing sense of, 122
    e-therapy, 151–152

insurance companies and third-
    party payers, 152
    limits to, 155–156
    police, 152–153
    relatives, 153–154
    with other social workers, 149
Private practice, 253–254
    client dumping, 253–254
    misrepresentation, 254
Privatization of services, 191–192
Privileged communication, 159–160
Professional associations, 272–273
Professional ethics, 14–16, 27–28,
    39–47
    codes of, 41–47
    defined, 8, 27–28
    and judgment, 121–122
    reasons for, 38–41
    and responsibility, 267–277
    teaching, 14–16
    and values, 23–49
Professional judgments, limitations
    on, 121–122
Professional relationships, 119–143,
    196–200
    client interests versus worker
        interests, 124–125
    with colleagues, 196–200
    compassion fatigue, 141–144
    diagnosis and misdiagnosis,
        138–141
    dual roles within, 125–128
    limits of, 122–124
    sexual relations with clients,
        128–132
    social relations, 133–134
    and special duties, 119–122
    students and sexual relations,
        132–133
    touching, 133
    truth telling and
        misrepresentation, 134–138
    at work, 196–200
Professional review (RPRs), 273–274
Professional values, 24–25, 65–69
    clarifying, 68–69
    defined, 24–25
Protect, duty to, 167–171
Protection of
    clients' rights, 74–75
    a family secret, 4
    human life, 80–81
    life, 260–261
    society's interests, 75–76
Psychological indifference, 141–143

Quality of life, 82
Questions for ethical dilemmas, 86

Relationships, See Professional
    relationships
Relatives, and privacy, 153–154
Religion and spirituality, 231–234
    and plurality of identities, 235–238
    and secularism, 231–233
    and social work practice, 233–234
Religious ethics, 58–59
Research and evaluation in practice
    settings, 248–250

Resources for ethical decision-making, 268–274
accountability systems, 271
agency appeals procedures, 272
agency risk audits, 268–270
clients' bill of rights, 268
NASW professional complaint procedures, 273–274
peer review and committee on ethics, 270–271
professional associations, 272–273
training and consultation, 271
Respondeat superior, 214–215
Responsibility for professional ethics, 267–277
ethics advocacy, 274–276
resources for ethical decision-making, 268–274
Right to privacy and confidentiality, 82
Rights revolution, 121–122
Role conflict, 12

Scarce resources, 174–180
Secondary traumatic stress, 141–143
Secularism, 231–233
Selected client groups, 217–239
clients with HIV and AIDS, 225–227
elder abuse, 220–222
end-of-life decisions, 222
intimate partner violence, 217–220
religion and spirituality, 231–234
technology in direct practice, 227–231
Self-determination
fostering, 81–82
and professional expertise, 96–101
Service, 24
Sexual relations
with clients, 128–132
and students, 132–133
Social justice, 24, 173–193, 261
and clinical social work, 186–187
commitment to, 174–183
discrimination and adoptions, 182–183

discrimination and diversity, 180–182
ethical dilemmas in advocacy, 187–193
inequality, 174
and limited resources, 184–186
and NASW, 264
principle, 81
scarce resources, 174–180
and time, 39, 174
Social relations with clients, 133–134
Social work
administration and supervision, 210–215
changing dilemmas in social work, 241–264
competencies and practice behaviors, 6–7
core values, 24–25
and the military, 204–206
participants in process of, 116
sources of help for social workers, 143
and time, 39, 174
with selected client groups, 217–239
Societal values, 68
Social Workers Helping Social Workers (SWHSW), 143
Sources of help for social workers, 143
Special duties, 119–122
Spirituality and religion, 231–234
Stress, 142
Supervision, 210–215
conflicting obligations, 212–214
dual-role relations with supervisors, 211–212
supervisor ethics and liabilities, 214–215

Tacit consent, 166
Teaching professional ethics, 14–16
Technology, 246–248
Technology in direct practice, 227–231
Temporary Assistance for Needy Families (TANF), 78

Textbook overview, 16–17
Third-party payers, 152
Time, 39, 174
Touching, 133
Training and consultation, 271
Truth telling and misrepresentation, 134–138

Uncertainty, 101–104
Unethical behavior
defined, 33
but legal, 20–30
and malpractice, 33–38
Uniform Health Care Decisions Act (1993), 97
U.S. codes of ethics, 44–47
USA Patriot Act (2001), 146

Value dilemma, 12–14
Value gap, client/worker, 107–109
Value imposition, 111–113
Value neutrality, 109–111
Values, 19, 21, 23–24, 53, 64–69
competing, 11
defined, 19–20, 23–24, 64–65
group, 67–68
imposition 111–113
inevitability of, 115–116
making judgments about, 114–115
neutrality, 109–111
personal, 65–67
professional, 24–25, 68–69
and professional ethics, 23–49
religious, 113
societal, 68
Virtue ethics, 40, 62–63
Voluntariness, 163–165

Ways of consenting, 166–167
direct or tacit consent, 166
rorced consent, 167
oral or written consent, 166–167
past or present consent, 167
present or future consent, 167
Whistleblowing, 190–191
Written consent, 166–167